What People Are Saying About

THE LAW OF MOSES VERSUS THE LAW OF MESSIAH

+++

The Torah-observant movement has for too long perpetrated the idea that Messianic believers need to keep Torah and all its commandments to please God.

As the author emphatically states, "It is impossible to keep Torah today!" He counters this with Scripture clearly showing that the Body of Messiah is under Messiah's Law rather than Moses' Law. He expertly intertwines other important topics like hermeneutics, the covenants [of God], and Dispensations to help us understand why we are all under Messiah's Law.

The "Snapshots" in the second part of the book also help us to understand this goal. This is a book that I would have liked to write myself; however, the author has done a great service to our movement. This is a book that I highly recommend for all who are engaged in the Messianic Jewish Movement of today and for all believers around the world. Our hope is that this movement will read it with an open heart and see the truth of God's Word that all believers of Yeshua are now found in the New Covenant under God's grace living a life of faith by the Spirit's power.

Dr. Richard Hill, Messianic Pastor of Beth Yeshua Messianic Congregation, Las Vegas, NV

+++

As a Jewish believer in Messiah Jesus, and having led a Messianic Congregation which was sound in doctrine, I know that this book is needed. Reading through the manuscript gives me hope that many who are uncertain about Law vs. Grace will see the overwhelming evidence that we come into the family of God through faith alone, and continue in that family by God's grace alone. This book is a packed spiritual meal. Enjoy!

Mottel Baleston, Messianic Jewish Teacher

The Hebrew Roots Movement has [unfortunately] made significant in-roads into both the Messianic Movement and Evangelical Christianity in particular. In every place, its teaching of Torah Observance as a means to the believer's sanctification, or to simply being "right with God," has brought confusion and division within the greater Body of Messiah. It is evident that such results indicate there is something wrong with this teaching, but a clear and biblical explanation has been difficult to find. John Metzger has given us not only a sound critique of the problems but also the correction in a proper understanding of the relationship of the Mosaic Covenant with the New Covenant and a thorough study of its Law of Messiah. For everyone who has sought an answer to the question of keeping the Law as a believer in Yeshua, this book is a must!

Randall Price, Ph.D., President, World of the Bible Ministries

+++

I am grateful for John Metzger's in-depth study and thoughtful insights regarding the error of imposing Torah observance on believers today. Those who teach this error infiltrate churches today and cause divisions by exporting this false teaching. Individual believers are stymied in their spiritual growth when they are taught they are saved by faith alone in Jesus Christ, but must live the Christian life by Torah observance. This book is an excellent tool for equipping pastors and individual believers to understand the issue and to refute the errors of this false teaching. I highly recommend this book.

Donnie Preslar, Grace Bible Church, Charlotte, NC

+++

The question of law, and its proper place within the Judeo-Christian tradition, certainly dates to the First Century, being a central topic for the Council of Jerusalem in light of the grace that was bestowed to *both* Jew and Gentile after Cornelius in Acts 10.

What are we to do with this "new thing" that the Jewish Messiah established, and what does it mean for covenant obedience?

"Law" and "covenant" are very loaded terms that touch major biblical subjects such as Israelology, Christology, Soteriology, Ecclesiology, and Eschatology (just to name a few). How are we to understand "law" in the current age, considering that which was conveyed through Moses at Sinai to the people of Israel versus that which Yeshua Himself conveyed in Jerusalem to the future judges of Israel (c.f. Matthew 19:28), the first leaders of His Church?

As Metzger rightly illuminates, one Torah [the Law of Moses] in the biblical canon was meant to point us to His better Torah [the New Covenant] (c.f. Hebrews 8). This book guides the reader in asking the proper "law" and "covenant" questions *within* God's text, so that they might find the proper answers *from* God's text. The countless hours of research put into this book have resulted in a biblical study aide that will guide its reader in better grasping the Torah of Messiah, and the blessed covenant that Yeshua established in His blood.

John Myles, Senior Pastor, Fellowship Chapel, Jarrettsville, MD

+++

Metzger has assembled an impressively comprehensive and cogently argued case regarding the place of the New Covenant and the role of Torah in the life of the believer. This work shines a necessary beacon to dispel the darkness and confusion that so often obscures this critical subject. This is clearly a passion project for the author who ... leaves no theological stone unturned in his quest for accurate, biblical answers. It should be considered essential reading for all interested in understanding messianic theological issues and their practical implications for followers of our Messiah.

Steven Ger, Director of Sojourner Ministries, Beth Sar Shalom Congregational Leader, TX

+++

Metzger explains very clearly why the Mosaic Covenant with its 613 Commandments has come to an end and has no more bearing on Jewish or Gentile believers in Messiah today. What has drawn me into John Metzger's book in the first place was a desire to learn and to understand why the Law of Moses is not in effect anymore and not binding on any believer and how to share this biblical truth with a Torah observant believer. To my delight, the author writes in such a way that it is not only very easy to follow and understand, but it also reads like the author is sitting right there with the reader, engaging in a thorough discussion on the subject. A must-read for any believer, and in particular for those who either encounter believers who believe in or teach Torah observance or are Torah observant and question it. Highly recommended.

Anja Vaughan, Friend

Other Books Authored by John B. Metzger

The Tri-unity of God is Jewish – 2004

Discovering the Mystery of the Unity of God – 2010

God in Eclipse: God Has Not Always Been Silent – 2013

    God in Eclipse in Russian – 2016

    God in Eclipse in Spanish – 2020

    God in Eclipse in Hebrew – 2023

    God in Eclipse in French – 2024

Israel's Only Hope: The New Covenant – 2015

Poking God's Eye: A Theological and Historical View of Anti-Semitism, Based on the Blessings and Cursings of Genesis 12:3 – 2018, 2025

The Law, Then and Now: What About Grace? – 2019

Work in Progress: *Jewish Study Bible*

Law of Moses

Ministration of Death and Condemnation
Validated in the Old Covenant to Israel Only
Genesis 3:18 Isaiah 53:6b

VERSUS

Law of Messiah

Ministration of Life – Abundant Life
Validated in the New Covenant
for all believers in Messiah

John 19:1-5   1 Peter 2:24

By John B. Metzger

The Law of Moses VERSUS the Law of Messiah: Ministration of Death and Condemnation vs. Ministration of Life

© 2025 by John B. Metzger, author, *www.PromisesToIsrael.org*

Published by JHousePublishing, Purple Raiment label, Keller, TX, *www.jhousepublishing.com*

ISBN: 978-1-950734-13-9

REL006090	**RELIGION** / Biblical Criticism & Interpretation / Old Testament
REL006100	**RELIGION** / Biblical Criticism & Interpretation / New Testament
REL101000	**RELIGION** / Messianic Judaism

All rights reserved. No part of this publication may be reproduced or transmitted in any form or by any means without written permission of the publisher.

Scripture in this book has been quoted from the King James Version (Public Domain), with modernization of the language by the author, unless otherwise noted.

As noted, Scripture taken from the New King James Version®. Copyright © 1982 by Thomas Nelson. Used by permission. All rights reserved.

Scriptures taken from the Holy Bible, New International Version®, NIV®. Copyright © 1973, 1978, 1984, 2011 by Biblica, Inc.™ Used by permission of Zondervan. All rights reserved worldwide. www.zondervan.com The "NIV" and "New International Version" are trademarks registered in the United States Patent and Trademark Office by Biblica, Inc.™

The Holy Bible, English Standard Version® (ESV®) © 2001 by Crossway, a publishing ministry of Good News Publishers. All rights reserved. The ESV text may not be quoted in any publication made available to the public by a Creative Commons license. The ESV may not be translated in whole or in part into any other language. ESV Text Edition: 2016

Cover design: Jesse Gonzales
Editor: Joni Prinjinski
Proofing: Sandy Van Heest
Paperback: Acid-free paper
Printed in the USA

Cover Note

Genesis 3:18 - *Thorns also and thistles shall it bring forth to you; and you shall eat the herb of the field;*

Isaiah 53:6b - *...and the* LORD *has laid on Him the iniquity of us all.*

John 19:1-5 - *Then Pilate therefore took Jesus, and scourged Him. And the soldiers platted a crown of thorns, and put it on His head, and they put on Him a purple robe, And said, Hail, King of the Jews! and they smote Him with their hands. Pilate therefore went forth again, and said to them, Behold, I bring Him forth to you, that you may know that I find no fault in Him. Then Jesus came forth, wearing the crown of thorns, and the purple robe. And Pilate said unto them, Behold the man!*

1 Peter 2:24 - *Who His own self bore our sins in His own body on the tree, that we, being dead to sins, should live unto righteousness: by whose stripes you were healed.*

What Does Our Cover Design Mean?

The Law of Moses VERSUS The Law of Messiah

Two great Laws dominate the Bible. One historically has far outweighed the other in use and understanding. Of these two laws, the **Law of Moses** is predominately referenced and used by both Judaism and Christianity to the absolute neglect of the current **Law of Messiah**. Observe the five points that the Cover Design encompasses:

First, notice the word in all <u>caps</u>, the word *VERSUS*.

> This is a **book of contrasts** showing that these two law systems are **at odds with one another**.
>
> They are **different**, with **different** purposes.
>
> One law, the **Mosaic Law**, deals with **one ethnic group called Israel,** and this law has been **fulfilled**.
>
> The other, the **current biblical law,** the **Law of Messiah**, **embraces all ethnic groups around the world.**

Second, notice that the **Law of Moses** presents a ministration of **death and condemnation**, while the **Law of Messiah** presents **life**.

> The **Law of Moses** was validated for use only in the Tanakh and Gospels and was impotent to produce righteousness.
>
> The biblical account thoroughly confirms **the Mosaic Law's lack of success** with an undeniable failure to produce a righteous people.
>
> On the other hand, the **Law of Messiah** presents **Life, the abundant Life** that **Yeshua (the Messiah)** spoke of.
>
> The **Law of Messiah** supersedes the **Mosaic Law**.
>
> The validity of the **Law of Messiah** was confirmed by the **inauguration** of the **New Covenant** by Yeshua ha Mashiach at a Jewish Seder, also known as the Last Supper, followed by His death, burial, resurrection and ascension.
>
> Yeshua (Jesus) actually **is the Author of both laws** that would accomplish difference results and purposes.

Third, the picture of the **thorns** symbolizes sin.

> The **sin nature** that indwells every individual because of Adam is illustrated by the **thorns and thistles** of Genesis 3:18, the curse.
>
> Yeshua had these thorns placed on His head at the crucifixion (John 19:1-5) as **He took on Himself our sin and all of God's wrath** as He mediated the New Covenant.

Fourth, Isaiah 53:6b and I Peter 2:24 state that the **Father** laid on Messiah Yeshua *the iniquity of us all*.

> While **Jews** are predominately the subjects in the context of **Isaiah 53**, the **New Testament reveals the mystery that God's salvation plan also includes the Gentiles.**
>
> Peter further amplifies that act of the Father that **Yeshua bore our sins** on the tree making us dead to sin.
>
> **Yeshua opened the door to all** that we may live unto righteousness through His mediation of the **New Covenant**.

Fifth, the cover picture is designed to show that the <u>Mosaic Covenant</u>, also called the *old covenant,* **was inadequate to give us new life in our Messiah.**

> The <u>Mosaic Law</u> **was powerless** to give anyone victory over sin.
>
> The <u>Law of Moses</u> **did not give righteousness** but was given to an unrighteous people.
>
> The old law imputed **death and condemnation**, which is unquestionably shown through 1500 years of Jewish history and since Adam in human history.
>
> In contrast, **the New Covenant and the <u>Law of Messiah</u>** that proceeds from it give every believer, both Jew and Gentile, the ability to **live in victory over sin** by yielding to the indwelling presence of the **Rauch ha-Kodesh (Holy Spirit)** in all believers.

Table of Contents

Dedication

Introduction xv
    The Law of Context xvii

Part One - What Is the Law of Messiah?

Chapter One Defining the Law of Messiah 1

Chapter Two Hermeneutics 9
    Literal, Historical/Grammatical Method 9
    Allegorical or Spiritualization Method 10
    The Use of the Term *Church* – the *Ekklesia* 14

Chapter Three What Is the Difference Between an Eternal and a Conditional Covenant? 17
    Progressive Revelation 17
    Definition of an Eternal Unconditional Covenant 19
    The Centrality of the Abrahamic Covenant 22
    Definition of a Conditional Covenant 24
    Purposes of the Law of Moses 25
    The Nine Purposes of the Law of Moses 27
    The Timing of the Law 28
    The Remedy for the Mosaic Law 30
    The Continued Value of the Law 32
    Does the Bible Warn Us to Stay Faithful to His Word? (Jer. 18:7-10) 36

Chapter Four Dispensations 39

Chapter Five The Hebrew Word *Olam* (Strong's H5769) עוֹלָם 45
    Application and Conclusions 50

Chapter Six The New Covenant 51
    Difference Between *New* and *Renew* 51
    Promises in the New Covenant 54
    New Covenant Passages 58

Chapter Seven Dealing with the Terms *Law*, *Torah*, and *Tanakh* 63

Chapter Eight Torah Observance and the Old Testament Pilgrim Feasts 65

Chapter Nine Christian Liberty for Jews and Gentiles 67

Chapter Ten Moral Law of Moses Is Carried over to the Law of Messiah 75
    Ten Commandments – Exodus 20:1-17; Deuteronomy 5:1-21 77

Chapter Eleven Rendered Inoperative 81

Part Two - Snapshots from God's Word About Messiah's Law

- Introduction: I Am Continually Surprised 91
- Snapshot from Genesis 94
  - Shabbat Observance: What Does the Old Testament Say? 94
- Snapshots by Yahweh in Exodus, Leviticus, and Numbers 97
  - The Torah: Who is the Author of the Law? 97
- Snapshot from Moses in Deuteronomy 101
- Snapshot from Jeremiah 103
- Snapshot from the Gospel of Matthew 106
- Snapshots from the Apostle John 112
- Snapshots from the Record of Luke in Acts 114
- Snapshots from Paul, Beginning with Romans 117
- Snapshots from Corinthians 136
- Snapshots from Galatians 145
- Snapshot from Ephesians 170
- Snapshots from Philippians 176
- Snapshots from Colossians 179
- Snapshot from I Timothy... 183
- Snapshot from II Timothy.. 186
- Snapshots from Titus 188
- Summary of Acts and Epistles 193
- Snapshots from the Letter to the Hebrews 195
  - Background and Foundational Emphasis of Hebrews 195
  - Superiority of the Messiah as Divine Revelation 198
  - Angels Are Servants; Yeshua Is the Son of God (1:4-14); Proofs of His Deity from the *Tanakh* 200
  - The Superiority of Messiah to Angels (2:1-18) 204
  - The Superiority of Messiah to Moses (3:1-6) 205
  - The Superiority of Messiah to Aaron (4:14-5:10) 209
  - Messiah Is after the Order of Melchizedek, Not of Aaron (7:1-28) 210
  - The Superiority of the New Covenant over the *Old Covenant* (8:1-13).... 225
  - Conclusion – 8:13 – The Temporary Ceases; The New Covenant Is Permanent 230
  - Summary of Main Points in Hebrews 232
  - The Superiority of the Messiah's Priestly Service (9:1-10) 232
  - The Ministry in the New Tabernacle (9:23-28)... 245
  - Conclusion of Hebrews... 246

APPENDIX ONE General Categories of the Law of Messiah	249
APPENDIX TWO Law of Messiah – Greek Imperative Commands	251
Gospels	251
Acts	252
Romans	261
I Corinthians	264
II Corinthians	269
Galatians	271
Ephesians	272
Philippians	274
Colossians	275
I Thessalonians	277
II Thessalonians	278
I Timothy	278
II Timothy	280
Titus	281
Philemon	282
Hebrews	282
James	285
I Peter	287
II Peter	289
I John	290
II John	291
III John	291
Jude	291
Revelation	291
APPENDIX THREE The *Tanakh* Is Not Neglected or Depreciated by the New Covenant	295
List of Used Passages in Hebrews from the Torah and *Tanakh*	296
List of Used Passages in Romans from the Torah and *Tanakh*	302
List of Used Passages in Galatians from the Torah and *Tanakh*	306
List of Used Passages in James from the Torah and *Tanakh*	306
List of Used Passages from I & II Peter from the Torah and *Tanakh*	307
List of Used Passages from the Torah and *Tanakh* in Revelation	308
APPENDIX FOUR Thirty-Three Positional Truths	313
APPENDIX FIVE The Eternal Nature of the Mosaic Law	325
Define Torah	325
Evidence from Language	326
Evidence from Jeremiah 31:31-34	328
Evidence From Rabbinic Literature	328
Return to Jeremiah 31:31-34	329
Evidence From Zechariah 14:16-19	331
Evidence from The Soncino Books of the Bible	332

The Position of the New Testament 332
   Conclusion 334
BIBLIOGRAPHY **335**

Dedication

This book is dedicated to the representatives of two former Christian youth organizations from the days of my youth back between 1959 and 1965.

The beginning of my accumulated knowledge of Scriptures began back in my youth as I attended The Christian Youth Crusade, which was headed up by Don Rosenberger and Irvin and Muriel Nase in Riverdale, MD.

I greatly benefitted spiritually from their quiz game called "Seventeen." It involved memorizing 150 items, each in five biblical categories: Places, Things, Events, Persons, and Bible Verses. The fellowship was wonderful.

Then my education continued with Youth For Christ (YFC) rallies in Wheaton, MD, with director Daniel P. Hill and his assistant Woody Schwartz. They both were a great blessing and encouragement to me in my teen years. I was also involved in YFC Clubs in my high school, Walt Whitman, in Bethesda, MD; but even more so was my involvement in YFC Quizzing where we memorized vast amounts of Scripture. It was in 1961 that I dedicated my life to serve Christ at the Capital Teen Youth Convention, with Billy Graham as the speaker, at the National Guard Armory in Washington, DC. A great highlight each year was a week with about 100 of us kids from our group attending the YFC Convention for a week at Ocean City, NJ, with several thousand other teen believers. I often wonder about the other young people that I fellowshipped with. Are they still walking with the LORD? These early years were used of God to encourage and strengthen me as a young believer in Christ, and the impact of those days was a foundation for my early Christian walk and spiritual growth in Christ. Couple those beginning days with the impact of my church, the Mclean Bible Church, and its pastor, J. Albert Ford, who guided and encouraged me to attend Washington Bible College, and you have a picture of the path that I traveled to be trained to serve the LORD for my life.

Introduction

Years ago, in 2010, I wrote a book *Discovering the Mystery of the Unity of God*, a 10-year study of the concept of the Triunity of God from a Jewish perspective; and for the first time I really grasped the plurality of the God-head as well as the deity of Messiah in the Old Testament (*Tanakh* or Hebrew Scriptures). What was especially exciting was seeing the activity of the Second Person of the Godhead, who we understand today to be the pre-incarnate Jesus (Yeshua) long before He arrived physically on the scene as a baby in a manager in Bethlehem. That was refreshing!

Then I wrote a book called *Israel's Only Hope: The New Covenant* (2015), and I came away from that study with a whole new appreciation and understanding of my salvation and all that God had provided in the **New Covenant** for me as a Gentile. I fell in love with my Lord all over again. Understanding the reality of what He did for me in the **New Covenant** still takes my breath away; I will never be the same again because of my richer understanding of the permanence of my relationship with my Lord and Saviour. In understanding the **New Covenant**, I came face to face with the reality of the Law of Christ (Law of Messiah) in understanding that as a believer in Christ Jesus (Yeshua the Messiah) I was not obligated to obey the Law of Moses, for Jesus Christ had replaced it with the Law of Messiah.

So as an outgrowth of the **New Covenant** book, I wrote a book called *The Law: Then and Now, What About Grace?* (2019) I made a study of the Old Testament Mosaic (*Tanakh*) Law, that is the *Then* in the title and how God replaced it with the Law of Christ (Messiah) which is the *Now* in the title. In the process, I made a study of the imperative commands in the Greek from Acts and the Epistles that relate to the conduct of believers; there are over 600 commands given to the Church to obey in place of the Mosaic Law system.

As I researched the Law of Messiah, I found almost no material on the subject; and even coming from a sound Bible-believing church since my youth, I do not ever remember any sermon given on the subject of the Law of Messiah and its relationship to the believer today! Beyond that, I could not find any books dealing with the subject. That intrigued me, so I began to study the subject. What I discovered was that most believers, when pressed, fall back to the Mosaic Law by default. This new Law system offers life, the abundant life that Yeshua spoke of, that is to be reflected in our Christian walk as we live for Him in yielding to the Holy Spirit (Ruach Ha-Kodesh). This also became an exciting study as I began to understand what God required of me as a follower of Yeshua that was very different from the Mosaic Law. It is about life and liberty as we labor for Him, as we prepare ourselves for His judgment seat (I Corinthians 3:12-16; II Corinthians 5:10), also called the Bema Seat

Judgment or its biblical name the Day of Christ (Day of Messiah). While we have been saved by Faith in Messiah; at the Bema Seat Judgment, we will be given rewards for our faithful walk in our earthly life, and these rewards will follow us into our lives in the Kingdom and in the Eternal Order. This also became an exciting and refreshing study for me.

Now I never planned it this way, but the **New Covenant** book (*Israel's Only Hope: The New Covenant*) and the recent book on the Law of Messiah have actually now become a triad of books when combined with this newest one, and they are all interrelated. This new book is called the *Law of Moses VERSUS the Law of Messiah* and deals with the central issue today in the Messianic Movement concerning Torah observance, and also with many believers in the Church who fall back on the Mosaic Law as their default system. Many people believe that they must observe Torah Law, even after believing in Messiah Yeshua, in order to be good Christians. They have opted out of Yeshua's system of Law for the default system of Law that is no longer required – the Law of Moses. Consequently, today many zealous Jewish and Gentile believers are involved in importing the Law of Moses into the Church when it was never given to the Church, causing divisions in the body of Messiah. The biggest offenders are Gentile believers who adopt a Law that was never given to them in the first place. It is also a complete diversion from the progressive revelation that God gave to us, as He has given us His completed revelation in our walk with Him in the age of Grace. We'll review more about the Church ages as we get into our study.

There is an urgency in the Body of Messiah, the believing Church, to clarify the doctrinal and spiritual detour concerning whether or not Torah[1] or Torah observance[2] is valid in the New Testament for observance by believers today; that is the theme of this book. On one hand, Torah-observant believers firmly believe that Jews and Gentiles are to observe the **Law of Moses**; while on the other hand, others firmly believe we are to walk and grow in Messiah through the guidance of the Ruach Ha-Kodesh (Holy Spirit) in the Law of Messiah. Believers have become sidetracked in their spiritual growth as some are focusing on the *old covenant*, the Mosaic Law. However, the *old covenant* never promised spiritual growth nor did it promise victory over sin; instead, we find in *the* **New Covenant** and the Law of Messiah that proceeds from it, promises given to us for abundant life (John 10:10) in Messiah when obeyed.

---

[1] **Torah**: Will be used to refer to the Books of Moses only, Genesis through Deuteronomy.

[2] **Torah Observance**: Is a term used by some believers to refer to the supposed necessity of believers in Messiah Yeshua to keep the 613 Laws of Moses. However, these Torah observant believers generally selectively pick the laws they wish to obey and ignore others. It is called cherry picking because they are extremely inconsistent and are literally violating the very Law of Moses (James 2:10) that they say they are upholding.

Gentile believers are walking around wearing yarmulke (kippah), tzitzit (fringes), and prayer shawls (tallit), some even with tefillin (ritual straps). Often these zealous Judaized Gentile Christians come into churches and sow discord as they try to export their belief in trying to convince other Christians to convert to Messianic Judaism, which is the height of spiritual ignorance. Beyond this there is a greater spiritual consequence in not knowing how to have victory over sin by walking in the Light of Messiah and yielding to the Ruach Ha-Kodesh by obeying Yeshua's new commandment (John 13:34) and the commandments (John 14:21) given to the Church by Him through His Apostles in the Law of Messiah for all believers from **all** ethnicities.

In viewing the subject of this book, we need to lay down some biblical boundaries so that we stay on track. We will define the term Law of Messiah.

Let us briefly deal with how to *interpret* Scripture, a method of study called *hermeneutics*. We should always take God at His Word and not follow the biases of so-called theologians and scholars. Remember that God is the Author of language and does not need the fickle intelligence of man to "help" Him interpret it. Because this rule has been violated repeatedly, entrenched in Christian theology are the false teachings of Replacement Theology (now called Fulfillment Theology), Amillennial Theology (Roman Catholic Theology), and Covenant Reform Theology. They all continue to use the allegorical method of interpretation, also called spiritualization, inaccurately placing the Church in the *Tanakh* and trying to rob Israel of the covenants made to Israel only. The same thing is true of Torah observant believers and the Hebrew Roots movement as they ignore, twist, and pervert Scripture to teach their false doctrine.

Understand that in interpreting Scripture, **CONTEXT IS KING**. Don't read into the text what is not there. If you go into your study of Scripture with any other method of interpretation, you will come out of your study time with an anti-biblical bias. If you violate literal interpretation and the context in which it is given, you can make the Bible say anything.

The Law of Context

Another very important rule of interpretation is the law that teaches a text apart from the context is a pretext. A verse can only mean what it means in its context and must not be taken out of its context. The rule of context: The meaning must be gathered from the context. Every word you read must be understood in the light of the words that come before and after it. Context is king! A prime example of not examining the context is how Zechariah 13:6 is used. This verse is often used as a prophecy of the Messiah. Many pull it out of its context; it does appear to refer to Yeshua on the surface. But the context of verses 2-6 is speaking of *false prophets*. Verse 6 cannot refer to Yeshua unless He is a false prophet. This is the danger of studying a verse by itself rather than in context. The common saying, "You can prove anything by the Bible," is only true when this law is violated.

Later as we get into Scripture directly, we will discuss Matthew 5:17 and how it is ripped out of context in an attempt to prove an unbiblical biased point concerning Torah observance and their emphasis on keeping the Mosaic Law. One quick point: The Gospels are NOT New Testament theology, but are theologically a continuation of the Dispensation of Law. The whole context of the Gospels is completely surrounded by Law keeping as Yeshua kept the Mosaic Law because it was still in full effect; but He disregarded Rabbinic Law. The Law ended with the Lamb of God's voluntary sacrifice on the Cross and the Church Age. The Age of Grace began on the Jewish Feast of Shavuot (Pentecost) in Acts 2.

When you study the Bible, focus on the foundational **covenants** that God made with man, not covenants that are assumed and undocumented in Scripture as taught by Covenant Reform Theology. We will examine these common errors.

Be aware of the different **economies** that God used in ruling over the sinful hearts of men. These economies are called Dispensations, and they address the ways that He managed a sinful world at different times throughout the history of the Bible.

In connection with the Covenants and Dispensations, we recognize that God revealed His will and Word progressively, called progressive revelation. He revealed His will and His Word in bits and pieces through 40-plus sub-authors over a period of sixteen centuries until the revelation was complete with the Book of Revelation. There has been NO further revelation from God whether it be so-called visions, or dreams, or feelings, which are very common and popular today, which is against the *thus says the LORD* principle.

We must understand the distinctions between Israel and the Church. Israel is NOT the Church and the Church is NOT Israel.

It is helpful to understand the Hebrew word *olam* and its definition. When we understand the terms *forever*, *everlasting*, and *eternity* in Hebrew, we see that they are governed by time. In Greek the meanings are very clear; those words involve infinity and are not qualified by time.

We must take into account the timing and implications of the Law with Adam. There are repeated patterns in the *Tanakh*, to illustrate: Adam had two laws (not to eat the fruit from the tree in the center of the garden, and to multiply and replenish the earth) and violated one of them; and he and Eve were banished from the Garden **eastward**. God gave Israel 613 laws, and Israel flagrantly violated His Law. God's banishment of people in the future mirrors the banishment of Adam and Eve **eastward**; that time it was **eastward** to Babylon. Now we have believers in Messiah who ignore His commands (the Law of Messiah) during the economy of Grace, and their works will be judged by Yeshua on the Day of Messiah in heaven, not their salvation, but their works will be judged and rewarded accordingly.

What is the difference between a **New Covenant** and a **renewed** covenant? There is a critical difference between these two terms and their implications are also critical in understanding God's plan through the ages.

Biblically the Church and the Dispensation of Grace are NOT antinomian (meaning "without law") even though we do not keep the Mosaic Law code. When Dispensations were changed by God from Law to Grace, the **New Covenant** given to us had the Law of Messiah embedded in it, so the Epistles to the Church do not teach lawlessness or antinomianism, which is defined as the freedom to act or do as you wish.

Can we grasp the significance of Christian Liberty? The Law of Moses has been a great asset in western culture, especially in the development of the laws and government of the United States in the past centuries; and our great legal framework is not devalued simply because God has moved us on from the Dispensation of Law to the Dispensation of Grace because of the gift of His Son. Of course, if one becomes anti-Dispensational, they may mistakenly become anti-God in designated areas of their theology. Some teachers even have the talent of using persuasive words that teach AGAINST God's plan and how He chose to work with man and sin. Let me explain. Man's depraved heart that God must deal with cannot be bridled on earth because He allows mankind free will. Although we in the age of Grace are no longer under the Law of Moses, we are not at liberty in this age to live an unbridled life of sin; God has not left us without His guidance. We are now at liberty to live a life walking abundantly in Messiah, complying with His ways while being nurtured and guided by the Holy Spirit.

It is my goal to be first of all up front and pointed about our great liberty in Christ Jesus (Yeshua); please be patient, as I realize that the idea of a Law of Messiah may seem strange. Secondly, it is my goal to assist you by showing what the Bible teaches about Messiah's new commandment, while keeping theology and hard-to-understand concepts to a minimum. Theology is important, of course, but the Bible speaks pretty clearly on how to walk with Messiah. Once you see it for yourself, it will open doors for your understanding and practice. Remember that Jesus (Yeshua) said, *Come to Me all you who labor and are heavy laden, and I will give you rest. Take My yoke* (teachings / disciplines) *upon you, and learn of Me; for I am meek and lowly in heart; and you shall find rest unto your souls. For My yoke is easy, and My burden is light* (Matthew 11:28-30). I remember as a youth, my pastor saying,

"Keep the cookies on the lower shelf so that everyone can reach them."

So I want to keep this as simple and uncomplicated as possible, but to the point. We will lay down the key principles of biblical understanding in the first section of the book before we go into a verse-by-verse study of the Epistles in the second half of the book concerning the fact that the New Testament DOES NOT validate the use of the Law of Moses today, but it does teach about Yeshua's easy yoke, the less-pondered <u>Law of Messiah</u>.

Part One
What Is the Law of Messiah?

Chapter One
Defining the Law of Messiah

There are two biblical ideas that work together, and they are the key topics of this book: the **New Covenant**, which introduces a new lifestyle and freedom from the old way of Law, and the teachings and example of Yeshua and His Apostles on how believers are to live under the **New Covenant**, which Paul called the Law of Christ (Law of Messiah). Before laying down the biblical boundaries of this book, the term Law of Messiah needs to be defined since it will be referenced heavily throughout the book. So, what is the Law of Messiah?

Technical answer: In the Greek there is a tense called an *imperative*; it comes in the form of a command in the Epistles for the body of believers in Messiah. These commands are just as weighty as if they came from Sinai. There are over 600 of these that apply directly to the believer in this economy or Dispensation, the Age of Grace, or the Church age.[3] They come in the form of warnings, telling us to beware of false teaching, how to interact with believers and the unsaved world, instruction on how to walk in Messiah, things to refrain from and things to yield to the Holy Spirit (Ruach Ha-Kodesh).[4] The nature of this Law of Messiah is to guide believers as *new creations* in Messiah Yeshua as we walk and yield to the Ruach Ha-Kodesh with no threats of judgment; however, there can be disciplinary action on God's part (Hebrews 12:5-8) to disobedient believers.

Practical answer: Yeshua in the Gospel of John 13:34 (14:15; 15:14-15) gave a new commandment which is also referenced by the Apostle John in his First Epistle in 2:7-8 and 3:11, 23-24; see these verses respectively before the Law of Messiah is defined.

> John 13: [34] *A new commandment* [singular] *I give unto you, that you love one another; as I have loved you, that you also love one another.* [35] *By this shall all men know that you are My disciples, if you have love one to another.*

---

3 See Appendix Two.
4 See Appendix One.

> John 14: ¹⁵ *If you love Me, keep My commandments [plural].*
>
> John 15: ¹⁴ *You are My friends, if you do whatsoever I command you.* ¹⁵ *From now on, I call you not servants; for the servant does not know what his lord does: but I have called you friends; for all things that I have heard of My Father I have made known unto you.*
>
> I John 2: ³ *And hereby we know that we know Him, if we keep His commandments [plural].* ⁴ *He that says, I know Him, and keeps not His commandments [plural], is a liar, and the Truth is not in him;*
>
> I John 2: ⁷ *Brethren, I write no new commandment unto you, but an old commandment which you had from the beginning. The old commandment is the word which you have heard from the beginning.* ⁸ *Again, a new commandment [singular] I write unto you, which thing is true in Him and in you: because the darkness is past, and the true Light now shines.*
>
> I John 3: ¹¹ *For this is the message that you heard from the beginning, that we should love one another.*
>
> I John 3: ²³ *And this is His commandment [singular], that we should believe on the Name of His Son Jesus Christ, and love one another, as He gave us commandment [single]* ²⁴ *And he that keeps His commandments [plural] dwells in Him, and He in him. And hereby we know that He abides in us, by the Spirit which He has given us.*

In this collection of verses from the Apostle John's Gospel and his Epistles, the subject is Yeshua's new commandment, which is an absolute imperative for all believers to obey. There is much that can be written on these verses, but I want to share just a couple of points. *First,* Yeshua gives a new commandment, and then John in his Epistles references it as an old commandment, that is still new. *Old* can be taken two ways, first it is *old* as to the timing being that it occurs first in Leviticus 19:17-18 (then is reflected later in Yeshua's Sermon on the Mount in Matthew 5:21-22):

> *"You shall not hate your brother in your heart, but you shall reason frankly with your neighbor, lest you incur sin because of him. You shall not take vengeance or bear a grudge against the sons of your own people, but you shall love your neighbor as yourself: I am the LORD."* (ESV)

Secondly, it is *old* since Yeshua gave it roughly 60 years earlier, during His ministry on earth, and John was now citing it in his Epistle as he looks back. Yeshua at that time took the *old* commandment from Leviticus and intensified it in the **New Covenant** as *I have loved you* in His statement in John 13:34-35 in the economy of Grace, making it totally unlike anything in the *Tanakh*. So, for the believers that

John is writing to in his Epistles it is *old*, for they have had it since the beginning of their walk in Messiah, but in another way it is forever *new*.

I will quote a statement from a Jewish believer[5] as he ties together a series of verses concerning this Law that Yeshua intensified in the **New Covenant**, pairing the *old* and *new*. First, this Jewish believer quotes Matthew 22:36-40 regarding the new commandment that Yeshua mentioned, and then he proceeds to share other related passages:

> One day a Pharisee asked our Lord:
>
>> *^{36} Master, which is the great commandment in the law? ^{37} Jesus said unto him, you shall love the LORD your God with all your heart, and with all they soul, and with all your mind. ^{38} This is the first and great commandment. ^{39} And the second is like unto it, you shall love your neighbor as yourself. ^{40} On these two commandments hang all the law and the prophets* (Matthew 22:36-40).
>
> And then our Lord added the following, in the parallel account by Mark:
>
>> *There is no other commandment greater than these* (Mark 12:31b).
>
> Then Paul added to that in Romans and Galatians:
>
>> *... for he that loves one another has fulfilled the law* (Romans 13:8).
>
>> *For all the law is fulfilled in one word, even in this; you shall love your neighbor as yourself* (Galatians 5:14).
>
> Then my friend quotes James:
>
>> *If you fulfill the royal law according to the scripture, you shall love your neighbor as yourself, you do well* (James 2:8).

---

[5] Lehman Strauss. *The Epistles of John*. Neptune, NJ: Loizeaux Brothers, 1972, p. 109.

Then back to Paul again:

> *Love works no ill to his neighbor: therefore love is the fulfilling of the Law* (Romans 13:10).
>
> *Now the end of the commandment is to love out of a pure heart, and of a good conscience, and of faith unfeigned* (I Timothy 1:5).

These passages teach us that the sum total of man's duty and moral obligation is expressed in one word, *love*. Love is the supreme thing. Notice the *change of motivation* in Yeshua's statement in John 13:34 when He said,

> *A new commandment I give unto you, that you love one another;* **as I have loved you***, that you also love one another.*

Observe in Leviticus it is brother showing love to brother, but it is greatly intensified in the **New Covenant** with Yeshua's statement of *as I have loved you*. Believers are to love each other sacrificially as He had demonstrated in His three years of ministry before His disciples, with His most recent display of washing the disciples' feet just before this teaching. Later that day He would demonstrate His sacrificial love for them on the Cross, the ultimate intensifying of His commandment. So, the newness of Yeshua's command is not the command itself; but the motivation and standard are pinpointed exactly. This is the way in which believers are to love each other. Love was required in the *Tanakh*, however, what was *new* was the degree of love that Yeshua commands; it is a much higher level because of His example on the Cross to us. His love for us was self-sacrificial; human fleshly love cannot and does not live up to that. For believers, this kind of love is now a command. So that is *first of all* to be our motivation before other believers and before the unsaved world.

Yeshua intensified a law originally given in the Mosaic code, so His words are not new in and of themselves. Rather His words emphasize a completely new pattern, standard, or model for believers' love for each other. It is the way in which we are to love that is different due to His First Coming. It never happened in human history before that God would literally come in the flesh (John 1:14) and demonstrate His love for us. He voluntarily sacrificed Himself on the Cross for depraved, sinful people so that we who were eternally separated from Him would now be guaranteed new life through the **New Covenant** and to live forever with Him, with our new everlasting life. Love was required prior to His First Coming, but not to this degree; this was something completely new. He changed our understanding and experience of love forever.

Now *second,* Yeshua states clearly that He no longer will call believers *servants*, but now He calls them *friends* (John 15:14). Paul and others called themselves *bondservants*, but after the inauguration of the **New Covenant,** believers are referred to by Yeshua as *friends*, *sons of God, the bride of Messiah,* having been adopted into

His own family. That is also a status change because of the **New Covenant**. This was never accomplished in and through the *old covenant*.

Third, on page 1, the difference between the terms *commandment* and *commandment<u>s</u>* is shown with the underlined and bolded <u>s</u> and is emphasized with the words *singular* or *plural*. Yeshua gave a singular commandment in John 13:34 and mentions plural commandments in John 14:15 and I John 2:3 and 3:23. John states that Yeshua gave plural commandments in John 14, meaning that Yeshua gave other commandments on two fronts when He mediated the **New Covenant**. First, He gave some of them Himself, especially in His Upper Room Discourse (John 13:31 – 15:26)[6]; but, secondly, He also gave commandments through His Apostles as they taught and developed the doctrines for the first-century believers on how to live out their Faith in Messiah through what He did in inaugurating the **New Covenant**. John in his First Epistle references that there are plural command<u>s</u> 60 years after Yeshua's ascension in AD 30. So, what are His command<u>s</u> that He gave through His Apostles? Remember the Scriptures make a transition from the *old covenant* (Mosaic Law), ending with the death, burial, and resurrection of Yeshua, to the **New Covenant** through His blood (Matthew 26:27-28; I Corinthians 11:25; Isaiah 42:6; 49:8) on the Jewish feast day of Shavuot, also known as Pentecost, in Acts 2. In the Epistles there are numerous topics that the <u>Law of Messiah</u> covers in teaching believers a brand-new standard of living. In Appendix One there are general topics of areas that are incorporated into the <u>Law of Messiah</u> as a direct result of the **New Covenant**. These commands are found in 614 verses in the books of Acts and the Epistles which are referenced 758 total times as imperative command*s*. In going through these commands, some do not directly apply to believers in the Church because they were personal requests. However, there are over 600 of these command<u>s</u> that the Apostles gave that apply directly to the Church and to every believer in Messiah.

What becomes a major issue today in the Messianic Movement is to understand how the commandment<u>s</u> of Yeshua relate to the Mosaic Law. Some want to make the <u>Law of Messiah</u> into a supplement to the Mosaic Law, while others disregard them altogether. Their reasoning is because they emphatically teach that the Mosaic Law is eternal and cannot be changed, while others modify the Mosaic Law so that it can be kept outside the Land without a Temple or priesthood.

The net result is that they depreciate the <u>Law of Messiah</u>, making it a supplement to the Mosaic code because they teach that the **New Covenant** is not *new* but a *renewed* covenant. In so doing they place Yeshua, *the Prophet like Moses,* under Moses, making His words less important than Moses' words, an approach which is diametrically opposed to Moses' words in Deuteronomy 18:18-19 when he spoke of

---

[6] Arnold G. Fruchtenbaum. *Yeshua: The Life of Messiah from a Messianic Jewish Perspective* – Abridged Version. San Antonio, TX: Ariel Ministries, 2017, Par #161-162, pp. 521-540. There are twenty-five promises and thirteen admonitions given.

the *Prophet Like Moses* who would come after Moses. Moses said that to Him and to Him alone are they then to hearken (listen and obey).

Two Jewish believers, Alan Poyner-Levison of Beit Shalom Ministries and Robert Morris of HaDavar Ministries, have set the tone for all believers on how we are to interact with the Law of Messiah given to them through Messiah.

> The Law [of Moses] has been a major stumbling stone to many in the Messianic Movement, even to many who have come from a Gentile background. They are mainly prone to error because they will not accept that the Law [of Moses] has been fulfilled by Yeshua; otherwise, why would He have come to die if it wasn't to fulfill Scripture? God sent Yeshua to confirm Scripture and to be the ultimate sacrifice, something that only the Son of God could ever fulfill, since nobody was ever found to be good enough (Revelation 5:4).[7]

> Jews and Gentiles who have placed their faith in *Yeshua* as their Savior should express their faith externally through obedience to the commands stated in the New Testament. Those imperatives, and there are over 600 of them, are titled in the New Testament under two names: 1) The Law of Christ (Galatians 6:2) and 2) The Law of the Spirit of Life [in Christ Jesus] (Romans 8:2). The document "A New Commandment I Give to You" is a compilation of those commandments found in the New Testament. These commands are the rule of life for the New Testament Believer today. Obeying them will lead to the "abundant life" *Yeshua* promises to those who trust and obey Him.[8]

> [Brackets are mine - I would add I Corinthians 9:21 which speaks of *the law to Messiah* as a third reference.]

In short, the motivating factor of our walk in Messiah is His work done in mediating the **New Covenant** and the new lifestyle that comes from it in the Law of Messiah.

In summary **our focus is to be on Messiah**, or should I say on *the Prophet Like Moses*, not Moses and the Law given at Sinai. **Our focus is on the Mediator** Who inaugurated the **New Covenant** and all its ramifications as opposed to the *old covenant* and its deficiencies because of our corruptible flesh. Understanding all the

---

[7] Alan Poyner-Levison. "The Law of Moses and the Law of Messiah." Messianic Jewish Author and Director and Messianic Teacher of Beit Shalom Ministries in the (Wakefield, Yorkshire) UK, n.d.

[8] Robert Morris. "The Eternal Nature of the Mosaic Law," unpublished manuscript used by permission.

multiple ramifications of what He did for us in transferring us from the kingdom of darkness to the kingdom of Light should change forever our motivation for our daily living and service to Him. The <u>Law of Messiah</u> is how we are to live and relate to Him, to the brethren, and to the unsaved world. The Christian life is not difficult; God planned it that way so all could walk in Him. The Christian life is not complicated nor hard to understand, so don't make it difficult. The <u>Law of Messiah</u> is our standard of how we are to live out our Faith through yielding to the ministry of the Ruach Ha-Kodesh (Holy Spirit). The <u>Law of Messiah</u> gives us our standard in living morally, socially, and ethically before mankind in this dark, corrupted, and twisted world. The Law of Moses is not to be lifted up above the Messiah Who birthed it, as the erroneous Torah observance folks have lifted it up over Messiah. This Law He gave at Sinai to serve its purpose until He, the Author of that Law, came in the fullness of time to fulfill and die to issue an even greater Law, the <u>Law of Messiah,</u> to be our guide in Messiah for all our days here on earth.

Chapter Two
Hermeneutics

Hermeneutics is a technical term used to explain how to interpret Scripture accurately using a proper method. There are numerous types of *hermeneutics* used in the Church today, but we will only focus on the two primary ones. Hermeneutics is one of the key foundations of understanding Scripture which theologians and scholars have greatly complicated by substituting spurious hermeneutics. Not every method is equally effective.

Literal, Historical/Grammatical Method

The primary and biblical hermeneutic is the **literal, historical/grammatical** method of interpreting Scripture. Simply put it is believing that God, who by the way is the Author of languages (Genesis 11:6-8), can speak clearly what He wants understood in the text without man inserting his own personal biases or theologies which are foreign to the context. Here is the Golden Rule of Interpretation that all need to memorize:

> When the plain sense of Scripture makes common sense, seek no other sense; therefore, take every word at its primary, ordinary, usual, literal meaning unless the facts of the immediate context, studied in the light of related passages and axiomatic[9] and fundamental truths, indicate clearly otherwise.[10]

---

[9] *Axiomatic* means "that which is taken for granted: Self Evident."

[10] David L. Cooper. *The God of Israel: Messianic Series Number One.* Los Angeles, CA: Biblical Research Society, 1945. This is a seven-volume set written by Cooper, the others are:
  Volume two: *Messiah: His Nature and Person,* 1933.
  Volume three: *Messiah: His Redemptive Career,* 1932.
  Volume four: *Messiah: His First Coming Scheduled,* 1939.
  Volume five: *Messiah: His Historical Appearance,* 1958.
  Volume six: *Messiah: His Glorious Appearance Imminent,* 1961.
  Volume seven: *Messiah: His Final Call to Israel,* 1962.
Numerous other books by David L. Cooper and the same publisher include:
  Future Events Revealed according to Matthew 24-25, 1935.
  The 70 Weeks of Daniel, 1941.
  When Will Wars Cease?, 1941.
  Why God's Interest Is in the Jew, 1941.

Scholars can complicate the Scriptures, which in places can be difficult to understand; but when using the literal method of interpretation as Dispensationalists[11] do and adding to that a Jewish perspective, many problem texts are remedied. Many people struggle with issues such as Torah observance and the whole Hebrew Roots movement which some Messianic Jewish and Gentile believers teach as an absolute necessity. Taking the Scriptures literally will eliminate much of the problem. The literal method of interpretation must be consistent throughout the biblical text as Michael Vlach notes in his contrast of literal and non-literal interpretations.

> Is literal interpretation unique to Dispensationalism? In one sense the answer is "No" since non-Dispensationalists also use the grammatical-historical method for much of Scripture. They apply it to historical narratives, legal literature, wisdom literature, the Gospels, and the Epistles. But the answer is "Yes" in another sense.
>
> Non-Dispensationalists often abandon literal or grammatical-historical hermeneutics concerning Old Testament prophecies, particularly restoration prophecies about Israel. They often will call for "symbolical interpretation" or "typological interpretation" or "a different kind of literal" or "spiritualization" of Old Testament prophecies. … What makes Dispensationalism unique is it attempts to be consistent with the literal method of interpretation, even with Old Testament prophecies about national Israel. Dispensationalism believes these are to be taken literally like other texts of Scripture. No need exists to shift to another hermeneutical method for Old Testament prophetic texts.[12]

Allegorical or Spiritualization Method

The second hermeneutic is called "allegorical" or "the spiritualization" of the biblical text. Again, simply put, theologians/scholars because of their theological bias, especially as it relates to Eschatology (the study of future things) and Israelology (the study of Israel) as well as Ecclesiology (the Study of the Church), are determined to

---

Man: His Creation, Fall, Redemption and Glorification, 1950.
What Men Must Believe or God's Gracious Provision for Man, 1953.
The Shepherd of Israel, 1962.
When Gog's Armies Meet the Almighty in the Land of Israel: Exposition of Ezekiel 38-39, 1970.
An Exposition of the Book of Revelation, 1972.

Also, on *www.PromisesToIsrael.org* under the banner David L. Cooper, there are over thirty brochures that he wrote that can be copied for free.

[11] Dispensationalism will be discussed in Chapter Three.
[12] Michael Vlach. *Dispensational Hermeneutics.* Theological Studies Press, 2023, p. 30.

read into the biblical text of the *Tanakh* their theological biases in replacing Israel with the Church and spiritualizing a multitude of Second Coming prophecies in the *Tanakh*. These people are non-Dispensationalists who are not consistent with their hermeneutic as pointed out in this quote:

> The non-Dispensationalist is a literalist in much of his interpretation of the Scriptures, but [critics] charge him with allegorizing or spiritualizing when it comes to the interpretation of prophecy. The Dispensationalist claims to be consistent in his use of this principle, and he accuses the non-Dispensationalist of being inconsistent in his use of it.[13]

Michael Vlach adds a comment regarding the importance of a consistent application of hermeneutics and a warning for those who would change it as follows:

> A proper contextual [hermeneutic] does not elevate man's reason over God's Revelation – it respects it … Many acknowledge the necessity of contextual hermeneutics for most Scripture including Old Testament narratives, the Gospels, Acts, and the Epistles. But many do not believe literal interpretation should apply to Old Testament prophetic sections, particularly prophecies about Israel's restoration.[14]

Most of Christian theology gives disrespect to God and His Word by not being consistent with His Word. For instance, we understand God uses allegory as in The Vision of the Valley of Dry Bones (Ezekiel 37), but then He interprets His own allegory. Paul in Galatians (4:22-31) does the same thing by stating he is using an allegory as he explains what it means. Nowhere in Scripture does God approve or authenticate fickle biases that men come up with on their own. Some even have many theological degrees behind their name but still go astray of God's own word by inserting their wildly fantastical spiritual meanings. In essence what they are doing is usurping God's authority with their own biased unbiblical authority in re-interpreting what the God of the Universe has clearly spoken. In a way, they are just like the Pharisees in Yeshua's day in how they used the Oral Law to work around the spirit of the written Law of Moses. J. C. Ryle makes an interesting observation:

> Time would fail me, if I attempted to quote all the passages of Scripture in which the future history of Israel is revealed. Isaiah, Jeremiah, Ezekiel, Hosea, Joel, Amos, Obadiah, Micah, Zephaniah, Zechariah all declare the same thing. All predict, with more or less

---

[13] Michael Vlach quotes from page 30 of Charles Ryrie's *Dispensationalism Today*. Chicago, IL: Moody Press, 1965, p. 89.

[14] Michael Vlach. *Dispensational Hermeneutics*. Theological Studies Press, 2023, pp. 31-32.

> particularity, that in the end of this Dispensation the Jews are to be restored to their own land and to the favor of God.[15]

Using allegory and spiritualization to interpret prophecies about Israel goes against the well-respected rules for using context, which means to rely on the sense of the overall story of the Scriptures to understand individual passages. For instance, we can mistakenly try to read New Testament Church truth back into the *Tanakh* (Old Testament). When we do this, we may believe that whenever the Bible makes a prophecy about Israel that it is not about Israel but has been magically transformed into a prophecy for the Church. This type of error is called *Replacement Theology*. By illustration, it is like seeing a digital clock hanging on the wall of Moses' home, totally out of place. If you are unaware that a digital clock did not exist before modern times, you may not realize how out of context it is. It is surprising how often Replacement Theology interferes with a believer's understanding of God's plan to restore Israel. When you move away from biblical context, you will arrive at a faulty and erroneous theology, especially as it relates to Israel and prophecy in the *Tanakh*. Three examples follow, of which many could be cited:

First, Yeshua said *upon this Rock I will build My Church* (Matthew 16:18). This is in the future tense NOT past or present tense. In other words, when Yeshua made that statement before AD 30, the Church was not in existence, so how does one confuse the Church as Israel in the *Tanakh*? So, if it was not in existence, with what authority can you read something that DID NOT exist back into the biblical text of the *Tanakh*? You can only ignore what Yeshua said if your bias is so strong that it does not accept what Yeshua literally said. Don't complicate Scripture!

I would recommend a simple Bible study presented as a book by Robert Morris that shows the significance of taking the Bible literally. It is called *Messiah and the Tabernacle,*[16] and it provides 18 easy lessons about the building of the Tabernacle in the wilderness that drive home the importance of context and literal interpretation of the Bible. It uses no fancy theology, and is ideal for a small group or individual Bible study that helps in understanding how the Bible was written, including the correct use of symbols and context. It is a fascinating and powerful study and easy to lead.

In a ***second example*** let me begin by defining the word *mystery*, for that is the word that Paul used in Ephesians 3:1-6 and Colossians 1:25-27. *Mystery* in our English language is something that is mysterious, something that cannot be known; it's a secret that secret societies hold. The use of *mystery* by Paul here refers to a *mystery*

---

[15] J.C. Ryle. *Are You Ready For The End of Time?* Fearn, Scotland: Christian Focus, reprint, 2001, p. 9.

[16] Robert Morris. *Messiah and the Tabernacle: Exodus 25-30, A 16-Part Bible Study.* Huntington Beach, CA: JHousePublishing (Purple Raiment label), 2010.

that was unknown to man in the *Tanakh* until God made it known by revelation. Vine Expository Dictionary states the following:

> In the New Testament it [the term *mystery*] denotes, not the mysterious (as with the English word), but that which, being outside the range of unassisted natural apprehension, can be made known only by Divine revelation, and is made known in a manner and at a time appointed by God.[17]

Paul clearly gives the meaning of this unique *mystery* not revealed in the *Tanakh* but now revealed in Ephesians 3:4-6 and Colossians 1:25-27 respectively:

> *[4] Whereby, when you read, you may understand my knowledge in the mystery of Messiah [5] which in other ages was not made known unto the sons of men, as it is now revealed unto His holy apostles and prophets by the Spirit; [6] That the Gentiles should be fellow heirs, and of the same body, and partakers of His promise in Messiah by the gospel.*
>
> *[25] Whereof I am made a minister, according to the Dispensation of God which is given to me for you, to fulfill the word of God; [26] Even the mystery which has been hidden from ages and from generations, but now is made manifest to His saints: [27] To whom God would make known what is the riches of the glory of this mystery among the Gentiles; which is Messiah in you, the hope of glory:*

What is the *mystery* revealed? It is not that Gentiles could be saved, but that both Jews and Gentiles are equally accepted into the body of Messiah as equal co-heirs with Him (Ephesians 2:11-22). That was not revealed in the *Tanakh;* those who read the Church back into the *Tanakh* have allowed their theological bias to read the Church back into the *Tanakh* when IT WAS NOT THERE! Could I say that when they are guilty of reading their theology back into the *Tanakh*, they are adding to Scripture, which the Scriptures condemn (Revelation 22:18). Those who say that the Church is really the Israel of the *old covenant* are just like the Pharisees who treated their Rabbinic Law (Oral Law) as weightier than Scripture itself.

*The **third*** and last example comes from Galatians 6:16 which will be dealt with later. Let me simply say here concerning that passage that Paul uses the phrase *the Israel of God*. Israel is referenced 69 times in the New Testament and 68 of those times it

---

[17] W. E. Vine. *Vine's Expository Dictionary of Old and New Testament Words*, Old Tappan, NJ: Fleming H. Revell Co, 1981. Vol 3, p. 97.

unquestionably refers to ethnic Israel.[18] In Galatians 6:16, Paul is speaking of *the Israel of God* referring to **the remnant of Israel**; *in this instance,* Jewish believers are being called *the Israel of God*. Paul reiterates in Romans 9:6 that only Jewish believers are the Israel of God. Again, to take this verse and read the Church back into the *Tanakh* is a violation of the Law of Context. We must pay attention to all the contextual road signs that help us understand what the text is referencing. This is especially true of understanding the difference between references to Israel and references to the Church.

The Use of the Term *Church* – the *Ekklesia*

Usage in the Tanakh

The word for Church, the *ekklesia*, means "assembly" and is used in the *Tanakh* (LXX – Greek Septuagint or *old testament* translation) in reference to people assembling together for corporate worship as at the Pilgrim Feasts three times a year in Jerusalem (Exodus 23:14-19; 34:18-23; Deuteronomy16:1-16). It is a compound word, *ek*, meaning "out of," and *klesis* meaning "a calling out." In the Hebrew text the word *ekklesia* was not used, for *ekklesia* is a Greek term, not Hebrew. In the Greco-Roman world, not in the Jewish world or in the *Tanakh*, it referred to a body of citizens gathered to discuss affairs of State as is reflected in Acts 19:39 in the context of the riot in Ephesus. In the Greek Septuagint (LXX), the term is used to designate the gathering of Israel, summoned for any definite purpose, or a gathering regarded as representative of the whole nation, as in Acts 6:12, in reference to the gathering of the Sanhedrin against Stephen to stone him.[19] *Ekklesia* generally references the assembly of God's people when it is used in the *Tanakh*. These assemblies developed into the Jewish synagogues as the gathering of the community of God in what has been called the silent years, the time period of 400 years between the completed writings of the *Tanakh* and the Gospels, with Messiah's First Coming. Only in Acts, authored by Luke and in the Epistles authored by Paul, do Luke and Paul use the specific technical term *ekklesia* to identify the body of Messiah.

---

[18] Arnold G. Fruchtenbaum, *Faith Alone: An Exposition of the Book of Galatians*. San Antonio, TX: Ariel Press, 2014, pp. 60-70 and *Israelology: The Missing Link in Systematic Theology*. San Antonio, TX: Ariel Press, 2018, pp. 660-667.

Michael Rydelnik & Michael Vanlaningham, *The Moody Bible Commentary*. Chicago, IL: Moody Press, 2014, p. 1842.

Robert Wilkin. *The Grace New Testament Commentary, Vol 2*. Denton, TX: Grace Evangelical Society, 2010, pp. 856-857.

[19] *Vine's Expository Dictionary of Old and New Testament Words*, Old Tappan, NJ: Fleming H. Revell Co., 1981, vol 1, pp. 82-83.

Usage in the New Testament

But while *ekklesia* may find its roots in the Greco-Roman world and the term used for the Jewish synagogue, it is not a subset of these, but becomes a new special term used for the gathering of believers in Messiah.[20] This came about largely as a Pauline term although it is used by Matthew in his Gospel (16:18; 18:17), by Luke in Acts (21 times), the author of the Book of Hebrews (2:12; 12:23) along with John in the Book of Revelation (Chapters 1-3 and 22:16). Paul gives the term *ekklesia* new meaning in reference to the body of Messiah that meets together physically, but it primarily means the Universal Church, the body of Messiah. Yeshua did the same thing with redefining the third cup in the Passover ceremony. Originally the wine referred to the blood of the Passover lamb of Exodus 12, but He used it to refer to His blood, the blood of the **New Covenant;** and we are thus called to remember Him and what He did for us.

---

[20] William Mounce, *Mounce's Complete Expository Dictionary of Old and New Testament Words*, Grand Rapids, MI: Zondervan Publishing, 2006, p. 110.

Chapter Three
What Is the Difference Between an Eternal and a Conditional Covenant?

There are eight covenants given by God through history and not three covenants as Covenant Reform Theology claims. The covenants given in the Bible are called the Edenic, Adamic, Noahic, Abrahamic, Mosaic, Land, Davidic, and **New Covenant**. Most believers are more familiar with the Mosaic and **New Covenant**s, but each one is an intentional promise that involves God and mankind at different times in human history. Covenant Reform Theology, on the other hand assumes events in the eternal past that were supposedly made between God the Father and God the Son but which have no biblical authentication, and they add another covenant between God and Adam, which is an implied agreement, without any covenant language.[21]

We will cover the significance of the biblical Covenants and the problems with Reform Theology in Chapter Four. Reform Theology tends to support the false claim that the Church of believers existed in the Old Testament. Included in Chapter Four is a chart that helps us recognize how theses covenants were introduced by God over time. The eight biblical covenants are divided into two groups: Eternal unconditional and conditional. Three covenants were given to humanity in general (Edenic, Adamic and Noahic) and the other five covenants (Abrahamic, Mosaic, Land, Davidic, and New covenants) were given to Jewish humanity.

Progressive Revelation

Before I move into a discussion of the Covenants and later into Dispensations, I need to explain the importance of how God revealed His Word over sixteen centuries comprising 40-plus authors to His people in the *Tanakh* and His people, true faithful believers in Messiah. Kenneth Symes expressed an important observation concerning progressive revelation:

> It is important, also, for us to understand that Dispensations are the only means of harmonizing all apparent contradictions that are

---

[21] For a good general understanding of Covenant Theology, read the following book: E. Showers. *There Really is a Difference!: A Comparison of Covenant and Dispensational Theology*. Bellmawr, NJ: Friends of Israel Gospel Ministry, 1990.

generally related to different actions in different time frames, thus enabling us to better understand Scripture.[22]

Hebrews 1:1-2 serves as a strategic passage in showing clearly that the Scriptures were revealed progressively to mankind. God did not reveal everything in His plan to Adam, nor did He to Enoch, Noah, Abraham, Moses, David, Isaiah, Jeremiah, Ezekiel, Daniel, or Zechariah. It was revealed in pieces or increments over the sixteen centuries by numerous inspired authors. So we read that Noah lived by Faith (Hebrews 11) and believed in what had been revealed to him in God's progressive revelation. He and all the others in the Books of Moses did not believe in the death, burial, and resurrection of Yeshua to be saved, because Yeshua's ministry had not yet been revealed through God's progressive revelation, contrary to the claims of Covenant Reform Theology. Look at the words of the author of Hebrews 1:1-2:

> *[1] God, who at many times and in various ways spoke in time past unto the fathers by the prophets, [2] has in these last days spoken unto us by His Son, whom He has appointed heir of all things, by whom also He made the worlds.*

Below is a chart to help explain progressive revelation. We understand the foundational precepts as they are developed through the Covenants and Dispensations to our fuller understanding of the revealed Word of God. The chart is an inverted pyramid with a key verse from Isaiah 28:9-10 used as an application.

> *[9] Whom shall he teach knowledge? And whom shall he make to understand doctrine? Them that are weaned from the milk, and drawn from the breasts. [10] For precept must be upon precept, precept upon precept; line upon line, line upon line; here a little, and there a little.*

This figure is a perfect illustration from Scripture as to how we learn, precept upon precept, or teach point upon teaching point, biblical truth upon biblical truth as we study, learning how to understand His Word that He gave us over a span of sixteen centuries.[23]

---

[22] Kenneth Symes, *Understanding God's Program for the Ages*. Bethel Baptist Printing Ministry: London, Ontario, Canada, 2012, p. 18. Chart on Foundational Precepts done by Ken Symes.

[23] Kenneth Symes. *Understanding God's Program for the Ages*. Printed in Canada by Bethel Baptist Printing Ministry, 2012, chart in back of book.

Definition of an Eternal Unconditional Covenant

An eternal, unconditional covenant[24] is a unilateral covenant, meaning it was made by one party, God, acting on behalf of another party with the following formula: "I will" followed by a promise.

Notice in the Abrahamic Covenant of Genesis 12:1-3, 7. There are five "I will's," meaning the promise is dependent on God and not Abraham and is confirmed in Genesis 15 by God alone. *I will* show you ***a Land***, a promise which is later developed by God into the **Land Covenant** (Deuteronomy 29-30). Again, the promise is dependent on God and not the faithfulness of Abraham, Yitzchak (Isaac), Yaakov (Jacob) or Israel. God's commitment is unconditional and eternal. While the ownership of the Land of Israel is not conditional, there is one contingency related to ownership. What was conditional was the possession of the Land, not ownership, by their obedience to the Law. However, Abraham and his descendants were given the title deed to the Land and will in the future possess all the Land promised. Much to the dismay of the promoters of false theologies such as those associated with Replacement/Fulfillment; Amillennial; and Covenant Reform Theologies,[25] as well

---

[24] For a full study of Eternal Unconditional Covenants and Conditional Covenants, see the *Come & See Series, The Word of God*, vol. 1, pp. 69-117, published by Ariel Press, *www.Ariel.org*. Also see DVDs by Mottel Baleston: *The Eight Covenants of the Bible* (four DVDs) and *The Plan of the Ages* (five DVDs) which may also be obtained through Ariel Ministries at *www.Ariel.org*.

[25] These three false theologies I sometimes call "the three wicked sisters" because none of them believe in a future for the nation of Israel. The Bible teaches that God will physically / literally establish His throne on earth under the rule of Messiah for 1000

as all anti-Semites, the Land of Israel including the West Bank and Gaza belongs to Israel. The world's two-state plan for Israel is dead on arrival with God. Notice the format and confirmation of the Abrahamic Covenant in Genesis 15 as well and that God made the covenant binding on Himself for fulfillment and not on Abraham and his descendants.

It's easy to see that if we believe what God says in the Bible that we can understand His faithfulness as we comprehend His hand at work. If He is good for His promises to the Jewish people, we can easily believe He will fulfill the promises we have from Him for eternal life because of Yeshua's death, burial, and resurrection.

Here is a brief summary of how God put forth His fulfillment of His promises to the Jewish people. *I will make you a* **great nation**, for at that time Abraham had no heir. God will later take this promise and give to Abraham a son, his seed. Then that aspect of the Seed, God will later develop into the Davidic Covenant. Abraham's seed, will be Isaac (Yitzchak). Then God will give a son to Yitzchak – Yaakov (Jacob) – and his twelve sons will become the future leaders of the twelve tribes. According to Ruth 4:17-22, from Yehuda, the fourth born of Yaakov out of Judah, will come the promised Seed, meaning the Messiah Yeshua. Genesis 22:18 refers to Abraham's Seed, meaning Yeshua, the one who shall bless all the families of the earth. This passage in Ruth traces Abraham's line to David, and to him (David) was given the Davidic Covenant. Galatians 3:16 also makes it clear that Messiah was promised to come from Abraham's line, referring to Him as the Christ (Messiah). We again see the promise to Abraham being fulfilled in the titles ascribed to Messiah Yeshua: son of Abraham, the son of David, the Son of God (Matthew 1:1-2; Luke 3:33-34). This action is God working through the lives of sinful man from Abraham to David using promises in the format of His *I will* statements. (II Samuel 7:12-14 presents five *I will's*: I Chronicles 17:11-14 repeats these five of God's *I will* statements. Putting all His *I will* statements together, we see that God established the **Seed line** through which Messiah would come (Luke 3:23-31, 32-34, 35-38). As with the Abrahamic Covenant, we once again see that the ***Davidic Covenant*** is dependent on God and not David.

An additional *I will* given to Abraham and his descendants by God pronounced curses and blessings on the Gentiles based on how they treat the Jewish people.[26] That *I will* is the promise of *blessing* through Abraham to all the families or ethnicities of the world, an aspect which God will develop later in Jeremiah (31:31-

---

years. This Messianic Kingdom, also known as the Millennial Kingdom, will be based in the literal, physical city of Jerusalem with Messiah, Himself, physically on the throne. Various errors taught are that the Kingdom is already here, that there will be no future kingdom, or that the Church fulfills this prophecy that was meant for the House of Israel.

[26] John B. Metzger, *Poking God's Eye: A Theological and Historical View of Anti-Semitism Based on the Blessings and Cursings of Genesis 12:3.* Keller, TX: JHousePublishing, 2018. Also available through Ariel Ministries at *www.Ariel.org.*

34; Ezekiel 36:26-28) in the **New Covenant**. Notice also when you read Jeremiah the promise of the **New Covenant** was given to Israel NOT when they were faithful, but when they were wicked and evil just before they were taken captive to Babylon and punished. This blessing on the Jewish people and on the Gentiles is completely dependent on God through the death, burial, and resurrection of the Messiah, for Messiah's blood is the blood of the **New Covenant** (Matthew 26:28); it is totally based on what God will do, not man. The **New Covenant** and our salvation are dependent on God; the FREE GIFT of salvation by His Grace is not based on our works or merit (Ephesians 2:8-10). Summary: In understanding the language of the Covenants, it was God obligating Himself to fulfill the Covenants, not on Abraham, not on David and not on Israel! As a result, it makes no sense to say that God would renege on His covenant promises to His people or to those who have received the **New Covenant**.

These are all unconditional, eternal covenants that God made initially through Abraham and David and to Israel. They completely, unquestionably, depend on God to fulfill His will and make salvation available to mankind (Isaiah 42:6; 49:6; Matthew 26:28; Romans 3:23-30; Heb 9:11-14). The ONLY cure for man's sin problem and his depraved heart is the **New Covenant**. Just a side point, if Israel has these everlasting covenants that totally depend on Him for fulfillment, and your salvation is a result of the **New Covenant**, part of the everlasting covenant, then your salvation is also dependent on Him, it is secure in HIM, not in your performance. You cannot lose it (as Arminianism teaches), nor do you have to persevere to keep your salvation (as Calvinism teaches), your salvation is ONLY dependent on Him alone, not your performance!! Yeshua promised by believing in Him you HAVE as a possession Everlasting Life (John 3:16, 36; 5:24; 20:31).

How egotistical and smug are Replacement, Amillennial, and Covenant Reform Theologians who say the Church has inherited the blessings of the covenants because of Israel's sin and unfaithfulness and their rejection of Messiah. They claim that Israel's shortfall caused God to "disown" them. But of course, in their opinion, Israel gets to keep the cursings that come with disobedience. How convenient for these biased theologians. This is the height of spiritual pride!! Haven't they looked in the mirror lately? The Church is wicked and evil (just as Yeshua predicted in the parables of Matthew 13 and to the Churches of Revelation). Just look at its history, a corrupt and wicked history with its Church dogmas, synods, popes, and councils like the Council of Trent (1545-1563), with its corrupted theology then and today. Even in the Protestant churches, sin has been multiplied. Today's churches in general are no different than Israel, just as unfaithful and sinful. Yet has God disinherited His church with ALL it sins??? It takes an enormous ego to conclude that the Church today is so wonderful, pure, and holy. As the saying goes today, really!![27]

---

[27] Please read the following books:

The Centrality of the Abrahamic Covenant

The Abrahamic Covenant of Genesis 12:1-3, 7 (13:14-18; 15:1-21; 17:1-22; 22:15-18; Galatians 3:8) is the first covenant given to the Jewish people, given to Abraham with its fourteen provisions, then to Yitzchak (Isaac) (Genesis 26:3-4) and to Yaakov (Jacob) (Genesis 28:13-14). This triad of names (Abraham, Isaac, and Jacob) is the core of Jewish identity. A Jewish person's identity comes from their ethnicity and not from the Mosaic Law or Rabbinic Laws. In Genesis 12:1-3, three key aspects are given to Abraham in God's eternal unconditional covenant:

- In verse 1 the promise of a **Land**;
- In verse 2 the promise of **Seed**;
- And in verse 3 the promise of **Blessing** through Abraham to all the families or ethnicities of the earth.

God will later take these three aspects of Land, Seed, and Blessing and develop them into three other eternal, unconditional covenants. There is one other covenant that God made with Israel, which is a conditional covenant made with Israel at Mount Sinai (Exodus 24:1-11). This covenant is known as the Mosaic Covenant and has to do with the giving of what is referred to as the Law. This will be discussed in the next section under the title Conditional Covenant. Misunderstanding about the temporary nature of the Mosaic Law is also the root source of Torah observance today. Someone has said: The Abrahamic Covenant is the most central portion of all Scripture; everything else is commentary on it!

The following figure gives a beautiful summary of God's promises to Abraham and his descendants (chart available free on the *www.PromisesToIsrael.org*).

William Heinrich, *In the Shame of Jesus: The Hidden Story of Church-Sponsored Anti-Semitism.* Witmer, PA: Evidence of Truth Ministries, 2016. (Available through *www.PromisesToIsrael.org*).

Andrew D. Robinson, *Israel Betrayed, Vol 1: The History of Replacement Theology.* San Antonio, TX: Ariel Ministries, 2018.

Michael L. Brown, *Our Hands are Stained with Blood: The Tragic Story of the "Church" and the Jewish People.* Shippensburg, PA: Destiny Image Publishers, 1990.

Earle E. Cairns, *Christianity Through the Centuries.* Grand Rapids, MI: Zondervan Press, 1967.

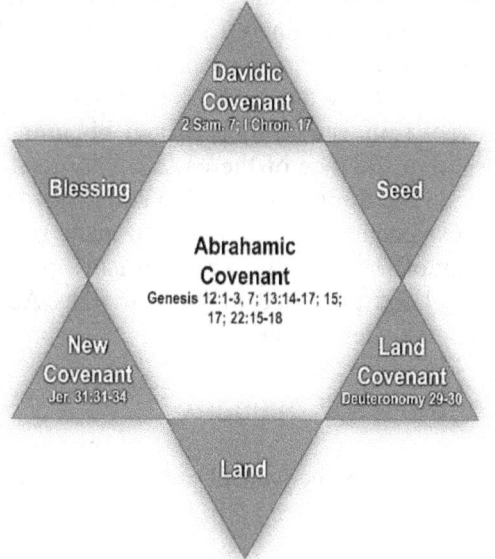

1. Father of a great nation 2. Land of Canaan 3. Abraham will be blessed 4. Name will be great 5. Abraham a blessing to others 6. Blessing for blessing

7. Cursing for cursing 8. Gentiles blessed 9. Sarah to have son 10. Egyptian bondage 11. Other nations 12. Name changed 13. Sarai-Sarah 14. Circumcision token

Contemplate the ramifications of that statement. Here is what is so powerful and central about the Abrahamic Covenant. Out of the three aspects highlighted above, God will make three more Eternal, Unconditional Covenants:

- The **Land** aspect God will develop into the **Land Covenant** – Deuteronomy 29.

- The **Seed** aspect God will develop into the **Davidic Covenant** – II Samuel 7:11-16 and I Chronicles 17:10-14. This will reflect the coming Seed line of Messiah from Genesis 3:15 through Malachi 3:1 into the Gospel in Matthew 1 (Solomon's line) and Luke 3 (Nathan, Solomon's brother's line).

- The **Blessing** aspect God will develop into the **New Covenant** – Jeremiah 31:31-34 and Ezekiel 36:26-28. This blessing includes the promise of a regenerated heart (a circumcised heart) (Colossians 2:11); the promise of the removal of sin, no longer just covered by animal blood; and the promise of the indwelling of the Holy Spirit for all believers, not just on a selected few as in the old economy.

With these three covenants, which all come from Genesis 12, we become aware of how these promises to Israel are central in our understanding of God. These central Covenant promises are to Israel, *not* the Church. There is *not* a non-Jewish recipient (Gentile) in any of these promises. Now all these covenants hinge on the **New Covenant** being fulfilled, and Gentile salvation is also guaranteed with the addition of the wild olive branch that is grafted in (Romans 11). The blood of Yeshua will regenerate Jew and Gentile; this was a mystery in the *Tanakh*. Now the ultimate fulfillment of the **New Covenant** is with Israel when Israel returns to God. That generation of Jewish people, who committed the unpardonable sin by rejecting their Messiah when He came to them (Matthew 12:22-32), will finally call for His return at the very end of the Tribulation period[28] when all Israel embraces Yeshua by Faith as their Messiah and LORD. Only then will Messiah return (Matthew 23:39; Psalm 118:26) and deliver Israel from the Anti-christ and his armies who will be set on annihilating every Jew from the face of the earth. Only then will Yeshua come as King and sit physically on the throne of David in Jerusalem for a literal 1000 years, fulfilling the Davidic Covenant. The Davidic Covenant promises that Israel will always have a descendant of David on the throne of Israel. At Yeshua's return, Israel will then receive all the Land promised to the patriarchs Abraham, Yitzchak, and Yaakov and all their believing descendants.

Definition of a Conditional Covenant

A conditional covenant is a bilateral covenant, meaning it is between two parties with the following formula: "If you will, then I will."

To illustrate, in Exodus 20-23 God lays down laws to be obeyed. In Exodus 24 you have *all* the people (v. 3) and the leaders of Israel agreeing to the covenant terms (vv. 6-8) set forth by God which were confirmed by blood and with a covenant meal (vv. 9-11). Their agreement with God's laws makes it a conditional covenant and ***not*** an eternal covenant, again illustrated in Deuteronomy 28. In verse 1 is the condition, *if you will hearken* or obey these laws, then God will bless His people beyond their wildest dreams, which is laid out in verses 1-14. But then you have the flip side of the agreement in verses Deuteronomy 28:15-68, *if you will not hearken* or obey the voice of the LORD your God, there are curses to endure. God proceeds to take the next 54 verses to describe just how He will punish and judge them beyond their wildest dreams.

In Leviticus 26:1-13 God again tells His people, the Israelites, how He will bless them *if you walk in My statutes, and keep My commandments, and do them* (v. 3). Once again God gives the flipside if they choose not to obey His commands (vv. 14-39). Notice what God said, ***but if you will not hearken unto Me, and will not do all***

---

[28] **Tribulation Period:** This is a seven-year period of judgment upon Israel, specifically, and the whole world in general, which is also called the Seventieth Week of Daniel (Daniel 9:24-27; Revelation chapters 6 through 19). It is also called the Time of Jacob's Trouble (Jeremiah 30:7) where God will purge Israel of its rebels (Zechariah 13:8) so that they will embrace Yeshua as their Messiah and LORD. It will **begin** with the signing of the covenant with the Anti-christ and **end** with the Second Coming of Messiah when Israel calls for His return to rescue them from the armies of the world who come together under the authority of the Anti-christ to annihilate Israel. Yeshua will then set up His Kingdom.

*these commandments; and **if you** shall despise My statutes, or **if your** soul abhor My judgments, so that **you will not do all** My commandments, but that you break My covenant* (vv. 14-15), then there were consequences. Israel failed to measure up, making the **New Covenant** a necessity (Jeremiah 31:32). The Law could not change their heart (Deuteronomy 10:16), but the **New Covenant** can and will change the heart (Deuteronomy 30:6; Jeremiah 31:31-34).

Moses forewarned His people of what was to come if they violated, broke His covenant and did not keep their end of the covenant. Moses in Leviticus 26:33-39 and Deuteronomy 28:63-67 tells them, both the Exodus generation and the wilderness generation, before they even entered the Land, what God would do to them when they violate His Law. God will finally forcibly remove them from the Land, scattering them into all the nations of the earth. But in Deuteronomy 30:1-6 Moses also states that God will gather them from wherever He had driven them and bring them back to the Land of Israel, the Land of their forefathers. They possessed the title deed for the Land in the Abrahamic Covenant, but because of violating His Law they did not possess the Land; and that has been their status for the last 2,500 years.

It is illustrated again *if they disobey,* which they did in Judges 2 as God laid out their fourfold cycle of sin, that when they repent God will send a judge to deliver them. This turned out to be the pattern of rebellion and repentance throughout most of the period of the monarchy of Israel and Judah with the downward spiral becoming deeper each time. Finally, there was NO remedy but total destruction of the ten tribes in the northern kingdom of Israel by God using the Assyrians to carry them away into captivity in 722 BC. Later, the kingdom of Judah and the city of Jerusalem were attacked, and the people were carried away from the Land by the Babylonians in 586 BC. To repeat: The tragic thing is that the cycle of sin deepened each time until their hearts were completely hardened.

This principle, that God punishes or rewards based on obedience, also lays down the overall principle that *ALL* God's commandments are to be obeyed, not just some of them (Matthew 5:19). So the issue became if anyone disobeyed one commandment, that person was guilty of breaking *all* of them (James 2:10; Galatians 5:3). This presented God's Law as a unit.

Purposes of the Law of Moses

The Law of Moses had certain specific purposes that guided and established the Jewish people.[29] These purposes are clearly taught in the pages of the Old Testament

---

[29] It would be to your advantage to go to YouTube and look up a message by Arnold Fruchtenbaum given in the fall of 2022 at Tacoma Bible Church on The Law of Moses and the Law of Messiah, *https://www.youtube.com/watch?v=Htd6lhigllY*. (Last accessed

and relate to God's relationship to His covenant people. Misapplying these purposes to other groups of people, such as the contemporary Christian Church, the USA, or other groups of people such as the Palestinians, creates errors in understanding God's purposes in general and His plan of redemption specifically.

The Law of Moses was given to the Jewish people (Exodus 19:3-8, 9-25; 20:22; 24:3-11 Deuteronomy 4:7-8; 18:15-16; Psalm 147:19-20; Malachi 4:4). Notice in the context of these passages that the Jewish people – the children[30] of Israel, the covenant people of God – are the only people being dealt with, not Gentiles or the Church. Adding other groups of people to God's plan in the Old Testament is a completely foreign concept to the covenant made with Israel in the whole *Tanakh*. People today use *eisegesis*,[31] which is to insert the idea of a multitude of peoples, the Church, into the text of the conditional, temporary Jewish Mosaic Covenant that was not written to them (today's Church and the Palestinians).

The ***Conditional*** aspect of the Law of Moses is seen in that they *agreed* to keep the Mosaic Law (Exodus 24:3-8; Deuteronomy 28:1-14, 15-68). It becomes clear that Israel put themselves voluntarily under the Law of Moses because they saw the miraculous works of God. We find in Deuteronomy 28 that the Law of Moses was a conditional covenant and NOT an eternal covenant made with Israel. The key phrase is when God says *If you will* obey My Law then *I will* bless you abundantly. However, in prophetic language (Deuteronomy 31:9 and 11) it clearly states that Moses wrote the Law, giving it to the Levites and that this Law was to be read before **all** Israel **in the Land**; **it was given to them only and to no one else!** Then God validates His words in the future tense that Israel would break His Law (Deuteronomy 31:16 and 20) throughout its history: in the wilderness generation, during the period of the judges, and under the kings into the first century AD. Then God, speaking in the past tense in Jeremiah 31:32, clearly states that Israel broke His Law. So both in the present tense with Moses and then in the past tense with Jeremiah, the Mosaic Law could not keep them from breaking His Law. We see that Paul clearly stated that the Law was an *administration of condemnation* and *death* (II Corinthians 3:6-9); the Law did not provide spiritual life (Romans 8:1-4).

5/26/2025.) It is well worth an hour and a quarter to listen to him as he clearly opens up the Scriptures on this subject.

[30] **Children:** In a future coming book, I will be expressing under the teaching of progressive revelation why God, when speaking of man refers to us as "children" and "sheep," and even as "children of God" in the Epistles. This is a very important concept that scholars in all shades of Replacement Theology need to understand as it affects how they interpret Scripture.

[31] An interpreter uses ***exegesis*** to lead to their conclusion by following the text of Scripture. However, in ***eisegesis***, the interpreter imports their own subjective interpretations into the biblical text, interpretations that are totally unsupported by the text itself.

> **Definition of the Law of Moses**
> **(John B. Metzger)**
>
> *The Law of Moses* was the term that included all 613 commandments applicable only to the Jewish people as a rule of life till Messiah died (Romans 7:1-4; Galatians 3:23-24; Hebrews 9:15-17).
>
> The Law of Moses was given to show the love of God to Israel to keep them a distinct and separate people from the pagan nations around them. The Law of Messiah is also designed to make believers distinct from the world on how we think and act in accordance to our relationship with Him. It is given to show how believers can live a Spirit-filled life.

The Nine Purposes of the Law of Moses

1. To reveal the holiness of God (Leviticus 11:44; 19:1-2, 37; I Peter 1:15-16). The Law itself was holy, and righteous, and good (Romans 7:12).

2. To provide the rule of conduct for the saints of the *Tanakh* (Leviticus 11:1-43; 19:2; 20:7-8, 26).

3. To provide for Israel occasions for individual and corporate worship three times a year, not every Sabbath (Leviticus 23).

4. To keep the Jewish people a distinct people (Leviticus 11:44-45; Deuteronomy 7:6; 14:1-2).

5. The Law was to serve as a middle wall of partition to keep the Gentiles out (Ephesians 2:11-16).

6. To reveal sin (Romans 3:19-20).

7. To cause one to sin more (Romans 4:15; 5:20).

8. To show Israel (the sinner) that there was nothing he could do on his own to please God with no ability to keep the Law perfectly or to attain the righteousness of the Law (Romans 7:14-25).

9. To drive one to faith, ultimately to faith in Messiah Yeshua (Romans 8:1-4; Galatians 3:24-25).[32]

---

[32] Arnold G. Fruchtenbaum. *Israelology: The Missing Link in Systematic Theology*, Tustin, CA: Ariel Press. 1994, pp. 590-593.

Israel's rebellion reflects the disobedience of Adam and Eve who had two commandments given to them; and they disobeyed, God dispersing them eastward from the Garden. Israel was given the Mosaic Law, all 613 commandments; and as Moses records, the LORD fully anticipated Israel violating them and that He would also disperse them eastward and then worldwide. Israel followed that same pattern of disobedience and being dispersed from the Land over a period of fifteen centuries, first being dispersed when the Babylonians took them eastward (Deuteronomy 29:22–30:6); and then, finally, when God used the Romans to disperse them worldwide (Deuteronomy 30:3-4; Isaiah 11:11; Ezekiel 37:14; Jeremiah 33:8; Zephaniah 3:20).

The Timing of the Law

The Law was made to be observed IN THE LAND OF ISRAEL, **not** in exile (Ezekiel 36) or outside the Land, for the Temple and the whole sacrificial system was located in the Land. The Law of Moses SIMPLY CANNOT BE KEPT OUTSIDE THE LAND OF ISRAEL. It was specifically made for Israel within the confines of their physical borders. It **cannot** be kept in the USA, Europe, Russia or any other place outside of the borders of the Land. Look at Ezekiel 36:16-28 where the prophet clearly states that Israel was living in Gentile lands because they *profaned God's Name* by their very existence in those lands which was a direct result of breaking God's covenant with them (Leviticus 26:14-41.)

> Notice the phrase in Leviticus 26:21: *walking contrary to ME.*
>
> In Deuteronomy 31:16: They will *forsake me, and break my covenant.*
>
> In Deuteronomy 31:20: They will *provoke Me, and break My covenant.*
> Isaiah 1:4:
>
>> *Alas, sinful nation,*
>> *A people laden with iniquity,*
>> *A brood of evildoers,*
>> *Children who are corrupters!*
>> *They have forsaken the LORD,*
>> *They have provoked to anger*
>>   *The Holy One of Israel,*
>> *They have turned away backward.*
>
> Jeremiah 31:32: *My covenant they broke.*

His people were living outside the Land because they had *profaned* [God's] *holy Name* among the Gentiles for they *defiled the land* by their evil and wicked lifestyle. Simply put, they violated God's covenant with them; and as God said to Moses, He would *vomit them out of the Land* (Leviticus 18:24-29; 20:22). To any Jewish believers who say they are Torah observant, do you think you can do better than your ancestors? And Gentiles are not even in the conversation! Let me ask a series of rhetorical questions, with a focus on the history of Israel.

- Did the Israelites keep the Law under Moses? NO, they broke it!

- Did they keep the Law when in the Land during the period of the Judges? NO, they broke it!

- Did they keep the Law during Israel's and Judah's monarchies? NO, they broke it!

- Did they keep the Law when in Assyrian and Babylonian lands! NO, they continued to break it.

- Did they keep the Law in the Intertestamental years? NO, they continued to break it!

- Did they keep the Law in the first century? NO, they insulated themselves with Rabbinic manmade laws, rejected the Messiah, and gave Him over to the Romans to crucify Him!

So over a very long period of time Israel did not keep the Law, and so God dispersed them into all the nations of the earth for their disobedience. They made for themselves manmade laws – Rabbinic Laws – which formed an unauthorized detour from God's plan.

To any Gentile Torah observers, I raise a question: Why is it now in the last century that you try to keep the Law when before that, from the first century AD into the twentieth century, Gentiles largely did not try to commit themselves to Mosaic Law keeping? Why after nearly 2,000 years would your leaders suddenly attempt to promote Law keeping by pushing and exporting Torah observance now? Gentiles through roughly twenty centuries, since the Messiah fulfilled the Law, had not even tried to keep the Law, nor did it come into their minds to do so. Logic is not on your side to insist on Gentile Law keeping that generally was not practiced before, say, the 1970s or '80s.

The Law since the death of Messiah has become outdated, inadequate, insufficient, and obsolete because it could not make Israel *holy, just,* or *good*. Why ignore biblical history? How does Torah keeping make anyone holy? To insist on Torah keeping is to depreciate the work of Messiah on the Cross. Look carefully at the writer of Hebrews who said (7:11-12, 18; 8:13) respectively,

> *7:11 Now if there was perfection through the Levitical priesthood (for under it has the people received the law), what further need was there that another priest should rise after the order of Melchizedek, and not be called after the order of Aaron? 12 For the priesthood being changed, there is made of necessity* **a change also of the law**.
>
> *7:18 For there is a disannulling of a foregoing commandment because of its weakness and unprofitableness ...*

> *8:13* In that he said, A New Covenant, He has made the first [covenant] old. Now that which decays and grows old is ready to vanish away.

Look at Deuteronomy where twenty times[33] God said He would place His Name in one location. That place became Jerusalem, not New York City, not London or Brussels, not Moscow or Buenos Aires or Cairo, and definitely not Brooklyn, NY. The Law was made to be lived out within the confines of the nation of Israel where God placed His Name.

God made it absolutely impossible for Israel to keep the Law by sending Israel into the Assyrian and Babylonian captivities. Only a few of the Jewish people returned to the Land while the rest remained voluntarily in Gentile lands, meaning much of the Law could not be kept. Then in AD 70 the Romans thoroughly dispersed Israel throughout the world and again, this time for almost 2,000 years. He has made it impossible to keep His Law because they violated His covenants. Notice I said He has now made it impossible to keep the Law, because the Temple, the center of the Mosaic Law, is now gone. The whole of the context of the *Tanakh* is that the Law was given to Israel and not to the world at large. Theological supersessionists, those who have invented Replacement Theology, may try to read themselves and the Church back into the Dispensation of the Law (the time when the Law of Moses could be practiced as given), but their logic does not stand up against what Scripture says.

The Remedy for the Mosaic Law

The remedy for the problem of the Law within the Torah is only found in the Messiah.[34] The remedy of sin is found in the blood of Messiah, not in keeping the Law; for it cannot be kept in human flesh (Acts 13:39; 15:10; Romans 8:1-13; 10:4; Galatians 2:16; 3:2-3). The remedy of the impossible standards of the Law in the Torah is found in the Messiah who by His blood became our sin bearer, not covering sin as the Law commanded, but by removing sin all together (Jeremiah 31:34; Ezekiel 36:25-26; Hebrews 9:11-14). Messiah did this through His blood of the **New Covenant**, creating a circumcised or a regenerated heart (Deuteronomy 30:6; Ezekiel 36:26; Colossians 2:11) for believers in Messiah. Our Messiah, and not the *old covenant* with Moses, mediated the **New Covenant** (Hebrews 9:15) and the <u>Law of Messiah</u> so that believers in Messiah can now walk in Him.

---

[33] Deuteronomy 12:5, 11, 14, 18, 21, 26; 14:23-25; 15:20; 16:2, 6, 11, 15-16; 17:8, 10; 18:6; 26:2.

[34] Seth Postell, Eitan Bar, and Erez Soref, *Reading Moses, Seeing Jesus*; Wooster, OH: Weaver Book Company, 2017, chapter 3.

The story line of the Torah (the Books of Moses) most certainly includes the giving of the Law, it also prophetically *anticipates* the breaking of that Law by Israel. The problem of sin set forth in Genesis 3 is the foundation of the sinful hearts that simply cannot keep the Law perfectly; we always fall short (Job 5:7; 14:1; Romans 3:9-20, 23; 6:23). Law keeping is not a remedy for getting rid of sin or for having victory over sin, nor does it have a provision for a victorious walk in Messiah. The goal is to be Messiah-like in our daily life, and not to be preoccupied with the old, failed Law that could not save sinners.

Now to be absolutely correct, the problem was not the Law, the problem was our depraved nature that is like a sewer with the raw sewage constantly seeping out of our lives and daily conduct. The problem does not come **from** the Law for *The Law is holy, and the commandment holy, and just, and good* (Romans 7:12), The simple problem is that mankind is totally depraved and cannot keep it. Why adopt a failed program that was used by God to draw man's attention to the fact that mankind cannot keep it? It was used by God as a schoolmaster to lead Israel to Messiah (Galatians 3:24). Remember the words at the Jerusalem Council in Acts 15:10 where Peter says,

> *Now therefore why do you tempt God*
> *To put a yoke upon the neck of the* [Gentile] *disciple,*
> *which neither our fathers nor we were able to bear?*

In this context, the word *disciple* refers directly to new Gentile believers and not to put a yoke around their necks, a yoke that historically Israel itself could not and would not keep and the Messianic Movement today cannot keep. Those who are teaching Torah observance today have resurrected a dead corpse in the twentieth century. How is it that advocates for Torah observance speak and write as if they have more insight and authority than the Apostles at the First Council in Jerusalem by directly contradicting the Apostles and Scripture?

Now I need to make something completely clear: I AM NOT ANTINOMIAN!!! I am NOT anti-*Tanakh*. Let me quote II Timothy 3:15-17 that specifically references the *Tanakh* and all that is in it:

> *[15] And that from a child you have known the holy Scriptures* [the *Tanakh*], *which are able to make you wise unto salvation through faith which is in Messiah Yeshua. [16] All Scripture is given by inspiration of God, and is profitable for doctrine, for reproof, for correction, for instruction in righteousness; [17] That the man of God may be perfect, thoroughly furnished unto all good works.*

Notice the **positive words**: *inspiration of God*; *profitable for doctrine*; *instruction in righteousness* and then the **negative words** *for reproof* and *correction* so that the two combined together would make us *thoroughly furnished unto all good works*. The *Tanakh* is not outdated, Paul used it as one of his examples of correct living when he taught the I Corinthians (10:1-11) and to the Romans (1:18-3:31. So did Peter (II Peter 3:4-9) and Jude (5-7, 11-15). The *Tanakh* is very positive and good, not to be cast aside or depreciated. But we also need to understand that when Messiah Yeshua came and fulfilled the Law (Matthew 5:17; Galatians 2:16; 3:11, 13), He rendered the *old covenant* system that He gave as inoperative, but NOT the *Tanakh*. What changed was God's economy; God pointed to the future for His people and a new economy. He prophesied through Moses, to a people who repetitively broke the Law and ultimately rejected the promised Messiah (Genesis 3:15; 22:18; 49:10) whose coming was prophesied by Moses (John 5:45-46), David (Psalm 22:14-18), Isaiah (7:14; 9:5-6; 50:1-6; 53:1-12), Jeremiah (23:5-6), Micah (5:2), and Zechariah (3:8-9; 6:12-13; 9:9; 11:4-14; 12:10; 13:7).

God's way of governing mankind, moved from the *holy, righteous, and just* (Romans 7:12) Law which failed to govern the uncircumcised heart of man (Deuteronomy 10:16; Jeremiah 4:3-4; 6:10; 9:26) to the free gift of salvation offered to all by Faith in Yeshua. This future economy offered a way of peace with God regardless of anyone's ethnicity (John 3:16; Acts 10:45-46; 16:31) through the blood of the **New Covenant**, the blood of Messiah, which He spoke of at His last Passover when He took the Third cup, the Cup of Redemption.

The Continued Value of the Law

The foundations of the Jewish laws have been incorporated into much of western civilization, although Globalists are quickly trying to eradicate their influence from the statutes and laws of our American Republic and western Europe. Where did our justice system come from that our forefathers created in the founding of the United States of America? Our foundation came straight from the Torah!

Where did our moral system come from that secularists and immoral people busily try to erase from our laws and society? With no moral absolutes and the substitution of Relativism, we are watching our country disintegrate before our eyes. That moral system of laws came straight from the Torah and the *Tanakh* as a whole.

Where did our once sound scientific discoveries come from? Scientists originally clearly understood from the Torah that God created the earth in six literal, 24-hour days and rested on the seventh. Real science did not arise from the unproven, satanic, evolutionary myths of Darwin that completely ignore Creation and the worldwide Flood as true science.[35] Science came from knowing the God of the

---

[35] Please see these challenging books:

    Ken Ham, *The Lie of Evolution*. Green Forest, AR: Masters Books, 2006

    Ken Ham, *Six Days: The Age of the Earth and the Decline of the Church*. Green Forest, AR: Masters Books, 2014.

    John C. Whitcomb and Henry M. Morris, *The Genesis Flood: The Biblical Record and its Scientific Implications*. Phillipsburg, NJ: P&R Publishing, 2011.

Tanakh. Without a biblical perspective, scientists believe man is just an evolved animal. However, when mankind acts like animals do, people who have been seduced into evolutionary thinking are shocked.

How did our forefathers come up with the Constitution; the Declaration of Independence; the Bill of Rights; the legislative, judicial, and executive branches of government; and a system of laws to control man's heart of depravity? Because our wise founding fathers knew that power corrupts, these three branches of government were put in place to be a deterrent to keep the depravity of human hearts at bay. Because of human depravity, they envisioned dividing power among the many and not just among a few intent on forcing only one political position. The problem is that for the last several decades, our sons and daughters have not been taught Civics, nor have they been instructed in the books of Proverbs and Ecclesiastes. Thus many citizens are lacking godly wisdom, having no understanding of the insight of our founding fathers who focused on and quoted the *Tanakh* more than any other source.[36] Some of these men were indeed Deists,[37] but the majority of them were believers in Christ.[38] Here are a few other quotations from David Gibbs:

> It has long been recognized that America is the only country in the history of the world that was deliberately founded on the Judeo-Christian principles of the Bible. During these early years of American history, the Bible was the source most often quoted in political writings of the day. [pgs. 34-35]
>
> *Newsweek Magazine* in 1982 stated the following: Now historians are discovering that the Bible, perhaps even more than the Constitution, is our founding document: the source of the powerful myth of the United States as a special, sacred nation, a people called by God to establish a model society, a beacon to the world [pg. 35].
>
> The biblical principles of government had been taught to the people by the patriotic Black Regiment, the name assigned to American's

---

Also see the Institute for Creation Research website in Dallas, TX. *https://discoverycenter.icr.org/* (Last accessed 05/26/2025.)

[36] David C. Gibbs, *Understanding the Constitution*. Flower Mound, TX: National Center of Life and Liberty, 2014.

[37] Deists: Deism is a system of thought that advances a natural religion. Deists did believe in the evidence of God in nature and that God did create the world, but then left it to operate under natural laws that He set in place. That means they believe that God is not personally active in His created world; He is not personally in control of the world He created.

[38] David C. Gibbs, *Understanding the Constitution*. Flower Mound, TX: National Center of Life and liberty, 2014.

colonial preachers because of the color of their robes. While most of these men never donned a military uniform during the Revolutionary War, their black pulpit robes identified them as being just as important to the success of the Revolution as those who wore military uniforms. [pg. 35]

The vast majority of the 55 state delegates who attended the meeting in Philadelphia, later known as the Constitutional Convention, were professing Christians. Only Benjamin Franklin and James Wilson of Pennsylvania were known to be Deists. [pg. 40]

But then the miracle happened! On that day, June 28, 1787, a breakthrough occurred. After weeks and weeks of frustratingly little progress, a wonderfully moving speech, made on the Convention floor, caused the tide to turn. Benjamin Franklin, who gave that speech, was a Deist. He was not one of the vast majority of Christian delegates to the Convention who believed strongly in the Judeo-Christian God of the Bible. Nevertheless, Franklin made an impassioned speech, reminding his fellow delegates that God had always answered their prayers as a nation, even when they were at war. Now that things were going so badly, should they not again turn to the Lord for help? Besides, asked Franklin, how could they expect to successfully create a new nation without God's help? [pg. 43]

The following article comes from the Oxford University Press and is material that most Americans today are not aware of because it has been removed by revisionists of American history.

Another often overlooked or discounted source of influence is the Bible. Its expansive influence on the political culture of the age should not surprise us because the population was overwhelmingly Protestant, and it informed significant aspects of public culture, including language, letters, education, and law. No book at the time was more accessible or familiar than the English Bible, specifically the King James Bible. And the people were biblically literate.

The discourse of the era amply documents the founders' many quotations from and allusions to both familiar and obscure biblical texts, confirming that they knew the Bible from cover to cover. Biblical language and themes liberally seasoned their rhetoric. The phrases and cadences of the King James Bible influenced their written and spoken words. Its ideas shaped their habits of mind and informed their political experiment in republican self-government.

The Bible left its mark on their political culture. Following an extensive survey of American political literature from 1760 to 1805, political scientist Donald S. Lutz reported that the Bible was cited more frequently than any European writer or even any European school of thought, such as Enlightenment liberalism or republicanism. The Bible, he reported, accounted for approximately one-third of the citations in the literature he surveyed. The book of Deuteronomy alone is the most frequently cited work, followed by Montesquieu's *The Spirit of the Laws*. In fact, Deuteronomy is referenced nearly twice as often as Locke's writings, and the Apostle Paul is mentioned about as frequently as Montesquieu.

Many in the founding generation – 98% or more of whom were affiliated with Protestant Christianity – regarded the Bible as indispensable to their political experiment in self-government. They valued the Bible not only for its rich literary qualities but also for its insights into human nature, civic virtue, social order, political authority and other concepts essential to the establishment of a political society. The Bible, many believed, provided instruction on the characteristics of a righteous civil magistrate, conceptions of liberty, and the rights and responsibilities of citizens, including the right of resistance to tyrannical rule. There was broad agreement that the Bible was essential for nurturing the civic virtues that give citizens the capacity for self-government. Many founders also saw in the Bible political and legal models – such as republicanism, separation of powers, federalism, and due process of law – they believed enjoyed divine favor and were worthy of emulation in their polities.

The political discourse of the founding, for one example, is replete with appeals to the Hebrew "republic" as a model for their own political experiment. In an influential 1775 Massachusetts election sermon, Samuel Langdon, the president of Harvard College and later a delegate to New Hampshire's constitution ratifying convention, opened: "The Jewish government, according to the original constitution, which was divinely established, ... was a perfect Republic ... The civil Polity of Israel is doubtless an excellent general model ...; at least some principal laws and orders of it may be copied, to great advantage, in more modern establishments." Most of what the founders knew about the Hebraic republic they learned from the Bible. These Americans were well aware that ideas like republicanism found expression in traditions apart from the Hebrew model, and, indeed, they studied these traditions both ancient and modern. The republican model found in the Hebrew Scriptures, however, reassured pious Americans that republicanism was a political system favored by God. [39]

To sum all these statements up, contrary to depreciating the Torah or the *Tanakh;* these men were firmly entrenched in the Scriptures and built a nation like no other outside of Israel itself. Yet, today in America and Europe, all the foundations of a law-abiding society are being removed by secularists with pagan globalism. In America, the Democratic Party and "Rino" Republicans (**R**epublicans **i**n **n**ame **o**nly) are anti-Bible, anti-morality, and anti-righteousness, to name just a couple of disconnects from our foundations. So you, Torah-observant proponents, I do not want to even hear that we in Dispensationalism depreciate the *Tanakh*. As my Dad used to say, they are "talking to hear their ears roar" – just saying empty words.

Does the Bible Warn Us to Stay Faithful to His Word? (Jer. 18:7-10)

> [7] *At what instant shall **I** speak concerning a nation, and concerning a kingdom, to pluck up, and to pull down, and to destroy it:* [8] *If that nation, against whom **I** have pronounced, turn from their evil, **I will** repent of the evil [calamity] that **I** thought to do unto them.* [9] *And what instant **I** shall speak concerning a nation, and concerning a kingdom, to build and to plant it:* [10] *If it does evil in **M**y sight, that it obeys not **M**y voice, then **I will** relent concerning the good with which **I** said **I** would benefit it.*

In viewing these verses, God is clearly referencing the Jewish nation. However, in a general sense, this passage can also apply to any nation **He** *raises up and plants;* and, at the same time, because of wickedness **He** can p*luck up and pull down and destroy* that nation. We can observe that Israel is a people specially called of God to be **His** instrument to reveal **Himself** to all the nations and peoples of the world. Through Israel, **He** introduces **His** plan of Redemption in the Abrahamic Covenant (Genesis 12:3; 26:4; 28:14), then ultimately **His** plan of Salvation through the Messiah. As Jeremiah announced the **New Covenant** (Jeremiah 31:31-34; Ezekiel 36:26-28), Yeshua inaugurated the **New Covenant** (Matthew 26:28;

---

[39] See these related online resources:

Oxford University Press blog entitled "How the Bible Influenced the Founding Fathers," *https://blog.oup.com/2016/11/bible-influenced-founding-fathers,* last accessed 5/26/2025.

C. S. Lewis Institute: Please see "The Bible and the American Founders," *https://www.cslewisinstitute.org/ resources/the-bible-and-the-american-founders/*, last accessed on 5/26/2025.

The *Federalist*: "How the Bible Inspired the American Founding from the Beginning," See *https://thefederalist.com/2020/11/23/how-the-bible-inspired-the-american-founding-from-the-beginning/*, last accessed 5/26/2025.

Hebrews 9:15) and will ratify that **New Covenant** when Israel in the future repents concerning the blasphemy against **Him** (when the leaders lied about Yeshua's power and identity and rejected Him as their Messiah on those false grounds). At the moment they repent of their blasphemy and welcome Him, Salvation will be given to the nation of Israel (Micah 2:12-13; Zechariah 3:9; Romans 11:26).

In the annals of nations over the centuries, there is only one other nation that has been blessed abundantly by God and was established on the Word of God – the Jewish Scriptures of the *old covenant* and **New Covenant** – and that is the United States of America. Today, because this nation has been weakened spiritually, most Americans do not know their own national heritage and background, that most of the founding fathers as Christians established the Constitution and Bill of Rights for a Republic based on the Hebrew Scriptures. Today, the enemies within our Republic have attempted to remove its biblical and spiritual history, causing the United States to be more like Sodom and Gomorrah with their complete depravity of the human heart than this once strongly Christian nation we remember. America today stands in its own sinful, septic sewer and does not even realize it.

There is a biblical picture that Jeremiah references in the books of Kings and Chronicles. Israel passed the point of spiritual return to its God in the reign of King Manasseh (II Kings 21; II Chronicles 33). Illustrated for us in our recent history of America, we also have had our own "King Manasseh" in the person of Barack Hussein Obama with his third term in Joseph R. Biden. These two men are the pinnacle of bringing out the sin of this country which was once in the shadows to now flaunting sin in the faces of all Americans. Please understand that the United States of America is NOT mentioned in prophecy; however, Jeremiah 18:7-10 reveals the principle of what God does with a nation that chooses to live righteously or chooses to live unrighteously in wickedness.

As we have seen just a glimpse of corruption through what the new U.S. Department of Government Efficiency (DOGE) has uncovered: massive fraud, promoting sin, and lack of accountability in our federal government, I fear we may have crossed God's red line of no return. Our Republic may be "time over." If we as a nation have chosen evil over righteousness, God will pluck our Republic up and pull it down and destroy it by His own hand, just as He did with Judah.

We need revival, but I do not see a national movement back to Him; instead, our Republic looks just like rebellious Judah in the days of Josiah, a righteous king (II Kings 22-23; II Chronicles 34-36). He was inspired to heart-felt fear of God and desire to lead Israel to turn from their rebellious ways when the Scriptures were rediscovered in the Temple. When the Law was read to him, he was overcome with a desire to end the steady path to destruction that Judah was following. (Ironically, at that moment, Josiah was set on a course to return money to the workers that had been wrongly taken when the Book of Law was discovered in the Temple.)

Despite Josiah's personal repentance and forceful attempt to stem the tide of evil in Judah under his reign, it was too late. The people were totally caught up in rebellion against their Creator. God rewarded Josiah's passion for confronting evil by allowing him to die in battle so he would not have to witness Judah's destruction. God plucked up and plowed under Judah due to their determined passion to rebel against Him.

Chapter Four
Dispensations

The economies that God used in working with man are called Dispensations. There are **Seven Dispensations** – Each Dispensation is a distinguishable economy in the outworking of God's purpose.[40] The Seven Dispensations are the following: Innocence, Conscience, Human Government, Promise, Mosaic Law, Grace, and Eternal Reign. In each of these ages, people were held accountable for God's new revealed revelation as to how they were to live towards Him in that economy. However, God provided different rules for each economy which involved that period of time. For instance, Adam and Eve had only two laws (Age of Innocence), but Israel had 613 Laws (Mosaic Law). As this book shows, in the age of Grace that we as believers in Yeshua our Messiah live in, we have over 600 Laws based on the teachings of Yeshua and His Apostles. How these laws are administered in each age is different.

> ***Definition of Dispensation***: *Oikonomia*, means "to manage, to regulate, to administer, and to plan." *Oikonomia* is a Greek compound word: *oikos* means "a house" and *nomos* means "law." Precise definition is: "to divide," "to apportion," "to administer," "to manage the affairs of an inhabited house."
>
> ***Progressive Revelation***: Means that in each Dispensation God revealed a little more of His plan for the ages. He did not dump on man all of His revelation at once, but through 40 plus authors over 1600 years, a work we call the Bible.

Dispensationalism is a view of the world as a household run by God. In this household – the world – God is dispensing or administering its affairs according to His own will, and in various stages of revelation in the process of time. These various stages mark off the different distinguishable economies in the outworking of God's total purpose. These economies are called Dispensations. The understanding of God's different economies is essential to a proper interpretation of His revelation within these various economies. If you disregard the Covenants (as mentioned in the previous chapter) and Dispensations, your theology at some point will be against what God has said and taught through His Prophets and Apostles.

---

[40] For a full study of Dispensations see the *Come & See Series, The Word of God*, vol. one, San Antonio, TX: Ariel Press, 2015, pp. 119-141.

Authors of pro-Torah-observance books try to validate Torah observance from the Epistles. I noticed that many of these authors are not Dispensationalists and look down on Dispensational teaching[41] as being erroneous and pre-Tribulation Rapture as dangerous,[42] when in reality Dispensationalism is the only approach that makes biblical sense and allows Scripture to fit together. In Scripture, God worked with people in different ages, requiring different things in obeying Him at the time, but ALWAYS trusting Him BY FAITH (Habakkuk 2:4; Hebrews 11). The Protestant Reformation was incomplete, specifically as it related to future things (Eschatology) and the study of Israel (Israelology). The Reformers interpreted the Bible literally in almost all areas, but did they continue to spiritualize or allegorize in the area of future things (Eschatology), especially as it related to the distinction of Israel and the Church? Dispensationalism is the completion of the Protestant Reformation[43] that Covenant Reform, Preterist, Amillennialists, and Replacement Theologies reject.

Dispensations make a clear distinction between ISRAEL and the CHURCH. The Church in Scripture is NEVER Israel; they are two distinct entities.

Here are some other observations of the significance of Israel and its continued literal understanding that are connected to Dispensationalism and how we interpret His Word. First let me quote from Mark Yarbrough, president of Dallas Theological Seminary:

> The Bible is a grand story and is a thoroughly Jewish contextualized presentation from beginning to end and has as its epicenter the work and deliverance offered by the promised Jewish Messiah.[44]

Did you see what he said? The grand story of the Bible is Israel from beginning to end. I have often asked pastors at conferences after they looked at Arnold Fruchtenbaum's book *Israelology* the following questions:

---

[41] I will develop in an upcoming book that all anti-Dispensationalists are actually practicing Dispensationalists every day of their married life. I will express this essential understanding which cannot be denied by them.

[42] **Pre-Tribulation Rapture:** The Scriptures of the Tanakh point toward the Millennial Reign of Messiah and its length is given as 1000 years (Revelation 20:3-7). Immediately preceding the Millennial Kingdom is the seven years of Tribulation upon the earth, which is also called the Seventieth Week of Daniel (Daniel 9:24-27). The catching up (Rapture) of the Bride of Messiah (the Church), which is called the Rapture, precedes the Tribulation period of God's wrath upon all earth dwellers. We believe that the Rapture of the Church is imminent but will occur before the signing of the covenant with the Anti-christ which sets off the Seventieth Week of Daniel.

[43] Andy Woods, *Ever Reforming*. Taos, NM: Dispensational Press, 2018.

[44] Mark Yarbrough, "Israel and the Story of the Bible," in *Israel the Church and the Middle East*, eds. Darrell L. Bock and Mitch Glaser. Grand Rapids, MI: Kregel Publishing, 2018, p. 51.

> If you take Israel out of the Bible, what do you have left? They normally answer correctly, "nothing, or very little."
>
> I then ask a follow up question: If Israel is so significant in Scripture, then why do our Bible Colleges and Seminaries ignore it?

Some schools would say we do not ignore it, but yes, they do by not emphasizing it or by directly subverting it. Israel and Dispensations tell the storyline from Creation (Genesis 1) to the new heavens and new earth (Revelation 22). God in Genesis 12:3 raises the standard, through Abraham (Israel), *I will bless all the families* (ethnicities) *of the earth.* How did He do that? Michael Vlach expresses it well:

> Israel was destined by God to bless the world ... God said, *in you all the families of the earth will be blessed.* This blessing occurs in three main ways. First, God used Israel to bring the Scriptures to the world (Romans 3:2). Second, Israel is the vessel for the Messiah (Romans 9:5), who will save and restore national Israel and bring blessing to the Gentiles (Isaiah 49:1-6). Third, Israel will be the geographical center of a worldwide earthly kingdom of the Messiah with a role of service to other nations (Isaiah 2 & 11). Israel's coming fullness will mean greater blessings for the world (Romans 11:12). Isaiah 14:1-6 reveals that Gentile nations will join Israel in being the people of God.
>
> But for Israel to fully complete its God-given destiny, Israel must be saved. That is why Dispensationalism also affirms a coming salvation of *all Israel*. While a present remnant of believing Israel exists, Israel as a whole will be saved (Romans 11:26; Zech 12:10). And this salvation is linked with restoration as a nation. The Apostles expected the coming restoration of national Israel when they asked, Lord, *is it at this time that You are restoring the kingdom to Israel?* (Acts 1:6).[45]
>
> Thus, Dispensationalists believe the hermeneutical principles they abide by arise from God and Scripture and are not imposed on Scripture [pg. 22].

Dispensationalism is not a created theological system per say, but it is how God has chosen to reveal Himself and His plan through progressive revelation through the ages to mankind from the very beginning of time till the very end of time. In it He is and will be glorified and praised.

Dispensations and the Covenants are central to a biblical hermeneutic. I recommend the following three books for a great background in the concepts of how God has chosen to reveal Himself differently in different ages.

---

[45] Michael Vlach. *Dispensational Hermeneutics.* Theological Studies Press, 2023, p. 17.

Dispensationalism before Darby by William C. Watson, Published by Lampion Press, Silverton, OR, 2015.

Forever Reforming by Andy Woods, Published by Dispensational Publishing House, Toas, NM, 2018.

Dispensational Hermeneutics by Michael Vlach, Published Theological Studies Press, 2023.

The following chart, used by permission of Mottel Baleston, provides a great overview of the eight Dispensations discussed in the Bible. Below the title of each of the eight Dispensations is the portion of Scripture that corresponds to each Dispensation. While the Scripture references do not overlap, the covenants that operated in these ages do overlap. A beautiful color version free to copy can be found on my website at *www.promisestoisrael.com* under Literature/charts Resources.

The Dispensations & Covenants

THE RELATIONSHIP OF THE DISPENSATIONS & COVENANTS

Each dispensation is a distinguishable economy in the outworking of God's purpose.

These eight covenants govern God's relationship with mankind.

Dispensation	Period	Reference
INNOCENCE	Adam to the Fall	Gen. 1:28 — 3:6
CONSCIENCE	Fall to Flood	Gen. 3:9 — 8:14
HUMAN GOVERNMENT	Flood to Babel	Gen. 8:15 — 11:9
PROMISE	Abram to Mosaic Law	Gen. 12:1 — Ex. 18:27
MOSAIC LAW	Sinai to Calvary	Ex. 19 — Acts 1:26
GRACE	Shavuot to Tribulation	Acts 2:1 — Rev. 19:21
KINGDOM REIGN	1,000 Years	Rev. 20:1-10

Covenants: EDENIC, ADAMIC, NOAHIC, ABRAHAMIC, MOSAIC, LAND, DAVIDIC, NEW

PAST — PRESENT — FUTURE

DISPENSATIONALISM IS DISTINGUISHED BY:

1. A literal interpretation of the Bible
2. A consistent distinction between Israel and the church and a recognition of God's everlasting Abrahamic Covenant with the Jewish people
3. An understanding that the glory of God is the theme of history

Chapter Five
The Hebrew Word *Olam*
(Strong's H5769) עוֹלָם

Judaism and much of Messianic Judaism teach that the Mosaic Law is eternal and will always be in force throughout time. When we understand the usage of the word *olam* as it is used in Hebrew, we discover that *olam* is always bound by time, except when it references God who created time and is outside of time. In Hebrew there are no words for eternity as in the Greek! The strongest reference for eternity in Hebrew would be the words *without end* or *no end* (Isaiah 9:7) found in the Prophets. The problem arises that Torah-observant believers have accepted a false teaching from apostate Rabbinic Judaism[46] concerning *olam* and have transferred that teaching into the Jewish Messianic Movement. The other problem is that the translators of our English Bibles have made a poor choice of words to express the meaning of *olam*. They have used the English words *everlasting, forever,* and *eternity* for the Hebrew word *olam*, which is very misleading and inaccurate.

Olam is a masculine noun with the meaning of a "long duration," "antiquity," or "future," used 405 times in the *Tanakh*. The term *olam* when confined to time has a limited and varied impact, whereas when used of God, who is outside time, it would then be literally "everlasting, eternal" as we in English understand the term. *Olam* when used in the context of man and time is limited and is not eternal. When used of God in the context of His eternality, *olam* means forever, in the sense of that which never ends. Not understanding that the Hebrew idea of lasting forever only applies to God, Judaism and many in the Jewish Messianic Movement teach that the Mosaic Law itself is eternal and thus setting the stage for their mental bias. They falsely teach that the Mosaic Law cannot be done away with and that it cannot be rendered inoperative as the New Testament teaches (Romans 7:1-6; 10:4; Hebrews 8:13; 9:15-17). A sampling will show that the concepts of *eternality, forever,* or *everlasting* are

---

[46] There are two forms of Judaism: First is biblical Judaism which involved only the Written Law of God that was fulfilled by Yeshua at the Cross when He inaugurated the **New Covenant** which replaced the Mosaic Law code system with an entirely new code of living in the ***Law of Messiah***. Second is Rabbinic Judaism which is based on elevating the Oral Law, the Mishnah, and all Rabbinic authority above the Written Law and by modifying the biblical Mosaic code at the Council of Yavne (AD 90) to be taught and lived without a Temple or Sacrifice in Jerusalem. The full emphasis is on apostate Rabbinic Law or manmade law being placed over the Mosaic Law which was rendered inoperative by the death of Yeshua at Calvary.

not in view in the context of the *Tanakh* as it relates to the activities of man, as viewed from the *Tanakh* but primarily here from the Mosaic Law.

> *My Spirit shall not always [olam] strive with man* – Genesis 6:3 – context is limited, not eternal.

> *This is the token of the covenant which I make between Me and you ... for perpetual [olam] generations* – Genesis 9:12 – context is limited to man's generations, not eternity.

> *everlasting covenant* – the rainbow, Genesis 9:16 used within the context of time.

> *You shall keep it a feast* [Passover] ... *by an ordinance forever [olam]* – Exodus 12:14 – and it was to be kept in the place where God would put His Name, which became Jerusalem (Deuteronomy 12:5, 11, 14, 18, 21, 26,). To keep Passover outside of Jerusalem is violating the Law and contrary to the Law passed on by the rabbis at the Council of Yavneh[47] after the fall of Jerusalem and destruction of the Temple, stating that the Law was retooled as to how the Jewish people could keep the Law. Passover was retooled to be celebrated wherever they lived in the Diaspora instead of always in Jerusalem. Louis Goldberg writes the following:

>> The solution to the problem came at the Council of Yavneh (A.D. 70-90), at which Israel's religious leaders structured a Judaism that made no provision for a substitute atonement, while at the same time insisting that the Mosaic Covenant was still in place, although in a modified form! Perhaps they thought the interval between the 2nd and 3rd Temples would be short, as it was for only 50 years between the 1st and 2nd Temples (586 to 536 BCE). But the years since the Yavneh Council have stretched out to centuries, with no opportunity to build a temple, and what has remained is the decision by the Yavneh Council regarding a so-called modified Mosaic Covenant.[48]

---

[47] **Council of Yavneh**: This is where the rabbis met from AD 70-90 to restructure the Law of Moses to function without a Temple and sacrifices; they remodified the Law.

[48] Louis Goldberg, *God, Torah, Messiah*. San Francisco, CA: Purple Pomegranate Productions, 2009, pp. 19-20.

Yet Jeremiah says the celebration of Passover of the Exodus will not be remembered in the future; in its place the regathering of the Jewish people from the north and throughout the world is what will be remembered (Jeremiah 16:14-15; 23:7-8). However, the remembrance of Passover will be kept in the Millennial Kingdom (Ezekiel 45:21). So, the Feast of Passover will not be kept forever for it, too, is limited to time and has not been biblically kept for 2000 years; it is not eternal.

> *All the males among the children of Aaron shall eat of it. It shall be a statute forever [olam] in your generations ...* (Leviticus 6:18) This statute God stopped in AD 70 with the destruction of the Temple and the sacrificial system; it was not eternal or everlasting.

> *This shall be a statute forever [olam] unto you: that in the seventh month, on the tenth day of the month, you shall afflict your souls ... And this shall be an everlasting statute unto you, to make an atonement for the children of Israel for all their sins once [echad] a year* (Leviticus 16:29a, 34a) God stopped the observance of Yom Kippur on two accounts: First, because of His acceptance of the blood of the **New Covenant** – the blood of Messiah – and, second, in AD 70 with the Roman destruction of the *city and the sanctuary* (Daniel 9:27) – it was not eternal.

> *The cities of the Levites, and the houses of the cities of their possession, may the Levites redeem at any time [olam]* – Leviticus 25:32 – This has not been kept for almost 2,000 years; it was not and is not eternal.

> The statute of the *shewbread* (or *showbread*) (Leviticus 24:8-9) and the oil for the menorah (Leviticus 24:3) in the Tabernacle/Temple was to be an *everlasting [olam] covenant* and *perpetual* practice. The statute of the shewbread and the oil for the lampstand ceased with the destruction of the Temple by the Romans; that too was not eternal.

> *Then you shall take an aul, and thrust it through his ear unto the door, and he shall be your servant forever [olam] ...* Deuteronomy 15:17 – This *olam* law was limited to a man's lifetime; this is not everlasting.

According to Leviticus, the sin offering – trespass offering – was *olam*, but these offerings ended for 70 years with the Babylonian Captivity and for now almost 2000 years since the Roman destruction of the Temple.

In Jeremiah 25:9, God says that He will make the Land of Israel a *perpetual* [*olam*] desolation. Yet in Jeremiah 29:10, God promises to bring His people back to the Land 70 years later. In this case, *olam* refers to a period of 70 years; therefore, it is not eternal.[49]

Hosea states that for many days, now between 2,000 to 2,500 years, that Israel will abide without a king, without a prince, without a sacrifice and without the priestly office (3:3-4). God Himself put an end to the Law and replaced it with the **New Covenant** (Jeremiah 31:31-34; Ezekiel 36:26-28; Hebrews 8:7-13; 9:15-17; 10:1-9) and with the high priestly order of Melchizedek in the person of Messiah Yeshua (Psalm 110:1-4; Zechariah 6:11-13; Hebrews 7:14-21).

If the Law of Moses is eternal, why did God put a stop to it and issue a **New Covenant**, a new High Priestly Order, and the **Law of Messiah** which the Book of Hebrews teaches is ***better***? Hebrews is clear that the *old covenant* vanished with the installation of the **New Covenant**. Thus the Law of Moses became *old* with Jeremiah and *vanished away* with the Messiah's death.[50]

Why does the writer of Hebrews state that a *change* to the priesthood of Yeshua demands a *change* in the Law system? God rendered the Mosaic Law inoperative, no longer a required system to be followed (Hebrews 7:14-21).

Words convey meaning and when you grapple with three languages – Hebrew, Greek, and English – it can get interesting; and words can be twisted to mean something they did not mean in the original language.

Let me illustrate by quoting extensively from Arnold Fruchtenbaum [Bracketed comments are mine].[51]:

> There are three key phrases found in conjunction with the Sabbath that are used as the basis for teaching that the Sabbath is perpetual. The ***first key phrase*** is *throughout your generations* (Exodus 31:13). The ***second key phrase*** is the term *perpetual* (Exodus 31:16), which is taken to mean "unending." The ***third key phrase*** is the term *forever* (Exodus 31:17), which is taken to mean "eternal," and therefore still mandatory today.
>
> The Hebrew word for the ***first key phrase*** *throughout your generations* is *ledorot*. While it is used of the Sabbath, this

---

[49] Seth Postell, Eitan Bar, and Erez Soref, *Reading Moses Seeing Jesus*, Wooster, OH: ONE FOR ISRAEL Ministry and Weaver Book Company, 2017, page 16.

[50] Arnold G. Fruchtenbaum. *The Sabbath*, San Antonio, TX: Ariel Press, 2012, p. 41.

[51] Arnold G. Fruchtenbaum. *The Sabbath*, San Antonio, TX: Ariel Press, 2012, pp. 35-37. [The comments in brackets are this author's words and not Fruchtenbaum's.]

expression is also used of a man's lifetime (Leviticus 25:30), of the Levitical Priesthood (Exodus 40.15; Leviticus 6:22; 10:9; Numbers 10:8; 18:23), of the ceremony of the lampstands (Exodus 27:21; Leviticus 24:3), of the service of the brazen laver (Exodus 30:21), of the meal-offering (Leviticus 6:18), and of the sacrificial system (Leviticus 7:36; Numbers 15:15). [All these noted ceremonies God had removed, thus it has not been done throughout their generations.]

The *second key phrase* used as a basis for teaching the perpetuity of the Sabbath is the term *perpetual*. The Hebrew word is either *tamid*, which means "perpetual," or *chok olam*, which means "a perpetual statute." This is not only used of the Sabbath, it is also used of the ceremony of the shewbread (Leviticus 24:9), which everybody agrees has ended with Messiah's death.

The *third key phrase* is *forever*. The simple, basic truth is that Classical Hebrew – the Hebrew of the *Tanakh* – has no term that carries the concept of "eternity." There are phrases that carry this concept, such as "without end," but there is not a single word that carries the concept of eternity as there is in English.

To focus on the meaning of the term *forever*, several things should be kept in mind. The Hebrew word is *olam*. The word itself simply means "long duration," "antiquity," "futurity," "until the end of a period of time," that period of time is determined by the context. Sometimes it is the length of a man's life, sometimes it is an age, sometimes, it is a Dispensation, and sometimes it refers to the end of human history.

There are two Hebrew forms of *olam*. The first form is *le-olam*, which means "unto an age." The second form is *ad-olam*, which means "until an age." However, neither of these forms carry the English meaning of "forever." Although it has been translated that way in English, the Hebrew does not carry the concept of eternity as the English word "forever" does.

The word *olam*, *le-olam*, or *ad-olam*, sometimes means only "up to the end of a man's life." For example, it is used of someone's lifetime (Exodus 14:13), of a slave's life (Exodus 21:6; Leviticus 25:46; Deuteronomy 15:17), of Samuel's life (I Samuel 1:22; 2:35), of the lifetimes of David and Jonathan (I Samuel 20:23), and of David's lifetime (I Samuel 27:12; 28:2; I Chronicles 28:4). While the English reads *forever*, obviously from the context it does not mean "forever" in the sense of eternity, but only up to the end of a person's life.

Olam sometimes means only "an age" or "Dispensation." For example, Deuteronomy 23:3 uses the term *forever* but limits the term to only ten generations. Here it obviously carries the concept of an age. In II Chronicles 7:16, it is used only for the period of the First Temple. So, again, the word *forever* in Hebrew does not mean "eternal" as it does in English; it means up to the end of a period of time, either a man's life or an age or a Dispensation.

The same word for "forever" is used of certain ceremonial facets of the Mosaic Law that everyone agrees have ended with the First Coming of Messiah. For example, the same word *forever* is used of the kindling of the Tabernacle lampstands (Exodus 27:20; Leviticus 24:3), of the ceremony of the shewbread (Leviticus 24:8), of the service of the brazen laver (Exodus 30:21), of the Levitical Priesthood and Levitical garments (Exodus 28:43; 40:15; Leviticus 6:18; 10:9; Numbers 10:8; 18:23; 25:13; Deuteronomy 18:5; I Chronicles 15:2; 23:13), of the sacrificial system, including the sacrifices and offerings (Exodus 29:28; Leviticus 7:34, 36; 10:15; 18:8, 11, 19; 19:10), of the Day of Atonement sacrifice (Leviticus 16:34), and of the red heifer offering (Numbers 19:10). [Once again, these events and ceremonies have ceased and are no longer practiced; these were not forever.]

The last thing to keep in mind is the application: If Sabbath-keeping were mandatory based upon the Hebrew term *forever*, then so are all the other facets of the Law of Moses. Yet even Sabbath-keepers claim that the Messiah has brought these other things to an end. Therefore, it is inconsistent for them to say that all the others have ended, but the Sabbath has not.

Application and Conclusions

If terms such as *forever*, *perpetual statute*, and *throughout your generations* mean that the Sabbath is still mandatory, then so are all those other facets of the Law of Moses. Yet even Sabbath keepers rule out the others but do not rule out the Sabbath, although the same words are used. Thus, they lose their main foundation for arguing of the perpetuity of the Sabbath day. It is inconsistent exegesis to insist on the basis of such terms as *forever*, *throughout your generations*, and *perpetual statute* that the Sabbath law is still mandatory, without incorporating all of those other elements from the Law of Moses for the same reason.

Chapter Six
The New Covenant

Difference Between *New* and *Renew*

To the Church this is not an issue; however, in Messianic circles it is an issue on how the terms *new* and *renew* are used and interpreted in relationship to the Jeremiah 31 passage. ***First***, Rabbinic Judaism looks at the **New Covenant** as an extension of the *old covenant* because they view the *old covenant* as eternal and that it can never be changed. The ***second*** issue is that Messianic Jewish believers who have accepted the rabbinic concept of the Law of Moses being eternal also believe it is necessary to be Torah observant, to keep the Law as a believer in Messiah. We will look at this from two perspectives:

1. First, how are the terms *new* and *renew* used in the biblical text?

2. Second, how are we to understand the usage of the term *olam* which is often translated in our English Bibles as "forever," "everlasting," or "eternal," which was covered in the previous section?

First let us look at the terms *new* and *renew* in the *Tanakh*.

In the Hebrew

The Hebrew word *chadash* (חָדָשׁ) means to "renew," "repair," "restore" and "be restored" in other places (I Samuel 11:14; II Chronicles 15:8; 24:4, 12; Psalm 51:10) as referenced in the King James Version and the New American Standard Version. In this sense, how should the term *New* be understood when we consider the **New Covenant**? In Jeremiah it simply does not fit the context to understand the meaning to be "renewed." Some take Jeremiah 31:31 and try to isolate it from both the immediate and the multitude of other related passages in both testaments that are connected to it. However, because the word *NEW* in this context is used as an adjective and not a noun, it is clearly seen as indicating something "**NEW**" and not "**renewed**."[52] Robert Morris quickly corrects this issue with the proper usage:

---

[52] According to Robert Morris of HaDavar Ministries as he deals with the charge of Anti-Missionaries concerning the eternality of the Law, which is a subject dealt with earlier on

Some like to claim that the word means to renew or repair and is therefore describing a renewed Mosaic Law in Jeremiah 31:31. Their mistake is to miss the fact that the form of the word in Jeremiah is an adjective. It is true that the noun form of the word means renew or repair but the noun is not in the text; the adjective is.[53]

The biblical evidence, rabbinic evidence, and historical evidence from the Septuagint (LXX) all point to understanding it as a brand NEW Covenant.

To *renew* the Mosaic Covenant makes no biblical sense, for the **New Covenant** of Jeremiah and Ezekiel promised three things that were not in the Mosaic Covenant; they were simply unknown in all of 613 commandments of the Law, a concept which will be developed a little later. The **New Covenant** in Jeremiah 31:31-34 is contrasted with the *old covenant*, and the language used by the rabbis who translated the Hebrew text into the Greek Septuagint (LXX) three centuries before the coming of Messiah gave a clear distinction between the *old covenant* (Mosaic Law) and the **New Covenant**. Robert Morris, a Jewish believer, makes a clear personal reference as he relates this passage to Israel as a whole:

> God will put into place a brand-new arrangement after Jeremiah's time (circa 600-580 BCE). It cannot be the Law of Moses. That Law was broken before Jeremiah's time. What is the Law he is referring to here if it is not the broken Law of Moses? A formal name is not given here, just a description regarding the nature of this brand new arrangement — it will be internal.[54]

In the Greek

In searching the Septuagint (38:31) the Greek word for NEW is *kalvos* which is the same in New Testament Greek in the Book of Hebrews which means NEW or fresh (8:8, 13; 9:15).[55] Robert Morris states further:

---

this subject. In Appendix Five of this book, Robert Morris's full unpublished manuscript called "The Eternal Nature of the Mosaic Law" is presented.

[53] Robert Morris, "The Eternal Nature of the Mosaic Law," unpublished manuscript used by permission.

[54] Robert Morris, "The Eternal Nature of the Mosaic Law," unpublished manuscript used by permission.

[55] (Strong's Greek lexicon Number – G2537. 2785):

Sir Lancelot C. L. Brenton, *The Septuagint with Apocrypha Greek and English*. Grand Rapids, MI: Zondervan Publishing House, 1980, p. 952.

The New Covenant is distinct from the Mosaic Covenant. Verse 32 is a reference to the Law of Moses given at Mount Sinai 430 years after the Abrahamic Covenant (Galatians 3:17). Please notice that God states that the Law of Moses was broken by the Jewish people. The problem did not lie with God; He was a (faithful) husband to us. The responsibility for breaking the Mosaic Covenant is ours; we became an adulterous wife (Jeremiah 5:7-8; 7:9; 9:2; Ezekiel 22:9-11; 23:9-12; Hosea 4:2-3).[56]

This is in contrast with the broken Law of Moses which was external in nature. Under the Mosaic Covenant it was incumbent upon man to place God's Word in his heart. A righteous man, like the psalmist, would do his best to accomplish that task through study, meditation, memorization, etc. (Psalm 119:11 says, "Your word I have treasured in my heart, that I may not sin against You.") But it was up to the man, and that means that his efforts, while admirable, would always fall short because of mankind's limitations. However, in Jeremiah 31:33, placing the New Covenant in the heart of man would not face human limitations because God states that He will personally do it (Deuteronomy 30:6). This statement emphasizes why the New Covenant is so new and different from what came before. Under the New Covenant God Himself takes the responsibility and task of placing His law within the core of a person's being. Due to the perfect all-powerful nature of God, we can be sure that His workmanship is complete and perfect. It will not fall short due to human limitations as the Mosaic Law did. The Mosaic Law is holy and righteous and good (Romans 7:12), but God never embued it with the power to enter a man's heart.[57]

In the Greek there are two words for *renew*, one a verb, *anakainizo* which is used by Paul in stating that *our inner man is **renewed** day by day* (II Corinthians 4:16). In Colossians Paul states that we are *to put on the new man, which is **renewed** in knowledge after the image of Him that created him* (3:10). The other word is a noun,

---

John R. Kohlenberger III, Edward W. Goodrick, and James A. Swanson, *The Greek English Concordance to the New Testament*. Grand Rapids, MI: Zondervan Publishing House, 1997, p.401.

[56] Robert Morris. "The Eternal Nature of the Mosaic Law," unpublished manuscript used by permission.

[57] Robert Morris. "The Eternal Nature of the Mosaic Law," unpublished manuscript used by permission.

anakainósis which is used by Paul in Romans 12:2 and Titus 3:5 respectively where he states the following:[58]

> ² *And be not conformed to this world but be you transformed by the renewing of your mind, that you may prove what is that good, and acceptable, and perfect, will of God.*

> ⁵ *Not by works of righteousness which we have done, but according to His mercy He saved us, by the washing of regeneration, and renewing of the Holy Spirit.*

When the Hebrew and the Greek words in the Septuagint (LXX) and New Testament used for *new* and *renew* are analyzed, it becomes increasingly clear what Jeremiah, Paul, and the author of Hebrews meant in the word *NEW* as it related to the **NEW Covenant** and not to the broken *old covenant*. (I am referencing the book of Hebrews where the *old covenant* is referenced as the "first covenant" or "testament," and the lowercase word *old* is based on Hebrews 8:13, *he hath made the first old,* so I simply use the term *old testament,* italicized.)

Now let me elaborate on the three promises that God made known through Jeremiah and Ezekiel that were completely NEW and different from anything that the Law of Moses gave. The ramifications of the **New Covenant** involve regeneration, justification, sanctification, reconciliation, and the imputing of Messiah's righteousness, being redeemed from the marketplace of sin and placed into the family of God by adoption. These are only some of the ramifications of the **New Covenant** inaugurated by Yeshua the Messiah with His blood, the blood of the covenant (Isaiah 42:6; 49:6; Matthew 26:28), the blood of the vicarious sacrifice (Isaiah 53) by the Lamb of God (John 1:29) on the Cross of Calvary.

Promises in the New Covenant

1. Regeneration of the Heart of Israel

The **first promise** in Jeremiah 31:33 is that the **New Covenant** would *regenerate*[59] or circumcise the uncircumcised heart (Deuteronomy 10:16; Jeremiah 4:4; 9:26) making the heart of Israel responsive in obedience to the commands of God.

---

[58] William D. Mounce. *Mounce's Complete Expository Dictionary of Old and New Testament Words.* Grand Rapids, MI: Zondervan Publishing House, 2006, p. 579.

[59] **Regenerate**: This is an interesting word. Before man sinned in Genesis 3, man's heart was alive unto God, but when sin entered the picture man died twice. First he died

> *But this shall be the covenant that I will make with the house of Israel; After those days, says the LORD, I will put My law in their inward parts, and write it in their hearts; and will be their God, and they shall be My people.*

The *old covenant* made no such provision in all the Mosaic Law. The **New Covenant** is an internal change of heart and not just an external command upon man. This change is reflected in Hosea 2:23[60] and Ezekiel 37:23 respectively which states:

> [2:23] *And I will sow her* [Israel] *unto Me in the earth* [Hosea in 1:4-5 called the first child Jezreel]; *and I will have mercy upon her that had not obtained mercy* [in Hosea 1:6-7, this child is called Lo-ruhamah]; *and I will say to them which were not My people, you are My people; and they shall say You are my God* [Hosea in 1:7-9 called the third child Lo-ammi].

> [37:23] *Neither shall they* [Israel] *defile themselves any more with their idols, nor with their detestable things, nor with any of their transgressions: but I will save them out of all their dwelling places, wherein they have sinned, and will cleanse them:* **so shall they** [Israel] **be My people, and I will be their God**.

Neither the Abrahamic Covenant nor the Mosaic Covenant were given as a recipe for salvation; they simply did not make any provision for regeneration of the heart. ONLY the **NEW Covenant** promises regeneration.

2. Removal of Sin

The second promise in Jeremiah 31:34 is that the **New Covenant** would *remove sin* never to be mentioned again against them. The *old covenant* only covered sin by the inferior blood of an animal; it simply could not remove it.[61] Whereas, the blood of

---

spiritually in his relationship to God, as he was separated from God. Second, man would die physically because death was passed on through Adam (Romans 5:12). The term *regenerate* means to take something that was dead and make it alive or to regenerate it, and that is exactly what God would do through the **New Covenant**, which again the *old covenant* had NO power to do.

[60] **The names of Hosea's three children** are named by God, for it speaks of what God will do with Israel in Hosea 2:23. *Jezreel* means "to scatter / sow," *Lo-ruhamah* means "no mercy," and *Lo-ammi* means "not My people." God will in the future "sow" Israel in the Land; He will have "mercy" on them; and they will be "His people" internally because of what God will provide for them through the **New Covenant** when they embrace the Messiah at His Second Coming.

[61] **Day of Atonement:** Once a year this was repeated for centuries because the blood of bulls and goats could NOT take away sin (Hebrews 8:11-14).

the Lamb of God (John 1:29; Romans 5:17-18; 8:1; Hebrews 9:11-14; Psalm 103:10-12) would remove sin, period.

> *And they shall teach no more every man his neighbor, and every man his brother, saying know the LORD: for they shall ALL know Me, from the least of them unto the greatest of them, says the LORD: for I will forgive their iniquity, and I will remember their sin no more (Jeremiah 31:34).*

The *old covenant* once again made no provision for the removal of sin, that is why saints in the *Tanakh* did not go to heaven when they died but to Paradise, part of Sheol (II Samuel 12:15-23; Luke 16:19-31), not hell.[62] Another aspect is clearly brought out by Robert Morris, and it relates to the fact that it will not be necessary for those under the **New Covenant** to teach their brother or neighbor, for they will all know Him:

> Two key features of the New Covenant are the knowledge of God and [His] forgiveness of sins which is the basis for the Spirit's indwelling. Again, this is very different from the Mosaic Covenant. Under the Mosaic Covenant the tribe of Levi was assigned the job of teaching his neighbor and brother (II Chronicles 17:8-9; 30:22; 35:3; Nehemiah 8:7). When the New Covenant is finally fulfilled, when all Israel enters into the New Covenant (Zechariah 3:9; Hosea 2:16-20; 5:15-6:2; Romans 11:25-27;), this teaching ministry will not be necessary.[63]

Israel will be *born again* even as Yeshua challenged Nicodemus (John 3:1-21); and God will remember their sin no more. The indwelling aspect of the **New Covenant** will be given as was stated prophetically by the prophet Ezekiel.

3. Indwelling of the Holy Spirit

The **third promise** is found in Ezekiel 36:26-28 where God through Ezekiel promises the indwelling of the Ruach Ha-Kodesh (Holy Spirit) in all believers.

> *[26] A new heart also will I give you, and a new Spirit will I put within you: and I will take away the stony heart out of your flesh, and I will give you heart of flesh. [27] I will put My Spirit within you, and cause you to walk in My statutes, and you shall keep My judgments and do*

---

[62] **Sheol / Paradise**: This is the holding place of believing Old Testament saints until Messiah Yeshua died on the cross.

[63] Robert Morris, "The Eternal Nature of the Mosaic Law," unpublished manuscript used by permission.

them. *²⁸ And you shall dwell in the Land that I gave to your fathers; and you shall be My people, and I will be your God.*

By contrast, under the *old covenant,* the Ruach Ha-Kodesh (Holy Spirit) only came upon a few selected people out of the vast majority of believing saints in the *Tanakh* and only for a designated period of time until the Ruach Ha-Kodesh's task was completed in their lives. For example, with Bezaleel (Exodus 31:1-6), the Holy Spirit came upon him to enable him to complete the task of making the metal objects for the Tabernacle. A second example was when the Ruach Ha-Kodesh came upon Samson when he went against the Philistines (Judges 13:25; 14:6, 19). A third example was King Saul who received the Spirit and because of his sin; the Spirit was removed from him (I Samuel 16:14). That does not mean he lost his salvation; he only lost the enablement of the Holy Spirit to work in his life. Now in the **NEW Covenant,** Yeshua promised the coming of the Ruach Ha-Kodesh to indwell ***all*** believers (John 14:17b); and, later, Paul repeated the promise of the indwelling of the Ruach Ha-Kodesh (Romans 8:9, 11; I Corinthians 3:16; 6:19; II Timothy 1:14). Again, the *old covenant* did not provide the abiding presence of the Holy Spirit for believers. Robert Morris summarizes this difference:

> From our New Testament perspective, we know what this law is. We can give it two names. It is the Law of the Messiah (Galatians 6:2) or The Law of the Spirit of Life (Romans 8:2) [I Corinthians 9:21 Law of Messiah – added]. The internal nature of the New Covenant is enabled because the New Covenant believer is indwelt by the Holy Spirit (John 14:17; Romans 8:9-11; I Corinthians 3:16-17; 6:19; II Corinthians 6:16; I John 2:27). When the New Covenant Believer is indwelt by the *Ruach Ha-Kodesh*, then God's law is truly in his heart.[64]

Morris then gives further evidence of the distinction between the *old covenant* and the **New Covenant** from Zechariah 14:16-19:

> If the Mosaic Law is not in effect during the Messianic Kingdom, then what law will be in effect? The answer is that the New Covenant or Millennial Law will be in effect at that time, just as Jeremiah stated. Just one example (of many) of the differences between Mosaic Law and New Covenant or Millennial Law is found at the end of the book of Zechariah. Under the Mosaic Law the Feast of Tabernacles was mandatory for the Jewish people only. However, under Millennial Law/New Covenant the observance of Tabernacles

---

[64] Robert Morris, "The Eternal Nature of the Mosaic Law," unpublished manuscript used by permission.

will be mandatory for the entire world. Any nation that does not obey will be punished.[65]

There is a contrast, a difference between the concept of *renew* and something *new* in Hebrew. In the Greek Septuagint, there are two different words: one for *new* and the other for *renew*, meaning the rabbis in the third century BC by their word usage understood this was a brand **NEW covenant**, not a *renewed* covenant. In verse 32 Jeremiah states that Israel had broken the *old covenant* repeatedly (Numbers 15:31; Leviticus 26:15; Deuteronomy 31:16, 20; Jeremiah 2:13; 11:10; Ezekiel 16:59; 44:7). This disobedience applied to the exodus generation, the wilderness generation, the period of the Judges, the monarchy period, the days of Ezra and Nehemiah, as well as in the first century with the rejection of the Messiah and continuing with all the antagonism against Messiah Yeshua to this very day. The rabbis from after the time of Ezra the Scribe to the destruction of the Temple usurped the Mosaic Law by insisting on their own Rabbinic Law (Oral Torah) over Mosaic Law. The Mosaic Law pointed to the Messiah, but the Rabbinic Law was a fabrication that did not point to the Messiah. This is one of the two primary reasons that the Sanhedrin rejected Yeshua, first because of His rejection of their Oral Law and second because Yeshua said that He and the Father were one (John 10:30-39).

New Covenant Passages

Now look at several **New Covenant** passages that use the word *Kainos*, which is a contrast between something *NEW* and something *old* that is *renewed*. The emphasis in these verses is something that is completely *NEW*.

Matthew 26:28

> *For this is My blood of the **NEW Covenant**, which is shed for many for the remission of sins.*

Luke 22:20

> *Likewise also the cup after supper, saying, This cup is the **NEW Covenant** in My blood, which is shed for you.*

John 13:34

> *A **NEW commandment** I give unto you, that you love one another, as I have loved you, that you also love one another.*

---

[65] Robert Morris, "The Eternal Nature of the Mosaic Law," unpublished manuscript used by permission.

I Corinthians 11:25

*After the same manner also He took the cup, when He had supped, saying, this cup is the **NEW Covenant** in My blood: do this, as often as you drink, it, in remembrance of Me.*

II Corinthians 3:6

*Who also has made us able ministers of the **NEW Covenant**; not of the letter, but of the spirit: for the letter kills, but the Spirit gives life.*

II Corinthians 5:17

*Therefore, if any man be in Messiah, he is a **NEW** creature, old things are passed away; behold, all things are become **NEW**.*

Ephesians 2:15

*Having abolished in His flesh the enmity, even the law of commandments contained in ordinances; for to make in Himself of two one **NEW man**, so making peace.*

Ephesians 4:24

*And that you put on the **NEW man**, which after God is created in righteousness and true holiness.*

Hebrews 8:8

*For finding fault with them, He said, Behold, the days come, says the LORD, when I will make a **NEW Covenant** with the house of Israel and with the house of Judah.*

Hebrews 8:13

*In that He said, a **NEW Covenant**, he has made the first old. Now that which decays and grows old is ready to vanish away.*

Hebrews 9:15

*And for this cause He is the mediator of the **NEW Covenant**, that by means of death, for the redemption of the transgressions that were under the first testament, they which are called might receive the promise of eternal inheritance.*

Hebrews 12:24

> *And to Yeshua the mediator of the **NEW Covenant**, and to the blood of sprinkling, that speaks better things than that of Abel.*

The Matthew, Luke, and I Corinthians 11 passages all refer to the Passover meal that Yeshua had with His disciples which resulted in the celebration of the communion table that we partake of in remembering Him. Notice the words ***NEW Covenant in His blood.*** This refers to the cup of wine, the third cup, in the Passover celebration. The wine in this cup symbolized the blood of the lamb from Exodus 12; but here Yeshua gives it a completely new meaning. He now referred to the wine in the cup as His blood, the blood of the **NEW Covenant**. It is something completely **NEW**, not renewed. It is a **NEW blood Covenant** in contrast to the violated *old covenant* (Exodus 24:1-8).

In John 13 believers are told to observe a **NEW Commandment**, to love one another as He loved us. That is also different from the Law in the Torah where they were told to love the LORD their God (Deuteronomy 6:5).

In II Corinthians (3:6) Paul tells Jewish and Gentile believers that they are together ministers of the **NEW Covenant**, absolutely unheard of in the *old covenant*. The letter of the Law kills, but the **NEW Covenant** gives forth life (Romans 8:1-2) more abundantly (John 10:7-10).

In II Corinthians (5:17), again Paul tells Jewish and Gentile believers that they are a **NEW creation** because now according to the Apostle John in his First Epistle, we have been given a **NEW nature,** one which does not sin (I John 3:6, 9; 5:18). We still carry the baggage of the flesh, the old nature (Romans 7:21-25), but we now have two natures; the *old* we will shed at death or at the coming Rapture of the Body of Messiah, for we will only then be like Him (I John 3:2), and this **NEW creation** will be eternal.

In Ephesians chapter 2, Paul speaks about the union of Jew and Gentile into one **NEW man** (2:15) which is the body of Messiah. This is something brand **NEW**; it is not renewed, for again this concept was unheard of in the *old covenant*, that Jew and Gentile would be united together as one **NEW man**. Then Paul tells the believers in Ephesians that they are to put on the **NEW man** and live in righteousness and holiness. We are told to do this because in the **NEW Covenant** we can.

Hebrews is loaded with information, but only three verses are quoted that have a direct bearing on the Greek word **NEW** (*Kainos*). In Hebrews 8 it is used twice, once in verse 8 repeating Jeremiah 31:31-34, and the term ***NEW Covenant*** is used in the Greek Septuagint (LXX), NOT as a renewed covenant. Also, in verse 13, again the author of Hebrews says **New Covenant** and refers to the Mosaic Covenant as *old, decaying, waxing old ready to disappear* which indeed it did in AD 70. In Hebrews 9:15, again the author says that Yeshua is the mediator of the **NEW Covenant** and not a renewed covenant. The evidence is clear that the **NEW Covenant,** whether in the *Tanakh* or the New Testament, is to be understood as a

NEW Covenant, even by the seventy rabbis that translated the Hebrew into Greek nearly three centuries before Yeshua became an issue.

Paul uses the word *renew* in several Epistles in the noun (*anakainósis*) and verb (*anakainizo* or *anakainoo*) forms. As you compare the Greek words for *new* and *renew* you can see a stark difference.

Romans 12:2 (noun)

> *And be not conformed to this world: but be transformed by the **renewing** of your mind, that you may prove what is that good, and acceptable, and perfect, will of God.*

II Corinthians 4:16 (verb)

> *For which cause we faint not; but though our outward man perish, yet the inward man is **renewed** day by day.*

Ephesians 4:23 (verb)

> *And be **renewed** in the spirit of your mind;*

Colossians 3:10 (verb)

> *And have put on the new man, which is **renewed** in knowledge after the image of Him that created him.*

Titus 3:5 (noun)

> *Not by works of righteousness which we have done, but according to His mercy He saved us, by the washing of regeneration, and **renewing** of the Holy Spirit.*

Chapter Seven
Dealing with the Terms
Law, Torah, and *Tanakh*

The words *Law* and *Torah* are used very carelessly as defined in Rabbinic Judaism; they are used very elastically. The *Law,* biblically in a very narrow sense, speaks of the Mosaic Law found in the books of Exodus, Leviticus, Numbers, and Deuteronomy. However, beyond that, Rabbinic Judaism refers to the Torah as the whole of the *Tanakh,* the Oral Rabbinic Law, the Mishnah, and even the Talmud[66] as Torah, a very elastic interpretation. In a strict interpretation, the Law refers only to the Mosaic Law and nothing more.

The term *Torah* refers to only the five Books of Moses which are largely narrative and which also incorporate the Law. The Hebrew word *Torah* means "teaching," "doctrine," or "instruction." It does not refer to the whole of the *Tanakh.* These words used by God and His sub-authors are very precise and clear; it is only man who changes its usage without God's authority.

The term *Tanakh* is an acronym that refers to the three divisions of the Old Testament.

> The first division is called the **Law** or **Torah** and is the *T* in *Tanakh.*
>
> The second division, the **Prophets,** in Hebrew is called the Nevi'im, the *N* in *Tanakh.*
>
> The third division is the **Writings,** called the *Kethuvim,* the *KH* in *Tanakh.*

This is what Yeshua referenced in Luke 24 when he spoke to the two men on the Emmaus Road (vv. 25-27) and then to the disciples (vv. 44-45). Each word has a precise and clear meaning and is not used elastically in Scripture.

---

[66] **Mishnah and Talmud:** The Mishnah is the full record of the Oral Law handed down by memory from the rabbis in their attempt to teach the meaning of the Law of Moses. It started after Ezra the Scribe and continued as an oral tradition into the second century after Messiah when Judah ha Nasi compiled it all together in written form. This Mishnah, or Oral Law, became equal to and then greater than the Law of Moses itself.

Talmud: This is the combination of all the oral traditions, discussions, and instruction of the great rabbis and scholars of Judaism, which today involves about twenty-two volumes of literature. Rabbinic Judaism today promotes the study of the Mishnah and Talmud to the neglect of the Mosaic Law and the whole of the Tanakh.

The Law, Prophets, and the Writings were given to Israel, not the Gentiles. The Law in the Torah contains the conditional Mosaic Law, and two other key unconditional covenants (Abrahamic and Land). The Law had no spiritual benefit to the Gentiles[67] in general because the Law and the keeping of it were designed literally as a middle wall of partition (Ephesians 2:11-15) to keep the Gentile away from the covenant promises given specifically to Israel. In light of this, God gave a huge incentive for the Jewish people in keeping the Law: the blessing of Deuteronomy 28:1-14. Literally everything the Jewish people would touch, God would bless. God would bless them in every area of their lives if they obeyed. Even the Gentile God-fearers in Acts (10:2; 13:16, 26) were attracted to the high morals of the moral law and the worship of one God, but they were not willing to submit to physical circumcision and place themselves under or obligate themselves to all the 613 regulations of the Law system. The Prophets record two other unconditional covenants (Davidic and **New Covenant**s) which again were given to Israel.

Concerning the Jewish doctrine of inspiration, they had three different levels of inspiration taught concerning the *Tanakh*. First the Torah which incorporates the Mosaic Law was the most inspired and given the highest authority. Next was the Prophets section of the Scriptures, also called the *Nevi'im*, which was inspired, but not as inspired as the Torah. The last section is the Writings section which was also called the *Kethuvim* which were inspired but not as inspired as the Prophets, which in turn was not as inspired at the Torah. This demonstrates the significance that Judaism gives to the Torah. Christianity believes that all Scripture is equally inspired of God and that every word (plenary inspiration) is inspired of God. No Scripture is weightier than any other concerning it being the God's Word. Actually, believers in Messiah have a higher view of the *Tanakh* than Judaism because they believe *all Scripture is given* (equally) *by inspiration of God* (I Timothy 3:16).

---

[67] The Law did have a moral benefit to Gentiles years ago and still does today. That is what attracted the God-fearers that Paul met in his three missionary journeys. According to I Timothy 1:8, Paul said the Law can be used lawfully to show Gentiles that they are sinners.

Chapter Eight
Torah Observance and the
Old Testament Pilgrim Feasts

The pilgrim feasts (Exodus 23:14-17; 34:18-23; Deuteronomy 16:1-15) were to be celebrated in Jerusalem where the Temple was, where God placed His Name (Deuteronomy 16:16). However, resulting from the rejection of Israel's Messiah, the Temple was destroyed because of their ultimate disobedience. So, if you are celebrating any other place than in Jerusalem regarding Passover, Shavuot (Pentecost) or Succoth (Tabernacles), you are acting in disobedience to the Law. So instead of being Torah observant you are violating the Torah, for you are only to be celebrate these pilgrim feasts in Jerusalem. This violation was made possible because the rabbis at Yavneh[68] who violated the Mosaic Law in modifying the Law so that it could be observed outside the Land, in the Diaspora. In celebrating these pilgrim feasts in the Americas or eastern/western Europe according to Ezekiel (36), they are in those countries to begin with because Israel repeatedly, unrepentantly violated the Law. Israel was there in the Diaspora because they profaned God's Name and defiled His Land.

Let me step back for a moment and speak to non-compliant Jewish believers (and Gentiles). If you are Jewish or want to teach how all seven feasts are a picture of the ministry of Yeshua, it is fine, because you're not trying to be Torah observant; you are instead lifting up Yeshua. If it is a means for you to identify with your culture and identify with the larger unbelieving Jewish community, it is fine. The key is your motivation for observing the feasts. I personally have done Passover demonstrations well over 100 times to teach what the Jewish Passover is and how Yeshua fulfilled the Passover and what all that means to believers. Now I will return to the issue of being Torah observant.

Can you imagine today flying to Tel Aviv and traveling to Jerusalem every time you sinned to make the required sin offering or trespass offering. How about traveling to the Temple in Jerusalem after the birth of every child to fulfill the law of purification (Leviticus 12:6-8; Luke 2:22-24) either 40 or 80 days after childbirth? Can you imagine flying to Jerusalem three more times a year to celebrate the pilgrim feasts when all males were to present themselves before the LORD (Exodus 23:14-17; Deuteronomy 16:16-17) in Jerusalem. Does that sound impossible, yes, if you live in North American, South America, Europe, Russia, India, China or Africa, and to

---

[68] **Yavneh**: The Council of Rabbis at Yavneh retooled the law or modified the law to survive without a temple and sacrifices in AD 70-90.

complicate that there has been no Temple or priesthood now for approximately 1950 years! Now go back several centuries before there were airplanes, cars, or trains. To travel from where you lived, it would have been a long, physically hard, and often impossible trip because of a lack of funds, getting time off from your employer, or nations at war, etc. As I said before the Mosaic Law was made for the people of Israel within the borders of Israel, not from other continents, nor from far away countries courtesy of the rabbis at Yavneh. There is nothing wrong with celebrating these laws as Hebrew culture, and Hebrew identity, but doing so is NOT being Torah observant!

Understand God did this because of Israel's sin. So now messianic Jews and Gentiles want to cherry pick what laws are convenient to obey and have the nerve to say they are Torah observant. Something is wrong with this picture.

The Law is obviously not practical for those who live outside of Israel whether hundreds or thousands of miles away to keep Torah. But today, even in Israel with no Temple or sacrifices, it is easy to cherry pick laws to obey or not to obey conforming to the Council of Yavneh. Doug Friedman in the winter issue [#21] 2016 of the Ariel Ministries magazine[69] researched all 613 laws of Moses and found that without the Temple and officiating priesthood it was absolutely impossible to keep 58% of the Mosaic Law. Here is the observation from the article:

1. Well over half [58%] of the 613 commandments cannot be observed by anyone today, even if they wanted to. Therefore, whoever claims to be Torah observant is not telling the truth.

2. Most believers – even church attendees who are not striving to observe the Mosaic Law – actually observe almost 30% [actually number is 28%].

3. Most Messianic believers only observe about 5% more than the non-Messianic church attendees.

4. Even those who are serious Messianic Torah Proponents [MTPs] fail to observe 8% of the commandments that they could observe.

The only thing that I can say about Torah observance is you have the liberty in Messiah to do them, but why do you export them and cause confusion and division in the Body of Messiah? Why is there no focus on knowing Messiah and allowing God to conform you to the image of His Son (Romans 8:28-29) and observing the <u>Law of Messiah</u> through the indwelling ministry of the Ruach Ha-Kodesh (Holy Spirit) that has far more benefits spiritually (Ephesians 1:3-14, 18-23)?

---

[69] Available online at *www.Ariel.org*. Click on *Resources*, then magazine and go to the winter of 2016.

Chapter Nine
Christian Liberty for Jews and Gentiles

While I have been critical of Jewish and Gentile believers who are exporting their pro-Torah-observance message, I also need to explain the Christian Liberty that we have as believers in the Body of Messiah. Some may say that I am antinomian because I see the Scriptures teaching that the Law of Moses has been rendered inoperative as a system to live by, having been replaced by the Law of Messiah through the **New Covenant**. However, believers in the economy of Grace are NOT without law, we are under the Law of Messiah.

First let us examine the Greek word *eleuqeria* (*eleutheria*) which is translated as "freedom" or "liberty." The meaning of this word can be twisted and abused by those who have a pro-Torah-observant agenda. It is important to see how Paul used these two words (*liberty* and *freedom*) in a Church context, for they were not used under the Mosaic Law. In I Corinthians 10:31 and Colossians 3:17, Paul laid down the ***underlying*** purpose of our liberty and freedom in Messiah.

> *So whether you eat or drink or whatsoever you do, do it all **to the glory of God*** (I Corinthians 10:31).

> *And whatsoever you do in word or deed, **do all in the Name of the Lord Yeshua**, giving thanks to God the Father by Him* (Colossians 3:17).

Notice you are to do all things in the Name of Yeshua, not in the name of Moses or the Mosaic Law system. ***The purpose*** in all that we do is to give glory to God, not to ourselves and not for our opinions or theological biases. Rather, all is to be done in the Name of Yeshua, who is the pinnacle of all the *Tanakh* and New Testament truth. It all culminates in Him and not Moses. Remember that Yeshua is *the Prophet like Moses* (Deuteronomy 18:18-19)! Glory and praise are for Him and to Him; it is not focused on us and our preferences, and every believer has preferences. ***Here is a principle*** laid down by Paul in Romans (14:13-15) as he deals with the Jewish and Gentile relationships and all the multiplicity of cultural backgrounds of the Gentiles:

> *[13] Let us not therefore judge one another anymore: but judge this rather, that no man put a stumbling block or an occasion to fall in his brother's way. [14] I know, and am persuaded by the Lord Yeshua, that there is nothing unclean of itself: but to him that esteems anything to be unclean, to him it is unclean. [15] But if your brother is grieved with your meat [that had been offered to idols] you are no*

> *longer walking in love. Do not destroy him with your meat, for whom Messiah died.*

In verse 13 we are not to judge each other in non-moral issues, for all servants of Messiah will stand before Him at His judgment seat or Bema Seat (Romans 14:10). I do not have to answer to God for you, I will have to answer to Him for myself, and so do you. So let us not judge each other on non-moral issues. To do so may put stumbling blocks before weaker believers who are not grounded and perhaps easily distracted, causing them to be sidetracked by majoring on non-moral issues that are not sin. Most of Torah observances are non-moral issues.

In Romans 14:14-15, the context is of meat offered to idols in Paul's day; but today because of a person's background, that person may be convinced that a non-moral issue like eating a certain food is wrong. Paul's advice is to not condemn that person. In your Christian liberty you would not take a former alcoholic to a restaurant that serves wine. Instead, in consideration for your brother and his weakness, you would avoid it because you love your brother. In your Christian liberty you would be sensitive to a person who has a weakness and not put him in an environment that would cause him to stumble and fall. If you did, you would be equally responsible for his fall as your brother would be before Yeshua at His Judgment Seat. The key is to be sensitive and discerning for each brother and sister on a multitude of issues that could cause them to sin. Be sensitive to issues that are stumbling blocks to weaker believers. So if you as the stronger brother would not take part in something that would cause a weaker brother to stumble, that is using your liberty in Messiah as Yeshua intended you to use it. There are many issues that I do not have a problem with; they are not sin to me, yet those issues may be a stumbling block for another believer. In my love for my fellow believer in Yeshua I will avoid anything that may cause them to stumble.

Now in our context here we are not talking about meat offered to idols, but we are talking about two different groups of persons: 1) the Covenant People of God (Jewish believers) and 2) the multiplicity of culture and customs of Gentiles who through the blood of the **New Covenant** are being blessed with salvation because of their Faith in Yeshua, not in Mosaic Law. They are followers of Yeshua, not Moses. Who is greater than Moses? Yeshua the Messiah!

Here is a principle to understand and to contemplate: **Total freedom is anarchy!** Freedom has limitations. To illustrate, you have the freedom to drive a car, but you do not have the freedom to drive recklessly and endanger another person's life. That principle can be multiplied in many areas of life. Now go back to Exodus 19-24 where there are absolutely no Gentiles included in the giving of the Mosaic Law to Israel alone. So why as Jewish believers in Messiah do you try to persuade Gentiles to keep something that was NOT given to them. Why do you attempt to persuade Gentiles that they must keep Torah when the Law was not given to them? Why have some of you Gentile believers in Messiah taken on your own personal "crusade" to convert other Gentile believers to Messianic Judaism? The point is, if you are a believer, you are already converted! If you teach now that all need to be re-converted to Messianic Judaism, that is blatant error when they have already been converted to

Messiah Yeshua, Who is far above Moses, as their personal Saviour from sin? Which is greater: the Mosaic Law or the God of Israel in the person of Yeshua who fulfilled it!? If it is the Law you push, then you are depreciating the Person and work of Messiah and bring Him down to the level of Moses, which is blasphemy. Who is better? Yeshua is better than angels, Moses, and the priesthood of Aaron (see the Book of Hebrews). Most of the Laws of Moses are non-moral issues that have absolutely nothing to do with a believer's walk and fellowship in the Light of Messiah as far as obeying His commandment, and commandments, the <u>Law of Messiah</u> (I John 1).

Nine of the Ten Commandments are carried over to the <u>Law of Messiah</u>, along with the laws against the occult and fornication and other sexual sins which are also forbidden in the <u>Law of Messiah</u>. Look at Paul's statement in I Corinthians 6:12:

> *All things are lawful unto me, but all things are not expedient: all things are lawful for me, but I will not be brought under the power of any.*

Many of the non-moral issues for Paul were not that important in Messiah. Paul's conclusion is that he would not be controlled by them. Paul as a Jew had the liberty or freedom in Messiah to personally observe parts of the Mosaic Law; and he did, but he never taught that Torah observance was necessary for Gentiles or for Jewish people. Here is a quote worthy of repeating via a Messianic Jewish believer:

> The biblical basis for the freedom to keep the law can be seen in the actions of Paul, the greatest exponent of freedom from the Law. His vow in Acts 18:18 is based on Numbers 6:2, 5, 9 and 18. His desire to be in Jerusalem for Pentecost in Acts 20:16 is based on Deuteronomy 16:16. The strongest passage is Acts 21:17-26, where Paul, the Apostle of freedom from the Law, is seen keeping part of the Law himself. The believer is free from the Law of Moses, but he is also free to keep parts of it. Thus, if a Jewish believer feels the need to refrain from eating unkosher food like pork, he is free to do so. The same is true for all the other commandments.[70]

Paul the Apostle of freedom from the Law made several statements in Galatians that apply to serving Messiah and not Moses, and not being entangled again with the yoke of bondage (Acts 15:10) to the Law, which they themselves could not keep for fifteen centuries. But you say, "I can obey the Law and serve Messiah as a Jew," and, yes, that is correct, you can; but it does not make you a better believer or more spiritual than the Gentile believer in Messiah who does not. Paul exhorts the Galatian Church:

---

[70] Arnold G. Fruchtenbaum, *Faith Alone: An Exposition of the Book of Galatians*. San Antonio, TX: Ariel Press, 2014, p. 89.

> *Stand fast therefore in the **liberty** wherewith Messiah has made **us** free and be not entangled again with the yoke of bondage* (Galatians 5:1).

> *You are **severed** from Messiah, you who would be justified by the law; you have fallen away from Grace (*Galatians 5:4 – ESV).

Notice the word *made US free*; Paul is speaking to Jewish believers and Gentile believers, warning that the Law for *us* as a working system is not the issue to dig our heels into! The issue that the Torah-observant folks don't mention is that the Law of Messiah is our guide to living a Spirit-filled life with its over 600 imperative commands that apply to believers in Yeshua.[71] The word translated "severed" or "fallen away" is *katargeo*, which means "to render inoperative." It is the same word used by Paul when a husband dies. In that case, the wife is severed or discharged (Romans 7:2) from the law of marriage to the husband. The law can rule only until the point of death, and when the husband dies the law of marriage to the husband no longer has any jurisdiction over the wife. This I will bring out in relationship to the Law of Moses: The *old covenant* has no more jurisdiction over the Jewish people, and it never had jurisdiction over the Gentiles because the Author (Yeshua) of the *old covenant* died (Hebrew 9:15-17). This I will cover in detail as I show who the Author of the Law is and Who the Mediator of the **New Covenant is**.

> *For you were called to freedom, brothers. Only do not use your freedom as an opportunity for the flesh, but through love serve one another* (Galatians 5:13 ESV).

Below are the words of a friend of mine who is in Jewish ministries as I am. He used an illustration of a Jewish believer who is a co-worker with him in CJF Ministries who states the following: Sometimes Christians criticized him for keeping kosher. They'd say, "You're a Christian now! You're not under the Law anymore! Go ahead and have some pork or lobster."

> But for this believer it wasn't about Law-keeping. It was more about culture and his Jewish heritage. In his way of thinking, he was Jewish, and Jewish people don't eat pork. He was well aware that he could eat pork and it wouldn't affect his standing before God one iota. But he chose not to eat pork. In fact, he told us many times that he had no desire whatsoever to eat anything unclean.

> He had no problem with His Messianic Jewish brethren who didn't keep kosher. He could take Moishe Rosen out for dinner, for example, and buy him a big, two-pound lobster – and they'd sit and

---

[71] See John Metzger, *The Law, Then and Now: What About Grace*? Larkspur, CO: Grace Acres Press, 2019, Chapters 14-20 and Imperative Commands in Appendix.

talk for hours and have a great time. He didn't care what anyone else did. But for him, he didn't want to eat anything that was biblically unclean."[72]

That is one of the best illustrations of the exercise of Christian Liberty on the parts of both Jewish believers. Neither one reprimanded the other over a non-moral matter; they respected each other and the biblical principle of the liberty that a believer has in Messiah.

However, in the Torah-observance movement that is not the case, for they encourage other Jewish believers to wear the Jewish religious garb and to encourage Gentiles to do the same. So their focus is on being more Jewish by selectively keeping parts of the Mosaic Law than on adhering wholly to the Law of Messiah, which is to be like Christ, their Messiah.

I have used the phrase and strongly implied in this book that we are not to be "Jewishlike," but Christlike! What do I mean by that? It can be misconstrued that Jewish believers in Messiah are to lay aside their Jewishness with all its culture and heritage and become like other Gentile believers in Messiah. That should NEVER be the case!

Biblically we are dealing with two different people groups from the Scriptures: Jews and Gentiles. We are also dealing with two totally different economies of God (Dispensations of Law or of Grace) and two totally different Covenants (Mosaic and **New Covenant**), with the first conditional or temporary and the other unconditional and eternal.

So let me deal with the Gentiles first. The Law of Moses was given to the Jewish people, for it was they who made the bilateral covenant with the LORD called the Mosaic Covenant (Exodus 24:3-11). So the Gentiles biblically were NOT told to adhere to the Law of Moses; but later, as followers of Yeshua, they were told to adhere to the Law of Messiah, because of the **New Covenant**. This book is dealing with the fact that Gentiles are to be Gentiles and Jews still are to be of Jewish ethnicity, for the Law of Moses is not for Gentiles. So the issue of whether or not Gentiles should be following the Mosaic Law should be moot; but it is not because Gentiles are being sucked into Torah observance, often by other Torah-observant Jewish and Gentile believers; **but the focus is on the wrong Law system!** Believers, both Jewish and Gentile, should focus completely and only on the Law of Messiah and all the command<u>s</u> in the Epistles directed to believers in Yeshua.

Now we come to the more difficult part, and that is that Jewish believers in Messiah called Messianic Jews are Hebrew Christians. In this context, the concept of Christian liberty that Paul taught to believers is very pertinent to both Jew and

---

[72] Personal communications with Gary Hedrick of CJF Ministries.

Gentile. However, the issue at hand is ***the statement that I have made in the context of Jewish believers: They are to be imitators of Messiah and not Jewishlike***. So what do I mean?

Many Jewish believers in Messiah have become very legalistic in teaching that the Law given to them is to be obeyed by Gentiles and by themselves as a necessary component of living out their Faith, a practice which the New Testament simply does not teach. Jewish believers in the Messiah have every right to practice and observe any of the Laws of Moses that they want to keep. They have that freedom in Messiah to do so. That is the teaching of Paul in Romans, First Corinthians, and Galatians. However, they – whether Jewish or Gentile believers – do not have the right to export it because the Law of Moses is not the active law system now; the Law of Messiah is now in effect. So to teach other Jewish and Gentile believers to keep the Torah of Moses is simply unbiblical; it is legalism and out of step with God.

Let me give a biblical illustration. In Deuteronomy, eighteen times God said that He would place His Name in one location, which was the Temple in Jerusalem. However, the people of Israel did not want to travel the long distance to Jerusalem so they made *high places* where they could worship the LORD. Now, they were worshipping the LORD, the true God, but at their place and not His place. Kings Hezekiah and Josiah removed the high places in being obedient to the Torah; however, other good kings such as Asa and Jehoshaphat were reluctant to do so. They worshipped God but disobeyed Him in where He was to be worshipped. That is what Torah observance is doing in worshipping Him through the Mosaic Law that HE, HIMSELF, LAID ASIDE, instead of according to the **New Covenant** and the Law of Messiah.

At the same time, for other Gentile believers to teach that Jewish people are to be like other Gentile believers and lay aside their culture and heritage is equally unbiblical. I have personal friends who are Jewish believers and keep kosher as well as other things in the Law because they are Jewish and want to identify with their Jewish roots and community. They have also told me that they know that it does not give them any extra righteous merit points with God; and they do not try to obligate others to observe what they are convicted to practice.

Principle of Freedom for Believers in Yeshua Messiah

(John B. Metzger)

Free from any obligation to keep any of the 613 commandments today.

Free to keep parts of the commandments that we might choose, which do not compromise New Testament truth.

1. Torah keeping has no value in our justification – We are saved by Grace through Faith plus absolutely NOTHING!

2. Torah keeping has no value in our sanctification – We are sanctified by means of the Law of Messiah and not the Law of Moses.

3. In selectively keeping parts of the Law of Moses there is no increase in spirituality and there is absolutely no merit before God because of the contradictions between the two law systems.

4. Keeping the Law of Moses does not add to Jewish identity or make a Gentile Jewishlike.

   One does not become more Jewish or spiritual by Torah keeping.

Chapter Ten
Moral Law of Moses Is Carried over to the Law of Messiah

Many people have divided the Law into three artificial divisions: moral, ceremonial, and civil. While doing so does make it easier to categorize the Law, this division did not come from God. Many people want to promote the moral law of the Mosaic Law as still valid. Nine of the Ten Commandments are valid only as they have been transferred over to a new law system, the <u>Law of Messiah,</u> through the **New Covenant,** by God. These folk do not understand the purpose of the economies of God (how God governs His people at different times in history). A definition of Dispensations or economies of God by Charles Ryrie is as follows:

> Dispensationalism views the world as a household run by God, and in this household world, God is dispensing or administering its affairs according to His own will and in various stages of revelation in the process of time. These various stages mark off the different distinguishable economies in the outworking of God's total purpose. These economies are the Dispensations. The understanding of God's different economies is essential to a proper interpretation of His revelation within these various economies.[73]

Arnold Fruchtenbaum adds an insightful observation:

> From God's viewpoint, a Dispensation is an economy. But from man's viewpoint, a Dispensation is a responsibility, because in each new economy God gave new revelation that requires a reaction from man.[74]

It can be concluded that these economies of God are the only system of theology that seriously deal with the issue of progressive revelation that we talked about in chapter two. These economies concern God revealing His person, nature, and will, bit by bit, piece by piece over a period of 1600 years, from Moses (1446 BC) to the Apostle John (AD 95). The content of each economy of God changes with new revelation, but man's responsibility is to be obedient (by Faith) to that new revelation. Salvation

---

[73] Charles Ryrie, *Dispensationalism*. Chicago, IL: Moody Press, 1995, pp. 23-43.

[74] Arnold G. Fruchtenbaum, *Come & See: The Word of God, vol 1*. San Antonio, TX: Ariel Press, 2015, p. 123.

NEVER changes; it is always *by Faith* (Habakkuk 2:4; Hebrews 11) in the LORD God.

When a Dispensation is given, there are four things that are variables, though this is an incomplete list. I provide my own summary of Fruchtenbaum's teaching here, from his book, *Israelogy: The Missing Link in Systematic Theology:*[75]

1. Any new revelation usually goes hand in hand with a continuation of certain things, meaning **some things remain the same**.

    - The ten commandments are carried over from the Law of Moses to the Law of Messiah, except for Sabbath observance.

2. It means an annulment of other things, meaning that these **things are removed**.

    - Concerning food: in the Edenic and Adamic Covenants people were vegetarians, in the Noahic Covenant animal meat could be eaten, and in the Mosaic Covenant only kosher food could be eaten. In the **New Covenant,** all things are clean to eat; and there are no more sacrifices for sin as in the Mosaic Covenant since the blood of Messiah is completely adequate.

3. New requirements are added because of new revelation, **brand new things**.

    - In the Mosaic Law there were forty-two commandments which you could be put to death for if you violated them; whereas, in the **New Covenant** the whole nature of the covenant has been transformed to focus on life and not death.

4. **Some things are modified or intensified or carried over from one economy to another**.

    - Some commandments in the Law of Moses are **intensified by the Law of Messiah.** The Law of Moses said *love your neighbor as yourself* (Leviticus 19:18), but the Law of Messiah says *love one another, even as I have loved you* (John 15:12). Also, the motivation changes from obeying the Law of Moses and being blessed; whereas, in the Law of Messiah the motivation is, you have been and are blessed, therefore do.

---

[75] Arnold Fruchtenbaum, Israelology: *The Missing Link in Systematic Theology.* San Antonio, TX: Ariel Press, 1993, adapted from p. 650.

Since the ceremonial and civil law can no longer be kept, the moral law (the Ten Commandments) has become the focus of theologians. However, in II Corinthians 3:7, Paul says that what was *engraven in stone* is now the *ministration of death*. So now let us compare the moral law in the Law of Moses and the Law of Messiah and see what changed, comparing apples with apples.

Ten Commandments – Exodus 20:1-17; Deuteronomy 5:1-21

When you look up the verses you will clearly see that nine of the Ten Commandments are repeated in the New Testament Epistles. Take a look:

1. You shall have no other gods before God – I Corinthians 8:6; I Timothy 2:5.

2. You shall not make or worship graven images – I John 5:21; I Corinthians 6:9; Ephesians 5:5; Revelation 21:8.

3. You shall not take God's name in vain – I Timothy 6:1.

4. Remember the Sabbath day and keep it holy – No References in **the New Covenant** - Why??? Because the Sabbath was a sign of the Mosaic Covenant – just as circumcision was a sign of the Abrahamic Covenant – and just as the rainbow was a token or sign of the Noahic Covenant – it is obvious that the Sabbath can only be related to Israel, since only Israel was set apart at Sinai and only Israel has been delivered from the land of Egypt. God never delivered the Church out of Egypt nor did He deliver the Seventh Day Adventist Church in particular out of Egypt. In the context of the Mosaic Law, the Sabbath and the reasons for the Sabbath can only be related to the Jewish nation. The reasons given for Sabbath observance in the Law of Moses include: a memorial of Creation, a memorial of the Exodus, a sign of Israel's sanctification or setting apart as a nation, and a sign of the Mosaic Covenant. No one single event is given as the subject of its observance, but instead several are alluded to. Because the Sabbath is a sign of the Mosaic Covenant, it is in force for the duration of that covenant. If there is a time when the covenant comes to an end, the sign would no longer be obligatory.[76]

5. Honor your father and mother – Ephesians 6:1-2.

6. You shall not murder – Romans 13:9; I Peter 4:15; Revelation 21:8.

7. You shall not commit adultery – Romans 13:9; I Corinthians 6:9; Ephesians 5:3; Colossians 3:5; Hebrews 13:4.

---

[76] Arnold Fruchtenbaum, *The Sabbath*. San Antonio, TX: Ariel Press, 2014, p. 33.

8. You shall not steal – Romans 13:9; I Corinthians 6:10; Ephesians 4:28; I Peter 4:15.

9. You shall not bear false witness (lie) – Romans 13:9; Ephesians 4:25; Revelation 21:8.

10. You shall not covet – Romans 7:7; 13:9; I Corinthians 6:10; Ephesians 5:3; Colossians 3:5; Hebrews 13:5.

What is nice about the Torah (the five Books of Moses) is that the Ten Commandments are concise and all together provided in two passages; whereas, in the Epistles they are scattered among seven Epistles. Nonetheless they are all carried over into the **New Covenant** because they are so foundational.

Notice that Paul in three verses identifies five of the Ten Commandments; and he instructs Timothy that the Law was not made for good persons but sinners (I Timothy 1:8-10 - NASB):

> *But we know that the Law is good, if one uses it lawfully, realizing the fact that law is not made for a righteous person, but for those who are lawless and rebellious, for the ungodly and sinners, for the unholy and profane,*
>
> *for those who kill their fathers or mothers* [5th and 6th commandments],
>
> *for murderers* [6th commandment]
>
> *and immoral men and homosexuals* [7th commandment]
>
> *and kidnappers* [8th commandment]
>
> *and liars and perjurers* [9th commandment], *and whatever else is contrary to sound teaching.*

Below is a chart that provides a summary of the comparison between the Ten Commandments and the Law of Messiah.

So the keeping of the Law, ceremonial, civil, and moral, all ceased as an operating system. With the change of economies through the blood of the Lamb of God, Messiah Yeshua, the Mosaic Law was rendered inoperative and was replaced with the Law of Messiah because of the **NEW Covenant**.

How the <u>Law of Messiah</u> and the Law of Moses Interact with Each Other
(John B. Metzger)

Commandments	*Law of Moses*	*Law of Messiah*
Many are the same	The Ten Commandments	Nine of the Ten Commandments
Many are different	Sabbath Law	No Sabbath Law – Romans 14:5; Colossians 2:16
	Dietary Code	No Dietary Code – Mark 7:19; Romans 14:20
Some are intensified	Love neighbor as yourself Leviticus 19:18	Love as Messiah has loved us John 15:12
Motivational difference	Do – In order to be blessed Deuteronomy 28:1-14	You are blessed – Therefore do Ephesians 1:3

Chapter Eleven
Rendered Inoperative

Because this term, *rendered inoperative,* is referred to so frequently throughout Part Two of this book it needs to be explained so that the significance of this word is understood. The Greek word is καταργέω (*katargeó*) meaning to "render inoperative" or "abolish." This is a Greek compound word, *kata* meaning "down" and *argeo* meaning "to be inactive" or "idle." The word appears in our English Bibles with some of the following terms:

> *abolished* or *abolishing,* to bring to an end, to do away, or done away, fading or fades away, to nullify, passing away, removed, render powerless, and to be severed.

There is an array of words used to express the Greek term *katargeo*, or **render inoperative** that will be referred to as we proceed through the chapter snapshots of the Epistles. In fact, the Theological Dictionary of the New Testament[77] gives the meaning "to make completely inoperative or to put out of use." It is a term used twenty-five times primarily by the Apostle Paul and once by Luke and the author of Hebrews. Strong's give the following word definitions of *katargeo*:

> to be (render) entirely idle (useless), abolish, cease, cumber,[78] deliver, destroy, do away, become (make) of no (none, without) effect, fail, loose, bring (come) to nought, put away (down), vanish away, make void.[79]

So when the words *rendered inoperative, terminated, annulled* are used, it simply means that it is no longer in effect, it is no longer applicable, it becomes moot. It is used both **positively** for the benefit of the believer (we are no longer under the Law) and **negatively** as it relates to the Law (it is of no effect) having been *rendered inoperative,* terminated or annulled. So, concerning the Law of Moses as the author of Hebrews related it in 8:13 (ESV), *In speaking of a **New Covenant** He makes the first one* [Mosaic Covenant] *obsolete. And what is becoming obsolete and growing*

---

[77] Gerhard Kittel, *Theological Dictionary of the New Testament.* Grand Rapids, MI: Eerdmans Publishing Co. vol. 1, 1964, p. 453.

[78] **Cumber**: The primary definition of the word means "trouble, harass, to hinder or encumber by being in the way."

[79] James Strong, *A Concise Dictionary of the Words in the Greek New Testament with their Renderings in the Authorized English Version.* Peabody, MA: Hendrickson Publishers, 1988.

old is ready to vanish away. This verse conveys the same idea as the *old covenant* being **rendered inoperative**; it is *old*, out of date because something brand new is now placed over it. Because this issue is so important, I will take the time to reference directly verses which include the concept of being **rendered inoperative**. Here is a list of most of the Bible verses that use the root word *katargeo* which all carry the idea of being **rendered inoperative,** or one of its related meanings described above.

Romans 3:3, 31

> ³ *For what if some* [Jewish people] *did not believe? Shall their unbelief make the faith of God **without effect** [καταργήσει]?* The answer is given in verse 4, *God forbid!*

> ³¹ *Do we* [believers] **then void** [καταργοῦμεν] *the law through faith? God forbid: yes, we establish the Law.* Answer given in the Snapshot on Romans after the block teaching on imputation (see page 118).

> Basically, while keeping the Law was never possible, the Law brought physical promises or blessings to the people of Israel upon their obedience. Their disobedience did not suspend or void the promises. The promises extended to the faithful. However, this was a general rule for when God judged His people as in the Book of Judges because they violated the Law. The promises or blessings were temporarily invalid because of the sin of the unfaithful nation, even spilling over to the faithful. Examples: Did not Israel's defeat at Ai (Joshua 7) come because of the unfaithfulness of Achan? The promises were temporarily suspended because of sin, and thirty-six soldiers died needlessly. Did not Ezekiel and Daniel suffer the consequences of the sin of the nation by being taken into Babylonian captivity? What the Law established was that although it (the Law) was *holy, and just, and good,* man is not unless he is walking by Faith.

Romans 4:14

> *For if they which are of the Law be heirs* [Jewish people], *faith is made void, and the promise made of **no effect*** [κατήργηται].

> If Jewish people obtain salvation – become heirs of salvation by the Law – then the promises of the covenants have been made of no effect, because they did not keep the Law. Therefore, they did not qualify to receive the blessings of the promises as Leviticus 26, Deuteronomy 28, and Judges 2 clearly show. The promises for obeying the Law of Moses are contingent upon Faith, not works.

Romans 6:6

Knowing this, that our old man [sin nature] is crucified with Him, that the body of sin might be destroyed [καταργηθῇ], that from here on out we should not serve sin.

Because our *old man* has been *crucified*, the umbilical cord of the sin nature has been cut, and the source of deadness through Satan will be eradicated. In the future, when we arrive in His presence, our sinful nature will be completely destroyed because of the Blood of the **New Covenant,** confirmed by His resurrection. We therefore should be living to serve Him and not sin.

Romans 7:2, 6

*² For the woman who has a husband is bound by the law to her husband so long as he lives; but if the husband dies, **she is loosed** [κατήργηται] from the law of her husband.*

*⁶ But now we are **delivered from** [κατηργήθημεν] the law, that being dead when we were held within it; that we should serve in newness of spirit, and not in the oldness of the letter.*

I Corinthians 1:28

*And base things of the world, and things which are despised, has God chosen, yes, and things which are not, to bring to **nought** [καταργήσῃ] things that are.*

The emphasis is on the word *nought* or καταργήσῃ, meaning the base things in life will be rendered inoperative, no longer in effect.

I Corinthians 2:6

*Yet we speak wisdom among them that are perfect [mature]: although it is not the wisdom of this age, nor of the princes of this age, that come to **nought** [καταργουμένων].*

I Corinthians 6:13

*"Food is meant for the belly, and the belly for food": But God shall **destroy** [καταργήσει] both it and them. Now the body is not meant for fornication, but for the Lord; and the Lord for the body.*

The emphasis is not on the belly or food, or fornication, but on the word *destroy* (καταργήσει), meaning that all these carnal things which apply in this life are temporary and will be invalidated in the future when we are with Him, so live for Him now. The key word is ***destroy***.

I Corinthians 13:8, 10-11

⁸ *Love never fails: but as for prophecies, **they shall fail** [καταργηθήσονται]; as for tongues, they shall cease; as for knowledge, **it shall vanish away** [καταργηθήσεται].*

¹⁰ *But when that which is perfect comes, then that which is partial shall be **done away** [καταργηθήσεται].* ¹¹ *When I was a child, I spoke as a child, I understood as a child, I thought as a child: but when I became a man, I **put away** [κατήργηκα] childish things.*

I Corinthians 15:24, 26

²⁴ *Then comes the end, when He delivers the kingdom to God, even the Father, when He shall have put **down** [καταργήσῃ] all rule and all authority and power.*

²⁶ *The last enemy that shall be **destroyed** [καταργεῖται] is death.*

II Corinthians 3:7, 11, 13-14

⁷ *But if the ministry of death, written and engraven in stones, was glorious, so that the children of Israel could not steadfastly behold the face of Moses for the glory of his countenance; which glory was to be **done away** [καταργουμένην].*

¹¹ *For if that which is **done away** [καταργούμενον] was glorious, much more will what is permanent be glorious.*

¹³ *And not as Moses, who put a veil over his face, that the children of Israel could not steadfastly look to the end of that which is **abolished** [καταργουμένου]:* ¹⁴ *But their minds were blinded: for until this day the same veil remains untaken away in the reading of the old testament; which veil is **done away** [καταργεῖται] in Messiah.*

Galatians 3:17

*And this I say that the [Abrahamic] covenant, that was confirmed before of God in Messiah, the Law [Mosaic Law], which was 430 years after [the Abrahamic Covenant], cannot disannul, that it should make the promise of **no effect** [καταργῆσαι].*

Because the Law was broken does not invalidate or cancel out the eternal unconditional covenant God made with Abraham. So, the economy of Promise to Abraham is NOT contingent on the covenant given through Moses in Law keeping. Again, the key word is ***no effect*** or **καταργῆσαι** meaning that even when the Mosaic Covenant was broken it DID NOT render the Abrahamic Covenant inoperative.

Galatians 5:4, 11

*[4] Messiah has become of **no effect** [κατηργήθητε] unto you, who would be justified by the law; you have fallen from grace.*

*[11] And I, brothers, if I yet preach circumcision, why do I yet suffer persecution? In that case the offense of the Cross **ceased** [κατήργηται].*

Ephesians 2:15

*Having **abolished** [κατήργηται] in His flesh the enmity, even the law of commandments contained in ordinances; for to make in Himself of two one new man, so making peace.*

II Thessalonians 2:8

*And then shall that wicked [one] be revealed, whom the Lord shall kill with the breath of His mouth and shall **destroy** [καταργήσει] with the brightness of His coming.*

Couple the understanding of *katargeo* with these verses into the context that Paul is writing in and it becomes abundantly clear that as *holy, just, and good* the Law of Moses was, it is completely inadequate to give salvation and victory over sin. This should especially be evident to us when we realize that the **New Covenant** and the Law of Messiah and all the superior spiritual benefits of what Messiah did for us on the Tree are all devalued by the false teaching of keeping Torah.

Review

In the first half of this book, we laid down the background, the preliminary material to be understood as we embark on our clear quest to show from the Scriptures that Torah observance is not validated in the New Testament Scriptures, with the emphasis on the Epistles to the New Testament believers:

> First, we reviewed the correct method of interpretation (Hermeneutics), which relies on the literal historical and grammatical method and understanding and the Law of Context. In that context, we can better understand the usage of the term *church* or *assembly*.

> Second, we examined the difference between conditional and unconditional covenants and the ramifications of each. By doing so, we can recognize that the Law is ***not*** eternal but temporary.

Third, we looked into the economies of God, known as Dispensations, and saw briefly how He administered His Word in each one.

Fourth, we studied the biblical usage of *renew* and *new* as used in the Hebrew and in the Greek as the terms relate to the **New Covenant** and the three unique promises of the **New Covenant** that those in the *old covenant* did not even imagine.

Fifth, we dealt with terms that have been confused.

Sixth, we realize that it is impractical if not impossible to keep the Law without a Temple and priesthood.

Seventh, we developed an understanding of the liberty that believers are to exercise between each other in the areas of non-moral issues as well as moral issues.

Last of all, we see the artificial division of the law into moral, civil, and ceremonial and realize that only the moral law, with the exception of Sabbath observance, was carried over to the **New Covenant**.

A helpful chart is included below to summarize what Scriptures say about the Law of Messiah versus the Mosaic Law.

In understanding these points, we are now ready to enter a verse-by-verse study within the Book of Acts and also of the Epistles that specifically relates to the recordings and teachings of Luke, Peter, James, Paul, and the author of Hebrews. In so doing, we will see that Torah observance is not authenticated or validated in the Acts of the Apostles and the Epistles of the New Testament and that we are to live daily in Messiah, not in Moses. Yeshua is the Mediator of the **New Covenant** and the Law of Messiah that is embedded in it. Let us begin.

Definition of Law of Messiah

The purpose of the Law of Moses was to reveal the standard of righteousness which God demanded for a proper relationship with Him. The Law of Messiah provides over 600 rules of life for New Testament believers beginning in Acts 2 and onwards. It is not a way of salvation, but it is evidence to show how we love the Messiah.

The many individual commandments from Messiah and the Apostles are applicable for New Testament believers to show our love and appreciation for all that He has done for us in the **New Covenant** with all its ramifications.

The Law of Messiah is designed to also make believers distinct from the world on how we think and act in accordance to our relationship with Him. It is given to show how believers can live a Spirit-filled life.

Observations concerning the Law of Messiah:*

1. Believers must clearly recognize that they are under Grace and not under the Mosaic Law (Romans 6:14). Believers must always remember that the life they now lead is not based on the Mosaic Law but the Grace of God **ALONE**. [Bold emphasis mine] Contrast: under the law, "do it in order to be blessed" whereas under Grace "do it because you have been blessed."

2. Believers are free from the Law of Moses, they are not free from law altogether. They must now operate under a different law, the Law of Messiah which Paul points out in I Corinthians 9:21 and Galatians 6:2 [and Romans 8:2].

3. Believers are confusing the matter. They often go back to the Mosaic Law, as a default system in order to find a rule of life which is the wrong place. Believers are no longer under the Mosaic Law but under Grace. Therefore, the law they should go to for a rule of life is the Law of the Messiah, which is a product of Grace.

4. The Law of Messiah can be classified in four distinct ways: a.) Positive commandments, b.) Negative commandments, c.) Principles [for living], and d.) Rules given by rulers or elders. [Brackets mine]

5. Believers with the Law of Messiah are given divine enablement to keep God's standards by the indwelling ministry of the Ruach HaKodesh [Holy Spirit]. Divine enablement is provided so that the believer can keep God's standards. On the one hand, God has given the Law of the Messiah, providing believers with the rules and regulations to obey, providing a rule of life for this [present] age. On the other hand, however, comes divine enablement, so that believers can keep the righteous standards of God. [See John 7:37-39; Romans 5:5; 8:9; I Corinthians 2:12; 6:19; Galatians 3:2; I Thessalonians 4:8; I John 3:24 and 4:13.]

6. The Law of the Messiah, which spells out the conduct of life that believers ought to lead. Just as the Law of Moses contained numerous individual commandments, so too does the Law of the Messiah.

* *Fruchtenbaum, Come and See Series, Vol 7, The Soteriology of the Bible*, pp. 68-74.

Part Two
Snapshots from God's Word about Messiah's Law

Introduction:
I Am Continually Surprised

Since my introduction to the Jewishness of Scripture at Camp Shoshanah in 1995 I am continually surprised at passages that I knew of but did not comprehend. They have been revealed to me through the illumination of the ministry of the Ruach Ha-Kodesh (Holy Spirit) as He has instructed and guided me into all truth (John 16:12-15; Romans 8:14), His Word.

Scriptural understanding of God's Word has purposely been placed by Him on different levels. I first discovered over fifty-five years ago, while in Child Evangelism Fellowship, that everyone can understand that we are sinners in need of a redeemer, even small children. My own children, Mark our oldest, came to Faith at age seven after my wife Sharon explained the Gospel to him. Several months later, with much urgency in his heart, he led his four-year-old brother Jonathan to the LORD. So whether you are an adult, a child, or even mentally challenged, the gospel is very simple to understand. God planned it that way.

That is the foundational level for all believers, they are babes in Messiah (I Corinthians 3:1). God instructs us to study the Word of God (II Timothy 2:15) and grow in grace. As we diligently "study hard and grow strong" in Messiah we enter new levels of understanding and comprehension of His Word guided by the principles of His Word discussed in Part One of this book. I do not know how many levels of understanding there are with the complexities of His Word, but this I do know: If it is our heart's desire to know Him (Psalm 37:4-5; Philippians 3:10), He through the Ruach Ha-Kodesh (Holy Spirit) will teach us and illuminate our hearts and minds through His Word (I Corinthians 2:9-16) as we become mature in our Faith in the Messiah.

I gaze in amazement at how complete and thorough God is in His Word. Within the Messianic Movement there is a tug of war between those who believe in Yeshua but also state unequivocally that we are to obey the Mosaic Law. On the other side are Messianic believers who say in order to be saved, you must believe in Yeshua, period. That means that our salvation is by Faith through Grace Alone. The necessity of the Mosaic Law has been rendered inoperative by the death of Yeshua on the Cross, by the blood of the Lamb of God. Paul and the author of Hebrews have clearly spelled it out in their Epistles that the Mosaic Law has been rendered inoperative by His death.

In my study, for the last eight years on the Ariel Jewish Study Bible, I have seen more clearly the issue concerning law keeping or Torah observance. I clearly believe that the Law of Moses was rendered inoperative by Yeshua with His death. Here are some of God's cumulative answers from His Word, that stack up in clear evidence, but that others seem to refuse to listen to and obey in His Word.

When reading Paul's Epistles, there is an undercurrent of attacks on Paul's work by Judaizers in places like Corinth, Ephesus, Philippi, and Colosse. Occasionally, the subject surfaces as Paul must deal with this heresy of the Judaizers in several churches. In the books of Acts and Galatians, Luke clearly records the events of Peter at Cornelius' house and what God did for the Gentiles by including them in salvation without any if's, and's, or but's; and Paul deals with the issue of Judaizers and Law keeping head on.

What do I mean by Judaizers? Simply they can involve several aspects of the same issue, which is the place of Jewish Law in a believer's life. ***One***, some teach that no one's salvation is complete without circumcision. Those are extreme Judaizers. ***Second***, some teach that to become a mature believer in Messiah a believer must observe the Mosaic Law in one's walk *in Christ*, the Messiah. That is the issue most often at hand today. Many believers who are Torah-observant "cherry pick" the laws they want to obey[80] but ignore other laws that they could keep and don't. The Law is a *unit*, and if you choose only to obey *certain* laws; you have automatically violated all of them (James 2:10; Galatians 5:3; Matthew 5:19). Another Jewish believer states the following:

> We are not permitted to cherry-pick which moral commands we think are still authoritative since the Mount Sinai Covenant was given as a unit and the commandments cannot be divided.[81]

Let us view this issue by taking snapshots from the Master Author, Messiah Yeshua, as He dealt with the issue throughout Scripture. We'll look at the Books of the Torah (Genesis, Exodus, Leviticus, Numbers, and Deuteronomy), the Gospel of Matthew, John's writings, Paul's writings, and the Letter to the Hebrews and gain understanding of how we should deal with the Law of Moses today.

One additional point before we begin with the Snapshots. The way our Bibles have been organized has been misleading for multiple centuries when we look at where the *Tanakh* (Old Testament) ends and the New Testament begins. Malachi is the end of the prophets at around 400 BC but it was not the end of the Law. The Law continued through more than 400 years between Malachi and Yochanan (John) the Immerser (Baptizer) through the crucifixion of Messiah. In fact, even though the Gospels were written by Matthew, Mark, Luke, and John after the beginning of the Church in

---

[80] See the cover story in the *Ariel Magazine,* Winter 2016, issue #21 entitled "The Mosaic Law: A New Perspective on an Old Problem" by Doug Friedman, https://magazine.ariel.org/winter-2021, last accessed 05/26/25.

[81] Sam Nadler, *The Messianic Ten Commandments: A Study in the Relationship Between Grace and Law.* Charlotte, NC: The Word of Messiah Ministries, 2023, p. 20.

Acts 2, during the first century, they are not, let me repeat they are NOT New Testament Truth! They are written concerning the fulfillment of the First Coming passages from the Law, Prophets and Writings, the promise of the coming Redeemer, the promised Son of David, Son of Abraham. So, theologically, the Old Testament ends with the Gospels, and the New Testament begins with Acts 2. The Gospels are theologically part of the Old Testament.

The following familiar quote was spoken to me over two decades ago:

Gospels

The Gospels are the hinges that the Old and New Testaments swing on.
Without the Gospels the Tanakh (Old Testament) is incomplete.
Without the Gospels the **New Covenant** (Testament) has no foundation

---

The Gospels are the pinnacle of the Story of Redemption; everything in the *Tanakh* builds towards the coming of the Messiah: All the covenants and Dispensations and all the prophetic promises of the coming *Seed of the Woman* in the *Tanakh* point to the Gospels. Understand that while the Gospels are NOT New Testament, they describe the ministry of Yeshua as He came and lived under the Law of Moses, for He had to fulfill that Law. Notice the whole context of the Gospels; they are all dealing with Law. All of Yeshua's (Jesus') interactions with the Pharisees and the Sadducees were dealing with the issues of the Rabbinic Law (a fence, the Oral Law) and Mosaic Law. The Church did not begin until Acts 2. This may be a shock to some of you, but look at the context of the Gospels; they are framed in the context of the Mosaic Law. Now let us begin with Snapshots from Genesis.

Snapshot from Genesis

Shabbat Observance: What Does the Old Testament Say?

Genesis 2:2-3

² And on the seventh day God finished His work which He had made; and He rested on the seventh day from all His work which He had made. ³ And God blessed the seventh day, and hallowed [sanctified] *it* [or made it holy]*; because on it He rested from all His work which God had created and made.*

Genesis is not a Law passage yet many people will appeal to it in their attempt to shore up their Sabbath observance teaching. I will let a Messianic Jew, Arnold Fruchtenbaum, explain the biblical position as he thoroughly explains this passage in the sections quoted below, entitled T*he Exposition* and *The Issue*:

The Exposition

Seven things should be noted concerning the exposition of the key passage.

1. First, with the end of the sixth day God finished His creative work.

2. Second, God then rested on the seventh day, not in the sense that He was tired, but in the sense of "ceasing." The Hebrew word *shabbat* means not only "to rest," it also means "to cease." God *sabbathed,* meaning He rested in the sense of ceasing from His labors or work.

3. Third, God did two things to the seventh day; He *blessed* it, and He *hallowed* or sanctified it.

4. Fourth, the reason He blessed it because God rested on that day; He ceased from all His creative work.

5. Fifth, this is the only reference to the Sabbath in the whole Book of Genesis, and it is not called a *Sabbath* but only *the seventh day*.

6. Sixth, there is no command to observe the Sabbath in Genesis.

7. Seventh, the emphasis is on rest and cessation, not on observance.

The Issue

Is the Sabbath a creation ordinance? At this point, let us assume that the Sabbath is a creation ordinance. If so, it would mean that it is obligatory for both Jews and Gentiles, since it was given before there was any distinction between Jews and Gentiles—a distinction that only began with Genesis 12, not Genesis 2.

Furthermore, even if it were a creation ordinance, it would not mean it is obligatory upon all. For example, one thing that certainly is a creation ordinance is marriage (Genesis 2:23-25). However, it is not mandatory for every individual because celibacy or singleness is a coequal, even a superior, option (Matthew 19:10-12; I Corinthians 7:1-7). If the Sabbath were a creation ordinance, then these things would also be true [mandatory].

However, the truth is that the Sabbath is not a creation ordinance, and this can be seen in six ways.

1. First, the crucial term *shabbat* or *Sabbath* is not even mentioned. At this point, there is no use of the word *shabbat;* the day is only referred to as *the seventh day*.

2. The second way this is seen is that there is no mention of man's being involved in the rest. There is only a mention of God's resting.

3. The third way this is seen is that the seventh day does mark a climax. However, the climax is not the creation of man, but it is God's own triumphal rest. God's own triumphal rest is what makes this day unique.

4. The fourth way this is seen is that there is no command in the Book of Genesis to observe the seventh day; it only states what God did on the seventh day. It is not found among the Noahic commandments or among the commands God gave to Abraham, Isaac, or Jacob. Furthermore, there is no record of its practice between Adam and Moses.

5. The fifth way this is seen is that the Sabbath is never treated as a creation ordinance in the New Testament. Mark 2:27 states:

    The sabbath was made for man, and not man for the sabbath.

    Some try to use this verse to prove that the Sabbath was a creation ordinance. However, the point of this verse is not to deal with the origin of the Sabbath, but to deal with the purpose of the Sabbath: *The sabbath was made for man*. Furthermore, what Yeshua said was to contradict the Pharisaic teaching that Israel was created for the purpose of honoring the Sabbath. A second passage used to try to prove that the Sabbath was a creation ordinance is Hebrews 4:3-4, but this passage is simply teaching about salvation rest on the basis of the Old Testament. The Book of Hebrews treats Genesis eschatologically for salvation rest, not as a creation ordinance. It also treats the Genesis Sabbath typologically of the future, heavenly rest.

6. Sixth, yes, God did bless and sanctify the Sabbath, but the blessing and sanctification of the seventh day was to emphasize rest and cessation of work, not as an observance.

Finally, six observations can be made on the issue of the Sabbath's being a creation ordinance.

1. *First*, the Sabbath rest law is not found in the Edenic Covenant, the covenant God made with Adam in Eden.

2. *Second*, it is not found in the Adamic Covenant, the covenant God made with Adam after his expulsion from the Garden.

3. *Third*, it is not found in the Noahic Covenant, the covenant God made with Noah after the Flood.

4. *Fourth*, it is not found in the Abrahamic Covenant, the covenant God made with Abraham, with whom the Jewish people began.

5. *Fifth*, there is no record of anyone's observing the Sabbath throughout the Book of Genesis, from Adam to Moses.

6. *Sixth*, there is the example of Job, a pre-Mosaic saint. There is no mention of the Sabbath, although Job does mention things in the Book of Genesis such as the Creation, the Flood, and many details concerning man's obligation to God.

So, concerning the issue: Is the Sabbath a creation ordinance? One can draw three conclusions: First, the Sabbath is not a creation ordinance; secondly, the institution of the Sabbath for the people of Israel was based on the creation account; and thirdly, it thus became an eschatological sign of salvation rest and God's redemptive goal for mankind.[82]

---

[82] Arnold G. Fruchtenbaum, *The Sabbath*, San Antonio, TX: Ariel Ministries, 2014, pp. 9-13.

Snapshots by Yahweh in Exodus, Leviticus, and Numbers

The Torah: Who is the Author of the Law?

Back in 2000 I began to research for a thesis paper on the Tri-unity of God in the Hebrew Scriptures. This in-depth study took me ten years and resulted in a 900-page theological study on the Person of Messiah in the *Tanakh*, called *Discovering the Mystery of the Unity of God*, which was published by Ariel Ministries. In it I did not reference the New Testament, just passages from the Hebrew Scriptures. Outside of seeing the multitude of plural references to the Person of God, I saw for the first time the activity of the Second Person of the Godhead who we understand to be the pre-incarnate Messiah.

I grew up understanding the many First Coming References to the Messiah in the *Tanakh*, but I never saw Him as an active participant in the pages of the Law (Torah), the Prophets (Nevi'im) and the Writings (Kethuvim). According to Yochanan the Immerser (John the Baptist) and Yeshua, I came to understand that the Son reveals the Father in the *Tanakh*. See John 1:18 and 5:37, 46 coupled with Isaiah 48:12-13, 16 where the Father and the Holy Spirit sent the Son.

> *No man has seen God at any time; the only begotten Son, which is in the bosom of the Father,* **He** [the Son] *has declared Him* [the Father] (John 1:18).

> *And the Father Himself, which has sent Me, has borne witness of Me. You have neither heard His voice at any time, nor seen His shape.* (John 5: 37)

> *For had you believed Moses, you would have believed Me; for he* [Moses] *wrote of Me* (John 5:46).

> [The Speaker] *Hearken* [listen] *unto Me, O Jacob and Israel, My called; I am He; I am the first, I also am the last.* [13] *Mine hand also has laid the foundation of the earth, and My right hand has spanned the heavens: when I call to them, they stand up together. ...* [16] *Come near unto Me* [the speaker], *hear this: I have not spoken in secret from the beginning; from the time that it was, there am I: and now the Lord GOD, and His Spirit, have* **sent Me** [the speaker]. (Isaiah 48:12-13, 16)

Yochanan (John) pointed out that God in His essence has *never* been seen by human eyes, period! The Son reveals the Father; this includes all the theophanies (appearances of the pre-incarnate Messiah) in the *Tanakh*. The Gospel of John also records forty-three times where the Son, Yeshua, says, the Father *sent Me*. Yeshua added to that by saying to the Pharisees specifically, and Israel in general, that they have *never* heard the voice of the Father, nor have they seen His shape. Then who did Abraham and Moses see??

Abraham saw a theophany of God on numerous occasions and Abraham entertained God with dinner (Genesis 18). The voice that Israel did hear was not the Father (Exodus 20), but a theophany of God in the Second Person of the Godhead as He spoke audibly to Israel. This theophany of God, the Second Person of the Godhead, the Shechinah, is the same one Who issued the Law of Moses. It is He who said concerning the Law, that they are **His** Statutes, **His** Ordinances, **His** Commandments; and **He** refers to them as **My** Law, **My** commandment and that Israel is **Mine**. So understand who is speaking to Moses at least 154 times as the Author of the Torah. What the elders of Israel saw (in Exodus 24) was the theophany of God in the Second Person of the Godhead, but they did not see God in His essence. Who did Moses see in Exodus 33 when God appeared to him in His essence? Moses could not see His Face and live. Moses saw the back of God, His afterglow, and as a result Moses' face glowed because of being in the presence of the Shechinah glory of God.

So, what am I getting at? As we focus on the Torah and the one Who is the Author, we see that the LORD interacted with Moses frequently; but the speaker was the theophany of God, who represented God, just like the Angel of the LORD did from Genesis through Zechariah. Please bear with me, for I am not trying to write a dissertation at this point.

Let's focus on the actual books of the Law: Exodus, Leviticus, Numbers, and Deuteronomy and understand Who is speaking. It starts in Exodus 3 with the burning bush incident, and the speaker is I AM THAT I AM. Once Israel is in the Land, notice again what the Angel of the LORD said to Israel in Judges 2:1:

> And an **Angel of the LORD** came up from Gilgal to Bochim, and said, I made you to go up out of Egypt, and have brought you unto the Land which I swore unto your fathers [Abraham, Isaac, and Jacob]; and I said, I will never break My covenant with you.

Here **the Angel of the LORD** distinctly states that He, not the Father, brought them from Egypt to the Promised Land which He swore to give to the patriarchs (Genesis 12:1-3, 7; 15:1-21; 26:3-5; 28:13-15) and that covenant He will ***NEVER*** break. It is key to understand that it was the Second Person of the Godhead that is actively engaged with Israel throughout the Torah. Before going through the Torah, we need to look at Numbers 12:5-8 to understand the parameters that the LORD gives:

> [5] And the LORD came down in the pillar of the cloud, and stood in the door of the tabernacle, and called Aaron and Miriam: and they both came forth. [6] And He said, hear now My words: If there be a

prophet among you, I the LORD will make Myself known unto him in a vision and will speak unto him in a dream. ⁷ *My servant Moses is not so, who is faithful in all My house.* ⁸ **With him will I speak Mouth to mouth** [Face to face], *even apparently, and not in dark speeches; and* **the similitude of the LORD shall he behold***: why then were you not afraid to speak against My servant Moshe?*

Two key points in verse 8: First, the LORD will speak with Moses Face to face and not through visions and dreams; and second, Moses will see, to a limited degree, the very essence of the LORD in all His Shechinah Glory. *None* of the prophets to Israel could put that on their personal resumes, *only* Moses.

Now let us focus on *Exodus* and review the personal discussion between the I AM (God) and Moses in chapters 3-4. God spoke personally to Moses as he challenged Pharaoh (Exodus 5-11). God personally gives the introduction concerning Passover in chapter 12. Both Chapters 13 and 14 of Exodus begin the same: *And the LORD spoke unto Moses, saying.* Look carefully as Moses headed for Mount Sinai and see how the LORD spoke to him directly. The principle is laid down for *the Prophet like Moses* described in Deuteronomy 18, according to Exodus 20:19: *And they said unto Moses, Speak with us, and we will hear: but let not God speak with us, lest we die.* Throughout the rest of Exodus, God is personally interacting with Moses from Mount Sinai and the Tent of Meeting concerning the Law, the Tabernacle, and the priestly garments. *I have found at least fifty-one divine utterances where the LORD personally interacted with Moses.*

Next we will focus on *Leviticus*. Israel spent a year at Mount Sinai, but Leviticus only involves an additional month at Sinai where the LORD on at least *thirty-five occasions gives Moses His divine utterances* as He instructs him on the use of the Tabernacle with the priesthood and the feasts of Israel. Now, between Exodus and Leviticus, we have at least *eighty-six personal interactive divine utterances between the LORD and Moses.*

Next, let us focus on *Numbers*. Israel journeyed through the wilderness accruing rebellion and disbelief towards the LORD and experiencing His disciplinary actions. We again have an additional *sixty-four times that the LORD personally interacted with Moshe.* That now totals *150 divine utterances where the LORD interacted personally with Moshe* over a period of 40 years.

Last of all, let us focus on *Deuteronomy*, also called the Second Law, which involved the wilderness generation about to enter the Promised Land. They had experienced thirty-eight years of God's discipline because of all the rebellions of the Exodus generation, specifically the rebellion of Kadesh-barnea (Numbers, Chapters 13 to 14). Moses recounted the rebellion of Israel and some of the laws, and added some new ones to the Mosaic code of Law. The book is a review of what the LORD said and did through Moses in Exodus, Leviticus, and Numbers.

So now consider the identity of Who was interacting with Moses throughout the period of the Exodus and Israel's journey to the Promised Land. We can understand that the theophanies of God are expressed in that He, the Father, spoke *through His Son*, who is also Yahweh (Genesis 19:24); *the Angel of the LORD* (Judges 2:1); and the Shechinah, Elohim, the Sent One of God (Isaiah 48:12-16 and the Gospel of John with forty-three references, too many to list here). So, what is the bottom line of all this? We see that the Second Person of the Godhead, not the Father, is the Author of the Mosaic Law. Understand it is not that the Father was not involved; He was, but through His only begotten Son. Put that in your memory bank as you proceed through the words of Yeshua in Matthew 5:17, the words of Peter in Acts 10 and 15, the words of the Jerusalem Council in Acts 15, and the multiple words of Paul in his letters to the Romans, Corinthians, Galatians, Ephesians, Philippians, and Colossians and to Timothy and Titus.

Also keep Yeshua versus the Law in mind as you read the words of the author of Hebrews, who gave the capstone as to the rank and position of Yeshua. Compared to the Law of Moses, Yeshua and His ministry is better. He is superior to Moses and to Aaron, superior to the inadequate Law of Moses, and superior to the priesthood that had to be continued on and on because of inevitable death of the high priest. Who does the writer of Hebrews exalt above all? Yeshua Ha-Mashiach. In Hebrews 9, the author points to Yeshua as the Author of the *first testament*, or the Mosaic Law, who made the Law (the will); and that Law was in effect until the Author died. But the LORD God cannot die! So, God became flesh and dwelt among us as Yeshua His Son (John 1:14) so that He could die, and in His death, the *first testament* or will was **rendered inoperative as a working system of law** (Romans 7:1-4). He, Yeshua, now has become the mediator of the **New Covenant** (Jeremiah 31:31-34; Ezekiel 36:26-27; Hebrews 9:15; Matthew 26:28; II Corinthians 3:6; Isaiah 42:6; 49:8).

Those who proscribe Law keeping, or Torah keeping for Gentiles are in total disobedience in multiple counts: They teach AGAINST the Creator of the Universe, The SAVIOUR; AGAINST Yeshua Himself; AGAINST Peter; AGAINST the Jerusalem Council; and AGAINST the Apostle Paul who repeatedly spoke of the Law of Moses being *rendered inoperative,* as well as AGAINST the author of the Book of Hebrews. The Law of Moses is not eternal; God has abandoned it for a far superior **New Covenant**. However, He did not leave us lawless; He gave a replacement: the Law of Messiah.

Snapshot from Moses in Deuteronomy

Deuteronomy 18:15-19

^{15} The LORD your God will raise up unto you a Prophet from the midst of you, of your brothers, like unto me; unto Him you shall listen;^{16} According to all that you desired of the LORD your God in Horeb in the day of the assembly, saying, Let me not hear again the voice of the LORD my God, neither let me see this great fire anymore, lest I die. ^{17} And the LORD said unto me [Moses], *they have well spoken that which they have spoken. ^{18} I will raise them up a Prophet from among their brothers, like unto you* [Moses], *and will put My words in His mouth; and He shall speak unto them* [Israel] *all that I shall command Him. ^{19} And it shall come to pass, that whosoever will not listen unto My words which He shall speak in My Name, I will require it of him.*

In verses 15 and 16 you have the announcement to Moses personally by God. Then God references the events of Exodus 19 when He appeared before Israel at Mount Sinai, and because of that Israel requested that God would speak no more to them but to Moses because they were terrified. They would rather hear from Moses, and they would obey him. In verse 17 God states that Israel has well-spoken and then gives the promise of *the Prophet Like Moses* to come.

Now regarding the promise in verses 18 and 19. God will raise up a *Prophet like Moses* from Israel's brethren. First notice the word prophet is singular and not plural since the rabbis like to teach that it is a series of prophets, plural. That does not agree with the text and Hebrew grammar!

So, the *Prophet like Moses* would speak to God Face to face as did Moses and He beheld the very form of God.[83] This *Prophet Like Moses* has the following descriptions in verses 18 and 19:

- *and* [I, God] *will put My words in His mouth;*
- *He shall speak unto them* [Israel] *all that I shall command Him,*

---

[83] Arnold G. Fruchtenbaum, *Ha Mashiach: The Messiah of the Hebrew Scriptures*. San Antonio, TX: Ariel Ministries Press, 2019, pp. 19-21.

- *Whosoever will not hearken unto My words which He shall speak in My Name,*
- *I will require it of him.*

This *Prophet Like Moses* who speaks directly to God and beholds the very form of God (John 1:18), He will come to Israel and God will hold Israel to account for every word that He speaks; that *Prophet Like Moses* was none other than Yeshua Ha-Mashiach (Colossians 1:15-19). So, when we speak of Yeshua and the Law of Moses, the messianic community today needs to understand Who Yeshua is and that He is the one Who is the Author of the Law! This will be dealt with in the Book of Hebrews.

Snapshot from Jeremiah

Jeremiah 31:33
But this shall be the covenant that I will make with the House of Israel; ***After those days****, says the LORD, I will put My law in their inward parts, and write it in their hearts; and will be their God, and they shall be My people.*

Jeremiah 31:33 references that God will put His Law in their (the people of Israel's) hearts. That did not happen in Jeremiah's day nor did it happen in Acts 2. This the prophet Jeremiah did not know anything about for it was an unrevealed mystery (Ephesians 3:4-9; Colossians 1:25-27). It did not become a reality in his day, nor did it become a reality in Acts 2 even though some of the features of the **New Covenant** became a reality in Acts 2; but the writing on their hearts did not occur then. There was going to be a period of time between the Law of Moses that was broken (31:32) and Kingdom Law of at least 3500 years before He would put it in their hearts. The following quote begins to capture the idea of a period of time between the First and Second Comings of Messiah:

> Everything was not fulfilled with Jesus' first coming. In some cases, complete fulfillment of the Old Testament passage awaits the second advent. And just as there is a gap in time between the first and second coming of Jesus, there can be a gap in time concerning the fulfillment of details in a prophetic passage. Thus, partial fulfillments of some Old Testament prophecies are linked with the fact there are two comings of Jesus.[84]

Concerning the work of Messiah, we see some patterns from the *old testament*. God on several occasions gave a period of time, unannounced to the prophets, concerning His timing of at least 2,000 years.

> Look at Daniel 9:25-27 there is a period of time between the Sixty-Ninth and Seventieth Weeks of Daniel. There is no period of time between the first seven weeks and the next sixty-two weeks, but there is between the Sixty-Ninth and Seventieth Weeks.
>
> Look at Isaiah 11:1-16, for according to Luke 4:16-20 Yeshua read verse one and the first part of verse two and said that they have been

---

[84] Michael J. Vlach, *Dispensational Hermeneutics*. Theological Studies Press, 2023, pp. 57-58.

fulfilled in His First Coming; but there is a period of time before the rest of the verses will be fulfilled during the Kingdom. Again, this is a period of at least 2,000 years.

In looking at Luke 4:16-21, we see Yeshua's actions fulfill the prophecy of Isaiah 61:1-2. Yeshua said this had just been fulfilled in their ears and then rolled up the scroll. He had stopped in the beginning of verse 2 because the rest of it will be fulfilled at His Second Coming. This involves another period of time, just like the other verses, of at least 2,000 years.

In Acts 15:14-18, we have another example of an unfulfilled and yet-to-be fulfilled passage.

James quotes Amos 9:11-12 which foretold Gentiles becoming God's people. But Amos 9:13-15 deals specifically with the agricultural prosperity and the rebuilding of Israel's cities because it is directed toward the Second Coming of the Kingdom of Messiah when Yeshua rebuilds the Davidic dynasty/kingdom after a period of judgment on Israel. Here again in quoting Amos it was approximately eight centuries before Messiah's First Coming and now well over 2700 years before the Kingdom will be realized in Messiah, again periods of time between the spoken prophecy, partial fulfillment in the First Coming, and the rest awaiting His Second Coming.

Observe Zechariah 9:9-17. Here again Yeshua fulfilled verse 9 when He rode into Jerusalem (Matthew 21:2-5; John 12:14-16; Luke 19:33-37), but again there is another period of time coming, of at least 2,000 years, before He fulfills the rest in establishing the Kingdom on earth.

Jeremiah 23:5-7 presents the Second Coming of Messiah except for one point. The Messiah, the Son of David, must be born first before He will reign on David's throne. There is at least another period of time of 500 years from the time that Jeremiah gave the prophecy until Yeshua's birth.

Have you considered Moses in Deuteronomy 18:18-19 concerning the *Prophet like Moses*? Moses referenced the Messiah, and it was a period of time of approximately 1500 years before Messiah Yeshua, the *Prophet like Moses,* appeared.

I believe by now you know what I am getting at: Often in Messianic prophesy, as well as other prophecies, there is a period of time between the promise and its completed reality. Jeremiah was speaking to a wicked, depraved, rebellious people who had a long history of breaking the *old covenant* going back to Exodus 32. It would be over 3,500 years before the **New Covenant** would become a reality to

Israel. From Jeremiah's day it was 500 years before Yeshua *inaugurated* the **New Covenant,** and it will be at least another 2,000 years from then before He will *ratify* that **New Covenant** at His Second Coming as promised to *the House of Judah* and *the House of Israel*. So, there is a period of time of 500 years between the *announcement* of the **New Covenant** to the *inauguration* of the **New Covenant** with His death, and at least another 2,000 years plus to the *ratification* of the **New Covenant** in the hearts of Israel.

Another mystery unknown to Jeremiah was that the *inauguration* of the **New Covenant** would fall between the end of the economy of Law to the beginning of the economy of the Kingdom, two distinct economies of God. In between those two economies He placed the economy of Grace which involves the Body of Messiah, the union of Jew and Gentile (Ephesians 2) with a limited fulfillment of the **New Covenant,** for the writing of the Law on their hearts did not occur then. Now the Church DOES NOT fulfill the **New Covenant**; that will ONLY be done with Israel when the prophecy in Jeremiah 31:31-34 is fulfilled completely with the regeneration of Israel's heart (Deuteronomy 30:4; Hosea 2:23) at the end of the Tribulation period, the Time of Jacob's Trouble (Jeremiah 30:7). At that point, God will write His Law upon Israel's heart, and not before then, not now in this age.

The bottom line of all this is that many in the Messianic Movement assume that God has written His Word on our hearts, NOT SO! He did regenerate us, He did remove our sins, and He did send the Ruach Ha-Kodesh to indwell every believer, but He DID NOT write His Law on Jewish (or Gentile) hearts. That is a future event to occur at the very end of the Tribulation. Only at that point will God write His Law on Jewish hearts. At that point He will return and set up His Kingdom and fulfill the Abrahamic, Land, Davidic and **New Covenants**. So, any argument that the *old covenant* is *renewed* in the **New Covenant** is riddled with problems. This reflects our studies in Chapters 6, 7, and 11 back in Part One of this book. The **New Covenant** and its fulfillment are unique.

Snapshot from the Gospel of Matthew

Matthew 5:17-19

17 Think not that I have come to destroy the law or the prophets: I have not come to destroy, but to fulfill. 18 For verily I say unto you, Till heaven and earth pass away, one jot or one tittle shall in no wise pass away from the law, till all things have been fulfilled [accomplished]. 19 Whosoever therefore shall break one of these least commandments, and shall teach men so, shall be called least in the kingdom of heaven: but whosoever shall do and teach them, he shall be called great in the kingdom of heaven.

Before I move on, let me define and explain the term *jot and tittle*. The jot is the smallest letter in the Hebrew alphabet of twenty-two letters. The tittle is the appendage on the end of the letter that distinguishes it from another Hebrew letter. Yeshua is strongly presenting that not only is every word inspired, but even the smallest designation between letters in the Hebrew alphabet will not disappear.

Let me give the setting and the background of this passage to help us understand what Yeshua was teaching. First, this is the beginning of the section often called the Sermon on the Mount from Matthew 5-7 and Luke 6:17-49. This title gives the location of the sermon and not its content. Actually, the whole context of this passage was given on a mountain plateau, and Yeshua was dealing with *the correct interpretation of the Mosaic Law*. The struggle then and now is the exalted place of Rabbinic Law over the God-given Mosaic Law at Mount Sinai. Actually, Yeshua's message is a unit; it is His interpretation of *the true righteousness of the Law in contrast to the Pharisaic interpretation of the righteousness of the Law*. Let me follow up with one further observation.

Under the surface of the Gospel text, Matthew is dealing with two laws: the Mosaic Law – all 613 laws included in it – and of Rabbinic, manmade law of which there are thousands of laws recorded in Jewish rabbinic writings. The Pharisees were accusing Yeshua of breaking their manmade laws. In my naivety for many years before I first went to Ariel's Camp Shoshanah in 1995 and came to understand the Jewish background of the text, this made absolutely no sense to me. How could Yeshua break the Law and yet keep the Law? I learned that behind the context generally unseen by Gentile eyes like mine that there were two sets of laws in the context:

Rabbinic manmade law derived from the Pharisees' religious sect of Judaism[85] and God's Law given at Mount Sinai. Yeshua did not keep man-made Rabbinic laws. In fact He even went out of His way to violate Pharisaic Law (Matthew 15:1-9; Mark 3:1-6; Luke 6:1-11 John 9:1-41)[86], but He completely kept all the 613 laws applicable to Him as a Jewish male. Now let me quote from Arnold Fruchtenbaum on this passage:

> People like to use this passage against the [verses quoted] above, because Jesus said that He did not come *to destroy* or to abolish the Law, but *to fulfill* it. Six things about this passage should be noted.
>
> > ***First***, this is the main passage people like to use to maintain the Sabbath law and other features of the [Mosaic] Law.
> >
> > ***Second***, while they emphasize verse 18, they tend to ignore verse 19 which adds: *these least commandments*. In other words, the context of Matthew 5:17-19 is not only concerned with the Sabbath law or only the Ten Commandments or only the major laws, but even the most minute laws, all 613 commandments. When verse 19 adds, *these least commandments*, it includes the entire Law, all 613 commandments.
> >
> > ***Third***, the Greek word for "fulfill" is *pleiroo*, which is used by Matthew in the sense of fulfilling prophecy, thus bringing that prophecy to an end. In Matthew 1:22-23, he used the term of the prophecy of Isaiah 7:14. He does not mean that Isaiah 7:14 can be fulfilled again in the future; he simply means that it is a fulfillment of prophecy, bringing it to an end.

Arnold adds to the previous quote at another time by referencing Matthew 2:6 which quotes Micah 5:2. Here Yeshua fulfilled the passage on His birthplace.[87] This passage will not be fulfilled again; that prophecy came to an end. As the next point

---

[85] To get a detailed but easy-to-understand explanation, read Paragraph 49 in *Yeshua: The Life of the Messiah from a Messianic Jewish Perspective,* Abridged Version, published by Ariel Press in San Antonio, TX, 2017.

[86] For further explanation, go to Arnold Fruchtenbaum's book *Yeshua: The Life of Messiah from a Messianic Jewish Perspective,* Abridged Version, and go to Paragraphs # 79, 51-52, 103, published by Ariel Press, San Antonio, TX, 2017.

[87] Arnold G. Fruchtenbaum, *The Law of Moses and The Law of Messiah,* in a YouTube message at Tacoma Bible Church in the Fall of 2022, *https://www.youtube.com/watch?v=Htd6lhigllY,* last accessed 05/26/2025.

shows, Yeshua also fulfilled this passage that Torah keepers abuse, He fulfilled it and brought it to an end. Now let us continue with Arnold Fruchtenbaum's quote:

> ***Fourth***, the word means the accomplishment of prophecy by fulfilling it, in contrast to its abolishment by failing to fulfill it. The point of Matthew is that the Messiah came to fulfill, not to abolish.
>
> ***Fifth***, these words were spoken during Jesus' lifetime when the Law was still in effect. As long as He was living, He still had to obey the [Mosaic] Law.
>
> ***Sixth***, the Law did not end with the coming of *Yeshua*; it ended with the His death. It was then that Law was rendered inoperative.[88] [brackets mine]

Look at this passage again and focus on the words ***destroy*** and ***fulfill***. They do not mean the same thing, as will be shown when we look together at these two words.

The Word *Destroy*

In the text we want to define the word *destroy* which is used twice in verse 17. Yeshua did not come to *destroy* the Law of Moses. The Greek word for *destroy* is *apollumi* (ἀπόλλυμι) which Vine's Expository Dictionary comments on as follows:

> To destroy utterly, to overthrow completely, is rendered *destroy,* as in Matthew 5:17.[89]

Mounce gives the basic meaning of the word *destroy,* using Matthew 5:17:

> Jesus contrasts His ministry of fulfilling the [Old Testament] teachings with the idea of invalidating them: *"Do not think that I have come to abolish the Law or the Prophets; I have not come to abolish them but to fulfill them"*[90] (NIV).

So Yeshua did not come to *destroy* or *abolish* the Law of Moses; for, as we saw, He, Himself, was the actual Author of that Law. He then qualified what He meant; He came to *fulfill,* which is a totally different concept than to *destroy* or *abolish*.

---

[88] Arnold G. Fruchtenbaum, *The Sabbath*, Manuscript #176, San Antonio, TX: Ariel Ministries, 2014, pp. 34-35.

[89] W. E. Vine, *Vine's Expository Dictionary of Old and New Testament words*. Old Tappan, NJ: Fleming H. Revell Company, 1981, vol 2, p. 302.

[90] William D. Mounce, *Mounce's Complete Expository Dictionary of Old and New Testament Words*. Grand Rapids, MI: Zondervan, 2006, p. 177.

The Word *Fulfill*

Now we need to define the word *fulfill*. The Greek word *pleeroō* (πλήρω) is explained in this following statement:

> It is a verb that means "to fill full," "to make full," "to fill up," "to complete," "to accomplish," "to execute," "to finish," "to verify," or "to coincide with a prediction."[91]

This term is often used in the New Testament to describe the fulfillment of prophecies, the completion of a task, or the satisfaction of a need. In the context of the Bible, πλήρω (pleeroō) is often used to describe the fulfillment of God's plans and purposes, as well as the completion of Yeshua's mission on earth as illustrated in Matthew 5:17-18, where Yeshua says:

> *"Do not think that I have come to abolish [apollumi / ἀπόλλυμι] the Law or the Prophets; I have not come to abolish [apollumi / ἀπόλλυμι] them but to fulfill [pleeroō / πλήρω] them. For truly I tell you, until heaven and earth disappear, not the smallest letter, not the least stroke of a pen, will by any means disappear from the Law until everything is accomplished" (NIV).*

Let me illustrate from the Gospel of Matthew how the word *fulfill* is used:

Matthew 1:22-23:	*"this was done, that **it might be fulfilled** which was spoken of the"* Prophet Isaiah (7:14)
Matthew 2:15:	*"death of Herod: that **it might be fulfilled** which was spoken of the"* Prophet Hosea (11:1)
Matthew 2:17:	*"Then **was fulfilled** that which was spoken by Jeremiah the prophet, saying,"* (Jeremiah 31:15)
Matthew 2:23:	*"called Nazarene: that **it might be fulfilled** which was spoken by the Prophets,"*
Matthew 4:14:	*"That **it might be fulfilled** which was spoken by Isaiah the prophet,"*
Matthew 5:17:	*"not come to destroy, but **to fulfill**."*

---

[91] Colin Brown, *New International Dictionary of New Testament Theology*, Grand Rapids, MI: Zondervan Publishing, 1986, vol. 1, pp. 733-734.

Matthew 8:17:	*"That **it might be fulfilled** which was spoken by Isaiah the prophet, saying,"* (Isaiah 53:4)
Matthew 12:17:	*"That **it might be fulfilled** which was spoken by Isaiah the prophet, saying,"* (Isa 42:1-4)
Matthew 13:35:	*"That **it might be fulfilled** which was spoken by the prophet, saying, I will open"* (Psalm 78:2)
Matthew 21:4:	*"this was done, that **it might be fulfilled** which was spoken by the prophet,"* (Zechariah 9:9)
Matthew 26:54:	*"then shall the Scriptures **be fulfilled,** that thus it must be?"*
Matthew 27:9:	*"Then **was fulfilled** that which was spoken by Jeremiah the prophet,"* (Zechariah 11:12-13)
Matthew 27:35:	*"casting lots: that **it might be fulfilled** which was spoken by the prophet,"* David in Psalm 22:18.

So erroneous teaching is put forth by other believers who are falsely teaching the need to keep Torah.

Now if you remember back in Part One of this book in Chapter Four, concerning "Dispensations," the economies of God come and go at His will and His timing! **The Gospels are NOT New Testament teaching but are dealing with the presentation of the Messiah to Israel** as their Redeemer, their Deliverer, the *Prophet Like Moses*. Yeshua was largely forced to deal with the difference between the Mosaic Law and the Rabbinic manmade law because of their unbelief and rebellion against Him. He would render inoperative the Mosaic code and render their man-made fictitious Law as heretical as He accused the Pharisees of blocking the people's entrance into the Kingdom (Matthew 23:13).

God, as in other new economies (Dispensations) gave *new* revelation and *new* requirements to be lived out BY FAITH;[92] the Gospels DID NOT do that. However, what transpired in Acts 2 was God changing His economy from Law to Grace when Yeshua meditated the **New Covenant** in His blood (I Timothy 2:5; Hebrews 8:6; 9:15). The context of Matthew, Mark, Luke, and John is Law, pure and simple.

---

[92] This is no different than when He moved from the Noahic Covenant (economy of Human government) to the Abrahamic Covenant and all His promises. Then He moved from those eternal promises to the conditional Law of Moses. His revelation changed again with the mediatorial work of Yeshua on the cross in rendering the *old covenant* inoperative and His mediation of the **New Covenant** and the Law of Messiah.

I have read Torah-observant authors and watched them try to wiggle and squirm around what the Creator of the Universe clearly stated, that salvation is by Faith and not by Law-keeping. I will not reference those authors because some of them are slick "wordsmiths" who would detour many immature believers from how to live out Messiah in our lives through the Ruach Ha-Kodesh (Holy Spirit). These authors are adamant that we will receive God's judgment if we do not adhere to the Mosaic Law, although in history it has clearly been shown to be impossible to keep! We in the New Testament (Acts and Epistles) are under His Grace, the **New Covenant**, and the Law of Messiah which supersede the Mosaic Law code. If anyone rejects God's economies or Dispensations their theology will be skewed at some point. When messianic Gentiles and Jews do this, they refuse to see what God did in His sovereignty for Gentiles and for Jewish believers.

Those who insist on Law keeping focus on the word *Torah*, meaning "instruction." Yes, God gave a law structure in the economy of Law through Moses, but He also gave new instruction on how to live under His **New Covenant** with the Law of Messiah through His Apostles in this present economy of Grace. He, Himself, will later give Kingdom Law during the Millennial Kingdom, which is also when the Law is planted in their heart (Jeremiah 31:33). As stated in Part One, the Law of Moses was given to Israel, NOT to Gentiles. Are there principles that are of value today? Of course, but the system of the Law has been ***rendered inoperative*** by a ***better*** blood sacrifice, meaning the blood of Messiah, the Lamb of God. Paul will later say that the proper use of the Law in this present economy of God is to convince man of his sin (I Timothy 1:8-9).

One further point, briefly, is that there are 613 laws in the Law of Moses, NOT ten. Yeshua in Matthew 5:18 states that even the least of the laws are part of the whole unit of the Law (James 2:10). By clear observation, would-be Torah keepers are not even close to keeping the Torah Commandments.

Where Does the *Tanakh* End & the New Testament Begin?

(John B. Metzger)

Early Church Fathers began to distort the Bible by removing the Jewishness from the biblical context. This is one of those points: Because they moved away from a Dispensational under-standing of the biblical text, they ended the "Old Testament" with the book of Malachi and then began the New Testament with the coming of Yeshua in the Gospels. Under the Dispensation of Law, the context of that Dispensation did not end until Acts 1, after the death, burial, resurrection, and ascension of Yeshua, not after Malachi 4. The New Testament does not begin with Matthew and the coming of Yeshua. He came and lived under the Law of Moses, the Dispensation of Law, and fulfilled it as He said that He would do in Matthew 5:17. The Law was in effect in all four Gospels – Matthew, Mark, Luke, and John – and into Acts 1. Acts 2 dispensationally begins the New Testament with the Dispensation of Grace on the Jewish feast day of Shavuot [Pentecost].

Snapshots from the Apostle John

As the <u>Law of Messiah</u> has already been mentioned, I will be intensifying its references as we move through the Epistles. The reason for this focus on the <u>Law of Messiah</u> is because Yeshua is God incarnate, the *Word of Life* that the Apostles *heard*, *saw* and Whom they *gazed upon*, **the Word of LIFE** (I John 1:1). He now becomes central in the believer's new lifestyle. Also notice the Apostolic *we*'s in I John, chapter 1, verses 2-7. John makes application concerning our *fellowship with* **Him** and our obedience to **His** Word:

> *² (For the life was manifested, and* **we** *have seen it, and bear witness, and show unto you that eternal life, which was with the Father, and was manifested unto us;) ³ That which* **we** *have seen and heard* **we** *declare unto you, that you also may have fellowship with us: and truly our fellowship is with the Father, and with His Son Yeshua the Messiah. ⁴ And these things* **we** *write unto you, that your joy may be full. ⁵ This then is the message which* **we** *have heard of* ***Him****, and declare unto you, that God is Light, and in* ***Him*** *is no darkness at all. ⁶ If* **we** *say that* **we** *have fellowship with* ***Him****, and walk in darkness,* **we** *lie, and do not practice the truth: ⁷ But if* **we** *walk in the light, as* ***He*** *is in the Light,* **we** *have fellowship one with another, and the blood of Yeshua the Messiah* ***His*** *Son cleanses us from all sin.*

According to 1 John 1, *He* is the Shechinah Glory that appeared to Moses and Israel, and **His Word** has become the whole issue to which we adhere. I summarize this important teaching below:

> He gave the Law of Moses, then at the cross **He** rendered it inoperative, setting it aside and issuing the <u>Law of Messiah</u> grounded in the **New Covenant,** that came from **His** mouth and from the mouths of the Apostles as the Holy Spirit gave them remembrance of what **He** said.

Why is that important? *He is the Author of both Laws*, first in **His** pre-incarnate state as the Shechinah Glory, and second in **His** incarnate state as the Son of God, the God/Man who rendered that Law, **His** first Law, inoperative through the Cross to issue His second, the <u>Law of Messiah</u>. Notice carefully His words from John 14:14, 23-24.

*If you love **Me**, keep **My commandments**.*
*If a man loves **Me**, he will keep **My words**.*
*He that loves **Me not**, keeps not **My sayings**.*

Don't filter **His** words through Torah-keeping lenses, for **He** is referencing the <u>Law of Messiah</u>. Remember Deuteronomy 18:15-19 and the *Prophet Like Moses;* the Father will hold them (Israel) and us (the Body of Messiah – His Church) accountable for everything **He** says. So do not disregard **His** *Word* that applies to the economy of Grace, for the economy of the Law was a failure. **He** did not fail!! Israel *failed* and believers today who attempt to keep Torah are presently in the state of *failing*. They cannot even keep **His** Law that they have modified.

Snapshots from the Record of Luke in Acts

Acts 10 and 11 are tied together as they give the testimony of Peter before the Church in Jerusalem (10:44 – 11:1-18), at the time described in 11:2 when the Circumcision (those insisting on circumcision for believers) contended with Peter. In disputing their position, Peter related the full account of the event and reminded them that God poured out His Spirit on the Gentiles (10:45 and 11:15) just as He did upon them in Acts 2. Peter continued to relate that God did so without being a respecter of persons (Deuteronomy 10:17; Acts 10:34; 15:9). What God did for the Jews in Acts 2, He repeated the same way for the Gentiles in Acts 10. Notice this was not just Peter's testimony, but the testimony of six other Jewish believers who were eyewitnesses (10:23; 11:12) that had accompanied Peter to Cornelius' house and who confirmed the fact that God put no extra requirements on the Gentiles. God did not require circumcision of Cornelius, nor did He require Law keeping for his salvation. Peter's testimony caused the Circumcision (those who had insisted on circumcision for believers) to glorify God that He had now opened the door of Salvation to Gentiles.[93] This event is CLEAR; God did not require these Gentiles to receive circumcision nor were they required to be Torah observant! We read here a full rebuke to modern day Torah keepers by God and Peter and later in Chapter 15 by the Jerusalem Council.

At the *Jerusalem Council in Acts 15*, both the pros and cons concerning Torah observance got a full hearing. The Circumcision Party, the believing sect of the Pharisees in Messiah, argued for these new Gentiles to be circumcised and to adhere to the Mosaic Law (15:5). Then Peter arose and declared that God through him preached the Gospel to the Gentiles and they believed; and notice clearly what Peter said in Acts 15:8-10:

> [8] *And God, who knows the hearts, bare them witness, giving them* [Gentiles] *the Ruach Ha-Kodesh* [Holy Spirit], *even as He did to us* [Jews in Acts 2]; [9] *and put no difference between us* [Jews] *and them* [Gentiles], *purifying their hearts by faith.* [10] *Now therefore why do you tempt* [94] *God, to put a yoke upon the neck of* [these new Gentile]

---

[93] Steven Ger, *The Book of Acts: Witnesses to the World*, Chattanooga, TN: AMG Publishers, 2004, pp. 150-172.

[94] **Tempt God:** Deuteronomy 6:16 and Isaiah 7:12 is where it says in the Law to not tempt God.

disciples, which neither our fathers nor we were able to bear? [bracketing mine]

The Apostle Peter clearly said not to put the burden of the Law upon the believing Gentiles (15:10) aided by the words of Barnabas and Paul (15:12) in their work in Antioch and the first missionary journey in Galatia. Then James, the LORD's half-brother recalls the words of Peter and quotes from Amos 9:11-12 that God took *out of them* [Gentiles] *a people for His Name.*

Then in unison with Peter, Barnabas, and Paul, with no verbal dissension, James states the position of the Jerusalem Council. Please read carefully Acts 15:19-27, for James gave NO wiggle room for circumcision or Torah observance to be practiced among the Gentiles:

> [19] *Wherefore my* [James'] *sentence is, that we not trouble them, which from among the Gentiles are turned to God:* [20] *But that we write unto them, that they* [Gentiles] *abstain from pollutions of idols, and from fornication, and from things strangled, and from blood.* [21] *For Moses of old time had in every city those who preach him, being read in the synagogues every Sabbath day.*
>
> [22] *Then it pleased the* **Apostles** *and* **Elders, with the whole church** [at Jerusalem], *to send chosen men of their own company to Antioch with Paul and Barnabas; namely, Judas surnamed Barsabas, and Silas, chief men among the brothers:* [23] *And they wrote letters by them after this manner: The Apostles and Elders of brothers send greeting unto the brothers who are of the Gentiles in Antioch and Syria and Cilicia.*
>
> [24] *For as much as we have heard, that certain ones who went out from us have troubled you with words, subverting your souls, saying, You must be circumcised, and keep the Law: to whom we gave no such commandment:* [25] *It seemed good unto us, being* **assembled with one accord***, to send chosen men unto you with our beloved Barnabas and Paul,* [26] *Men that have hazarded their lives for the Name of our Lord Yeshua the Messiah.* [27] *We have sent there Judas and Silas, who shall also tell you the same things by mouth.* [28] *For it seemed good to the Ruach Ha-Kodesh* [Holy Spirit]*, and to us, to lay upon you no greater burden than these necessary things;* [29] *That you* [Gentiles] *abstain from meats offered to idols, and from blood, and from things strangled, and from fornication: from which if you keep yourselves, you shall do well ...*

Notice the Circumcision Party was involved in the debate, and after the presentation they were then silent. James says they acted in *one accord* in unison even with the sending of the letter around AD 49 to Gentile believers stating that circumcision and Law keeping would not be required of them by the Jerusalem Council. So those today who promote Torah observance are not only going against Peter, the Apostle to the Jews (Galatians 2:7), but are blatantly defying the Apostles at the Jerusalem Council and their letter. They are in complete rebellion against what God did even to this day. It is interesting how the Judaizers of today will attempt to overwhelm believers with Greek words and arguments about why it is sinful and that God will judge Gentiles who do not keep Torah. These leaders continue to teach and subvert believers into a false gospel (Galatians 1:6-9) of believing in Yeshua and the keeping the Law, rebelliously going against the clear statement of the Jerusalem Council.

In Paul's day this teaching did not go away, as Paul had to deal with it as he faced off with the Circumcision Party throughout his ministry. These Judaizers were deceptive, supposedly agreeing with the Council and then sending out letters of their own to the Gentile believers to subvert the Apostles and the Jerusalem Council. Yet later they sent their own representatives out to actively subvert God, the Ruach Ha-Kodesh, the Apostles, and the whole of the Jerusalem Council. The issue of Torah observance should have been buried as an unclean thing and not even be touched again. The issue of Torah observance for Gentiles should have been laid to rest in the first century, but it has been "resurrected" again in the twentieth century and has become a completely unnecessary issue in the Body of Messiah today.

Snapshots from Paul, Beginning with Romans

As I cover the Epistles, we will not be taking them in chronological order, but in the order that they appear in the New Testament.

As a preface to the Epistles, I am writing not to complicate it with hard-to-understand theological terms; instead, I want it to be easily understood and made practical. I have seen and read Torah observance teachers setting up a straw man, which is always easy to knock down. They use verses that are against Torah observance, then agree with the straw man on some issues followed by contradicting the straw man to teach their own twisted heretical view of Torah observance. Leaning to this heresy robs all believers of their victory over sin in Messiah through the power of the Ruach Ha-Kodesh by uplifting Torah observance and depressing the **New Covenant** and the Law of Messiah.

Now let us look at several passages in Romans as we zero in on the contexts of Jeremiah, Yeshua, Peter and the other Apostles, and Apostle Paul and see how they really treated the Law of Moses.

See Romans 3:20

Therefore by the deeds of the law shall no flesh [human being] *be justified in His sight; For by the Law is the knowledge of sin.*

If you cannot be justified by the Law, then why practice it when God has provided a *new* and *better* law, the Law of Messiah, to follow. Chapters 1 to 3 deal with the fact that all are sinners (3:23): *for all have sinned and fall short of the glory of God.* All are under the condemnation of God (Romans 5:18; 6:23; John 3:18). The pagans are guilty because they have the witness of creation (1:18-32), the moralists because they have the witness of their conscience to condemn them (2:1-15). The Jews are guilty because they have the witness of the Scriptures and in particular the Mosaic Law to condemn them (2:16-29).

Sanford Mills, a Jewish believer, makes the following observation concerning Israel's unrepentant heart:

> It took God approximately 900 years to bring Israel out of idolatry, from the Exodus in Egypt to the deliverance out of the Babylonian Dispersion. When Israel came out of Babylon, she became a

monotheistic nation and left the polytheistic practices of the heathen Gentiles. It is now 2,500 years that God has been trying to bring Israel to her senses, and nearly 2,000 years to accept the Lord Jesus Christ as her promised Messiah.[95]

Paul clearly enunciates that all flesh whether Jewish or Gentile are under sin (3:9-20, 23) and will be judged by God. The Law of Moses cannot make us right with God; that was not its purpose! One of its purposes was that it identified sin and condemned the sinner. It is only *by Faith* (Habakkuk 2:4; Hebrews 11) in Messiah through His shed blood, the blood of the **New Covenant,** that man can have the righteousness of Messiah *imputed*[96] (4:24; 5:21) to him.

Imputation

The word *imputation* means "to reckon over to one," or "to set down to one's account."

On the *debit side* is the sin debt we owe that cannot be paid by us – Romans 5:12-19a. It also made us spiritually dead. Our sin was imputed to Messiah on the cross by the Father.

On the *credit side,* we have had His righteousness credited to our account – Romans 5:19b; Isaiah 53:6b. We, through Him, have had His righteousness imputed to us – II Corinthians 5:21.

The act that set the righteousness of Messiah to our account is an act of free grace.

[From pp. 40-49, J. Dwight Pentecost. *Things Which Become Sound Doctrine – Imputation*]

As we look at the Book of Romans, we see these doctrines taught:

Chapters 1-3 Man is totally depraved, without any righteousness before God.

---

[95] Sanford C. Mills, *A Hebrew Christian Looks at Romans*. Grand Rapids, MI: Durham Publishing, 1968, p. 88.

[96] **Imputation**: See teaching block in the text. Dwight Pentecost, *Things Which Become Sound Doctrine – Imputation – Chapter 4*. Westwood, NJ: Fleming Revell Publishing, 1965, pp. 40-49. All of these doctrinal words in teaching blocks come from Dwight Pentecost's book.

Chapters 3-5	Man can only be justified by God because of Yeshua's finished work on the Cross.
Chapters 6-8	Man can only be sanctified through the voluntary offering of Messiah combined with the indwelling and enabling ministry of the Ruach Ha-Kodesh (Holy Spirit).
Chapter 8	Based on Yeshua's work on the Cross and the sanctifying work of the Ruach Ha-Kodesh, we will someday be conformed to the image of Messiah (8:29); we will experience His **Glorification**.

The Greek word καταργήσει (root word is *katargeó*) is used to show that God did not ***void out*** or ***render inoperative*** the promises given in the covenants to Israel in Romans 3:3. Fruchtenbaum and Wuest give a paraphrase of this verse by saying:

> It is not true that Jewish unbelief has canceled [καταργήσει] out the promises to Israel contained in the oracles of God? Never may it be [*me genoito* meaning "God forbid"].[97]

> Well then – if as is the case, certain ones did not exercise faith. Their [Jewish] unbelief will not render the faithfulness of God inefficient [inoperative], will it? May such a thing never occur.[98] [brackets mine]

Then in Romans 3:31 Paul uses the word καταργοῦμεν (root word is *katargeó*) in saying that salvation ***by Faith*** does not void (καταργοῦμεν) the Law of Moses but established that even in the economy of Law you were saved ***by Faith*** and not by obedience to the Law of Moses. So, salvation ***by Faith*** alone establishes that the Law of Moses does not contribute anything to salvation; it is ***by Faith*** alone.

Two quotes from Sanford Mills that have valuable thoughts:

> The Law was never given for the purpose of making man just before God, but rather to show man his inability to keep the Law and cause Him to cry out, Abba, Father (Romans 8:15).

---

[97] Arnold Fruchtenbaum, *The Book of Romans: Exposition from a Messianic Jewish Perspective*. San Antonio, TX: Ariel Press. 2022, p. 84.

[98] Kenneth Wuest, *Wuest Word Studies in the Greek New Testament: Romans*. Grand Rapids, MI: Eerdmans Publishing Company, 1966, Vol. 1, p. 53.

> Man is incapable of keeping the laws of his own human government, let alone trying to keep God's laws.[99]

Now what I have seen in the following verses to be quoted is that the Law revealed our sin and it convicted us without question of our sin(s). Torah keepers have now resurrected an old heresy that the Jerusalem Council, Peter, Paul, and James and the other Apostles had remedied. Torah observance, which embodies rebellion against the Jerusalem Council concerning Law keeping, is biblically ludicrous. Romans 3:31 was not a recipe to try to keep or teach Torah observance. Have you considered that the resurgence of Torah observance teaching is only at the most a little over 65 years old (from the 1960s), if that? Yet they will try to convince Gentile believers that Torah observance is necessary for the believer to walk in the abundant life in Messiah. The Law cannot, has not, and will not, transform our thoughts and attitudes; it is only the **New Covenant** and His spiritual *regeneration* of our hearts with the indwelling work of Ruach Ha-Kodesh (Holy Spirit) that will transform our thoughts and attitudes in our personal relationship with Messiah Yeshua as we meditate on His Word (Romans 12:2).

Using Romans 3:28, some drag Torah observance into the discussion with a verse that has nothing to do with their Torah observance. The verse says *that a man is justified by faith without from the deeds of the Law*. One author said in so many words that our Faith in Yeshua does not abolish the need to follow the Law of Moses. Such teachers do so because they do not recognize the differences in the economies of God but blend the whole Bible into one theological stew or *pottage*. Remember progressive revelation? Remember the writer of Hebrews (1:2) that God said in different times in different ways? He revealed His revelation to man, but *in these last days He has spoken to us* through His Son in inaugurating the **New Covenant** at the Cross, laying aside permanently the *old covenant*. By doing so, God established our new standard of living, the <u>Law of Messiah</u>, for Jews and Gentiles together.

See Romans 4:5

But to him that works not, but believes on Him that justifies the ungodly, his faith is counted for righteousness.

Here Paul is referencing Abraham who lived 600 years before the Law of Moses (1446 BC); he was justified because he believed in the revealed will of God (progressive revelation) given to him through the Angel of the LORD.[100] Abraham believed God and his works showed it even as James said (James 2:18-23). Abraham believed God in the birth of Isaac (Genesis 18), and he believed the words of God so

---

[99] Sanford C. Mills, *A Hebrew Christian Looks at Romans*. Grand Rapids, MI: Durham Publishing, 1968, pp. 90-91.

[100] **The Angel of the LORD** is the pre-incarnate Christ. See John B. Metzger, *Discovering the Mystery of the Unity of God*. San Antonio, TX: Ariel Press, 2010.

much that he was willing to offer his son Isaac as a sacrifice (Genesis 22), and he believed God that he and his 318 men could recapture Lot and destroy the five kings of Mesopotamia (Genesis 14). His works backed up his Faith in God, and God declared him righteous (Genesis 15:6; James 2:23). So, this verse has absolutely nothing to do with Torah observance. Again, it was a different economy of God; it was the Dispensation of Promise, not the Dispensation of Law. Paul states in Romans 4:14:

> *For if they which are of the law be heirs, faith is made void and the promise made of **no effect** [κατήργηται] (KJV).*
>
> *For if it is the adherents of the Law who are to be the heirs, faith is null and the promise is void* (ESV).

This is also a repudiation of Replacement Theology. The keeping of Law for salvation or for justification and sanctification would then render inoperative the promises of the covenants to Israel as well as all the ramifications of the **New Covenant** to Gentile believers. So if Jewish or Gentile Torah observance of the Law is key, and Israelites (Jews) are heirs **without Faith**, then Faith has been rendered inoperative (κατήργηται). But again, salvation is by Faith Alone, not Law, not Torah keeping. Torah keeping disqualifies Faith and has dramatically reduced the significance of the **New Covenant** and the <u>Law of Messiah</u>.

Now we need to understand the Dispensation of Grace in place of Law. The Bible teaches that the Grace of God given to us is FREE, and I strongly believe in Free Grace Theology. The salvation that we receive is free to us, but very costly to God. One Torah observant author who is extreme in promoting the keeping of the Law of Moses mentions that some people do not believe works are important; and, thus, he says we open the door to sin without the Mosaic Law, so he keeps Torah. On the extreme opposite end of the spectrum, other Christians "think" now that they are saved *spiritually*, they can do anything they want, sin or not sin. They have been mistaught or are still on babies' milk spiritually. Those who say we can sin to our heart's desire are living and teaching completely by and in the flesh. There is NOTHING godly in their words. According to those who advocate for lawlessness, works are of zero value in connection to our salvation and justification, again zero. However, works are extremely important because our position in the Kingdom to come and perhaps in the Eternal Order are based on our walk (and works) and our faithfulness to Him in the here and now on earth. Paul in I Corinthians 3:12-16 states the following:

> [12] *Now if any man builds upon this foundation with gold, silver, precious stones, wood, hay, stubble;* [13] *Every man's work shall be made manifest* [be revealed]: *For the day shall declare it, because it shall be revealed by fire; and the fire shall try every man's work of what **sort** it is.* [14] *If any man's work abides* [survives] *which he has built upon, he shall receive a reward.* [15] *If any man's work shall be burned up, he shall suffer loss: But he himself shall be saved, yet so*

> *as by fire.* ¹⁶ *Don't you know that you are the temple of God, and that the Spirit of God dwells in you?*

There is a time after the Rapture of the Church, called the Day of Messiah (Christ) (I Corinthians 1:8; 5:5; II Corinthians 1:14; 5:10; Philippians 1:6, 10; 2:16; Revelation 2:23; 22:12), which is also called the Bema Seat of Messiah or the Judgment Seat of Messiah. There He will judge our works in heaven. Did you catch that? Our works are judged, not us, for Yeshua has taken all the wrath of God upon Himself (Isaiah 53:6) for us. He will judge our works to see what sort of works they are. Are they *gold, silver, and precious stones?* That would be because we acted in Faith and our works and our motivation matched our Faith. Or will our works be *wood, hay, and stubble* because of living for self and worldly pleasures? Burned up, nothing left? It is my opinion, perhaps the *wood, hay, and stubble* will be much larger than we ever imagined. Our works will be a mixture of both gold, silver, precious stone as well as wood, hay and stubble. Notice what Paul said in verse 15, you will suffer loss – loss of rewards – NOT loss of salvation, if you were not a good and faithful servant; but you will still be saved.

The standard for building good works for Messiah is NOT based on the Law of Moses by being Torah observant, for that has been **rendered inoperative**. But our focus is on this economy of God, the economy of Grace founded on the **New Covenant**, with our standard of living being the <u>Law of Messiah</u>. These laws given in the New Testament Epistles as commands, numbering over 600 commands given to the Church directly on how believers are to live out their Faith in Messiah in this economy of God.[101]

In Romans Chapters 6 through 8

There is much in these three chapters; therefore, I am only focusing on the Torah-observant issue. Paul is clear that there is a tug of war being waged in every believer's heart. The flesh and the Law become a dual force joined together to produce the works of the flesh (Galatians 5:19-21); they do not produce righteousness. But then you have *the Law of the Spirit of LIFE in Messiah* (Romans 8:2) that does produce righteousness (Galatians 5:22-24). This whole section clearly states that the flesh and Torah Law keeping does not give life and victory in Messiah. We will look at some clear passages in Romans 6-8.

Romans 6:6, 14

> ⁶ *Knowing this, that our old man is crucified with Him, that the body of sin might be destroyed [καταργηθῇ], that from here on forward we should not serve sin.*

---

[101] John B. Metzger, *The Law, Then and Now: What about Grace?* Larkspur, CO: Grace Acres Press, 2019.

> *¹⁴ For sin shall not have dominion over you: for you are **not under the Law,** but under grace.*

The term *destroyed* in Romans 6:6 speaks to the fact that the *old man,* our *body of sin,* is rendered inoperative, without power; its power lines have been cut. Believers are no longer tied to the kingdom of darkness, and we can make the choice not to serve sin through yielding to the power of the Ruach Ha-Kodesh. What an awesome promise that is ours because of the Messiah and His blood, the blood of the **New Covenant.** As Paul develops his argument, the flesh is tied to the Law; and it no longer has to rule over us! The choice is now yours: either yield to the Ruach Ha-Kodesh or yield to Satan in the flesh, which has been fueled by the Law. Satan, your fleshly appeal and Law is now the loser; and so will anyone be who yields to one's *old man.* Again, Paul is not dealing with loss of salvation but loss of unproductive works of the flesh.

Torah-observant believers claim that not being under the Law does not mean you are not to obey the Law. As an old, Native American saying goes, "He speaks with a forked tongue!" Why obey something if you are no longer under it??? Because of the **New Covenant,** we are to obey the Law of Messiah. Why have you transferred laws from the inferior Law of Moses which had NO strength, to add to or supplant the superior or *better* Law of Messiah? Remember what was emphasized in Part One of this book: The Law was not given to the Gentiles to begin with. If you once were a citizen of Germany (or any other country) and you now are a citizen, instead, of the United States, it would be ludicrous to continue to live under the laws of Germany since you are now exclusively a citizen of the United States. You would agree that it makes absolutely no sense to continue to live under German law, and you would be right. It makes NO sense. However, when you read the Scriptures and it says you are no longer under the Law of Moses because your Saviour has mediated a better Law (Galatians 3:9-10; I Timothy 2:5; Hebrews 8:6; 9:15; 12:24), the **New Covenant** Law, the Law of Messiah, because He has redeemed you and placed you into the Body of Messiah (1 Corinthians 12:13) and not in Moses! Why would anyone refuse to live under the New Law that Messiah gave through the **New Covenant** in the Law of Messiah? Why do you go back to the *old covenant* that did not *regenerate* your heart? It also ***did not*** remove your sins and ***did not*** give you the permanent indwelling of the Ruach Ha-Kodesh. The Law ***did not*** give you victory over sin, but His shed blood removed your sin. The Law only covered your sin with inferior animal blood. But the Blood of the **New Covenant** removed your sin with superior Blood!

Why live under a limited ministry of the Ruach Ha-Kodesh under the *old covenant,* the Law which ***did not*** give saints in the *Tanakh* permanent indwelling of the Ruach Ha-Kodesh (Holy Spirit) of God, when through the Blood of the **New Covenant** the Ruach Ha-Kodesh is your seal of His *redemption* in you (Ephesians 1:13-14)? Saints in the *Tanakh* by the Law ***did not*** secure their immediate entrance into heaven (II Samuel 12:23; Luke 16:19-31; 23:39-43). That came only by the Blood of the Lamb of God whose Blood again is superior to animal blood; it is better Blood (Hebrews 12:24; Revelation 1:5-6). However, if you have been misguided or have a misguided agenda that the Law is eternal, and there are no economies of God

(Dispensations), you have forced your erroneous view into the text, thus subverting the meaning and thrust of the Author of the text, YAHWEH!

Sanford Mills, a Jewish believer, understands the thrust of Paul as he writes to the Corinthians:

> The Greek word *wherefore* proceeds to explain more clearly the analogy between the Christian's death to the Law through the death of Christ and the death of the husband which frees the wife from *the law of the husband. You also were made dead.* The Greek for this statement expresses a past action viewed in its entirety. It is a once-for-all-time statement, and means exactly what it says, [that is], we were put to death to the Law. The Law is not what was put to death to the believer, but, rather, the believer was put to death to the Law through the body of Christ. The meaning of the phrase, *the body of Christ*, is the crucified body of Christ. The believer participates in the death of the Saviour by dying with Him. The old sinful nature is crucified with Christ (Romans 6:6).[102]

Now let us move on to Romans 7 and the beautiful word picture of the Law being **rendered inoperative**.

Romans 7:2-6

> *² For the woman which has a husband is bound by the Law to her husband so long as he lives; but if the husband dies, she is loosed [κατήργηται] from the Law of her husband. ³ So then if, while her husband lives, she marries another man, she shall be called an adulteress: But if her husband dies, she is free from the Law; so that she is no adulteress, though she married another man. ⁴ In the same way, my brothers, **you also have died to the Law** [of Moses] by the [crucified] body of Messiah, so that you should be married to another [Messiah], even to Him who is raised from the dead so that we should bring forth fruit unto God. ⁵ For when we were in the flesh, the motions of sins, which were by the Law, did work in our members to bring forth fruit unto death. ⁶ But now we are delivered [κατηργήθημεν] from the Law, that being dead wherein we were held; that we should serve in newness of spirit, and not in the oldness of the letter.*

---

[102] Sanford C. Mills, *A Hebrew Christian Looks at Romans*. Grand Rapids, MI: Durham Publishing, 1968, p. 206.

Mills brings up Paul's illustration concerning the law of the husband. In Romans 7:2, when the husband dies, *she is loosed*. The word *loosed* means the law which held her has now been **rendered inoperative** (κατήργηται).

Arnold Fruchtenbaum, a Jewish believer, writes:

> ... This fact explains why Paul used the wife as an illustration for the point he was trying to make. A woman could only be freed from the control of the law by the death of her husband. Once the husband died, she was "discharged" from the law of the husband. The Greek term for discharged *katargeo*, means "***to render inoperative***" or "to abolish" ... The conjunction *wherefore* indicates that the subsequent statement reveals the consequence of what was said previously. The Greek term for *were made dead, ethanatōthēte*, is the aorist indicative passive tense of the verb *thanatoó*, which means "to put to death." The aorist tense emphasizes that the death described is a once-and-for-all event. The passive voice indicates that the death is brought upon the person.[103]

Now look again, as Paul uses the illustration of the marriage bond to drive home the point that when the husband (or wife) dies, the remaining spouse is free from that bond of marriage, free to remarry. Paul moves from a physical bond of marriage to a spiritual bond of being in Messiah in verse 4.

> *So, my brothers and sisters, you also died to the Law* [of Moses] *through the body of Christ, that you might belong to another* [Messiah], *to Him who was raised from the dead, in order that we might bear fruit for God* (NIV).

Paul then in Romans 7:6 gives the climax of what happens when believers are *loosed* (κατήργηται) from the law of the husband and move to the spiritual impact of that reality:

> *But we are* [now] ***delivered*** [κατηργήθημεν] *from the Law* [of Moses] *that being dead wherein we are held; that we should serve in newness of spirit, and not in the oldness of the letter.*

Notice in verses 2 and 6 Paul uses the word *katargeo* twice in cementing the teaching that the law was ***rendered inoperative***. Paul's argument against Torah observance is powerful, but still some will twist the words of Paul into erroneous teaching. I will pick up this analogy later when I get to the Book of Hebrews. Paul is clearly

---

[103] Arnold Fruchtenbaum, *The Book of Romans: Exposition from a Messianic Jewish Perspective*. San Antonio, TX: Ariel Press, 2022, pp. 138-139.

teaching that the Law has no rule over you, because Messiah has **rendered it inoperative** by His blood, the blood of the **New Covenant**. So, why did Torah observers, in all practicality, count His blood as an unworthy thing and walk all over it (Hebrews 10:29), desecrating Him and His finished work? Why bring shame to the Name of Yeshua, whom they say that they believe in, because they want to exalt the Mosaic code in rebellion to Yeshua and the Jerusalem Council? That makes absolutely no sense.

I have read one Torah-observant author who wrote eight pages to wiggle, squirm, and twist around what Paul said to meet that author's carnal agenda. He taught that believers are to lift up the Torah by Faith and that the eternal Torah is to be fulfilled in us; and he continues to teach that if the law is dead, then it would contradict the words of Yeshua in Matthew 5:17: *Think not that I have come to destroy the Law, or the Prophets: I have not come to destroy, but to fulfill.* They simply do not understand the context of Matthew 5:17 and want to pull it out of context to meet their erroneous agenda. This teacher is in blatant error and totally ignoring the fact that the Law was not and is not eternal! The *old covenant* was **rendered inoperative**, fulfilled, brought to an end, and replaced by the Law of Messiah, which is a different economy of God given to the body of Messiah.

Romans 8:2-3

*² For the law of the Spirit of life in Messiah Yeshua has made me **free** from the Law of sin and death. ³For what the Law could not do, in that it was weak through the flesh, God sending His own Son in the likeness of sinful flesh, and for sin, condemned sin in the flesh.*

The Ruach Ha-Kodesh (Holy Spirit) guides believers into keeping the Law of Messiah in this economy (Dispensation) of Grace, not in the economy (Dispensation) of Law. The Ruach Ha-Kodesh did not have that kind of ministry in the *Tanakh*. The Law of Moses in the Torah did not bring life; instead, it brought *condemnation and death*, but Messiah gives life and frees us. The Law of Moses is **not** a living Torah, but the Law of Messiah is living. Arnold Fruchtenbaum expresses in a few sentences these two verses in Romans 8:

> Paul explained why there is no more condemnation for believers. The Greek term *gar* (for) introduces the explanation. Besides the principle of indwelling sin that was detailed in the previous chapter [Romans 7], there is another principle working inside the believer: the principle of the law of the Spirit of life in Messiah. This is the law that has set the believer free. The Greek term for *made free*, *eleutheroo*, is in the aorist tense, which indicates that the liberation was a once-and-for-all event.
>
> The believer has been set free from the law of sin and death forever. While the sin nature is still in the believer, it no longer has any legal authority over him. The believer has been freed from its power altogether. ... [The] reason for the liberty from the law ... Paul

> clearly stated that the problem was not with the Law but with whom the law had to work: the *weak*. The Mosaic Law itself was not weak. It was the flesh that was weak. God solved this problem by sending His Son in the likeness of sinful flesh. The Greek term for *likeness, homoióma*, means "that which is made like something else." It refers to a form or similitude, meaning a resemblance. The Messiah did not have sinful flesh, ... but He also came for sin. The Greek expression here is *peri hamartias*, which in the Septuagint is a technical phrase for the sin offering. Messiah came in order to deal with the problem of sin. In so doing, He *condemned sin in the flesh.*[104]

In reading this quote there is no way to artificially place Torah observance in this passage. That context has absolutely nothing to do with this context. Messiah came as our sin offering to remove the plague of sin upon us and the Law that highlighted our sin. Look once again to Sanford Mill and his understanding of the passage:

> The reason for there being *no condemnation to them that are in Christ Jesus* is that the believer has died with Christ and is *free from the law of sin and of death*. Here, as in [Romans] chapter 7, Paul speaks of Law. He has used the word *Law* repeatedly, that is, the law of the mind; the law of sin; the law of God; the law of the husband; and to this list must be added the Law of Moses or the Decalogue. In verse 2, it is the law of *the Spirit of life*. [brackets mine]
>
> The law of the Spirit of life operates in the life of the believer, and this law is life activated by the Spirit of God. ... Whenever He enters a person, it is for the purpose of giving life (Genesis 2:7); or for the purpose of creating eternal life (John 3:5-6); or for the purpose of calling one to receive the Word of God (Exodus 19:9); or for the ministry of the Gospel (Acts 13:2-4). In Romans 8:2 it is for the purpose of leading the believer to live a righteous life in Christ.
>
> The contrast between the law of the *Spirit of life* and the law of *sin and of death* is strikingly obvious. The old Law brought with it the thunderous *Thou shall not's* of Sinai. That Law brought sin to the forefront, and vividly exhibited the evil nature in man. Man is incapable of meeting the requirements of the Holy Law of righteousness through his sinful flesh alone. This law condemns him

---

[104] Arnold Fruchtenbaum, *The Book of Romans: Exposition from a Messianic Jewish Perspective*. San Antonio, TX: Ariel Press, 2022, pp. 149-150.

(Romans 7:9b) and makes his sinful flesh fearfully aware of its existence.[105]

But even with all this, it does not stop the Torah observance arguments from being inserted artificially into the context, as is done next. They insert that one needs to turn to the Sermon on the Mount to have the Law of Messiah defined as they attempt to propagate it. Again, they ignore, because of unbelief, the economies of God! The Law of Messiah is not predicated on the continued validity of Moses' teaching. Sorry to repeat, but the Sermon on the Mount is in the same economy as the Law, not in the economy of Grace. They are making a theological stew in throwing all the Bible references into the same brew with no distinction between the God-given markers of time in Dispensations. Yes, in Matthew, Chapters 5 to 7, Yeshua was speaking of the Law of Moses; but in His whole life, Yeshua did not break one of the Mosaic Laws. In less than three short years from His message on the Mount, He would fulfill every jot and tittle[106] of the Law in His death, burial, and resurrection. In Matthew, Chapters 5 through 7, Yeshua is contrasting the Law of Moses with Rabbinic manmade law to determine true righteousness. The Law ended with the death of Messiah as the perfect Lamb of God. Yeshua was the Author of that Law and when He died, he freed Israel from the curse of that Law and mediated another law, Law of Messiah, within another new economy of God, the Dispensation of Grace through the **New Covenant**.

The Law brought death in certain commandments. In fact, there are forty-two of those laws that required immediate death for violating them, usually by stoning. As stated before, there is absolutely NOTHING wrong with the Law. The problem lies with sinful man and his complete and constant inability to keep it, but Torah keepers seem to ignore the Law and its purposes. Please let me remind you, the Law was given to Israel and not to Gentiles. Yet Torah observance teaches on one hand a high standard, but on the other hand it is offering *death and condemnation* (II Corinthians 3:7, 9) to those who violate that Law. Now they want to transfer the Law to Gentiles who were never in the equation to begin with in Exodus 19-24. Paul clearly states that Messiah *made us free from the Law of sin and death.* The Law was not the cause of death; sin was! But the Law made man aware that he cannot keep it, so man brought death upon himself because of his sinful nature. The law merely mirrors who man is and that he is totally unable to keep it; it showed his *weakness*. Again, I appeal to the history of Israel in the wilderness, during the time of the Judges, during the monarchy up through the first century with the coming of the

---

[105] Sanford C. Mills, *A Hebrew Christian Looks at Romans*. Grand Rapids, MI: Durham Publishing, 1968, p. 237.

[106] **Jot & Tittle**: The Jot is the smallest letter of the 22 letters in the Hebrew alphabet. Whereas the Tittle is the small tail on three letters that distinguishes them from three other letters that are almost the same. So not the smallest letter in the Hebrew alphabet will fail, not even the small tail on the end of a letter will disappear until all be fulfilled. See chart of the Jot and Tittle in Matthew 5:19 section, page 102.

promised Redeemer. The Law stood as the standard that was impossible to keep, which Peter called a yoke upon their necks (Acts 15:10). It showed the inability of man to keep the Law. Paul will later say in II Corinthians 3 that the law was an administration of *death* and *condemnation*, but here he states that the Law of Messiah brings life.

So because of the finished work of Messiah in inaugurating the New Covenant, we in the economy (Dispensation) of Grace are not condemned because we are in Christ. He came in the likeness of sinful flesh and ***fulfilled*** every jot and tittle of the Law because we could not, and He provided a better way if we choose to walk in the Spirit and not in our old nature and sinful flesh. Paul says that man is free from the Law of sin and death.

In Romans 10:4

*For Messiah is the **end** of the Law for righteousness to everyone who believes.*

This is the second passage that Torah observant folk like to point to, along with Matthew 5:17, to try and shore up their position of Law (νόμου) keeping that is built on shifting sand and not on the Rock (Matthew 7:24-27; Deuteronomy 32:4,15). In this passage, the word under discussion is *telos* which is translated *end*. First, before we discuss the meaning of *telos* (τέλος), look at the uniformity of almost all translations and even paraphrases that focus on the primary meaning *end*, except for Messianic versions that want to emphasize the meaning as goal:

The Translation of the Term *Telos* in Various Bible Versions

Translations

King James Version	KJV	End
New King James Version	NKJV	End
1901 American Standard Version	ASV	End
New American Standard Version	NASV	End
Revised Standard Version	RSV	End
English Standard Version	ESV	End
New English Bible	NEB	Ends
Legacy Standard Bible	LSB	End
Berean Stand Bible	BSB	End
NET Bible (New English Translation)	NET	Goal or fulfillment of [which means it ends]
Weymouth New Testament	WNT	Termination
Holman Christian Standard Bible	HCSB	End – or end goal
New International Version	NIV	Culmination
Peshitta -Eastern Orthodox Text from the Aramaic		End
Contemporary English Version	CEV	No longer necessary

Paraphrase Bibles

Amplified Bible	AMP	End
Message	MSG	Intended simply to get us ready for the Messiah
New Living Translation (New Living Bible)	NLT	Ends
Phillips New Testament	PHILLIPS	End
Good News for Modern Man (Good News Transl.)	GNT	End

Messianic Jewish Bibles

Stern Complete Jewish Bible	CJB	Goal
Tree of Life Version	TLV	Goal or end goal

Notice on the surface the overwhelming translation of the *telos* is *end, termination, no longer necessary* and one use of culmination. The translation of *goal* is only found in Messianic Bibles, which in this case have a Messianic Jewish emphasis, which are generally good unless you have a Torah emphasis. They alone use *goal* except for a footnote in the Holman Bible. So what is the meaning of *telos* from Greek lexicons? First let me quote from Arnold Fruchtenbaum and then from Sanford Mills to give the best possible interpretation of the word *telos:*

> In the Greek, the first word is *telos*, translated as *end*. The order of words puts the focus on this term. *Telos* can mean two things. First it can mean "termination": Messiah is the termination of the Law; He brought the end of the Law. This is the primary meaning of the term [Thayer]. Second, *telos* can also mean "goal": The goal of the Law was the Messiah; the Law was not an end in itself, but it was intended to bring one to faith in the Messiah. From other passages, it is clear that both of these meanings apply in this verse. The Messiah was the goal of the Law, to bring one to faith (Galatians 3:10-4:7), The death of Yeshua also brought the Law to an end (Romans 7:1-6; Hebrews 7:11-19; II Corinthians 3:1-18). In either case, Israel as a whole failed on both counts.
>
> The nation failed to realize that the goal of the law was faith in the Messiah and that the law had ended as a rule of life. Israel also failed to understand that the law was never a means of salvation but a rule of life for those who were already saved. The law was rendered inoperative because Messiah was to be seen as the One through whom man attains righteousness. He brought a new law, the Law of Messiah (Galatians 6:2; Romans 8:1-2), which is now the rule of life for those who believes.[107]

According to Sanford C. Mills:

> Christ is the culmination of our fondest hope, the consummation of the highest law, the realization of life's grandest goal, the acme [summit] of human destiny, ... righteousness; or, as verse 4 describes it, *the end of the Law unto righteousness*. The accomplishments of the Cross not only "rent the veil" of the Law, but they swept aside the barrier separating God and man and cleared the way for direct communication between God's children and their heavenly Father. Christ fulfilled the purpose of every *jot* and *tittle* of

---

[107] Arnold Fruchtenbaum, *The Book of Romans: Exposition from a Messianic Jewish Perspective.* San Antonio, TX: Ariel Press, 2022, pp. 200-201.

the Law. In His person and in His work, He is the personification of virtue, *the way, and the truth, and the life.*[108]

The Greek word for *end*, *telos*, can mean either "termination" or "goal." However, the evidence clearly favors the meaning of end. For example, Thayer[109] gives the primary meaning of *telos* as: ... end, i.e. a. termination, the limit at which a thing ceases to be, ... in the Scriptures also of a temporal end; ... Christ has brought the Law to an end ... Nor is "goal" listed as a secondary or even a third in priority of usage; it is fourth on the list.

Fruchtenbaum quotes Arndt and Gingrich:

> [W. F.] Arndt and [F. W.] Gingrich[110] give the primary meaning of the verbal form as "bring to an end, finish, complete." The nominal *telos* is given the primary meaning of: "end ... in the sense of termination, cessation." They too list Romans 10:4 as being in this category and list the meaning of "goal" as being third on the list.[111]

These interpretations emphasize two meanings – *end* and *goal* and the language puts the understanding on *end* and *goal*, although *goal* has meaning in relation to Messiah in the Scriptures as Freeman understands it:

> Christ being the "goal" of the Law, while not the primary meaning in Romans 10:4, nevertheless is taught elsewhere in Scripture and must be understood in light of what the believing Israelite under the Mosaic Law comprehended. They knew that it was not doing the works of the Law that made them right in God's sight, but rather God's gracious acceptance of the animal sacrifice as payment for their sins that brought them righteousness. That was what Paul is alluding to when he says in Galatians 3:24-25:[112]

---

[108] Sanford C. Mills, *A Hebrew Christian Looks at Romans*. Grand Rapids, MI: Durham Publishing, 1968, pp. 337-338.

[109] *Thayer's Greek-English Lexicon of the New Testament*. Grand Rapids, MI: Zondervan Publishing House, 1963, pp. 619-620.

[110] Walter Bauer; William F. Arndt and F. Wilbur Gingrich, eds., *A Greek-English Lexicon of the New Testament and Other Early Christian Literature*. Chicago, IL: University of Chicago Press, 1957, p 818.

[111] Arnold Fruchtenbaum. *Israelology: The Missing Link in Systematic Theology*. San Antonio, TX: Ariel Press, 1993, pp. 643-644.

[112] Richard Freeman, *The Heart of the Apostle*. Published by *InstantPublisher.com*, 2007, p. 42. Available at Chosen People Ministries *www.chosenpeople.com*.

> *Therefore, the law was our tutor to bring us to Christ, that we might be justified by faith. But after faith has come, we are no longer under a tutor.*

This verse we will explain when we get to the Book of Galatians. As said before, Torah-observant adherents attack this verse along with Matthew 5:17 in a hopeless argument. Paul clearly states in the context of preceding chapters and surrounding verses that the Messiah is the *end of the Law* and that is the overarching view in the *Tanakh*, Gospels, and New Testament. You are biblically misleading believers if you teach that Yeshua, based on Matthew 5:17, directed NON-JEWISH people to uphold and continue to teach the Law of Moses. They even refer to verse 19, that they are instructing others to observe the least of the commandments. They have totally, let me say again, they have totally misunderstood and misinterpreted Matthew 5:17, because Yeshua in the economy of Law did uphold the Law of Moses, but He at the Cross brought an end to the Mosaic Law by mediating the **New Covenant.** This **New Covenant** contains the Law of Messiah in a new and different economy of God, the economy of Grace. If they are teaching others to obey the Law, they again are living a falsehood, because in verse 19 Yeshua did teach the fact that even the least important laws were to be obeyed; yet, these so-called Torah-observant believers "cherry pick" the laws they want to obey and modify the Law to suit their biases and disregard laws they could obey. Fifty-eight percent of the Law of Moses is completely impossible to keep by the direct hand of God (see page 226 for more info). What hypocrisy!

So, in Romans 10:4, they try to wiggle around the Law ending by saying Messiah was the *goal* of the Law. But as we saw earlier in this section, if Messiah was the goal of the Law, then Messiah crossed the finish line of the goal and He ***rendered*** the Law ***inoperative*** at the Cross with His death, burial, and resurrection. So, either way you go with it, whether *the end* or "the goal," the Mosaic Law is no longer a system to be obeyed because of Messiah's finished work on the Cross. He fulfilled and has ***rendered it inoperative*** for the body of Messiah, especially for Gentile believers, because it was NEVER given to them in the first place.

One final quote from a Jewish believer stating that the Law of Moses has been terminated in Messiah:

> Moving on to verse 4 we learn that the Messiah is the end of the Law: *For Christ is the end of the Law for righteousness to everyone who believes*. Yeshua is the termination or goal of the Law (*telos* in Greek) to everyone who believes. The law was not given to the

Gentiles, nor to the Church, but to Israel. They need to know that the law was fulfilled by the coming of the Messiah.[113]

Actually Matthew 5:17 and Romans 10:4 are in complete agreement: Messiah came to fulfill the Law, to bring it to an end; and in Romans 10:4, Messiah is the *telos* or end of the law; He caused it to cease as an operating system or rule of life. It is also interesting to note if you have followed Paul in his presentation throughout Romans concerning sin, the flesh, and the Law, he teaches that Messiah fulfilled the Law and brought it to an end. It cannot be re-fulfilled, a fact that I documented with Scripture in the "Snapshot from Matthew" section (starting on p. 106). Messiah fulfilled the Law, which will never be repeated, period! It is not to be continued by well-meaning but naive Messianic believers, whether Jewish or Gentile. Notice as Luke records the sermon of Paul in the Jewish synagogue in Antioch of Pisidia in Acts 13:39:

> *And by Him all that believe are justified from all things, from which you could not be justified by the Law of Moses.*

Please note the Law of Moses cannot justify anyone; it is impotent; it has no power or strength to be of any spiritual benefit to believers in the economy of the Law or the economy of Grace. Paul's teaching is airtight. When we get to Hebrews we find the case for the superiority of Messiah to angels, sacrifices, Moses, priests, and Aaron as being not only airtight, but air-locked; there is no wiggle room.

See Romans 11:6

> *And if by **grace**, then is it no more* [on the basis] *of works: otherwise, **grace** is no more grace. But if it be of works, then it is no more grace: otherwise work is no more work.* [brackets mine]

This verse has nothing to do with Torah observance, but it is only referenced because such adherents want to say that we teach that God's **grace** was not given in the text of the *Tanakh*. That is not true, and their intent is to reflect negatively on Dispensationalists. God's display of His **grace** and mercy has always been evident in the *Tanakh*, as is vividly shown when God in His grace dealt with Ahab, King of Israel, (I Kings 18-22 through II Kings 2 in the ministry of Elijah) as well as His grace shown to Ahab's son (II Kings 3, 6 in the ministry of Elisha). So the New Testament does not have the only rights to that word. First let me give several examples of God's **grace** being shown in the *Tanakh:*

After the fall of man into sin, God removed Adam and Eve from the Garden so that they could not partake of *the tree of life* and live forever in the state of sin

---

[113] Gideon Levytam. *I Am Not Ashamed of the Gospel of Messiah: Romans 1:16*. Hawkesbury, Ontario, Canada: The Holy Scriptures and the Israel Bible Society of Canada, 2013, p. 186.

(Genesis 3:22). That was a display of God's *grace* in the *Tanakh* to Adam and Eve and to all of mankind.

In Genesis 6:8 the text says that *Noah found grace in the eyes of the LORD.* That did not mean that he and his family were sinless, but it does mean that they obeyed God according to His revealed Word.

Noah and his family were sheltered from the worldwide flood, and that was God's *grace* in action. Also, God showed His *grace* to the other sinful inhabitants of the world in giving them 120 years to believe in Noah's preaching of the coming judgment.

The Law required a murderer (Exodus 21:12; Leviticus 24:17) and adulterer (Leviticus 20:10) to be killed. In the Mosaic Law there was no sin or trespass offering for those sins. Yet God showed His *grace* to David in letting him live (II Samuel 12:14) after his sins of murder and adultery, but not without paying for the consequences of his hideous actions (II Samuel 12:9-12).

The events of the King of Israel, Ahab by name, revealed he was a very wicked king and deserved God's judgment. God worked with him through Elijah, but with all the acts of God to convince Ahab who God was, he refused to accept the *grace* that God was giving him in letting him live as long as he did. God time and time again showed Ahab His *grace,* and he refused to follow the LORD.

Lastly, the Law of Moses was an act of God's *grace* upon Israel. Whereas in the pagan cultures around Israel when bad things happened to them, they had no idea what offended their gods that brought famine or military defeat. Israel, by God's *grace,* knew exactly why God had been punishing them; they could go to the exact law. The giving of the Law in one sense was a blessing; however, when they disobeyed, it would also begin God's curse upon them.

Kings Hezekiah and Josiah are both examples of God giving His *grace* to them in their circumstances. God in His *grace* gave Hezekiah fifteen more years of life (II Kings 20:1-11). As for Judah, it was going to be judged by God with the Babylonians, but God showed His *grace* to Josiah because of his obedience and faithfulness to God, so that it would not happen in his lifetime (II Kings 22:11-20). There are endless examples of God showing His *grace* to individuals and even to Gentile nations like Nineveh (Jonah 4).

So God's Grace is not exclusively a New Testament teaching; it is in the *Tanakh*. So how is it different?

In the *Tanakh,* God dispensed His undeserved favor (His grace) on Israel, but it was not the standard for Israel to live by as in the current Dispensation of Grace. The system that God used largely in the *Tanakh* was the Dispensation of Law, and God repeatedly judged Israel by His Law.

In the New Testament, *grace* (and mercy) is the unconditional love of God towards a sinner who does not deserve His *grace*; God's Grace and mercy are completely 100 percent unmerited. His Grace is given freely to all who believe, and is the standard of the New Testament. By God's *grace,* He dispensed His love to sinners, on all who embraced Him as their personal Saviour from sin. According to Ephesians 4:7, *grace* is a gift from God. God's *grace* is not a loan which needs to be paid back; it is a free gift from the donor, God, to the recipient, man. It is free to us; it costs us nothing, but it cost God the sending of His Son in order to dispense His *grace* in love. It was very costly to Him for it involved His Son's death on the cruel Cross. Once a gift is given by God, it cannot be taken back, for the Gospel of John records that believers in Messiah Yeshua have eternal life as a possession (John 3:16; 5:24; 20:31). This free gift involved an unconditional **New Covenant** of Grace; whereas, in the *Tanakh,* what was unconditional was the Abrahamic Covenant; it cannot be changed. What was conditional and temporary in the *Tanakh* was the Dispensation of Law; it would end.

So the standard in the *Tanakh* was Law, and judgment when the Law was violated, with a mixture of some Grace as God dealt with Israel. However, in the New Testament, the standard is His Grace to all, all the time. There is judgment in the Dispensation of Grace on two fronts and for two distinct purposes. First, Messiah took all of God's wrath upon Himself (Romans 3:24-26; 5:8-10; Colossians 1:20-22) so that we are free from His wrath. However, secondly, after the Rapture, our works will be judged (I Corinthians 3:13-15), for we personally cannot be judged, just our works on the Day of Messiah (I Corinthians 1:8; 5:5; II Corinthians 1:14; Philippians 1:6, 10; 2:16; II Timothy 1:18, 4:8). So, the false charge that we teach there is no Grace in the *Tanakh* is fruitless and a waste of words.

Next is a walk through the other Letters from Apostle Paul that speak to the Law of Messiah. We'll keep the Book of Hebrews, which has a different human author, for last. The Bible does not state the author of Hebrews, but it has a wealth of information regarding why the Law of Messiah is superior to the Law of Moses. We've already covered Romans, so next are the letters to the Corinthians and Paul's other Epistles.

Snapshots from Corinthians

After Paul ministered in Corinth for eighteen months, there came in after him false apostles, Judaizers claiming credentials from Jerusalem; however, the original letter from the Jerusalem Council (Acts 15) would completely refute their claims.

Torah observance folks today present the idea of what Paul said (6:12; 10:23) that if the Law of Moses is not upheld, then believers can easily say, "I can do what I want since I do not have the Mosaic Law to obey." They insinuate that since the moral law of the Mosaic Law is not in effect according to Dispensationalists, then believers are free to steal, burglarize, lie, and bear false witness in court. According to this deception, believers have no sexual restraints; they can have pre-marital, extra-marital affairs and even commit homosexual, lesbian, transgender sins. They suggest that murder would no longer be a deterrent because we say that the Law has been **rendered inoperative**, terminated. Look at the two verses below, for the Torah-observant folk say we have opened the door to sin freely, when the opposite is true:

All things are lawful unto me, but not all things are expedient [profitable].
All things are lawful for me, but I will not be brought under the power [mastered] *of anything.*
(I Corinthians 6:12)

All things are lawful for me, but all things are not expedient [helpful]:
All things are lawful for me, but not all things edify [build up].
(I Corinthians 10:23)

Those who are willfully blind say that now *all things are lawful for me* to commit because we are free and not constrained by the Mosaic Law. But Paul clearly refutes that suggestion on four accounts when he says in the same verses that while all things maybe lawful for him, (1) they are not all profitable, (2) not all are expedient, and (3) he will not be mastered by them; because (4) they do not all edify the body of Messiah. As I stated in Part One of this book, we are NOT under the Mosaic code, but we are under the Law of Messiah; and all the sins we need to avoid and many more are taught in the Law of Messiah in the **New Covenant**. But some will not acknowledge the Law of Messiah, for it will destroy their unbiblical position of Torah observance.[114]

---

[114] Concerning the Moral Law under the Law of Messiah, believers today are under nine of the Ten Commandments of the Moral Law, so the argument that Torah-observant teachers

I have often said Judaism has lassoed a dead horse, meaning the Law of Moses; for it will never get up again. As believers, their complete focus is on the Mosaic Law, the *old covenant* and not on the **New Covenant** and the Law of Messiah that it presents. Likewise, promoting Torah observance is still like trying to lasso the same dead horse because they believe that horse is eternal and they refuse to accept the Law of Messiah in its place. We are NOT free to sin, we are free to serve Him, for we are now under the Law of Messiah and the nature of this law is completely different, as it edifies the body of Messiah.

We as Dispensationalists are not ingrates concerning His Grace, for we understand all that God has done for us. We stand in awe of His Grace. Our motivation of love for Him constrains us to live for Him in all aspects of our daily lives because we understand many things that our ***Redemption*** involved, what it cost Him to ***Reconcile*** us to Himself, and that He has ***Imputed His righteousness*** to our account. He has satisfied all of God's holy righteous demands [***Propitiation***] so He can act on our behalf; and He has ***Sanctified*** us in the present, and will completely sanctify us, called ***Glorification***, in the future. So because of all these things, we live to honor Him and not to disgrace His Name before the world. We do NOT live unto ourselves, but under Him. So, their argument that we are lawless is completely biblically baseless.

II Corinthians 3:6-9

Now we move forward from Peter's testimony and the verdict of the Jerusalem Counsel, on to the masterful doctrinal treatise of Paul in Romans. Let's take a look at II Corinthians 3:6-14 concerning the Law issue as these Judaizers resurface where Paul refers to the Law as a ministry of *death* (v. 7) and *condemnation* (v. 9) but contrasts it with the *ministration of the Spirit and righteousness*, for the letter of the law has no life, it kills and is incapable of producing life. In 11:13-15 the Judaizers surface again and Paul called them *false apostles, deceitful workers, transforming themselves into the apostles of Messiah*. Yet Torah keepers will take verses where Paul deals negatively with them and they sugarcoat themselves and twist the text to avoid what the Scripture clearly says. Look at verses 6-9 and understand that the Mosaic Law is terminated, producing only *death* and *condemnation*.

> *⁶ Who also has made **us** able ministers of the **New Covenant**; not of the letter, but of the spirit: for the letter kills, but the spirit gives life.*
> *⁷ But if the **ministry of death, written and engraved in stones, was glorious, so that the** children of Israel could not steadfastly behold the face of Moses for the glory of his countenance; which glory was to be done away: ⁸ How shall not the **ministry of the spirit** be rather*

---

make is nothing more than speaking hot air. Go back and review Part 1, Chapter 10 entitled "Moral Law of Moses Is Carried over to the Law of Messiah."

glorious? ⁹ *For if the **ministry of condemnation** has glory, much more does the **ministry of righteousness** exceed in glory.*

Notice in verse 6, Paul includes both Jewish and Gentile believers in saying that they are ministers of the **New Covenant** and not of the *old covenant*. I can't help asking the Torah observant folks, "Do you see that you are to be ministers of, the **New Covenant** and not the *old covenant*?" Paul admonishes them in verse 6 that the letter of the Law kills but God's Spirit gives life. As Paul asked later in Galatians 3:2, "Were you saved by the hearing of the Law or by the Spirit? It is interesting to note in one of the larger Torah-observant books that I have read, this passage (vv. 6-9) of Scripture is ignored. Instead, they focus on many passages that are not even relevant to the text to push Torah observance. Torah observance teaching is layered superficially upon the text in question, in the same way that Judaism overlays Scripture with the Oral Rabbinic Law and the Catholic Church does this with their unbiblical traditions. Evidently, this passage, II Corinthians 3:6-9, does not give them any wiggle room to twist their false theology and conform it to their Torah bias. Read II Corinthians 5:17-21 and answer the questions after the quoted passage:

> ¹⁷ *Therefore if any man be in Messiah, he is a **new creature**: old things have passed away; behold, all things have become new.* ¹⁸ *And all things are of God, who has **reconciled us to Himself** by Yeshua ha-Mashiach and has **given to us the ministry of reconciliation**;* ¹⁹ *That is to say God was in Messiah, reconciling the world unto Himself, not imputing their trespasses unto them; and has committed unto us **the word of reconciliation**.* ²⁰ *Now then **we are ambassadors for Messiah**, as though God did beseech you by us: we pray you in Messiah's stead, **be reconciled to God** [in your daily life].* ²¹ *For He has made Him to be sin for us, who knew no sin; that we might be **made the righteousness of God in Him**.* [bolding and brackets mine]

- Did the Law of Moses make you a new creation? NO!
- Did the Law of Moses make you new? NO!
- Were you reconciled to God by Moses? NO!
- Did Moses give you the ministry of reconciliation? NO!
- Did Moses give you the word of reconciliation? NO!
- Are you an ambassador of Moses? NO!
- Did you receive the righteousness of God through Moses? NO!

	II Corinthians 3:2-11	
	(John B. Metzger)	
Law of Moses	**_Ten Commandments_**	**_Law of Messiah_**
Ministration of Death – v. 7	Spotlight on Them "Pass away" "Engraven on stones" "Done away" (vv. 3, 7)	Superior
Ministration of Condemnation – v. 9	Katargeo: Means "to render inoperative." Law of Moses has been rendered inoperative	Law of Messiah will never be rendered inoperative.
	Applies to Jews – Israel	Applies to the Church – All believers both Jews and Gentiles of all ethnicities

So, are you living a reconciled life in Moses or in Messiah? – Who is greater?

Why would anyone insist on clutching onto the *old covenant* with a death grip that only produced *death* and *condemnation*? It could not, and did not save anyone or make anyone more righteous! Why not choose life and redemption? Our LORD Yeshua *mediated* the **New Covenant,** a new standard of living in Him called the <u>Law of Messiah</u>. Let me follow up with additional questions based on other verses:

- In whose *Name* were the Apostles persecuted, in the name of Moses or the Name of Yeshua? (See Acts 2:38; 3:6, 16; 4:7, 10, 12, 17-18, 30; 5:28, 40-41; 8:12, 16; 9:14-16, 21, 28-29; 10:43, 48; 15:14, 17, 26; 16:18; 19:5; 21:13; 22:16.)
- In whose *Name* did the Apostles preach? Yeshua Ha-Mashiach! (Jesus the Messiah!)

Shall we go on?

- In whose *Name* were you *justified*, Yeshua or Moses?
- In whose *Name* were you *redeemed*, Yeshua or Moses?
- In whose *Name* did you find *propitiation*, Yeshua or Moses?

  [Definition of *propitiation*: To satisfy all of God's holy righteous demands enabling Him to act on your behalf.]

- In whose *Blood* were you cleansed of your sin, Yeshua or animals?
- **Who** *blessed* you with *all spiritual blessings* in heavenly places, Yeshua or Moses?
- **Who** made *peace* between the offending sinner and God, Yeshua or Moses?

- Through whom do you have the *indwelling*, *sealing*, *filling* and *baptism* of the Ruach Ha-Kodesh (Holy Spirit), Yeshua or Moses?
- **Who** *reconciled* you to God, Yeshua or Moses?
- **Who** made you *one* in Messiah (Ephesians 2:11-22), Yeshua or Moses?
- **Who** is the *foundation* of the body of Messiah, Yeshua or Moses?
- **Who** said to the Pharisees *and he wrote of Me* (John 5:46)? Yeshua or Moses?
- **Who** is central to all our spiritual heritage in Scripture? Yeshua or Moses?
- **Who** is the pinnacle of the words of Moses (Genesis 49:10; Deuteronomy 18:15-19)?
- **Who** is the focus of David throughout his Messianic psalms? Yeshua or Moses?
- **Who** is the *ultimate focus* of the Prophets (Deuteronomy 18:18-19)?

Isaiah	(7:14; 9:5-6; 11:1-2; 42:1-6; 48:12-16; 49:1-8; 50:1-6; 52:13 - 53:12; 61:1-2)
Jeremiah	(23:5-6)
Micah	(5:2)
Daniel	(2:34-35, 44-45; 7:13-14; 9:24-27)
Hosea	(5:15-6:3)
Zechariah	(3:1-10; 6:11-13; 9:9-10; 11:4-14; 12:1-10; 13:7; 14:1-4)
Malachi	(3:1)

- **Who** is *The Angel of the LORD* (Genesis 18:1-33; Exodus 23:20-23; Judges 2:1-4)?
- **Who** is the *BRANCH* (Isaiah 4:2; Jeremiah 23:5-6; Zechariah 3:8-9; 6:12-13)?

Now look closely at Deuteronomy 18:18-19. **Who** is God referring to? YESHUA, *the Prophet Like Moses!* Are you listening to *the Prophet Like Moses* or to Moses??? God will require of you to be obedient to *the Prophet Like Moses* and NOT to Moses who was a faithful servant over the house. *The Prophet Like Moses* was the builder of the house of Israel (Hebrews 3:1-6), NOT Moses! Note what Deuteronomy 18:18-19 says:

> [18] *I will raise them up a **Prophet** from among their brothers* [Israel], *like unto you* [Moses], *and will put My words in His mouth: And He*

> *shall speak unto them* [Israel] *all that I shall command Him.* ¹⁹ *And it shall come to pass, that* **whosoever will not hearken unto** [listen to and conform to] ***My words which He shall speak in My Name, I will require it of him.***

Do you see what God said through Moses? There will be One *like* him (Moses) coming, and He (Yeshua) came. God said He (Yeshua) would speak God's words, and God will require everything of you that Yeshua says to you. His words, actions, and ministry are recorded in the Gospels. At the last Passover, Yeshua announced to His disciples the establishment of the **New Covenant**, NOT a renewed one, but a **NEW** one. In that **New Covenant,** He has given us through His Apostles the <u>Law of Messiah</u>, a new and *better* standard to live by which the Book of Hebrew reiterates over and over again. So, in clinging to the Mosaic Covenant and not accepting the **New Covenant** that He mediated with His Blood on the cruel Roman Cross, God will require of you everything Yeshua said, taught, and did. Torah observance teaches willfully reducing His *Word* by diminishing[115] the authority of His *Word* (John 1:1-2; Genesis 15:1, 4: I Samuel 3:21; II Samuel 7:4-5; I John 1:1-4; Revelation 19:13).

II Corinthians 3:14

> *But their minds were blinded* [hardened]; *for until this day the same veil remains unlifted in the reading of the **old covenant**, which veil **is removed in Messiah.***

Yet, Torah observers ignore this main section in II Corinthians 3. They avoid using expository teaching to understand this passage, but instead use their own theological reasoning to come in the back door, as if attacking the Bible truths from the rear. First let me give a quote from Michael Vanlaningham, professor at Moody Bible Institute:

> Why then were so many Israelites rejecting Christ? Their minds continued to be hardened (See Romans 11:7-27). This is evident because the veil (representing Israel's hardness) remained over their heart when Moses (read the *old covenant* v. 15). The hardness is only removed when they embrace Christ as Savior. Just as Moses used to remove the veil to behold the glory of God (Exodus 34:34), so Jewish people now have the veil of hardness [which will be] removed when they repent and see the glory of God in the person of Jesus (v. 16). … Just as Moses removed the veil in the presence of

---

[115] **Diminish**: Meaning to make smaller or less; reduce, to detract from the authority, reputation, or prestige of.

God, so people [will] throw off their hardness of heart when they turn to God.[116] [brackets mine]

Vanlaningham explains well the meaning of II Corinthians 3:14-16. Now I am going to rephrase another quotation of a Torah-observant author so *he*[117] can reason in silence like *he* does by setting up a straw man, the words of an unknown pastor, so he can knock his position down. Before we tackle it, let me remind you that *he* does not believe in economies of God (Dispensations) and how God has chosen to work with His creation. Also, while it is unspoken here but alluded to, *he* insists on teaching two flawed areas: (1) *he* insists on the Torah being eternal (please check the chapter on *olam* in Part One of this book, starting on p. 45); and (2) *he* also insists on rejecting the teaching of Scripture that the **New Covenant** is a completely NEW and not a renewed or a modified *old covenant*.

Now concerning *his* teaching: *He* says it is pointless to say that the **New Covenant** was not enacted on believers in the Messiah. That is correct, for the **New Covenant** was obviously for all believers, which should be accepted without any controversy. But then *he* continues to say that these redeemed Dispensationalists who teach the abolishment of the Law of Moses are blatantly wrong to divorce the **New Covenant** from the Mosaic Law standard of living in Messiah. *He* then asserts that the Law (meaning the Mosaic Law) will be put in our hearts. The answer is that while the **New Covenant** has regenerated our uncircumcised hearts, the Word has not yet been planted in our hearts for we still do battle daily with our old nature (Romans 7) and will do so until the Rapture or our death. Only then will we have His Word implanted in our hearts; it will NOT be the Mosaic Law! This **New Covenant** was given to Israel (Jeremiah 31:31, 33), and believing Gentiles will be grafted in through the Messiah (Romans 11:13-25). *He* refuses to recognize that God often places a period of time between application and fulfillment throughout His prophetic history as pointed out earlier in this book. *He* does not include a period of time between these actual events:

- **Announcement** of the **New Covenant** by Jeremiah.

- The **inauguration** of the **New Covenant** by Yeshua on the Cross with His death.

- The **ratification** of the **New Covenant** when all Israel will be saved and have His Word implanted in their hearts (Isaiah 66:8; Hosea 5:15-6:3; Zechariah 3:9; Romans 11:26-27), but only when all Israel embraces Him (Matthew 23:39). We as Dispensationalists also teach living a holy life (I Corinthians 3:17; Ephesians 1:4; 2:21; 5:27; Colossians 1:22; 3:12;

---

[116] Michael Rydelnik and Michael Vanlaningham, *The Moody Bible Commentary*. Chicago, IL: Moody Press, 2014, p. 1812.

[117] **He:** This is a reference to the author of a Gentile Torah-Observant belief.

I Thessalonians 3:11-13; Hebrews 12:3-13; I Peter 1:15-16) on the bases of the **New Covenant** for the Law of Messiah is *better* than and superior to the *old covenant* (Hebrews).[118]

In reading all of these theological reasonings of Torah observance I have been struck with this thought. As I read and listen to Replacement, Amillennial, and Covenant Reform Theology proponents concerning prophecies of Israel's future, I am reminded that they are replacing what the Scriptures say with their own biases. They read the plain sense of Scripture and then spiritualize a large percentage of the *Tanakh* away from the intended understanding of the Author, Who is YAHWEH. Torah observance adherents do the same. There are so many passages against promoting Torah observance, but they wiggle around to get away from the impact of the **New Covenant** and the Law of Messiah replacing the *old covenant* Law.

- Hebrews (8:13) says that the *old covenant* in the first century was *decaying and waxing old, ready to vanish away* and it did physically in AD 70 as far as the ability to practice it biblically.

- God had already decreed it terminated at the death of Messiah forty years previously when *Yeshua inaugurated the New Covenant* making the first one *old*.

Why did the *old covenant* pass away? **Because the Author, God, Himself, rendered the Law of Moses inoperative**; He terminated it; He abolished it. We Dispensationalists did not do that; we simply have taken YAHWEH, the Author, at His word (Golden Rule of Interpretation) and believed it and acted upon His **unalterable** Word. The **New Covenant** does not reestablish the Law of Moses or the *old covenant*, for the Law of Messiah will enable believers, both Jew and Gentile, through the Ruach Ha-Kodesh (Holy Spirit), to live a holy life; and we as Dispensationalists do teach and live a *holy* life before our Master and LORD, Yeshua. Also, today, the law of the **New Covenant** has not been written on our hearts at this point in time, or else all of Paul's imperative commands would not be necessary.

> *And be not conformed to this world: but be transformed by the **renewing of your mind**, that you may prove what is that good, and acceptable, and perfect, will of God* (Romans 12:2).

If we were implanted with His Word (His Law) at salvation, then why are we commanded to renew our minds? Here is a principle of the value of the *Tanakh* in

---

[118] The Book of Hebrews presents Yeshua as BETTER than angels (1:4-14), BETTER than Moses (3:1-6), and BETTER than the high priesthood and sacrifices (5:1-10; 7:1-10:18). Since Yeshua is better, why cling to that which is inferior?

Joshua 1:8 and Psalm 1:2. These two verses are the seams[119] between the Law and the Prophets and between the Prophets and the Writings. These two verses link the three divisions of the *Tanakh* (Law, Prophets, and the Writings) together and tell us to meditate on His Word *day and night*. Why would Paul again emphasize to the Philippian believers to *think on these things* if our minds and hearts were only thinking God's Word in our hearts? Obviously, we are not!

> *Finally, brethren, whatsoever things are true, whatsoever thing are honest, whatsoever things are just, whatsoever things are pure, whatsoever things are lovely, whatsoever things are of good report; if there be any virtue, and if there be any praise,* **think** *on these things* (Philippians 4:8).

These words would be nonsense if His Word had already been implanted in our hearts. The word *think* in this verse is a Greek imperative command, part of the Law of Messiah.

No, this prophecy of having God's Word implanted in their hearts will be fulfilled only to physical, earthly **national Israel** when they accept Yeshua, whom they rejected in His earthly ministry, when they embrace Him as their Messiah, LORD, and Master. This will only happen at the end of *the Time of Jacob's Trouble* (Jeremiah 30:7), the Tribulation period which is still in the future. THEN Jeremiah 31:33 will be fulfilled in that God's Law will be written in their heart – Israel's hearts – and not before. The Church, the body of Messiah, will have it written on their hearts at death and/or at the Rapture when we stand before Him, a totally different time before Israel is redeemed as a nation.

---

[119] Michael Rydelnik, *The Messianic Hope: Is the Hebrew Bible Really Messianic?* Nashville, TN: B&H Publishing Group, 2010, pp. 66-69.

Snapshots from Galatians

In the Book of Galatians, which Paul (Sha'ul) wrote probably around the time of the Jerusalem Council in Acts 15, Paul is extremely clear on the fact that the Mosaic Law cannot give victory over sin; it cannot enhance salvation or justification. Paul would later, in the Book of Romans (chapters 6 to 8), deal with the issue of the Law and the flesh in contrast to the work of the Ruach Ha-Kodesh (Holy Spirit).

It is because of this Letter to the Galatians that Paul wrote that he was disliked by some Messianic Jewish believers of his day because of his strong language against Judaizers; for instance, when he opposed their teaching that circumcision was necessary to become a believer in Messiah. This same dislike occurs today among those who take issue with Paul's stance against Judaizers. In the same token, others in Paul's day took offense at his strong statements against Torah observance as well as against legalism.[120] He majored on the fact that the Law of Moses had been terminated, abolished, or *rendered inoperative* and that the new standard of living was found in the Law of Messiah.

I have read in Torah-observant books that they try to affirm Torah observance with an array of theological reasoning, using very smooth language. However, they do not deal with the text honestly because they have a preconceived bias that the Torah is eternal and that will not allow them to accept the plain sense of Scripture and interpret the Word of God as He gave it. As a result, we will be spending some time in this difficult, yet rewarding book as Paul guides believers away from being sidetracked by the Mosaic Law and toward the new economy of God called the Dispensation of Grace. The new economy of Grace came to believers as a direct result of the **New Covenant**. Paul then guided them toward the Law of Messiah, and away from being entangled with Torah observance. Acts 15:10 raises the question this way: *Now therefore, why tempt God, to put a yoke upon the neck of the disciples, which neither our fathers nor we were able to bear?*

In Galatians 1:6-9

Paul places a curse on Judaizers who insist on circumcision and observance of the Mosaic Law. First look at the passage:

---

[120] **Practical Definition of Legalism:** Because of Christian Liberty, believers have personal convictions not based on Scripture which Paul says is okay as long as they do not make it their mission in life to impose their personal view upon others, thereby insisting that others MUST adhere to their belief.

> *⁶ I marvel that you are so soon removed from Him that called you into grace of Messiah unto another* [ἕτερος / *heteros*] *gospel:* ⁷ *Which is not another* [ἄλλος / *allos*]; *but there be some who trouble you and would pervert* [μεταστρέψαι / *metastrepho*] *the gospel of Messiah.* ⁸ *But though we, or an angel* [ἄγγελος / *aggelos*] *from heaven, preach any other gospel unto you than that which we have preached unto you, let him be accursed* [ἀνάθεμα / *anathema*]. ⁹ *As we said before, so say I now again, if any man preach any other gospel unto you than that you have received, let him be accursed* [ἀνάθεμα / *anathema*].

Now let us look at each verse and the words that Paul used. In verse 6, Paul is amazed that they so soon had removed themselves from Grace, the result of the **New Covenant** that Yeshua gave to them, to another [ἕτερος / *heteros*] gospel. The word *heteros* means "another of a different kind." This was a different kind of gospel. They did present a Gospel of salvation in Messiah, but it was embedded with working out their salvation with "works, works, works" of the Law and that was NOT the Grace of the **New Covenant**. But a Faith intermingled with obeying the works of the Mosaic Law was NOT the Gospel that Paul preached, that the Galatians had believed, and that placed them into the body of Messiah. In verse 7, Paul used another word for *another* that is ἄλλος / *allos,* and it means "another of the *same kind.*" So they went from one kind of Gospel to a different kind of gospel. Paul is telling them that believing Judaizers had come in behind him and preached a perverted kind of gospel. *Perverted,* in the Greek *metastrepho,* means to turn away or to overturn and to completely twist something around. Let's quote Arnold Fruchtenbaum on these verses:

> In verse 7, he says that this new gospel is not another gospel but a perversion of the true gospel. There are two Greek words that mean "another." One term means *"another of the same kind,"* and the second term means *"another of a different kind."* The Greek word Paul used here means *"another gospel of a different kind."* In other words, they were not receiving another gospel of the *same kind*, a similar gospel, but they were deceived by another gospel of a *different kind*, a gospel totally different from the one they had believed earlier. This is a *different gospel* than the gospel of grace. This is not even another gospel of the same kind, but it is another gospel of a *different kind*.
>
> The Greek word for *pervert* [metastrepho] means "to twist something around," "to reverse it." It means that they are not denying it; rather, they are destroying it by adding to it. They are taking true things and destroying them. Throughout the letter, these perversions are seen in at least four areas.
>
>> *First*, they believe in the perfection of the flesh (Galatians 3:3).

> *Second*, they believe in the obligatory observance of days, months, and seasons, and years (Galatians 4:10).
>
> *Third*, they believe in being justified by the law (Galatians 5:4).
>
> And *fourth*, they believe in mandatory circumcision (Galatians 5:2). So, by these things the gospel was being perverted.[121]

So these believers were being convinced by others, believing the Pharisees' faction of the early Church that to believe in Messiah was great, but to be real believers you needed to be circumcised and observe and obey all the Torah. That would have changed the whole course of the body of Messiah in history, and it would have become just another branch of Judaism, which is what some Messianic believers are trying to do today by calling themselves the Fourth Branch of Judaism.

A Messianic Pastor of a congregation in Nevada echoes what Fruchtenbaum says with this following statement:

> When a soldier in an army takes a leave of absence without getting approval from the commander, they are considered to be AWOL which means *a*bsent *w*ithout *l*eave. A soldier that is AWOL is considered to be a deserter and is in much trouble with the army. Sha'ul [Paul] had considered the Galatians AWOL and was encouraging them to come back from deserting the Lord. What was the terrible action they had performed? They turned from the good news message of the grace of Yeshua to "another gospel." ... Sha'ul tells the Galatians with one word that they were deserting Yeshua not for another gospel of the same kind but for another gospel of a different kind. In essence, they abandoned the good news of grace for the bad news of legalism.[122]

Paul got more serious about the teaching of Torah observance when he said that even if an angel[123] from heaven would teach this, do NOT believe it. An interesting observation is that no angel from God's heaven would ever contradict their Master's

---

[121] Arnold Fruchtenbaum, *Faith Alone: The Condition of Our Salvation – An Exposition of the Book of Galatians*. San Antonio, TX: Ariel Press, 2014, p. 12.

[122] Richard Hill, *Freedom in Messiah: A Messianic Jewish Roots Commentary on the Book of Galatians*. Las Vegas, NV: S-E-L-F Publishing, 2015, p. 32.

[123] **Angel**: ἄγγελος / aggelos – means "messenger," and it can be a human or angelic messenger. In Scripture I am not aware of demons being called messengers, but we do know they convey the heart of Satan in deceiving mankind to rebel against the LORD of Creation.

word, so is it probable that a messenger who would teach against the Gospel of Messiah could be a messenger of Satan, a fallen angel who would have no qualms about teaching against the Gospel of Messiah? Perhaps the angel who taught Muhammad the false Islamic religion was the same angel that taught Joseph Smith the book of Mormon.

Now as if that is not serious enough, Paul ups the ante when he *curses* the teachers of the Judaizers, including their teaching of circumcision for Gentiles as well as Torah observance, obeying the Law of Moses. They rejected the Law of Messiah brought to them by the **New Covenant** at a high price. They endorsed legalism, which is an artificial manmade law, to keep believers in bondage to the Law. Let me reference Kenneth Wuest:

> *Let him be accursed.* The word *accursed* is from [ἀνάθεμα] *anathema*. It is a word used in the LXX [Septuagint] of a person or thing set apart and devoted to destruction, because [it is] hateful to God. Hence in a spiritual sense it denotes one who is alienated from God by sin.[124]

Another observation in connection with the word *curse* refers to Jericho. The city and items of the city were pledged to destruction. In Joshua 7:12 in the Septuagint the same word ἀνάθεμα is used which brought about Israel's defeat at the city of Ai and the judgment on the house of Achan who was stoned to death, *so that the LORD turned from the fierceness of His anger* (Joshua 7:26).

Now let us recap what Paul said in Galatians 1:6-9 concerning how to deal with the Judaizers:

> ***First,*** understand that they are accursed for presenting ***another different kind of gospel***.
>
> ***Second***, realize that they have ***perverted*** the Gospel of Messiah.
>
> ***Third,*** even if an angel came to them and contradicted the message of the Gospel, they are not to believe it.
>
> ***Finally***, Paul says twice in verses 8-9 that anyone who teaches this ***different kind of gospel*** is to be ***accursed***. This is not a matter to be overlooked or dismissed!

Galatians 2:16-18

In ***Galatians 2:16-18*** Paul clearly states that absolutely NO justification comes from law keeping; *by the works of the law shall NO flesh be justified*. Justification is by

---

[124] Kenneth Wuest, *Wuest's Word Studies: Vol. one, Galatians*. Grand Rapids, MI: Eerdmans Publishing Co, 1969, p. 40.

Faith in the finished work of Messiah on the Cross. We are saved by Grace through Faith ALONE, NOT by law keeping, nor do we get merit points with God for Torah keeping. First let me quote for you the passage to be discussed:

> [16] *Knowing that a man is NOT **justified** by the works of the law, but by the faith of Yeshua Ha-Mashiach, even we have believed in Yeshua Ha-Mashiach, that we might be **justified** by the faith of Messiah, and NOT by the works of the Law: for by the works of the Law shall no flesh be **justified**.* [17] *But if, while we seek to be justified by Messiah, we ourselves also are found sinners, is therefore Messiah the minister of sin? God forbid.* [18] *For if I build again the things which I destroyed, I make myself a transgressor.*

Today some have twisted their message to teach that the Law was needed to justify a believer. Now they subtly shift from teaching the necessity of Law keeping for justification to teaching that the Torah is eternal, and that since Yeshua kept the Law, every good believer needs to keep the Law like Yeshua did as our example. This is only one of the numerous ways in which they twist and turn in their attempt to make Law keeping a necessity for believers' growth in Messiah.

As we dive into this passage let me give you the definition for *dikaioo*, the Greek word for *justified*. It means to "declare to be just; and in relation to God and the divine Law, it means to declare righteousness, to regard as pious."[125]

> *Our justification is God's declaration that the demands of His Law have been fulfilled in righteousness of His Son. ... When God justifies, He charges the sin of man to Christ and credits the righteousness of Christ to the believer (II Corinthians 5:21).*[126]

Could the Law do this? NO! Now I will quote a lengthy passage from Richard Hill, spiritual leader of Beth Yeshua Messianic Congregation in Las Vegas:[127]

> After revealing to the Messianic Jews that their separation from the Gentile believers at Antioch was a dramatic sin of hypocrisy [Galatians 2:11-14], Sha'ul [Apostle Paul] then made his strongest declaration concerning the Law that should send fear into the hearts of the Messianic Jewish Movement and anyone who is trying to be Torah observant. He declares that no man is justified by the works

---

[125] Richard Hill, *Freedom in Messiah: A Messianic Jewish Roots Commentary on the Book of Galatians.* Las Vegas, NV: S-E-L-F Publishing, 2015, p. 74.

[126] Ronald F. Youngblood, *Nelson's New Illustrated Bible Dictionary.* Nashville, TN: Nelson Publishers, 1986, page 721.

[127] Richard Hill, *Freedom in Messiah: A Messianic Jewish Roots Commentary on the Book of Galatians.* Las Vegas, NV: S-E-L-F Publishing, 2015, pp. 75-76.

of the Law. Anyone who tries to be justified by their good works is only fooling themselves because in God's eyes these efforts are fruitless. Sha'ul is so emphatic about this theology that he repeats the statement three times.

Sha'ul is obviously stating that anyone who wants to be declared righteous by God has to approach Him through faith in Yeshua Ha-Mashiach. *Justified* is used three times in this verse and the Greek grammar shows that it is used in three different ways.

The first justified is in the indicative mood, present tense and middle voice.

> The ***indicative mood indicates*** a positive and clear-cut statement is made. Sha'ul is absolutely sure that no one can be justified by the Law.
>
> The ***present tense*** shows a continuous action is in progress. Therefore, a believer in the present is continuously not justified by the works of the Law.
>
> ... ***The middle voice*** specifies that the subject is acting in reference to himself. Here, *a man* is trying to show he is justified by his own workings of the Law. Sha'ul states this is impossible because we can only do this by faith in Yeshua.

The second justified is in the subjunctive mood, aorist tense and passive voice.

> The ***subjunctive mood*** indicates a doubtful or hesitant statement. Sha'ul has doubt that everyone included in the *we* are truly believers. He may also be including the group of unsaved Legalizers who instigated the separation.
>
> ***The aorist tense*** reveals an action as a point in past time. Sha'ul is saying that the true believers were justified by their one past action of faith in Yeshua. In other words, Sha'ul is saying the believers were justified in the past when they acted on their faith in Yeshua for salvation.
>
> ***The passive voice*** shows the subject is the receiver of the action but received their justification from God through their faith in Yeshua.

***The third* justified** is in the indicative mood, future tense and passive voice.

> The ***indicative mood*** reveals a positive and clear-cut statement. Sha'ul is sure that no man will be justified by the works of the Law.
>
> The ***future tense*** indicates an action as a point in future time. Sha'ul is saying no man will be justified in the future by the works of the Law.
>
> The ***passive voice*** shows the subject is the receiver of the action. Here, God performs the justification upon the believer through faith and not by works of the Law.
>
> Taken collectively, the Greek grammar in this verse emphatically reveals Sha'ul's theology on how a man can or cannot be justified. No man can be justified in the past, present or future by the works of the Law. No man can even perform good works of the Law to earn justification from God. However, a man can be justified in the past, present or future through faith in Yeshua.
>
> My question to the Torah observant of the Messianic Jewish Movement is, "Why are you trying to become justified in God's eyes through your Torah observance when Galatians 2:16 is so clear that to be justified by God it is necessary to only have faith in Yeshua and to live by this faith and not by the works of the Law?" Hebrews 11:6 encourages all believers, but especially Messianic Jews, to live by faith: *and without faith it is impossible to please Him ...*

In verse 18, Paul uses two words that need to be noted. He said to be *built again* (*oikodomeo*) means to render or declare valid. If you try to revalidate something that was already destroyed, you are sinning! The word *destroyed* (*kataluo*) means to abolish, to annul, and bring to an end. So what was destroyed was the false concept that justification and godly living came by the Law. It cannot again be rebuilt. It is over; it is done; we have a new law, the Law of Messiah and the indwelling presence of the Ruach Ha-Kodesh.

In saying all this I want to pointedly ask Torah observant folks who know that their justification is in Messiah alone, why they yet bristle at the thought that Messiah has **rendered inoperative** His *old covenant*, the Law. Yeshua has personally made it impossible to keep it in three ways:

- First, when He died on the Cross, He inaugurated the **New Covenant**.

- Second, because of what the Pharisees did in Matthew 12, when they attributed everything Yeshua said and did to Beelzebub (Satan), they committed the Unpardonable Sin. He in judgment then allowed the Romans to destroy the City of Jerusalem and the Sanctuary (Temple).

- Third, with the destruction of the Temple, meaning there are no more sacrifices, He made the priesthood obsolete in this economy.

Yet they continue in practice to lift the Torah up over the Messiah who was the Author of the Law in the first place to Israel alone. This we will cover later when we get to Hebrews. One final quote from Kenneth Wuest to Judaizers today:

> Paul repudiates the false assumption of the Judaizers who charged that Christ is the promoter and encourager of sin in that He causes the Jew to abandon the Law as a justifying agency, and in doing so, put Himself on the common plane of a Gentile whom he calls a sinner and a dog. The Judaizers argued that in view of the fact that violation of the Law is sin; therefore, abandonment of the Law in an effort to be justified in Christ is also sin. Thus, Christ is the promoter of sin.[128]

Galatians 3:2

In Galatians 3:2 Paul asks a very straightforward, probing question: Did you receive *the Spirit by the works of the Law or by the hearing of faith*? Even more forcefully, Paul states in verse 11 that *no man is justified by the Law in the sight of God*. Why? Because *the just shall live by faith*, as Paul quotes from Habakkuk 2:4. All the twenty old testament saints listed in Hebrew 11, the Bible's "Hall of Fame," were saved by Faith, plus all the others at that time who are unnamed (vv. 33-40). They were saved by Faith in God and His revealed Word. First, we need to see that verse 2 is part of a unit of six rhetorical questions that all require the answer NO. So, let's read Galatians 3: 1-5:

> *¹ O foolish Galatians, who has bewitched you, that you should not obey the truth, before whose eyes Yeshua Messiah has been openly set forth, crucified among you? ² This only would I learn from you. Did you receive the Spirit by the works of the Law, or by the hearing of faith? ³ Are you so foolish? Having begun in the Spirit, are you now perfected by the flesh* [human works]*? ⁴ Did you suffer so many things in vain? If it is indeed in vain. ⁵ He therefore that supplies to you the Spirit, and works miracles among you, does He do it by the works of the Law, or by the hearing of faith?*

One of the first things that I notice in a book that pushes Torah observance is that there are no references to these verses, because these verses do not promote the bias towards Torah observance; the passage instead goes completely against their thrust.

---

[128] Kenneth Wuest, *Wuest's Word Studies: Vol. one, Galatians*. Grand Rapids, MI: Eerdmans Publishing Co, 1969, p.78.

Another Messianic author tries to deflect or soften the passage by promoting the idea that these Judaizers were most "likely" believers who were probably Gentile proselytes in Galatia that were saved and became so enamored with the "beauty" of Judaism that they began teaching Torah observance.

The fact is not difficult; these foolish Galatians were simply from the Pharisees' sect of believers that came in behind Paul and began teaching that, yes, it is in important to believe in Yeshua, but you also must be circumcised and become Torah observant. This approach was anti-Gospel that they preached to them, because they were adding works to Faith. So, look at this passage to clearly see what Paul was presenting to the believers in Galatia. There are six rhetorical questions in this passage that require a negative answer. We will look at the questions first and then comment on them later:

> In verse 1, the *first question* is, "Are you so foolish?"
>
> In verse 2, the *second question* is, "Did you receive the Spirit by the works of the law or by the hearing of faith?"
>
> In verse 3a, the *third question* is a repeated question, "Are you so foolish? Having begun in the Spirit?"
>
> In verse 3b, the *fourth question* is, "Can you finish in the flesh what you have begun in the Spirit?"
>
> In verse 4, the *fifth question* is, "Have you suffered so many things in vain?"
>
> In verse 5, the *sixth question* is, "Who gave you the Spirit and who worked miracles among you? The works of the law or the hearing of faith?"[129]

Here is a summary of what is at stake in the Church of Galatia as their Faith is being undermined by the Judaizers:

> For the Christian to abandon faith and grace for Law and works is to lose everything exciting that the Christian can experience in his daily fellowship with the Lord. The Law cannot justify the sinner (Galatians 2:16); neither can it give him righteousness (2:21).
>
> The Law cannot give the gift of the Spirit (3:2), nor can it guarantee the spiritual inheritance that belongs to God's children (3:18). The

---

[129] Arnold Fruchtenbaum. *Faith Alone: The Condition of Our Salvation – An Exposition of the Book of Galatians.* San Antonio, TX: Ariel Press, 2014, pp. 24-25.

Law cannot give life (3:21), and the Law cannot give liberty (4:8-10). Why, then, go back to the Law?[130]

One additional item can be added to Wiersbe's list: The Law cannot provide powerful miracles either (3:5). Sha'ul was very defensive concerning his ministry in the first two chapters of this Letter; now he will go on the offensive by first calling the Galatians *foolish*.

In verse 1 the Greek word *anoetos* is an adjective which means "foolish and senseless."[131] It does not mean "a lack of intelligence" or "being stupid." Based on all that is involved, however, it is a stupid response. It is like a person who looks into the heavens and says there is no God, whose response is stupid (Psalms 10:4; 19:1; 53:1-4), or for a person to look at the complexity of the human body and say that it all occurred over time by evolution, or one who denies the wonder of God creating humankind in His image in Genesis 1:26-27; 2:7. Again, it is not saying that they are unintelligent – some are very intelligent – but wanting to deny God because of one's own spiritual blindness and reject and deny what God has clearly said is an unintelligent response for a believer. So Paul presents all the scriptural facts concerning being born again by the Ruach Ha-Kodesh, and then they turn around and try to finish what God has begun by being Torah observant. These deceived believers are unintelligent and stupid in their response. Likewise, present-day Torah observance was birthed out of the same mode.

The second word in the first rhetorical question is the word *bewitch*, as in *who bewitched you*. It is only used once and is the Greek word *baskaino* which means "to slander, to prate about anyone; then to bring evil on a person by feigned praise, or misleading by an evil eye, and so to charm, bewitch." *Bewitch* is used figuratively in verse 1 of someone leading another into evil doctrine.[132] It also includes the idea of being hypnotized, being fascinated as in a trance, being deluded as some today with the "beauty" of Judaism. The bottom line is that Yeshua was publicly crucified; He the God/Man is ALL sufficient. In that day and in this day, there is absolutely no need for the works of the Law, however it is packaged or disguised. There is NO comparison between the terminated Law and the death of Messiah and His *inauguration* of the **New Covenant** with a new standard of living in the Law of Messiah, all empowered by the Ruach Ha-Kodesh which the Law never had.

---

[130] Warren Wiersbe, *Be Free: A New Testament Study on Galatians*. Colorado Springs, CO: Chariot Victor Publishing, 1975, p. 41.

[131] William D. Mounce, *Mounce's Complete Expository Dictionary of Old and New Testament Words*. Grand Rapids, MI: Zondervan Publishing House, 2006, p. 263.

[132] W. E. Vine, *Vine's Expository Dictionary of Old and New Testament Words*. Old Tappen, NJ: Fleming H. Revell Co, 1971, p. 125.

Now concerning the ***second rhetorical question*** of Paul, a very straightforward question:

> On what basis did you receive the Holy Spirit? Did you receive it on the basis of the works of the law? NO! On the basis of the hearing of Faith? YES. There is clear superiority of Faith over works. Paul also makes this point in Romans 10:13-17.[133]

This statement is so clear that no further comment is needed. Then Paul moves into the ***third rhetorical question***, and again he repeats the word *foolish* which was dealt with in the first question. He then references the second rhetorical question by saying, "You began in the Spirit are you now going to bring to perfection in the flesh that which the Creator God started?" The flesh and the Law are incapable of bringing in perfection. ONLY Messiah in establishing the **New Covenant** through His blood could bring in that which is perfect, NOT Moses. An orange tree will always produce oranges and not apples. The work of Messiah in ***inaugurating*** the **New Covenant** will bring perfection; the works of the Law cannot in any form, day, or age bring in perfection. Again, let me quote a Pastor from a Messianic congregation:

> The meaning of *perfect epiteleo* is "to finish, complete, perfect." First Sha'ul [Paul] tells the Galatians that they became born again and started their walk with the Lord when they received the Ruach. So having begun in the Spirit, are they now going to complete their walk with the Lord by following Torah? The obvious answer, again, is NO.
>
> Flesh, *sarx* means "flesh, human, moral nature, physical life … Therefore, *sarx* signifies man's sinful nature, the seat of sinful desires and passions. In this sense flesh includes not only the physical body but the spiritual side as well.[134]

The flesh is terminal; it is cancerous (Isaiah 1:4-6); it WILL die; it cannot produce life, only death. But because of the **New Covenant,** believers are given a new nature. By the way, in repeating what was covered in Part One of the book, through the **New Covenant** we did not get a renewed old nature but a brand-new nature that does not sin (II Corinthians 5:17; I John 3:6, 9; 5:18). The **New Covenant** is exactly that, a NEW and not renewed covenant. Why do you think Paul said the following in Philippians 1:21 and Galatians 2:20:

---

[133] Arnold Fruchtenbaum. *Faith Alone: The Condition of Our Salvation – An Exposition of the Book of Galatians.* San Antonio, TX: Ariel Press, 2014, p. 25.

[134] Richard Hill, *Freedom in Messiah: A Messianic Jewish Roots Commentary on the Book of Galatians. Las Vegas,* NV: S-E-L-F Publishing, 2015, pp. 87-88.

> *For me to live is Messiah, to die is gain.* (Philippians 1:21)
>
> *I am crucified with Messiah: nevertheless, I live; yet not I, but Messiah lives in me: and the life which I now live in the flesh I live by the faith of the Son of God, who loved me, and gave Himself for me.* (Galatians 2:20)

If your goal in life is to be a faithful Torah observer, your flesh WILL fail you; and the fault lies with *you* and not with the Law of Moses, for it was *holy, just and good* (Romans 7:12). God knowing all this gave us the **New Covenant** which involved a New Nature and has empowered you to live in obedience when you yield to the Ruach Ha-Kodesh (Romans 6:11-14). He perfects, but the flesh does not! In this section I have also been answering the *fourth rhetorical question*. The flesh accomplished nothing but death, but the Spirit gave us life, will fulfill it, and finish it in us (Romans 8:29).

In the *fifth rhetorical question,* Paul dealt with the extreme Judaizer concerning circumcision. Today, in our century, the issue encompasses teachings on degrees of Torah observance, such as the Hebrew Roots Movement, legalism, as well as wearing all the religious garb that observance involves. Again, a quote from Arnold Fruchtenbaum addresses this issue:

> You have suffered so much for your faith. Was it all for nothing since you cannot be saved until you are circumcised? The thrust of the question is: You did not suffer so many things for nothing, did you? If up to now they are still unsaved because they have not yet been circumcised, it means they have suffered all those persecutions as believers for nothing.

Fruchtenbaum states it well concerning the extreme Judaizer then and today. But in this present day in the "religious" Messianic climate, you are looked down upon because you do not keep Sabbath, because you do not wear a head covering called a kippah (yarmulke), or tzitziot (called the *fringes* in gospels) nor use the tefillin (phylacteries) or at least wear the prayer shawl (Tallit) on the Sabbath in worship. There are some that wear these items and observe certain laws out of their Christian Liberty and to be identified with the larger Jewish community. That is fine as long as that does not lead to promoting the practice as making anyone a better believer for doing so.

However, many within the Messianic Jewish Movement have been persuaded to become Torah observant; and then they exert pressure to convince other believers to do so, which is unbiblical. The other sad statistic is that many of the exporters are Gentiles, and the Law was never given to them in the first place; they are not even Jewish. Some have even gone so far as to "convert" to Messianic Judaism. If you "converted" as a Gentile to follow Messiah initially, it is a step backward to "convert" again to something lesser than what you have in Messiah. While Gentiles can play at being Jewish, the Law was never for them.

Do not be deceived into believing that to be a good "Messianic" you must keep Torah. You can do all the spiritual twisting and turning you want, but when you stand before Messiah in *the Day of Messiah* (I Corinthians 1:8; Philippians 1:6, 10), your beliefs and practices of keeping the Torah for justification will be as *wood, hay, and stubble* (I Corinthians 3:12-15) because your motivation and purpose is biblically wrong.

The ***sixth rhetorical question*** that Paul asks is whether the miracles that were done among the Galatians were done by the Law or by the Spirit who ministered among you? The word *miracles* gives the wrong emphasis. The word *dunamis* means "power, might, ability, force." The emphasis is on the power that the Ruach Ha-Kodesh worked among them which was exhibited to them in two miracles. In Acts 14 when Paul first preached in Derbe and Lystra, the power of the Ruach was exhibited in two miracles, the impotent man who was crippled from birth (14:8-10) and the stoning of Paul who was left for dead but arose and entered into the city (14:19-20). Who performed these works of *dunamis*: *the works of the Law or by the hearing of faith*? On six counts, Paul reasons with them to help them understand that it was not the Law in any of the cases but the hearing of Faith. Torah observance is a spiritual distraction from the real emphasis of what God is doing through Messiah and the **New Covenant**, and the Law of Messiah that came from it.

Galatians 3:13a

Paul continues by saying *Messiah has redeemed us from the curse of the Law*. *Redeemed* is the Greek word *exagorazo* meaning "to redeem, deliver, buy back, or rescue." It denotes "to release by paying a ransom price," and the price that was paid was the blood of the **New Covenant**, the Lamb of God that would satisfy the holy demands of a holy God (propitiation).[135]

Propitiation
I John 2:1-10

Propitiation is the work of Christ that satisfies all the claims of divine holiness, righteousness, and justice, so that God is free to act on behalf of sinners.

p. 95, J. Dwight Pentecost. *Things Which Become Sound Doctrine; Propitiation.*

---

[135] Dwight Pentecost, *Things Which Become Sound Doctrine; Propitiation.* Westwood, NJ: Fleming Revell Co, 1965, pp. 93-101.

Remember, Abraham was justified before God by Faith 645 years[136] before there was the Mosaic Law (Romans 4:2-5), as Paul mentions in Galatians 3:17:

> *And this I say, that the Law, that was confirmed before of God in Messiah, the Law, which was four hundred and thirty years after, cannot disannul, that it should make the promise of none effect.*

If you are a sinner; and, yes, every one of us is a sinner – even Torah-observant sinners need to be redeemed – the law could not and did not redeem sinners. Only the blood of the **NEW Covenant**, the blood of the Lamb of God, can redeem all of us when we embrace Him by Faith (Habakkuk 2:4; Galatians 3:11; Romans 1:17; Hebrews 10:38). Torah observant folks, I ask if the Law could redeem sinners? It could not redeem anyone, so why hold onto it with a vise grip? Because they have been convinced by the misuse of Scripture that the curse of the Law can by no means be the Torah, that the Torah never becomes unimportant or irrelevant to its followers. Again, I will repeat that there is nothing wrong with the Law; it is *holy just and good* (Romans 7:12). The problem is that you and I are enslaved by our sin nature, and the Law in the Torah cannot release us from that! The Torah had a purpose, which we will get into shortly; but the purpose was fulfilled in Messiah (Matthew 5:17). He as the Author, brought His own Law, the Mosaic Law, to an end AND replaced it through the blood of the **New Covenant;** and a whole new standard of law in the <u>Law of Messiah</u> was given. Now look at the whole previous context in Galatians 3:13-16:

> *¹³ Messiah has redeemed[137] us from the curse of the Law, being made a curse for us: for it is written* [Deuteronomy 21:23], *cursed is every one that hangs on a tree*: *¹⁴ That the blessing of Abraham might come on the Gentiles* [Genesis 12:3; 26:4; 28:14] *through Yeshua Ha-Mashiach* (Isaiah 42:6; 49:6); *that we might receive the promise of the Spirit through faith. ¹⁵ Brothers, I speak after the manner of men; Though it be but a man's covenant, yet if it be confirmed, no man disannuls, or adds to it. ¹⁶ Now to Abraham and his seed were the promises made. He said not, and to seeds, as of many; but as of one, and to your* **SEED**,[138] *which is Messiah.*

---

[136] **Date problem:** From the time of Genesis 12 when the Abrahamic Covenant was made would be approximately 645 years to the giving of the Mosaic Law in 1446 BC. However, Paul uses the figure of 430 years. We know that Israel spent 430 years in Egypt. So most likely Paul is referring to the confirmation of The Abrahamic Covenant to Jacob before he entered Egypt (Genesis 46:1-4).

[137] J. Dwight Pentecost, *Things Which Become Sound Doctrine; Redeemed/Redemption*. Westwood, NJ: Fleming Revell Co., 1965, pp. 73-82.

[138] **Seed**: The word *seed* can be used two ways: (1) as a ***compound singular*** meaning many, or (2) an ***absolute singular*** referring to only one - the *SEED*. Illustration: In Genesis 12:7

> **Redeemed / Redemption**
> **I Peter 1:3-20**
>
> *Redeemed* is a word that emphasizes an act: it is the act of setting free, the act of liberating.
>
> It is the word which means "to go shopping" or "to go into the market to purchase." ... It is a redemption by purchase, and the purchase price is stated – it is redemption by blood. ... When we were purchased out from the curse of the law and bondage to sin we were purchased out so completely and effectively that we can never be returned to that slave market again.
>
> p. 75, J. Dwight Pentecost. *Things Which Become Sound Doctrine; Redeemed/Redemption, p. 75.*

In Galatians 3:13, Yeshua became a curse because He took our sin upon Himself (II Corinthians 5:21) and took your place on the cursed tree.[139] The Law in the Torah was impotent to do anything for us; it just pointed out our sin and condemned us as unholy, unjust, and not good. It was a pointer to Messiah who fulfilled it (Matthew 5:17) and brought an end to the curse through the **New Covenant**. What was the purpose of Yeshua redeeming[140] us from the curse? Get ready, it is not difficult: to bring the blessing of Abraham to the Gentiles (Genesis 12:3) and to the Jewish people as verse 14 states. Yeshua's "calling was not only to bless Jewish people but also to be a *covenant* and a *light to the Gentiles* (Isaiah 42:5-6; 49:6)."[141]

We see in verse 15 how certain God's provision is. If a legal agreement cannot be broken among men, then God who made an unconditional legal contract with Abraham, He being a holy God, even more so cannot break it, nor can it be spiritualized away by Replacement (Fulfilled), Amillenial, or Covenant Reform

---

the word *seed* is a compound singular meaning the future descendants of Abraham; whereas, here it is an ***absolute singular*** meaning only *one* – The Messiah – as used in Genesis 22:18. (See Arnold Fruchtenbaum's *Ha-Mashiach: The Messiah of the Hebrew Scriptures.* San Antonio, TX: Ariel Press, 2019. p. 9.)

[139] **Tree**: The Greek word is *xulon* which means "wood, timber, and tree"; now that is obvious, isn't it? Now for some background in Joshua (10:22-27), the five Canaanite kings were killed and hung on trees. First, when the kings were alive, the soldiers put their feet on their necks to show complete subjection and victory. Then, being cursed, the kings were killed, each body was hung on a tree, then they were buried in the morning in accordance with Deuteronomy 21:22-23.

[140] **Redemption / Redeemed**: Dwight Pentecost, *Things Which Become Sound Doctrine.* Westwood, NJ: Fleming Revell Co., 1965, pp.73-82.

[141] Richard Hill, *Freedom in Messiah: A Messianic Jewish Roots Commentary on the Book of Galatians.* Las Vegas, NV: S-E-L-F Publishing, 2015, pp. 112-113.

theologies. Now God made a covenant with Abraham that through him all the families (ethnicities) of the earth will be blessed, having the opportunity given to them to be *redeemed* when believing on Him in Faith. They are blessed through the Messiah in the **New Covenant**, not through Moses! and not through the Law! Before moving on to the next section of verses, we need to start with verse 19; for Paul uses three words closely knit together, and they are *added, till* and ***SEED****:*

> *What purpose does the Law then serve? It was **added** because of transgressions, **till** the **SEED** should come to whom the promise was made; and it was ordained by angels in the hand of a mediator.*
> [bold print mine]

Let me give you some excerpts from another Jewish believer in his commentary on Galatians:

> *Wherefore then serves the law?* If the law has no place in salvation, why did God bother to give it? If the law cannot justify a person, why was it ordered in the first place? This is an intelligent question when we consider that it is being asked by one [Paul] who had been all his lifetime in bondage to the Law.
>
> The answer to this seemingly baffling question is provided for us in the very Scriptures of the Law. Before the Scriptures present to us the Law of Sinai, they tell us of the Covenant of Grace [Promise], God's free promise to Abraham and to his Seed, which promise is fulfilled in Christ. Yet the Mosaic Code had a divine mission to perform. ... *It was added because of transgressions, till the Seed should come to whom the promise was made; and it was ordained by angels in the hand of a mediator.*
>
> The next phrase, till the **Seed** should come to whom the promise was made, shows that the Law was a temporary arrangement, extending from Moses to Jesus Christ, for our Lord is that **Seed** to whom the promise was made. ... It was a temporary covenant given for temporary purposes, and when Christ the **Seed** came, He fulfilled the Law (Matthew 5:17-20), ... The law remains in force to condemn the wicked (I Timothy 1:8-14) .... The law had its commencement at Sinai through Moses and its consummation at Calvary through Jesus Christ. ... the Law had no power in itself to declare the sinner righteous, ... the Law has no power to impart life or to justify. ...
> [bolding mine]
>
> We have a law against stealing; still men steal. Why? Because the Law can neither break the habit of stealing in a man nor can it force him to quit stealing. It can exact the penalty for its violations, but it cannot change the heart of man in begetting a desire to keep the law.

> The words, *we were kept in ward* [Galatians 3:23], mean that we were perpetual prisoners under the Law before the death and resurrection of Jesus Christ and the coming of the Holy Spirit at Pentecost. The idea expressed is that of a military term, and it suggests that we were held in bondage by the Law. Here is a prison scene in which Israel, to whom the Law was given, is primarily in view, since the Gentiles were never under the Law at any time. As long as Israel was under the Law she was guarded as a prisoner in bondage by the Law. But during the Dispensation of Law the coming of Messiah was kept before the people as imminent, each generation living in expectancy of this prophesied event. However, when Jesus came and revealed the Faith which was once delivered to the saints, He led out from the bondage of the Law all who heard His voice and followed Him.[142] [bracketed verse is mine]

I challenge you to consider his evaluation of the Law and that it is a futile exercise to try and keep it instead of abiding in the **New Covenant** and the Law of Messiah.

The Greek word *till* is *achri;* when followed by the word *hou*, it means "as long as" or "until." Until what? Until the **SEED** comes, Messiah.[143] Two other observations, first by John MacArthur, for the Jewish people should have known that the Law was not eternal but temporary and they should have understood the purpose of the Law:

> The Law ... was added to show the depth of man's transgressions against God. It was given to drive him to desperate guilt and the awareness of his need for a Deliverer.[144]

The second observation comes from Hogg & Vine and Wuest in stating the words *it was added* is the Greek word *prostithemi* meaning "to place beside."[145] So the Law of Moses was added because of man's transgressions until the promised Deliverer would come. The Law was not eternal; it was temporary, added or placed beside until the Redeemer / Deliverer would come.

---

[142] Lehman Strauss, *Galatians & Ephesians*. Port Colborne, Ontario, Canada: Gospel Folio Press, 2010, pp. 47-51.

[143] Richard Hill, *Freedom in Messiah: A Messianic Jewish Roots Commentary on the Book of Galatians*. Las Vegas, NV: S-E-L-F Publishing, 2015, p. 124.

[144] John MacArthur, *The MacArthur New Testament Commentary* [on] *Galatians*. Chicago, IL: Moody Press, 1987, p. 86.

[145] C. F. Hogg & W. E. Vine. *The Epistle to the Galatians*. Grand Rapids, MI: Kregel Publications, 1921, p. 149.

Kenneth S. Wuest. *Wuest's Word Studies in the Greek New Testament – Galatians*. Grand Rapids, MI: Eerdmans Publishing Co., 1966, p. 105.

The end of verse 19 is very interesting concerning the fact that *it* [the Law] *was ordained by angels in the hand of a mediator.* Scriptures clearly tell us that angels were involved in the giving of the Law (Acts 7:53, Hebrews 2:2); however, when we go through Exodus chapters 19 through 20 and following there is no mention of any angels, only fire, cloud, and smoke. We recognize these phenomena as the Shechinah glory of God in the Second Person of the Godhead, which we understand through progressive Scripture to be the pre-incarnate Yeshua Ha-Mashiach Who is also revealed to man as The Angel of the LORD, but that reference is singular and not plural. So, angels were involved; but the Scriptures do not give us details as to how. So Paul says that the Law was *ordained by angels* **and** then Paul continues by saying *in the hand of a mediator.* Who is the mediator? The first mediator of the Law was Moses, for he acted as a mediator between Israel and God; whereas, angels also acted as mediators between God and Moses. Now in the **New Covenant**, the Mediator between Israel and God is not Moses, but the God/Man, Yeshua, Who *inaugurated* the **New Covenant** (I Timothy 2:5; Hebrews 8:6; 9:15; 12:24).[146]

As Paul piles the facts and the evidence together in chapter 3, he is clearly teaching that the Law was *holy, just and good*, but man is unholy, unjust, and anything but good. The Law points to one Who would fulfill it, and that One was Yeshua and His work on the cursed tree that ended, terminated, ***rendered inoperative*** the Law of Moses in the Torah. The focus in the New Testament is not on Moses but on Messiah. We are not to be imitators of Moses, but imitators of Messiah. Moses and the Law, which is embedded in the Torah, does not even come close in dealing with the total and complete depravity of man and the abundant new life given in the **New Covenant** by the Messiah in the law that He issued through the Apostles, the Law of Messiah.

Now we will move onto the next few verses, to which I have particularly alluded, where Paul adds an unbelievable number of facts that reveal that the Law was completely replaced by Messiah. Let's continue.

Galatians 3:19-29

In *Galatians 3:19-29*

Before entering into this section, there is one very important word that Paul uses ten times between Galatians 3:14, 16-19, 21-22, and 29 with two times in chapter 4 (4:23, 29). First, we must describe what the ***Promise*** to Abraham included. This is the word used for the Dispensation of Promise, given to Abraham. Arnold Fruchtenbaum points out that there are fourteen provisions to the Abrahamic

---

[146] Arnold Fruchtenbaum, *Faith Alone: The Condition of Our Salvation – An Exposition of the Book of Galatians.* San Antonio, TX: Ariel Press, 2014, p. 32.

Covenant.[147] One of those provisions or *promises* dealt specifically with salvation to both Jewish people and Gentiles as recorded in Genesis 12:3b: *and in you [Abraham] shall all the families [ethnicities] of the earth be blessed,* coupled with Genesis 22:18: *and in your* **SEED** *shall all the nations of the earth be blessed.* This will be directly fulfilled in the **New Covenant** of Jeremiah 31. Salvation will come through the Jewish people to the Gentiles through Abraham in the absolute singular **SEED** (Genesis 22:18; Galatians 3:16, 19), Who is Messiah Yeshua. This *promise* of the **SEED** and Salvation becomes central to belief. For mankind to be *justified and sanctified*[148] comes ONLY through that **SEED** by Grace through Faith (Ephesians 2:8-9). The Law had absolutely no effect on the fulfillment of God's *promises* through the Abrahamic Covenant for there is a 430 year gap of time between the two covenants, and the Mosaic Law is a mere **temporary** supplement under the Abrahamic Covenant *until the fulness of time*. Paul references that a contract on a human level cannot be altered once made (Galatians 3:15). God made an unconditional covenant with Abraham leaving no obligations upon Abraham because he was already justified by Faith before God (Genesis 15:6). God made the *Promises* and obligated Himself, not Abraham.

Justification
Romans 3:21 – 4:8

Justification is the divine pronouncement that the one who is in Christ Jesus is fully acceptable to God, Himself; we have been declared righteous when believing on Him.

Sanctification
I Corinthians 1:1-3, 26-31

This involves three aspects:

First at salvation, in our past we have been *set apart* unto God upon believing in the finished work of Messiah on the cross. Our *position* is that we are holy, saints because of His work.

Second is the experiential side of sanctification in the *present*; we are exhorted to let our position presently be conformed to our position as being set apart in Messiah.

Third is our *future* sanctification at the Rapture or death, when we will be sanctified in the future.

---

[147] Arnold Fruchtenbaum. *Israelology: The Missing Link in Systematic Theology.* San Antonio, TX: Ariel Press, 2018, pp. 552-553.

[148] See Teaching Block on Justification & Sanctification (p. 155): J. Dwight Pentecost, *Things Which Become Sound Doctrine.* Westwood, NJ: Fleming Revell Company, 1965, pp. 102-122 and 113-122.

One other fact before moving on, remember that Abraham when he was justified by Faith (Genesis 15:6) was an uncircumcised Gentile, and that fact did not change until Genesis 17. He was circumcised a year before the birth of the promised son Yitzchak (Isaac) through whom centuries later Messiah would come. It also means that Yitzchak was a product of a circumcised Abraham (Genesis 21) also 400-plus years before the Law, and that Ishmael was the product of his uncircumcision (Genesis 16). This subject will come into play later in Galatians 4:22-31. Now let us look at the passage at hand, Galatians 3:20-29:

> *[20] Now a mediator is not a mediator of one, but God is one. [21] Is the law then against the promises of God? God forbid: for if there had been a Law given which could have given life, verily righteousness should have been by the Law. [22] But the scripture [Tanakh] has concluded all under sin, that the promise by faith of Yeshua Ha-Mashiach might be given to them that believe. [23] But before faith came, we were kept under the Law, shut up unto the faith which should afterwards be revealed. [24] For this reason the Law was our schoolmaster [pedagogue] to bring us unto Messiah, that we might be justified by faith. [25] But after that faith has come, we are no longer under a schoolmaster. [26] For you are all the children of God[149] by faith in Messiah Yeshua. [27] For as many of you as have been baptized into Messiah have put on Messiah. [28] There is neither Jew nor Greek, there is neither bond nor free, there is neither male nor female: for you are all one in Messiah Yeshua. [29] And if you are Messiah's, then are you Abraham's seed, and heirs according to the promise.*

In verse 18 *inheritance* is the Greek word *kleronomia* and means "possession," or "portion." Simply put, the believer's inheritance of salvation is by the means of the Promise, NOT by means of the Law, the Law does not annul the Promise. So, the Promise given to Abraham has priority over the Mosaic Law. The Promise was that justification would come by Faith, not by Law.

Verse 19 three significant words used by Paul are repeated again to show their significance and importance. He repeatedly uses the words ***added***, ***till*** or until, and the ***SEED***. These three words are very closely knitted together, as David Levy, another Jewish believer with Friends of Israel Gospel Ministry, points out.

> ***First***, Paul states: *it* [the Law] *was **added** because of transgression*, not for salvation or godly living. The giving of the Law had the

---

[149] **Children of God**: Just a seed thought that will be explained in my next book: Why are Israel and believers today called "children"? Worse yet, why are Israel and believers called "sheep"? There is a reason why believers in the *Tanakh* and believers in the New Testament are likened unto *children* and *sheep*.

specific purpose of showing sin for what sin is. This purpose of the Law is also given in Romans 3:20 and 5:20. ***Second***, is the Greek word *achri* meaning ***till*** or until. *Till* what? The law was an addition to the Abrahamic Covenant and so it had a definite beginning point; it was not always operative. The very word *till*, or until, emphasizes the fact that the Mosaic Law was intended to be temporary! How Temporary? This is brought out by his ***third*** point, *till the seed should come*. It was temporary; it was in effect only until the *seed* came. Once the *seed* came, the Law would no longer be in effect. In verse 16, Paul identified the seed to be the Messiah. The Law came to an end with the death of Yeshua, the Messiah.[150] [bolding mine]

The word *added* has the idea of being placed alongside the covenant of promise, meaning that the Law was supplementary and subordinate to it and in no way added conditions for salvation.[151]

The word **SEED** in Greek is *sperma*, and in Hebrew is *zera*. This word SEED Paul referenced comes from Genesis 22:18 which refers directly to Messiah. So, the Law was a temporary addition, supplemental material because of sin (transgressions), **added until** the **SEED** came. It had absolutely no bearing on the Abrahamic Covenant.

The Law was ordained by Angel*s* (Acts 7:53; Hebrews 2:2), separated by two mediators: Angels mediated between God and the Jewish people, and the other *in the hand of a mediator* – this was Moses. Both mediators acted on behalf of God to the Jewish people.

Verse 21 The Law is not in conflict with the Promise. If the Law could have produced life, then righteousness would have been through the Law. But righteousness did not and could not come from the Law. The law pointed out sin and condemned the sinner, but it did not produce life. Only *the Prophet Like Moses* (Deuteronomy 18:18-19) could produce that (John 10:10); the Mosaic Law produced the exact opposite, *death* and *condemnation* (II Corinthians 3:7, 9).

Verse 22 points out from the *Tanakh* that *all are under sin*; we are sinners. The value of the *Tanakh* is of utmost importance. Because the Law system of the Torah was **rendered inoperative** does not mean that the *Tanakh* is now unimportant. The *Tanakh* is extremely important on multifaceted points, as referenced in Part One of

---

[150] Arnold Fruchtenbaum, *Faith Alone: The Condition of Our Salvation – An Exposition of the Book of Galatians.* San Antonio, TX: Ariel Press, 2014, p. 32.

[151] David Levy. *Guarding the Gospel of Grace.* Bellmawr, NJ: Friends of Israel Gospel Ministry, 1997, p. 70. Levy quoted from Fred Dickason, Jr. *From Bondage to Freedom: Studies in Galatians, part 1.* Chicago, IL: Moody Bible Institute, 1963, p. 28.

this book. But in this context, it is the Promise of salvation that comes through Yeshua Ha-Mashiach that supersedes the Law that is here in view.

Verse 23:

> *Kept under the Law – Kept* in Greek is *phroureo* and means to guard and keep watch over. *Phroureo* is found to be in the indicative mood, imperfect tense, and passive voice. This means that it is a positive and clear-cut statement with continuous action in the past where we are the receivers of the action. The Greek grammar is very clear in that we had no choice in the matter: The Law performed the action in that it continuously was our master and guard over us making sure we stayed prisoners to our sin. The Law did nothing to help us escape our sin but in fact helped us to stay prisoner to our sin. This is the very reason God promised that the **Seed** would come. ... Not only were we kept in imprisonment under the Law, but we were *shut up* to the Faith as well.[152] [Bold print mine]

> *Shut up* is the Greek word *sunkleio* meaning "to enclose, imprison, or consign." Paul pictures the Law as a jailer. What did the Law do? It kept them in jail. It carries the idea of being kept under special military guard. The Law was bondage that Jewish people were *shut up* under till they are released by Messiah and by believing in Him and His finished work on the Cross.

Verse 25 The Faith – includes the definite article in the Greek.

> *Under* is the Greek word *hupo* which has many meanings, but this word indicates subordination as under the schoolmaster or *pedagogue*.

In *verses 24-25* Paul uses the illustration of the Law being a guardian of a child[153] until he comes of age. The Greek word *pedagogue* means far more than a schoolmaster, as reflected by a Jewish believer:

> The Law functioned as a Pedagogue, for *the Law was our schoolmaster to bring us to Christ, that we might be justified by faith.* The word schoolmaster does not provide a proper concept of the Greek word *paidagogos*, which means a child custodian or disciplinarian. The *pedagogue* was a slave, not a teacher, who governed children between the ages of 6-16 for wealthy Greek and Roman households. The *pedagogue's* function was to take the

---

[152] Richard Hill, *Freedom in Messiah: A Messianic Jewish Roots Commentary on the Book of Galatians.* Las Vegas, NV: S-E-L-F Publishing, 2015, p. 128.

[153] **Child:** Here the word *child* in verse 26 is understood. Why?

children to school, correct their moral behavior, protect them from harm, and prepare them for adulthood. In like manner, the Law functioned as a temporary custodian restricting sinful mankind under its provisions, so that only through Christ could people be justified by Faith.[154]

Another Jewish believer states:

> The Law could not impart eternal life like the promise did. However, the Law could lead us to Messiah [which is described in the word *paidagogos* above]. ... the Law was to be our strict supervisor or guide to bring us to the saving grace of Messiah through faith.[155] [brackets mine]

So, the point is when *a pedagogue* has fulfilled his responsibility, he as the guardian is no longer needed. The Messiah has come who fulfilled the Law, and in fulfilling the Law He brought it to an end, every *jot and tittle* of the Law (Matthew 5:17-18), so the *pedagogue* – the Law – is no longer needed.

One Torah observant author took eight pages to try and get around the obvious, that when the *pedagogue* was come there was no further need of the Law. Now, in Galatians 3 ***verse 27***, Gentile and Jewish believers have been *baptized into Messiah*. This is in keeping with I Corinthians 12:13 that speaks of the moment a person believes, *For by one Spirit* [the Ruach Ha-Kodesh] *we are all baptized into the one body* of Messiah. Galatians 3:27 says, *For as many of you have been baptized into Messiah have put on Messiah.* For Jewish people, that means laying aside the Law; as for the Gentile, the Law was NEVER given to them. Baptism is illustrated in I Corinthians 12:13 and also in Romans 6:3-4:

> [13] *For by one Ruach* [Spirit] *are we all baptized into one body, whether we be Jews or Gentiles, whether we be bond* [slaves] *or free; and have been all made to drink into one spirit.*
> (I Corinthians 12:13)
>
> [3] *Don't you know, that so many of us as were baptized into Yeshua Messiah were baptized into His death?* [4] *Therefore, we are buried with Him by baptism into death: that like as Messiah was raised up from the dead by the glory of the Father, even so we also should walk in newness of life.* (Romans 6:3-4)

---

[154] David Levy, *Guarding the Gospel of Grace*. Bellmawr, NJ: Friends of Israel Gospel Ministry, 1997, p. 72.

[155] Richard Hill, Freedom in Messiah: A Messianic Jewish Roots Commentary on the Book of Galatians. Las Vegas, NV: S-E-L-F Publishing, 2015, pp. 129-130.

We as believers are to *walk in the newness of life*, and not by the letter of the Law which kills (II Corinthians 3:6). We do not now walk in the Law of Moses but *walk in the newness of life* provided by the Mediator of the **New Covenant**. That **New Covenant** does not leave us without law! For the **New Covenant** provided the Law of Messiah to walk in as we walk in the newness of His life, not in the life of Moses who did not provide life or salvation.

Paul tells the Romans (13:14) to *put on Messiah*, and not to continue to put on the Law of Moses. He tells the Ephesians (4:24) and Colossians (3:10-12) to *put on the new Man,* a reference to man's New nature in Messiah, how to live the new life in Messiah. Paul also reminds them of the things they are to *put off* and *put away*, things to *mortify* and *put off*.

> *But **put on** the Lord Yeshua Messiah, and make no provision for the flesh, to fulfill the lusts thereof* (Romans 13:14).
>
> *And that you **put on** the New man, created after the likeness of God in righteousness and true holiness* (Ephesians 4:24).
>
> [10] *And have **put on** the New man, which is renewed in knowledge after the image of Him that created him:* [11] *Where there is neither Greek nor Jew, circumcision nor uncircumcision, Barbarian, Scythian, bond nor free: but Messiah is all, and in all.* [12] ***Put on** therefore, as the elect of God, holy and beloved, compassionate hearts, kindness, humbleness of mind, meekness, and patience …* (Colossians 3:10-12).

Does Moses cause you to *put on the New man,* or is it the Messiah, *the Prophet like Moses* who directs and enables us to do this?

The Romans, Ephesians, and Colossians and Torah-observant folks should note, you are to *put on* Messiah and make no provision for the flesh which works hand in glove with the Law of Moses (Romans 6-8). To the Ephesians, note that you are NOW *created in righteousness and true holiness* by the Mediator of the **New Covenant**, and not by the mediator of the *old covenant*.

The Colossians are prompted to be *renewed in knowledge after the image of* Messiah by living out that newness of life on a daily basis, not living out the inferior Law of Moses. Nowhere in the Gospels or the Epistles of the New Testament is any believer told or commanded to put on Moses!

Putting on Messiah and walking in the newness of life does not involve the Mosaic Law, but it does involve the Law of Messiah and Yeshua's commandment (John 13:34):

> *A new commandment I give unto you, that you love one another; as I have loved you, that you also love one another.*

The truth of Messiah's new commandment *is verified by His ministry and through the writings of His Apostles.* Out of His **new** commandment (John 13:34), and then through His Apostles, come His commandment**s**, which are referenced by John in his First Epistle (I John 2:3-8).

> *³ And hereby we do know that we know Him, if we keep His commandment**s**. ⁴ He that says, I know Him, and does not keep His commandment**s**, is a liar, and the truth is not in him. ⁵ But whoever keeps His word, in him truly is the love of God perfected: by this we know that we are in Him. ⁶ Whoever says he abides in Him ought to walk in the same way in which He walked. ⁷ Brethren, I write no new commandment unto, but an old commandment that you had from the beginning. The old commandment is the word which you have heard from the beginning. ⁸ Again, a new commandment I am writing to you, which is true in Him and in you: because the darkness is past, and the true light now shines.* [Emphasis mine]

As we have moved through the issue that Torah observance is NOT validated in the Epistles to the Church, whether in Peter's and Paul's testimony at the Jerusalem Council, whether to the Romans or the Corinthians, or even in the heavy weight of evidence from the Book of Galatians.

Snapshot from Ephesians

In Ephesians 2:4-22 Paul states that we were made alive, ***regenerated***[156] – the Jews (who were *near*) and Gentiles (who were *far*) – by Messiah who brought both into union together in the body of Messiah by Grace through Faith.

Regeneration

Regeneration is that act of God whereby He regenerates our soul and makes us alive spiritually to Him. The word means to be "born again, born a second time" (John 3:7). Once man was alive spiritually to God at Creation, but with the fall of man in the Garden man became spiritually dead, which was carried over to all men (Romans 5:12). The concept of *regeneration* is the taking of someone who was alive to God, but died spiritually because of sin, but was transformed by God through the finished work of Messiah at Calvary. He made us alive in Him (Ephesians 2:1-6), regenerating the heart to living eternally. We are now new Creations (II Corinthians 5:17).

I wonder if Torah observant readers have read the History in the *Tanakh* and the Gospels, and how it has proven that the Law cannot produce life and righteousness by the works of flesh? The standard of the Law is no longer necessary because the Messiah has now provided a new standard with *life* and *righteousness,* the <u>Law of Messiah,</u> by being the *Mediator* of the **New Covenant.** For the Law of Moses never did and could not produce either righteousness or life. Both Jews and Gentiles are now *one New man* in Messiah; no works of the Law are involved or necessary. In Ephesians 3:2-9, Paul presents the Mystery, unseen by Moses and the Prophets, the union of Jews and Gentiles without any qualifiers; instead, the fulfillment of Genesis 12:3 is in process where it says through *you all the families of the earth will be blessed.*

Both Jews and Gentiles were *dead*[157] *in trespasses and sins,* and history clearly presents that Jews and Gentile *walked according to the course of this world*, according to its master, the *prince of the power of the air*. Even walking in the law of Moses cannot quicken you or make you alive spiritually. You needed to be quickened, made alive, ***regenerated*** (Jeremiah 31:34; Titus 3:5), and that did not come through Moses and Torah keeping, it came through the Mediator of the **New**

---

[156] See teaching block above. Dwight Pentecost, *Things Which Become Sound Doctrine: Regeneration.* Westwood, NJ: Fleming Revell Publishers, 1965, pp. 30-39.

[157] **Dead**: This is referring to being spiritually dead before God.

Covenant Who promised a *regenerated* heart. Lehman Strauss, a Jewish believer states:

> The verses before us contain a triad of evil and a triad of good:
>
> > (a) The three ravaging forces are the world, the flesh, and the devil (Ephesians 2:1-3).
> >
> > (b) The three redeeming facts are mercy, love, and grace (Ephesians 2:4-5).
> >
> > (c) The three resulting features are – (Ephesians 2:5-6)
> >
> > That the saints are made alive together with Christ,
> > Raised up together with Christ,
> > And made to sit together in heavenly places in Christ.[158]

Now look at this triad of triads, my dear fellow believers who may be tempted to practice Torah observance. Did the Law free you from this wicked age? Did it free you from your flesh and the old nature? Did it free you from the devil's dominion over you to whom you belonged before the finished work of Messiah at Calvary in *inaugurating* the **New Covenant**? The answer to all three questions is No.

Did you receive God's unmerited favor from the Law? No! Did the Law benefit you in His love when you diminished His free gift of salvation in Messiah Yeshua alone? No! Did the Law give you His grace, His unmerited favor; for by His Grace were you saved through Faith, Faith in Who? – Messiah Yeshua. Did the Law do that? No! Have you ever studied the benefits received in the Jewish **New Covenant** versus the *condemnation* and *death* of the Jewish *old covenant*? Now let us look together at the rest of Ephesians 2.

> *⁶ And has raised us up together, and made us sit together in heavenly places in Messiah Yeshua. ⁷ That in the ages to come He might show the exceeding riches of His grace in His kindness toward us through Messiah Yeshua.*

Verses 6-7 from Wuest's Expanded Greek Translation[159] is absolutely fascinating; it takes my breath away in wonder. Wuest in his translation is very sensitive to the Greek language and its tenses.

---

[158] Lehman Strauss, *Galatians & Ephesians*. Port Colborne, Ontario, Canada: Gospel Folio Press, 2010, p. 133.

> *⁶ And raised us with Him and seated us with Him in the heavenly places in Messiah Yeshua, ⁷ in order that He might exhibit for His own glory in the ages that will pile themselves one upon another in continuous succession, the surpassing wealth of His grace in kindness to us in Messiah Yeshua.*

Now you Judaizers and Torah observant folks, could the *old covenant* of the Law do any of that? Could Moses whom you revere in respect and honor do that? The answer is obviously a resounding NO. Now let us move on to Ephesians 2:8-16:

> *⁸ For by grace are you saved through faith; and that not of yourselves: it is the gift of God: ⁹ **Not of works**, lest any man should boast. ¹⁰ For we are His workmanship, created in Messiah Yeshua unto good works, which God has before ordained that we should walk in them. ¹¹ Wherefore remember, that you being in time past **Gentiles** in the flesh, who are called **Uncircumcision** by that which is called the Circumcision in the flesh made by hands; ¹² That at that time you were **without** Messiah, being **aliens** from the commonwealth of Israel, and strangers from the **covenants of promise**, having **no hope**, and **without God** in the world: ¹³ But now in Messiah Yeshua you who sometimes were **far off** are made nigh by the blood of Christ. ¹⁴ For He is our peace, Who has made both one, and has broken down the **middle wall of partition between us**; ¹⁵ Having **abolished** in His flesh the enmity, even the Law of commandments contained in ordinances; for to make in Himself of two, one New man, so making peace; ¹⁶ And that He might **reconcile**[160] both unto God in one body by the Cross, thereby killing the hostility.*

Look at the absolutely hopeless situation of Gentiles without the **New Covenant** as Paul piles one fact upon another fact to show their hopelessness. Let's list their situation before the **New Covenant** was *inaugurated*:

- You were a *Gentile,* often referred to with a very unflattering word by the Circumcision, as *dogs.*
- You were an *uncircumcised,* heathen Gentile, as even David referred to Goliath.
- You as a Gentile were *without Messiah.*

---

[159] Kenneth Wuest, *New Testament an Expanded Translation.* Grand Rapids, MI: Eerdmans Publishing Co, 1962, pp. 450-451.

[160] Teaching Block on **R**econciliation: J. Dwight Pentecost. *Things Which Become Sound Doctrine.* Westwood, NJ: Fleming Revell Company, 1965, pp. 83-92. (See p. 152 of this book for the teaching block.)

- You were *aliens from the commonwealth of Israel.*
- You were a *stranger* from the Covenants and Promises given to Israel by God.
- You were absolutely *without hope* spiritually.
- You were *without God* to trust in, with only your pagan idols.
- You were a *far off*, everything was against you as a Gentile.
- The very thing that made you hopeless was the Law that was not yours in the first place. Messiah, through the **New Covenant**, broke down that *middle wall of partition*, the Law that some want to go back and cling to. The commandments and ordinances that you may want to tenaciously hold on to and observe have been abolished.

I want to focus a few moments on Ephesians 2, verse 10. Messiah Yeshua *created* you *unto good works* – what good works? The good works of the Law? Or the good works produced by the ministry of the Ruach Ha-Kodesh as we yield to Him (Romans 6:11-14)? Observance of the works of the Law in the flesh have been repeatedly condemned in the Epistles. So, what Paul is referencing are the works produced by our New Nature (II Corinthians 5:17) through the Ruach Ha-Kodesh. These are the works that when tried by Messiah at His judgment seat will be found to be *gold, silver, and precious stones* (I Corinthians 3:12-15). Whereas, the works of the flesh in the Law (Romans 6-8) because of our wrong motivation will be *wood, hay, and stubble* that will be devoured by the fire of His holiness as each one of them are evaluated by Him, the Word (Hebrews 4:12). Paul is clearly referring to the works produced by the **New Covenant** as He had created us unto good works. Also notice in verse 10 that you and I have been ordained to produce the kinds of works that the **New Covenant** and the Law of Messiah command and to walk in them. In that powerful verse, the works produced by the terminated Mosaic Law are not even in the context.

Now let me amplify the last two points of Paul to the Ephesians so that we do not miss his point. What is the *middle wall of partition,* and what does it reflect? It has great significance for Gentiles. **First,** it reflects the wall in the Temple that kept the Gentiles separated from the Jewish worshippers and the covenants and promises that were theirs (given to Israel). The middle wall of partition was the Mosaic Law. Second, there was another wall that kept all the Jewish people separated from contact with their God in the Holy of holies. That separation was the veil, which no one could enter through except the high priest once a year, and not without blood. We also recognize that it was that veil which was torn from top to bottom (Matthew 27:51) on Passover when Yeshua died on the cursed tree. Hebrews 10:20 speaks to the fact that the veil represented His flesh; therefore, now all believers have access to the throne of God through the torn veil, His flesh. So now because of Yeshua we are no longer *hopeless* but have been given access to enter the very presence of God, in His throne room. May I be redundant and ask again, did the Law do that for you as a Gentile?? NO, but Yeshua did, so why cling to the Law of Moses that locked Jews and Gentiles out, making them prisoners to the Law, when Yeshua has opened the door (veil) and has given us *better* access to the throne room of God that no one had under the Mosaic Law?

You have been lifted to a new standard in being ***reconciled*** by the blood of the **New Covenant** in Messiah. You are to conform to the **New Covenant** and adjust to a new standard, the Law of Messiah as opposed to the *old* standard.

Notice you are His *workmanship,* the Greek word *poiema* which means "something that is made." You are now created unto good works, not for the works of the *old covenant*, but unto your obedience to the works of the Law of Messiah. Notice in Ephesians 2:1-2, in the past we walked in sin; but because of Him, according to Ephesians 2:10, we now are to walk in good works through and because of Messiah, not because of Moses. Michael Rydelnik, a Jewish believer, gives a short summary of these verses:

> In presenting God's purposes for Jews and Gentiles, Paul moves from describing Gentile alienation from both God and the Jewish people (Ephesians 2:11-12) to their reconciliation to the Lord and the Jewish people (Ephesians 2:13-18). Ultimately, he reveals the unification of believing Jews and Gentiles in a new body, namely the Church.[161]

Reconcile / Reconciliation
II Corinthians 5:14-21

The word in the Scriptures means "to cause to conform to a standard, to be adjusted to a specified standard."

The Scriptural teaching on reconciliation: God is always the Reconciler and man the offending enemy is always the one who is reconciled to God. God brings us to Himself and causes us to be adjusted to His standards.

pp. 83-92, J. Dwight Pentecost, *Things Which Become Sound Doctrine; Redeemed/Redemption.*

Even though you were not born Jewish or became a proselyte to Judaism, you are now circumcised, but notice how. Jewish people are circumcised ***by hands***, you are now circumcised ***without hands*** because of the blood of the **New Covenant** in Messiah as stated in Colossians 2:11:

---

[161] Michael Rydelnik & Michael Vanlaningham, eds. *The Moody Bible Commentary.* Chicago, IL: Moody Press, 2014, p. 1849.

In whom also you are circumcised with the circumcision made without hands, in putting off the body of the sins of the flesh by the circumcision of Messiah.

The **New Covenant** and the Law of Messiah by far outweigh the limited and restricted benefits of keeping Torah.

Snapshots from Philippians

In Philippians 3:1-3, Paul gives a warning regarding Judaizers to the believers in Philippi: ***Beware*** *of dogs,* ***beware*** *of evil workers,* ***beware*** *of those who mutilate the flesh* (act of circumcision). The word *beware* in the Greek is an imperative command, part of the Law of Messiah given as a warning to believers. Today it is the Torah observers and Hebrew Roots movement who want to add works to Faith and to the Grace of God. But some of them speak out of both sides of their mouths saying that works have no effect on salvation and then teaching the necessity of being Torah observant, totally ignoring all the extremely clear passages in the book of Acts and the Epistles that teach the termination of the Law by its fulfillment when Yeshua inaugurated the **New Covenant**. We do not depreciate the *Tanakh* as I clearly laid out in Part One of this book; it is very valuable, nor do we depreciate the Torah. However, the Mosaic code within the Torah has been *rendered inoperative* by the Messiah in the **New Covenant**. There is a lawful way to use the Law with unsaved people to point out their sin before a holy God (I Timothy 1:8-9). Paul very strongly presents his Jewish pedigree (3:4-6) which was precious to him; yet when he looks at what Yeshua did in *inaugurating* the **New Covenant** and these new benefits, he emphasizes that his life in the **New Covenant** outstrips his benefits as a Jew under the *old covenant*. When Paul analyzes the difference, he makes an even stronger statement. Those things which were important to him as a plus, he is now counting them as loss for Messiah. He gets even stronger by calling it dung – human, smelly waste that men bury in the ground (Philippians 3:7-9). Look what Paul says:

> *⁷ But what things were gain to me, those I counted loss for Messiah. ⁸ Yet doubtless, and I count all things but loss for the excellency of the knowledge of Messiah Yeshua my Lord: for whom I have suffered the loss of all things, and do count them but dung, that I may win Messiah, ⁹ And be found in Him, not having my own righteousness, which is of the Law, but that which is through the faith of Messiah, the righteousness which is of God by faith.*

Paul counted the cost by analyzing the two systems, adhering to the Mosaic Law of the *old covenant* and now adhering to the Law of Messiah because of the **New Covenant** and all the things that God has blessed us with in the present. He regarded these blessings only to be magnified beyond comparison in the future in the heavenlies (Ephesians 1), our eternal state and position. Torah-observant believers of every stripe have not made this comparison! How excited would you be if you won $10,000 in the lottery versus winning $100,000,000 in the state lottery (as an illustration, not that we should be involved in the lottery or gambling). Can you compare the two? The benefits of the larger by far outweighs the limited and fading benefits of the other. Yet Torah-observant adherents gravitate to the small amount (the Mosaic Law of the *older covenant*) regardless of the intensity of involvement in law keeping. They ignore the greater benefit of the larger amount based on the **New Covenant** and the Law of Messiah.

In reading one of the books promoting Torah observance, I stand amazed at the author's belief of what Messiah has done for us, but that salvation has nothing to do with being Torah observant. He insists on being obedient to a system God, Himself, is responsible for laying aside. God did so because Messiah fulfilled (and brought to an end, never to be done again) the Law of Moses through Messiah's sacrifice, the death, burial, and the resurrection (I Corinthians 15:3-4).

The *old covenant* no longer has ANY relevance to us who are in Messiah Yeshua because of Him being the Mediator of the **New Covenant**. You say, "You repeat and repeat the same thing." I say, yes, I do, for repetition is still the mother of learning, yet you repetitively return to the *dung* like a dog to vomit (Proverbs 26:11) and like a cleaned up "pig" returning to the mud (II Peter 2:22). Now let's look at the three warning statements that Paul gives to the Philippians who had been infected by Judaizers. Paul calls them three unflattering names in Philippians 3:2.

> **Dogs**: Jewish people called Gentile pagans dogs. These were not cute pets that people rave about; these dogs ran in packs. They were scavengers for garbage food, and would even attack people. This then was applied to the Gentiles who afflicted[162] Israel as a pack of wild dogs. However, Paul turns this around and applies it to the Judaizers, who like a pack of dogs were spiritual scavengers feeding off of believers by pulling them into their legalistic heretical camp.
>
> **Evil workers**: Now Paul ups the warning a second time to believers. These dogs preached another gospel (Galatians 1:6-9) by attacking the Gospel of God's Grace obtained by Messiah and through the Ruach Ha-Kodesh (Galatians 3:2). Paul refers to them as evil workers, unclean spiritually, not biblically kosher. Their works from the very beginning in Acts 10 and 15 were against God's plan and purpose.
>
> *Concisionists* means "those who mutilate the flesh." In Paul's context, he was referring to the act of circumcision that the Judaizers promoted to Gentile believers. Here Paul ups the warning again, the third time intensifying the warning, referring to them as *mutilators* (Galatians 5:12). Spiritually, they were just like the pagan religions. To them circumcision had lost its meaning and significance that God had placed on it (Genesis 17:1-14). So Paul characterizes them not as true circumcision, but merely mutilators of the flesh. Paul is

---

[162] **Affliction:** This is the state of being afflicted; the cause of persistent pain or distress resulting in great suffering.

saying that these Judaizers were mutilating the message of the Gospel of Messiah by adding Law to Grace.

Circumcision: Paul explains in Colossians (2:11) that God has circumcised our hearts in Messiah. It is the result of *regeneration* promised by the **New Covenant** (Jeremiah 31:31-34; Ezekiel 36:26-27). Now God circumcised both Jews and Gentiles together into the body of Messiah (Ephesians 2), circumcised *without hands*. It is now a spiritual transaction that God did in the heart which He will also do at the end of the Tribulation period (Deuteronomy 30:6) for all Israel when they embrace Messiah as Saviour and LORD. The works of the flesh CANNOT give us any confidence in the flesh. God is the one who justifies us by the finished work of Messiah on the tree.

Snapshots from Colossians

Torah observant believers hold that the obvious statement of Paul in Colossian 2:14 does not mean that the Law of Moses was *nailed on the Cross* with Messiah. They make such statements as, was the Law really nailed to the Cross? They say that the Law with its "high and holy standard" that we are to live by was not terminated after the resurrection of Yeshua onward. They are blind to the Scriptures and are teaching sighted believers to be blind like themselves. Read these verses (Colossians 2:9-14), and then I'll share a couple of observations:

> *9 For in Him dwells all the fullness of the Godhead bodily. 10 And you are complete in Him, Who is the head of all principality and power: 11 In whom also you are circumcised with the **circumcision made without hands**, in putting off the body of the sins of the flesh by the **circumcision of Messiah**. 12 Buried with Him in baptism, wherein also you are risen with Him through the faith of the operation of God, who has raised Him from the dead. 13 And you, being dead in your sins and the uncircumcision of your flesh, has He quickened* [regenerated] *together with Him having forgiven you all trespasses; 14 Blotting out the handwriting of ordinances* [of the Law] *that was against us, which was contrary to us, and took it out of the way, nailing it to His Cross.* [brackets mine]

In Yeshua *dwells all the fullness of the Godhead bodily.* We are *complete in Him* who is all powerful and *in whom* we are **regenerated**, circumcised in our hearts *without hands,* in contrast to physical circumcision which was a sign of Jewishness under the Abrahamic Covenant (Genesis 17:11; Acts 7:8). Circumcision was also a sign of placing oneself under the Law of Moses as a son of the commandments (Leviticus 12:3; Numbers 15:37-41). To avoid any misunderstanding, let me quote from another Jewish believer:

> Circumcision was prescribed under the Abrahamic Covenant, but it was also prescribed under the Mosaic Covenant, though the significance was not the same. Under the Abrahamic Covenant, it was **mandatory for Jews only** and it was a sign of their Jewishness. Under the Law of Moses, it was **mandatory for** both Jews and [proselyte] Gentiles and it was a means of **submission to the Law**. It

> obligated the one circumcised to keep the whole Law, according to Galatians 5:3.[163] [bracket and bolding mine]

This circumcision of the heart involves our *baptism* into the body of Messiah (I Corinthians 12:13) as illustrated in Romans (6:3-4), and He delivered us from the bondage of the Law (Acts 15:10; Romans 7:1-4) and placed us under the <u>Law of Messiah</u> as our new standard of living, replacing the "high" and completely impossible standards of the *old covenant*. Remember, spiritually, the *old covenant* could do nothing for those yoked by it but sentence them to death! According to Colossians 2:14, in the **New Covenant** all our sins have been *blotted out;* the *ordinances* of the Law *that were against us* were nailed to His Cross.

We walk in Messiah, not Moses. Moses did not deliver us by *putting off the body of sins in the flesh.* Moses did not regenerate you; Yeshua did through the **New Covenant**. As *holy, just and good* as the Law was (Romans 7:12), it was inadequate to change our behavior or deliver us. It could point out our sin and condemn us to death as a violator; but it could not redeem us and give us life. So, why hang on to the *old covenant* Law system that was completely inadequate to deliver you from your sins? Remember, the sacrifices of the Mosaic system only covered sin (Hebrews 9:11-14), a shadow of something greater to come – the blood of the Lamb of God. Sacrifices and the law did not remove our sin; only the blood of the Lamb of God through the **New Covenant** could do that.

I have been pouring over verse after verse in this study where Paul clearly stated that the Law, which was *holy, just and good* (Romans 7:12), was terminated, ***rendered inoperative***, nullified as a working system by Messiah, by the Author of the Law, on the Cross because its purpose was fulfilled according to Galatians (3:23-25) when He inaugurated the **New Covenant**. The new standard of living for believers today in this Dispensation is called the <u>Law of Messiah</u>. I have looked at Acts with Peter and Paul's testimonies, the verdict of the Jerusalem Council (Acts chapters 10 and 15), at Romans, the two books of Corinthians, and the letters to the Galatians, Ephesians, and now Colossians, with more to follow as we proceed through the Epistles. How many times does Paul have to say something before he is recognized by those who insist they know more than Paul? These rebels pervert the clear sense of Scripture despite the fact that Paul received this direct revelation from the LORD (Galatians 1:11-12). Paul was a sub-author of Scripture under the direction of the Ruach Ha-Kodesh.

Before I ask you another question, let's look together at II Corinthians 12:1-4, 7 (KJV):

---

[163] Arnold Fruchtenbaum, *Israelology: The Missing Link in Systematic Theology.* San Antonio, TX: Ariel Press, 1994, p. 593.

> *¹ It is not expedient for me doubtless to glory. I will come to visions and revelations of the Lord. ² I knew a man in Messiah about fourteen years ago, (whether in the body, I cannot tell; or whether out of the body, I cannot tell: God knows) such a one caught up to the third heaven. ³ And I knew such a man, (whether in the body, or out of the body, I cannot tell: God knows) ⁴ How that he was caught up into paradise, and heard unspeakable words, which is not lawful for a man to utter. ...*
>
> *⁷ And lest I should be exalted above measure through the abundance of the revelations, there was given to me a thorn in the flesh, the messenger of Satan to buffet me, less I should be exalted above measure.*

Here is my question, which is addressed to anyone who is tempted to follow the Mosaic Law instead of walking in the Law of Messiah: Who appeared to Paul on the Damascus Road and spoke audibly to him (Acts 9:3-6, 15-16), as it were, *Face to face* just as Moses experienced? Whether they like it or not, Paul was authorized to write New Testament Epistles in the Age of Grace in a similar way that Moses was authorized to write the Torah. How many of you have been to the third heaven and have *heard unspeakable words, which is not lawful for a man to utter* (II Corinthians 12:1-4, 7)? How many of you have experienced a literal conversation with Yeshua and received a direct commission and an abundance of revelations? Since you have not, how is it that you can ignore and twist the very revelation given to Paul? You are no different than the rabbis who built a fence (the Mishnah) around the Law, subverting the Law, and the rabbis who modified the Law against the words of Moses (Deuteronomy 4:2) at Yavna in AD 90. What Paul received – to use a human illustration – is far, very far above any of our pay grades! As Hebrews will later bear out, Torah-observant proponents DO NOT fall into that class!

It appears that Torah-observant folks are no different than Belshazzar, a Babylonian king, who did not understand the handwriting on the wall (Daniel 5:5, 24) by the finger of God (Exodus 31:18; John 8:6). They have chosen by their own free will not to recognize the handwriting on the wall, meaning the Scripture by the **Author** of the Law (Yeshua Ha-Mashiach). They do not need a Daniel to interpret and explain what it means when Paul, who stands in a category by himself in his understanding of Scripture, shares with them the truth given to him by the very same **Author** of Scripture. Instead of receiving this teaching, they wiggle and twist against God's Holy Word like a soft pretzel to suit their bias of trying to keep the Mosaic Law, which promotes death instead of life.

In Colossians 1:24-27 (and Ephesians 3:1-6), Paul again references the *mystery* of Jews and Gentiles being brought together in union in the body of Messiah. Everywhere Paul teaches, he condemns works for salvation and justification, and excludes works from salvation and justification. Some Torah-observant adherents agree with the above statement, but then do an about-face and say you must keep the Law to be a "good" Christian. In Colossians 2:11 Paul states that all believers in Messiah are *circumcised*, spiritual circumcision *made without hands*. There is no physical circumcision required nor is Law keeping required for Gentile believers as a prerequisite for salvation or justification or to be a "good" Christian.

> ^{24} *Who now rejoice in my sufferings for you, and fill up that which is behind of the afflictions of Messiah in my flesh for His body's sake, which is the Church:* ^{25} *Whereof I am made a minister, according to the* **Dispensation of God which is given to me for you**, *to fulfill the word of God;* ^{26} *Even the mystery which has been hid from ages and from generations, but now is made manifest to His saints:* ^{27} *To whom God would make known what the riches of the glory is of this mystery among the Gentiles; which is Messiah in you, the hope of glory* (Colossians 1:24-27).

Please notice, the ramifications of the Dispensation of Grace and Dispensations in general that many reject, these were given to Paul by the Creator of the Universe Whom you have accepted as your Saviour and Lord. Now, Who saved you? Paul did not invent this Dispensation that was hidden from the ages; it was given to him by Yeshua Ha-Mashiach, the Author of the Mosaic Law Who fulfilled His own Law. Moses, himself, and the Prophets attested to this Law repeatedly throughout the pages of the Torah, Nevi'im, and Ketuvim of the *Tanakh* as did Matthew, Mark, Luke and John in their Gospels. Yeshua then, at His death, inaugurated the **New Covenant** and His new Law for this economy of Grace, the Law of Messiah.

- Who is the real authority: You or Yeshua Ha-Mashiach?
- Again, who placed you in the body of Messiah?
- Who died for your sin?
- Who kept the Law perfectly?
- Who has given you abundant life?
- Who was it that changed the Dispensation of Law to the Dispensation of Grace?

It was **not** Moses; it was **not** Torah-observant "scholars." Law-keeping did **not** save you; Law keeping did **not** regenerate you. Law keeping never gave you victory over sin! Who was it? It was Messiah, Messiah, Messiah!

Snapshot from I Timothy

I Timothy 1:7-9

⁷ Desiring to be teachers of the Law; though they understand neither what they say, nor about the things they confidently affirm. ⁸ But we know that the Law is good, if a man uses it lawfully, ⁹ as knowing this, that law is not made for a righteous man, but for the lawless and disobedient, for the ungodly and for sinners, for unholy and profane, for murderers of fathers and murderers of mothers, for manslayers.

As I read these verses and the comments of Torah keepers, I am evermore amazed that they absolutely, completely ignore the <u>Law of Messiah</u> and all the instructions that God gave to the Church. It does not mean that the Law is "useless" with "no importance" to the believer today. Let me illustrate, since 1776 we as a nation are no longer under British law, but we are under American law. That does not mean that British law is useless or unimportant, but it does mean that we do not live under British law but under American law. Likewise, as I said several times before, the Law of the *old covenant* is *holy, just, and good,* and it is!! But we are NOT under the *old covenant*, we are under a new governing economy, the **NEW COVENANT**. Why adhere to a law we as a nation have not been under since 1776? Likewise, why spiritually live under a Law that we are spiritually no longer under since AD 30, for it was under a different governing economy of God. Yet Torah keepers insist on going back to the old economy, the *old covenant* which gave us NO spiritual benefits, only *death* and *condemnation*. The Mosaic Law was always pointing out our sin with no remedy. God's people had only a Promise, and when the Promise came, those who clung to the Law despised all that He had done for them by the **New Covenant**. Also let me re-emphasize, as Gentiles we were NEVER under the Law of Moses to begin with! So, it should be a moot issue.

We as Dispensationalists DO NOT diminish the *Tanakh* or the Torah, even though the Law system in the Torah of the *old covenant* is no longer the standard of life. Dear Torah-keeping brothers in Messiah, do you think that the <u>Law of Messiah</u> does not tell us how to live, nor warn us of impending dangers from false teaching and from our old fleshly sin nature? The <u>Law of Messiah</u> tells us how to interact with other believers in need of physical and spiritual help. The <u>Law of Messiah</u> tells us how to conduct ourselves with Gentiles (Romans 12:9-16) in this pagan, wicked, corrupted world (Romans 12:17-21) and under a corrupted government (Romans 13:1-7). It tells us how we can live a holy life before God by the empowering of the Ruach Ha-Kodesh if we yield to Him (Romans 6:11-13). It also tells us how to live and walk with our spouse, our children and our employers and employees (Ephesians 5:18-6:9; Colossians 3:18-4:6). Your insistence on Law keeping tells me you have NEVER STUDIED the <u>Law of Messiah</u> nor the **New Covenant**; you are totally unfamiliar with this new lifestyle that Yeshua gave us

2,000 years ago through the **New Covenant** and its over 600 commands for us to obey.

Why is it after 2,000 years of Church history, the pulpits in our Churches are completely ignorant of some very important doctrines like (1) all the ramifications of the **New Covenant,** or (2) standing before Messiah at His judgment (Bema) seat in having our works judged to see what kinds of works they were. If we understood the significance of the **New Covenant** and the Law of Messiah for the last 2,000 years there would be no platform for the spiritually distracting Torah-observance teaching. Remember, exporting Torah keeping is in violation of Peter, Paul and the Jerusalem Council and of Yeshua Himself.

So let me address I Timothy 1:8 and its relevance today. When the Mosaic Law is used in submission to the **New Covenant** and the Law of Messiah, there is no problem because it is not the predominant law system. One of the similarities is when Dispensations change things, some things remain the same, like nine of the Ten Commandments – so use them *lawfully*, now in accordance with the Law of Messiah. Let me restate, Paul is not anti-Torah, but in our Christian Liberty Jewish brothers in Messiah have the liberty to practice Jewish Law personally as Paul did (Acts 18:18) as long as they do not export it to others to practice it, because it then becomes legalism. As for the Gentiles, we were never under the Law of Moses to begin with, and this is not a difficult lesson. Read Exodus chapters 19 through 24 again and see who is addressed by God – Jews, not Gentiles! To those of us who are Gentile believers in Messiah, we are free from the yoke of the Law, for we were never under it in the first place. However, now both Jew and Gentile have now been given a new Law to obey, both of us together, the Law of Messiah.

How is the Law used *lawfully?* The term *lawfully* is couched in the context of the Mosaic Law, and it was made for unrighteous mankind. The Law can be used to convince mankind today in this sinful world that they are indeed sinners and separated from a holy God who has spelled out His holy Law to sinful mankind. So, it is *lawful* to use the Law for that purpose, as well as all the *Tanakh,* to illustrate to sinful mankind that they are in desperate need of salvation and justification before God.

Since the Law of Moses was made for unrighteous Israel, and they have demonstrated that same unrighteousness throughout the *Tanakh* into the Gospels, are you implying by your insistence on observing Torah that your standing is also in unrighteousness? Do you need a schoolmaster to guard you while allowing it to condemn you and shut you up into a spiritual prison (Galatians 3:19-29)?

> *[19] What purpose then does the law serve? It was added because of transgressions, till the Seed* [Messiah] *should come to whom the promise was made; and it was appointed through angels by the hand of a mediator* [Moses]. *[20] Now a mediator does not mediate for one only, but God is one.*

> *^{21} Is the law then against the promises of God? Certainly not! For if there had been a law given which could have given life, truly righteousness would have been by the law. ^{22} But the Scripture has confined all under sin, that the promise of faith in Yeshua Messiah might be given to those who believe. ^{23} But before faith came, we were kept under guard by the law, kept for the faith which would afterward be revealed. ^{24} Therefore the law was our tutor to bring us to Messiah, that we might be justified by faith. ^{25} But after faith has come, we are no longer under a tutor.*
>
> *^{26} For you are all sons of God through faith in Messiah Yeshua. ^{27} For as many of you as were baptized into Messiah have put on Messiah. ^{28} There is neither Jew nor Greek, there is neither slave nor free, there is neither male nor female; for you are all one in Messiah Yeshua. ^{29} And if you are Messiah's then you are Abraham's seed, and heirs according to the promise.*

If so, and you do not understand the impact of your choice, then today you are in reality walking as a spiritual schizophrenic with two natures, one that sins – your <u>old sinful nature</u> – and your <u>new nature</u> that lives unto righteousness because we now have the spirit of Messiah living within us. In the presence of the Holy Spirit (Ruach Ha-Kodesh), we learn to yield to the Holy Spirit. Now our salvation is no longer foreshadowed by the blood of an animal. Instead, now we can have victory over sin ONLY through the **New Covenant** in the sacrificial death of Messiah Yeshua.

Because of our new walk in **New Covenant** faith, we have the indwelling (I Corinthians 3:16; 6:19-20), sealing (II Corinthians 1:22; 5:5; Ephesians 1:13-14; 4:30), baptism (I Corinthians 12:13), and filling (Ephesians 5:18) of the Ruach Ha-Kodesh. Do you still want to live under the *old covenant*? If that is the case you are saying that you only want the Holy Spirit to come upon you in a limited way. That was the case with most believers in the *Tanakh* who never experienced the filling with the Holy Spirit, for to them He only came upon a limited number of them for a limited period of time.

If you want both Grace and Law, that is impossible; they are like oil and water: they do not mix. You cannot have your cake and eat it too. It is impossible! So, in Grace we are free to use the Law lawfully to convict sinful mankind that they fall short of all of God's holy righteous demands. However, it is unlawful to use it as a system of Law to be kept today when we have the *Law of Messiah* to edify us in the body of Messiah.

Snapshot from II Timothy

II Timothy 1:9
Who has saved us, and called us with a holy calling, not according to our works, but according to His own purpose and grace, which was given us in Messiah Yeshua before the world began.

Here Torah keepers key off on the aspect of living holy lives, living according to Messiah, for Yeshua lived according to the Law of Moses, which He was required to do under the Law. The Law being incorporated in the Torah, and since He did fulfill it, they say we are supposed to live according to the same Law. Now, are they saying that those who follow Yeshua's commands of the Law of Messiah in Acts of the Apostles and according to the Epistles cannot live holy and separated lives to Him and before the world because we do not adhere to the Mosaic Law? Are they then discounting the indwelling, sealing, baptism, and filling of the Ruach Ha-Kodesh which the *old covenant* did not have? In effect, that *is* what they are saying.

In perusing a pro-Torah-observant website I found all kinds of books on how to eat kosher by following the Mosaic dietary commandments, how to practice Sabbath-keeping, and all kinds of "messianic aids" to help people get into their "Jewish roots" so that they can "follow Yeshua" in what they would call their living standard. What is meant by "Jewish roots," and how should we understand that statement?

God wrote the Bible through Jewish lenses, not Gentile lenses. Because the Jewish lens is undeniable, it is incumbent upon us to understand the Jewish background of the Scriptures. That is the perspective of the *Tanakh*, Gospels, and New Testament when written. We understand through the Abrahamic Covenant that God chose to reveal Himself through the Jewish people for which we, as Gentile believers in Messiah, are indebted (Romans 11:11-32). For through the Jewish people, we have ***His written Word*** from a Jewish context and understanding, and through the Jewish people came ***the Promise*** of the Messiah (Genesis 3:15; 49:9-10). Understanding the Jewish background relates to everything taught in the Bible, whether it is the Dispensation of Law or the Dispensation of Grace.

In the Dispensation of Grace, the requirements for obedience have changed; but this does not mean that the Jewish background is no longer important – it is very important!! As a personal testimony, I became a believer at the age of 14 (1960) at the Christian Youth Crusade in Riverdale, MD, and then spent my teenage years at McLean Bible Church in Virginia, graduating from Washington Bible College (Lanham, MD) in 1970 and from Lancaster Bible College and Graduate School with a Masters in 2004. I had spent twenty-five years in ministry when I discovered the Jewish background of Scripture at Ariel's Camp Shoshanah in 1995 as I sat under Dr. Arnold Fruchtenbaum in his class on the Life of Messiah from a Jewish perspective. I was not a novice in Scripture, but I had no concept of the Jewish background; and this discovery revolutionized my whole concept of Scripture. I already knew of the distinctions in the Dispensations, that it was not important to do Jewish stuff as a Gentile; but it was very important to understand the Scripture as God wrote it from a Jewish perspective.

For me, the Scriptures came alive in such a fresh new way after perceiving and studying the Jewish background of the Bible, and this approach has been transforming my understanding now for almost 30 years. Here is a statement that is foundational in understanding the Jewish background of Scripture that I learned that first year at Camp Shoshanah.[164] So, if we want to say who is obedient, I dedicated my life to serve the LORD in December of 1961 at the Youth For Christ Capital Teen Convention in Washington D.C. Because of that commitment to HIM, I have channeled my whole life toward Messiah to live a holy life before Him. Am I a second-class believer because I do not observe Torah? I think NOT!! I am not Charismatic, but I learned something important from Charismatic believers: "Do not put God in a box." I do believe that my Torah-keeping brothers and sisters are putting God in a box, by not allowing Him to speak and move from one economy to another different and improved economy. I will submit to the Law of Messiah, for that is the system that God has placed in our lives in this economy.

In summing up this section, I want to paraphrase the statement and goal concerning the viability of the Law from the perspective of Torah-observant believers today. They want people, often Gentile believers, to obey the Laws of Moses so that they can imitate Messiah's observance of Mosaic Law by living holy lives in this day. They desire for the Gentiles to be separated from the world and to be following the theological footprints of the Creator, Yeshua. Their desire is correct; but now Yeshua, Himself, has replaced that Law that He authored which had no spiritual benefits, with the new system He enacted, called the **New Covenant**. To live out the **New Covenant** through the Law of Messiah leads unto an abundant life full of our spiritual blessing in heavenly places.

Who are we told to imitate? Not Moses! Instead, we should focus on Yeshua who went outside of the box of Torah keeping and gave us a superior **New Covenant** and the ability to live His abundant life by being in submission and yielding to the Ruach Ha-Kodesh in living by the Law of Messiah.

---

[164] Camp Shoshanah is now the Ariel School of Messianic Studies.

Snapshots from Titus

Titus 1:10-16

*¹⁰ For there are many unruly and vain talkers and deceivers, especially those of the **circumcision**: ¹¹ Whose mouths must be stopped, who subvert whole houses, teaching things which they ought not, for filthy lucre's sake. ¹² One of themselves [a Cretan], even a prophet of their own, said, the Cretians are always liars, evil beasts, slow bellies.¹³ This witness is true. For this reason rebuke them sharply, that they may be sound in the faith; ¹⁴ Not giving heed to Jewish fables, and commandments of men, that turn from the truth. ¹⁵ Unto the pure, all things are pure: but unto them that are defiled and unbelieving nothing is pure; but even their mind and conscience is defiled. ¹⁶ They profess that they know God; but in works they deny Him, being abominable, and disobedient, and unto every good work reprobate* [unfit for any good work]. [bolding mine]

Paul as he references Judaizers does not mince words here to Titus as he ministers in Crete. It is a very serious issue with Paul, who refers to *unruly vain talkers and deceivers* in verse 10 whose *mouths must be stopped* for they subvert whole families, and are doing so for money's sake (verse 11). Today I do not know about an issue that Torah keepers are doing it because it is financially profitable, but I do know that they often will infiltrate churches to export and spread their false teaching. Paul then picks up in verse 14 concerning Jewish fables and commandments of men, known as legalism, which is also in some sectors of Messianics, but legion in Rabbinic writings. In verse 15, for those who are defiled, all things are "defiled" because their *conscience is defiled*. Finally in verse 16, Paul calls their actions *abominable, disobedient*, and in their good works they are *reprobate* (unprincipled, wicked). If you look back in Corinthians, Paul calls them *false apostles*. In Galatians, he says let them be *cursed* for teaching *another gospel*. In Philippians, he calls them *dogs, evil workers* and those that mutilate the flesh (circumcision). These references are quite an indictment to Judaizers whatever shade or stripe, which includes Torah keepers; it is all a perversion of the truth of the Gospel.

Titus 2:11-15

¹¹ For the grace of God that brings salvation has appeared to all men, ¹² Teaching us that, denying ungodliness and worldly lusts, we should live soberly, righteously, and godly, in this present world; ¹³ Looking for the blessed hope, and the glorious appearing of the great God and our Saviour Yeshua Ha-Mashiach; ¹⁴ Who gave Himself for us, that He might redeem us from all iniquity, and purify unto Himself a peculiar people [a people for His own possession],

> *zealous of good works. ¹⁵ These things speak, and exhort, and rebuke with all authority. Let no man despise you.*

Here is the **New Covenant** and the Law of Messiah in action, Paul did not mention the "necessity" of keeping Mosaic Law!!! Notice that Paul said the *Grace of God* brought *salvation* through the **New Covenant**; he did not say that in the context of the *old covenant*. Grace was given at times and under certain instances in the *Tanakh*. But Grace was not given as it is to the Church in this Dispensation, to all believers in Messiah Yeshua. What does Grace do? ***It teaches*** us to deny *ungodliness* and *worldly desires*, to live *righteously* and *godly*. It activates our minds and hearts through His Word (Romans 12:2; Hebrews 4:12) and makes our consciences sharp as we face the challenges of life in Him. We are to be focused, YES, but not on the Law of Moses; we are to be ***focused on Messiah's appearing*** – YES HIM, not on Mosaic Law. Yeshua Ha-Mashiach redeems us from all iniquity and purifies us unto Himself, a people who will be like Him in character. Notice Paul does not attribute this spiritual walk to the Mosaic Law but to Grace and walking in His Law, the Law of Messiah (John 13:34-35; I John 2:1-8). In verse 15, the words *speak*, *exhort,* and *rebuke* are all imperative commands, part of the Law of Messiah. Have you ever read in the *Tanakh* these kinds of words? Below you will find a chart[165] that I made to help explain the Grace of God in this economy of God: the Dispensation of Grace.

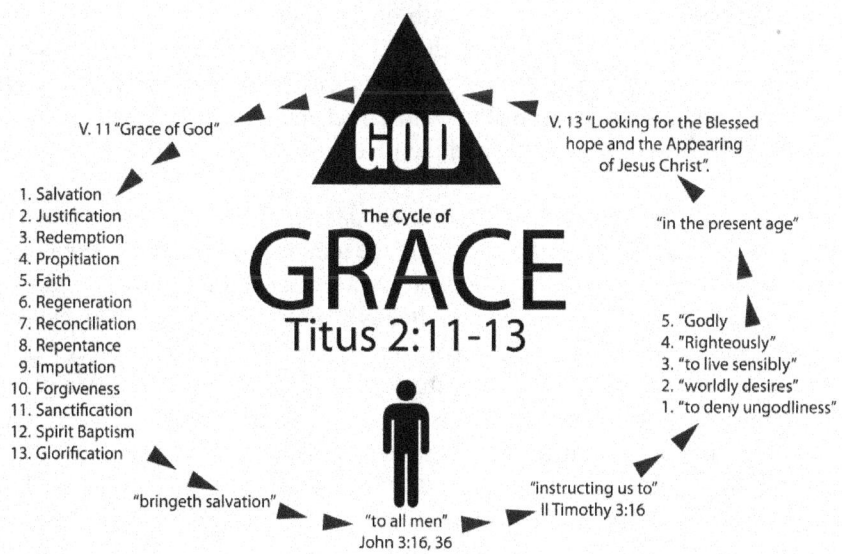

---

[165] This chart can be downloaded for FREE from my website: *www.PromisesToIsrael.org*.

Titus 3:5-9

*⁵ Not by works of righteousness which we have done, but according to His mercy He saved us, by the **washing of regeneration**, and **renewing of the Holy Spirit**; ⁶ Which He shed on us abundantly through Yeshua Ha-Mashiach our Saviour: ⁷ That being justified by His grace, we should be made heirs according to the hope of eternal life [Hebrews 9:15]. ⁸ This is a faithful saying, and these things I want you to affirm constantly, so that those who have believed in God might be careful to maintain good works. These things are good and profitable unto men. ⁹ But **avoid foolish questions**, and genealogies, and contentions, **and strivings about the Law**; for **they are unprofitable and vain**.* [bolding mine]

The *washing of regeneration* is the **New Covenant** and the ministry of the Ruach Ha-Kodesh Who has taken our spiritual deadness from the Fall in Genesis 3 that Paul states was passed on to us through Adam (Romans 5:12; 7:4-6). But now we have been *regenerated*, renewed by the power of the Ruach Ha-Kodesh. The **New Covenant** promises that His law will be implanted in Israel's heart (Jeremiah 31:34), and it will be, but *not* until the Kingdom of Messiah. It did not happen in Jeremiah's day; it did not happen in Yeshua's day; and it did not happen in Acts 2 at Shavuot (Pentecost); for in the Law of Messiah we are still told today to let His Word *transform* us *by the renewing [anakainizo] of our minds* (Romans 12:2). It will not happen for the body of Messiah until death or the Rapture, and it will not happen to Israel until the end of the Tribulation, the Time of Jacob's Trouble, the Seventieth Week of Daniel when all Israel will be saved in a day (Zechariah 3:9). Then Messiah will come and deliver Israel from the Anti-christ and his armies trying to destroy them. He will destroy those armies, and then He will set up the Millennial Kingdom.

Notice that the word *renew* (*anakainizo*) is a separate Greek word from *new* (*kalvos*) as mentioned in Part One of this book in the context of the word *new* for **New Covenant** and not a *renewed* old covenant. Notice as well that nowhere do you see the *old covenant* playing a part in the believer's present life. Paul excludes it! Torah-observant believers use a diplomacy of words to slip it into the context when interpreting a biblical text to the unsuspecting Gentile reader. Many Gentile believers cannot biblically discern the subtlety of these words because they have never been taught sound doctrine and the ability to discern false teaching. That is the complete failure of the pulpits and Sunday School teachers in Yeshua's Church to teach sound biblical doctrine. The Church today is too busy having an experience or mimicking worship.

Paul expresses that we are to maintain *good works* because we have been *justified* and have *the hope of eternal life*. The Law of Messiah spells out what good works are to be, along with warnings, exhortations, and commands. God has placed us, because of the **New Covenant**, into a new relationship with Him that we did not have before; and the Law of Messiah spells out how we are to live. The last part of verse 9 is applicable today that there should not be a *striving about the Law*, for it has been terminated, *rendered inoperative,* with Paul stating that to do such striving is *unprofitable and vain* spiritually.

Torah keepers have several overarching themes that overshadow all concrete proofs against Torah observance that we lay before them. *First*, they are not Dispensational, and so they pull a verse like Matthew 5:17 out of their theological pottage (stew), pull it out of its Law context, and try to say that it is expedient for all believers in Messiah today to practice and to emulate Yeshua as our example. Again, if you do not honor the Law of Context, you can make the Bible prove any spurious point. *Second*, they have the misconception that the Law of Moses is eternal, everlasting, and forever, by pointing to a term which in the Hebrew always indicates "limited in time," whereas in the Greek the term infers "infinity." *Third*, here is a paraphrase of one of their statements:

> They encourage Torah keeping so that people can emulate and follow Yeshua's example. By so doing they say that we can be holy and live separated lives by understanding the very character of God. They believe that since Yeshua followed the Law perfectly that we are to follow His lead in obeying the 613 laws of Moses so that we can be holy and separate in this world.

Again, those who teach this "other" gospel show dishonor and disrespect for what Yeshua did at the Cross in mediating the **New Covenant**. Also, they lay aside the eternality of the Son, making Him equal to Moses instead of elevating Him as *the Prophet like Moses*, being the Creator, Who ministers together with the Father and the Ruach Ha-Kodesh as One; HE IS GOD. What He said and did is not to be toyed with by using our finite, depraved minds in the name of religion. In so many words they have thrown aside the **New Covenant** and the Law of Messiah so that they can cleverly insert Torah keeping into the Christian's life to sidetrack and stunt spiritual growth in Messiah by the ministry of the Ruach Ha-Kodesh.

If you have been reading carefully, you have seen many verses that speak to the opposite of their false teachings. Look at the chart of the Cycle of Grace (above) and see the *thirteen things* that the Grace of God did in bringing us salvation. That does not even include other points made in the thirty-three positional truths[166] that Yeshua established through the **New Covenant**. Did the Law of Moses accomplish this? NO. As to living godly and separate lives, look at the *five things* given by Paul that we are to be instructed by: *to deny ungodliness, worldly desires, to live sensibly, righteously, and godly*. Just like the Pharisees of old, they have taken that which was *holy, just and good* and supplanted it with teachings that have been *rendered inoperable* by not embracing the **New Covenant**. Instead of practicing the Law of Moses, we are to be obeying Yeshua Ha-Mashiach's new commandment to love one

---

[166] Arnold Fruchtenbaum, Manuscript #110 – *Thirty-Three Things: A Study of Positional Truth.* San Antonio, TX: Ariel Press, n.d.

another as He loved us and the commandments that He authorized through His Apostles, the Law of Messiah.

Summary of Acts and Epistles

So whether Luke records the events at Cornelius' house or at the Jerusalem Council, the agreement that the Law was *rendered inoperative* by Yeshua was forged in those two initial head-to-head conflicts over the heresy in Acts 10 and 15. Paul taught decisively in Galatians that Judaizers were and are in complete rebellion against God, clearly alluding to the issue in his Epistles, clearly stating that the Law is *rendered inoperative*. Though the Law *was holy, just and good* (Romans 7:12) it was completely inadequate to produce life and spiritual vitality for the believer in one's walk in Messiah. Most Torah keepers recognize that the Law of Moses cannot give salvation and justification because it has absolutely NO foundation to justify anyone before a holy God, so why follow it?

Two final reminders on the Epistles. *First*, the testimonies of Peter and the Jerusalem Council should have put an end to Torah keeping, but it has not. Should I list the references for you in the writings of Paul? In almost every Epistle that he wrote, he repetitively condemned Mosaic Law keeping. And you think that I was repetitious; Paul was even more so. Just like the political climate today, you can give undeniable theological facts from the Scriptures, and from the Author of the Law of Moses and Mediator of the **New Covenant**; but because some have swallowed the "Kool-Aid" of Torah observance, they will not hear you, nor do they hear the *Prophet Like Moses* (Yeshua) in the Word that speaks of HIM.

> Romans 3:20; 4:5; 6:14; 7:2-4; 8:2-3; 10:4; 11:6; 13:14.
> II Corinthians 3:6-9, 14; 11:13-15.
> Galatians 1:6-9; 2:16-18; 3:1-5, 13-16, 19-29.
> Ephesians 2:6-7, 8-16; 4:24.
> Philippians 3:1-3, 7-9.
> Colossians 1:24-27; 2:9-14; 3:10-12.
> I Timothy 1:7-9.
> II Timothy 1:9.
> Titus 1:10-16; 2:11-15; 3:5-9.

How many times through the Book of Acts and then in nine of Paul's thirteen Epistles does he speak to the fact that the Law was *rendered inoperative*, not by Dispensationalists, but by Yeshua Ha-Mashiach, the Creator and Author of both Law systems, the One who is equal in all aspects of deity with the Father and the Ruach Ha-Kodesh. Is it possible that your hearts are *dull of hearing* (Jeremiah 6:10; Amos 8:11; Matthew 13:15; Hebrews 5:11) as the Prophets Jeremiah and Amos accused Israel of, and as Yeshua accused *that generation*, that generation that rejected Him, and as the author of Hebrews also rebuked believers? Paul again and again emphasized that the Law was *holy, just and good*, but was incapable of producing life in the economy of Law. If the Mosaic Law could not do it in the past, it cannot do it in the present under the economy of Grace.

As a Second reminder, have you studied the theological words given in the block teaching sections scattered throughout the book, terms like:

> *Regeneration, Imputation, Propitiation, Redemption,*
> *Justification, Sanctification,* and *Reconciliation.*

Did the Law give any of these? NO. Where would you be without all the ramifications of the **New Covenant** and the Law of Messiah that comes from it. You would still be lost in your sins.

Now we will move into the final book of interest, Hebrews, to show that the *old covenant* is no longer valid for believers today. Hebrews is an Epistle probably not written by Paul, but by another Jewish author whose Letter ties together all the theological points of Paul and, as it were, seals the deal concerning Who and what we are to obey.

Snapshots from the Letter to the Hebrews

Background and Foundational Emphasis of Hebrews

There are two foundational keys to understanding the Book of Hebrews. First, it was written to Jewish believers in Judea who because of the persecution of the Jewish Church by their fellow countrymen, were considering returning to Judaism. These were Jewish believers who were not participating in the Temple worship who had cut their ties to Judaism, specifically Rabbinic Judaism. Second, Hebrews was written by an unknown author just before the *destruction of the city and sanctuary*. These believers knew the writer, but he did not mention his personal name in the text. Different authors have been suggested, but the bottom line is no one knows who the author was.

The theme of Hebrews is that Yeshua Ha-Mashiach is **better** (or superior) to the Law of Moses, for He is the express image of God, He is the very essence of God (Colossians 1:15)! He is **better** than angels (1:4-14), **better** than Moses (3:1-6), **better** than Aaron and the priesthood and sacrifices (5:1 – 8:13). Messiah is of another priestly order, a **better** priesthood, the *order of Melchizedek* (Psalm 110:1-4; Hebrews 7:11-28). The old order with the Temple was in spiritual *decay and waxed old, ready to vanish* (8:13) and would be completely destroyed by the Romans in AD 70. God through the Romans removed the genealogical records, the ability of the priest to officiate, and removed Herod's Temple almost 2000 years ago. Hebrews 7:11-28 is a very powerful passage that deals with the Law having no salvific (saving) qualities and being incapable of justifying anyone before God. We see a system of Law that now has been **rendered inoperative** BY the Author of God's Word, the Messiah, Who at the Cross replaced the *old covenant* with a **better** covenant, the **NEW COVENANT**.

With this background, I want to reference a passage in the *Tanakh* that is not quoted in the Gospels. However, it is alluded to by the Pharisees in connection with John the Baptist (John 1:21) and by the Samaritan woman (John 4:25). This particular passage is directly referenced twice in the Book of Acts, once by Peter (Acts 3:22-24) and once by Stephen (Acts 7:37),[167] but this passage is the underpinning to all prophesies of Messiah except for the Abrahamic Covenant. The passage is Deuteronomy 18:15-19:

---

[167] Jim Sibley, "Serving Messiah, Serving Yeshua," *Ariel Magazine*, Winter issue, 2023. Go to *www.Ariel.org* click on "Ariel Magazine" button.

> *¹⁵ The LORD your God will raise up unto you a Prophet from the midst of you, of your brothers, like unto Me; unto Him you shall listen; ¹⁶ According to all that you desired of the LORD your God in Horeb in the day of the assembly, saying, Let me not hear again the voice of the LORD my God, neither let me see this great fire anymore, lest I die. ¹⁷ And the LORD said to me, They have spoken well that which they have spoken. ¹⁸ I will raise them up a Prophet from among their brethren, like unto you, and will put my words in His mouth; and He shall speak unto them all that I shall command Him. ¹⁹ And it shall come to pass, that whosoever will not listen to My words that He shall speak in My Name, I will require it of him.*

Another key passage that the author of Hebrews references is in regards to the Melchizedekian Priestly order (Psalm 110:4; Hebrews 5:6; 6:20; 7:21) which the author greatly expands. This *Prophet Like Moses,* though not mentioned again after it was given by Moses, echoes off all the *Tanakh* and the Gospels. After Yeshua opened the disciples' minds (Luke 24:45; Acts 1:3) of the reality of this passage and all other messianic passages, it became the foundation stone of the Apostles as they presented Messiah in the early history of the Church to the Jewish people.

This strategic passage in Deuteronomy 18:15-19 above goes back to Part Two of this book in the Snapshot from Deuteronomy. It becomes of central importance as we enter the Book of Hebrews. This *Prophet Like Moses* passage is a broad and deep vein of gold that the author of Hebrews begins to mine. As he proceeds through his letter to the Hebrews, the author picks up other jewels concerning the supremacy of the Messiah. This concept of the *Prophet Like Moses,* Who is the Creator/Redeemer/Deliverer, speaks of His absolute authority to give originally the Mosaic Law to Moses and Israel and to make a brand-**New Covenant.** He mediates between Israel and their God and uses His authority to replace the *old covenant,* which was inferior, with a now **better covenant** since the *old covenant's purpose* (Galatians 3:19-25) has been fulfilled (brought to an end). In everything that the author of Hebrews touches, he shows that Yeshua is **better**, He is **superior**, that there is no one to compare Him to; He stands **supreme**. He has the **pre-eminence**.

As we enter the book of Hebrews, I want to reference three resources for your personal use, which are as follows (with additional information in the Bibliography), for I will be quoting and alluding to these often:

- Arnold G. Fruchtenbaum. *Messianic Jewish Epistles,* published by Ariel Press.
- Steven Ger. *The Book of Hebrews: Christ is Greater,* published by AMG Publishers.
- David L. Allen. *The New American Commentary: Hebrews* published by B&H Publishers.

The Letter to the Hebrews was written to Jewish believers in Messiah who lived in Judea who were strongly considering going back to Rabbinic Judaism because of persecution, which oddly enough was coming from Pharisaic Rabbinic Judaism. The Book of Hebrews has five warning passages listed below.

Five Warning Passages

First Warning of Danger: Concerning Drifting from the Messianic Faith (2:1-4).

Second Warning of Danger: Concerning Disobedience and Doubt (3:7-4:13).

Third Warning of Danger: Concerning Spiritual Stagnation (5:11-6:20).

Fourth Warning of Danger: Concerning the Inferior Lifestyle of Faithlessness (10:26-31).

Fifth Warning of Danger: Concerning Spiritual Insensitivity (12:25-29).

by Steven Ger, *The Book of Hebrews: Christ is Greater*. Chattanooga, TN: AMG Publishers, 2009, p. 59.

This Book of Hebrews is emphasized because it literally is the capstone of all that Paul also taught in his Epistles. The theme of the Book is the *supremacy* of Messiah Yeshua, the *pre-eminence* of the Son, meaning He is *superior* in all areas of His character and work, but also in all areas that deal with the *old economy* of Law. The points below come from a contemporary Jewish believer in his commentary on Hebrews showing that Yeshua Ha-Mashiach is *superior* to all the *old covenant* standards. Notice carefully his points:

1. The *Superiority* of the Messiah as Divine Revelation (1:1-3).
2. Angels are the Servants of God: Yeshua is the Son of God (1:4-14).
3. The *Superiority* of Messiah to Angels (2:1-18).
4. The *Superiority* of Messiah to Moses (3:1-6).
5. The *Superiority* of Messiah to Aaron (4:14-5:10).
6. Messiah is after the Order of Melchizedek, not Aaron (7:1-28).
7. The *Superiority* of the **New Covenant** over the *old covenant* (8:1-13).
8. The *Superiority* of the Messiah's Priestly Service (9:1-10).
9. The *Superiority* of Messiah's Sacrifice (9:11-28).
10. Messiah's Sacrifice is Sufficient (10:1-18).[168] [*bolding* mine]

---

[168] Steven Ger, *The Book of Hebrews: Christ is Greater*. Chattanooga, TN: AMG Publishers, 2009, contents xi, x.

The theme of the Epistle to the Hebrews is that Yeshua Ha-Mashiach is ***superior*** to the *old covenant* system to which some Jewish believers considered returning. The author of Hebrews refers to all five books of Moses, called the Torah.

- From Genesis, he references Melchizedek and Esau.
- From Exodus, he references the Tabernacle.
- From Leviticus, he references the sacrifices and the priesthood.
- From Numbers, he references Moses (chapter 12) and Kadesh-Barnea.
- Finally, from Deuteronomy, he references the Law of Moses.

Yet we see as the author tackles the superiority of Messiah over everything in the Torah – even over Torah observance – he shows that Yeshua dismantled and fulfilled everything in the Torah, because everything compared to Yeshua is inferior (Deuteronomy 18:18-19).

Superiority of the Messiah as Divine Revelation

In Hebrews 1:1-3, the author makes a theological declaration of the supremacy of the Messiah, Who is the focus and spotlight of this Epistle.

> *¹ God who at sundry [many] times and in many ways spoke in time past unto the fathers by the Prophets, ² Has in these last days spoken unto us by His Son, whom He has appointed heir of all things, by whom also He made the worlds; ³ Who being the brightness of His glory, and the express image of His person, and upholding all things by the word of His power, when He had by Himself purged our sins, sat down on the right hand of the Majesty on high;*

I will spotlight some comments once again by Steven Ger, a Jewish believer, on these three verses as we see in the author's "dense thicket of messianic doctrine":

> The superiority of the Messiah as divine revelation. While over the past fifteen centuries God had progressively revealed Himself to Israel through the agency of a series of Prophets whom He employed and deployed in various ways, in this new, current era, He has revealed Himself with decisive finality in His Son ... God revealed Himself to Israel through two related means.
>
> The first, *polumeros*, [meaning] "in many portions," refers to the series of Prophets who had successively communicated God's Word over a roughly fifteen-century period as recorded in various books of the Old Testament ... The use of the term the fathers, indicates Israel's ancestors ... not limited to the three Hebrew patriarchs, Abraham, Isaac, and Jacob.
>
> [Second], ... in *polutropos* [meaning] "in many ways or means." ... [This would include] types, covenants, a legal code, a burning bush, angels, pillars of fire and cloud, a quaking, fiery mountain, dreams,

visions, signs and wonders, a still small voice, and in other ways. ... A new time calls for new tactics. In these last days or in these final days is a specific Jewish idiom for the Messianic age, the time for the fulfillment of God's yet unfulfilled promises. The Greek word here for last is *eschatos*, from which is derived the term eschatology, the study of the final (days of things). This Messianic age stands in contrast to palaios, "times past" or "long ago." If the author had meant to simply indicate a neutral, "the old days," it is far more likely that he would have used the term *archaios* (from which we get our word archaic). However, the loaded term he chose means "old in point of use, worn out, ready to be displaced by something new. A new and improved era, a new age or Dispensation, has dawned through the revelation of the Messiah. ...

God's Son [*huios*] is not merely the instrument through which God's message is communicated, [just] as were the Prophets. Uniquely, He Himself is also the message. God's final revelation is the person of the Son. In summary, God's revelation to us through His Son is superior to that received in Israel's past through the Prophets in three ways. **First**, while His previous revelation was fragmentary, addressed through many prophets, the new mode of revelation is through one individual. **Second**, while His previous revelation was through diverse means and various ways, the new revelation is through one means and one way only. **Finally**, while prior revelation was progressive and disclosed over centuries, the Son is God's final and conclusive revelation of Himself.[169] [Italics are mine.]

God's Superior Revelation	
In the Past	**In These Last Days**
Addressed to the fathers	Addressed to us
Through many prophets	Through one Son
Through diverse means	Through one means
In various ways	In one way
Revelation was progressive	Revelation is final

---

[169] Steven Ger, *The Book of Hebrews: Christ is Greater*. Chattanooga, TN: AMG Publishers, 2009, pp. 27-30. Also including the chart.

I spent some extra time on the introduction because it yields fruit regarding the **New Covenant** that far surpasses the *old covenant*, the Mosaic Law. This will be clearly and unquestionably seen in the following excerpts from the Epistle to the Hebrews. All of Scripture points to Yeshua, not to Moses or the Mosaic Law. Understand that in Matthew 5:17, Yeshua was being accused by the Pharisees of violating the Law, but that Law was Rabbinic manmade law and NOT the Mosaic Law. He came as *the Prophet Like Moses* (Deuteronomy 18:18-19), and all ears are to be fastened to His words; for the Father will require (hold accountable) the Jewish people for ALL His words. Application to the Gentiles who were not under the Law, they too need to be focused on what the Messiah said. His words will also be required of them as the **New Covenant** unfolds. He came to fulfill the *holy, just, and good* Law which everyone has failed to keep since its inauguration at Mount Sinai (Exodus 20-24). He fulfilled every *jot and title* of it, and **rendered** the Law of the *old covenant inoperative* when He **inaugurated** the **New Covenant** with its commands, comprising the Law of Messiah. Yeshua is the focus of all Scripture; all things build toward His Coming from Genesis through Malachi (Chronicles in the Jewish Bible) continuing through the Gospels. But with Israel's rejection of His First Coming, the actual fulfillment of the Promises in the Covenants has been postponed, put on hold, and will await His Second Coming when they ultimately will be completely fulfilled. He is the pinnacle of God's plan, not Moses or the Law.

Angels Are Servants; Yeshua Is the Son of God (1:4-14); Proofs of His Deity from the *Tanakh*

First-century Judaism had three pillars: angels, Moses, and the priesthood. In this section the author deals with the supremacy of Yeshua over angels. Verse 4 stands as a transitional verse between verses 1-3 and what he will develop in verses 5-14. The phrase *inheritance obtained a more excellent Name than they* refers directly to the Prophets, to the world He created and upholds (Colossians 1:15-18) by the Word of His power. Because of these things, the author then proceeds to quote seven passages in the *Tanakh* to show Messiah's superiority to angels. These seven passages are held by many to be Messianic in nature; that is, they point to Israel's Promised Messiah. Notice how the author quotes from these seven passages in the noted verses in Hebrews.

Hebrews 1:5 Compared with Psalm 2:7

For unto which of the angels said He at any time, You are My Son, this day have I begotten You? And again, I will be to Him a Father, and He shall be to Me a Son? (Hebrews 1:5)

"'I will declare the decree: the LORD has said to Me, 'You are My Son; Today I have begotten You.'" (Psalm 2:7)

Here I add some insight about the term *only,* which though this phrase is not used in this text, points to His uniqueness as the *only* one like Him, as reflected in John 1:18; 3:16; 1 John 4:9; and Hebrews 11:17 (by comparison to Isaac) that do reference Him as the "Only Begotten." This term *only begotten* is a legal term that stresses the rights of the firstborn, which points to the Messiah as heir, His special Sonship, and His position with the Father. The expression *only begotten* does not emphasize birth or origin but is a legal term that stresses His rights as the firstborn.

Hebrews 1:5 Compared with II Samuel 7:14 & I Chronicles 17:13

For unto which of the angels said He at any time, You are My Son, this day have I begotten You? And again, I will be to Him a Father, and He shall be to Me a Son. (Hebrews 1:5)

I will be his Father, and he [Solomon] *shall be My son. If he commit iniquity, I will chasten him with the rod of men, and with the stripes of the children of men;* (II Samuel 7:14)

I will be his Father, and he shall be My son; and I will not take My mercy away from him [David], *as I took it from him that was before you* [Saul] (I Chronicles 17:13).

The position of Son emphasizes Messiah as the One Who will fulfill the Davidic Covenant. The II Samuel passage emphasizes the line of Solomon (Matthew 1); whereas, the I Chronicles passage emphasizes Nathan, the brother of Solomon (Luke 3) through whom Messiah has a biological connection. Yeshua had no biological connection with Joseph. Yeshua is the Son of David through Mary, her Hebrew name being *Miriam* (Isaiah 7:14), who was of the line of David through Nathan (Luke 3:23-34); this Son of Mary will fulfill the covenant to David as the Eternal King, in the Eternal Kingdom and on the Eternal throne, for He is the Eternal Son.

Hebrews 1:6 Compared with Deuteronomy 32:43 (LXX) or Psalm 97:7

And again, when he brings in the firstborn into the world, He says, And let all the angels of God worship Him (Hebrews 1:6).

Rejoice, O nations [Gentiles], *with His people: for He will avenge the blood of His servants, and will render vengeance to His adversaries, and will be merciful unto His land, and to His people"* (Deuteronomy 32:43).

Rejoice, you heavens, with Him, and <u>let all the angels of God worship Him</u>; rejoice you Gentiles, with His people, (Deuteronomy 32:43a from the Septuagint - LXX).

Confounded be all who serve graven images, who boast of idols: Worship Him, all you gods. (Psalm 97:7)

Both passages in the Greek Septuagint (LXX)[170] emphasize that the Son is the final revelation of God and that ***the angels are to worship Him*** as the author states in verse Hebrews 1:6. This worship of the eternal Son shows that He is deity; the angels were created beings and are thus inferior to Him and worship Him. You will not find this verse particularly in Deuteronomy for it is not in the Masoretic Text[171] which is the basis for all our English Bibles; however, you will find it in the Septuagint Text translated from the Hebrew into Greek around 250 BC by seventy rabbis who translated from an older Hebrew text over 1000 years before the Masoretic Text.

Hebrews 1:7 Compared with Psalm 104:4

And of the angels He says, Who makes His angels spirits, and His ministers a flame of fire (Hebrews 1:7).

Who makes His angels spirits; His ministers a flaming fire: (Psalm 104:4)

This verse from Psalms emphasizes the transitory nature of angels who were created to serve their Master, the Son. They are His servants in the sense of being religiously devoted to Him.

Hebrews 1:8 Compared to Psalm 45:6-8

But unto the Son He says, Your throne, O God, is forever and ever: a scepter of righteousness is the scepter of Your kingdom. (Hebrews 1:8)

⁶ Your throne, O God, is forever and ever: the scepter of Your kingdom is a right scepter. ⁷ You love righteousness, and hate wickedness: therefore God, Your God, has anointed You with the oil of gladness more than Your companions. ⁸ All Your garments are scented with myrrh, and aloes, and cassia, out of the ivory palaces, by which they have made You glad. (Psalm 45:6-8)

These verses emphasize both the deity of the Son and His authority in the Messianic Kingdom. Again, the contrast is between the eternality and the deity of the Son and the transitory nature of the angels. He is God; and, therefore, He is both the Creator and Master of all the angels. He also has an Eternal throne, which no angel has. In this passage there are five specific ramifications combining the *Tanakh* context and what the writer says here: (1) The Father addresses the Son as *O God*, showing His

---

[170] The Septuagint reference is also found in the Dead Sea Scrolls. David Allen. *The New American Commentary: Hebrews*. Nashville, TN: B&H Publishers, 2010, pp. 172-173.

[171] The Masoretic Text is dated around AD 900, which was over 1100 years after the Septuagint text was translated by seventy Rabbis around 250 BC in Alexandria, Egypt.

deity and co-equality with the Father; (2) The Son is destined to have an Eternal throne and kingdom; (3) His reign will be righteous; (4) His reign will be righteous because He loves righteousness and hates iniquity; and (5) The Son is exalted above all.

Hebrews 1:10-12 Compared with Psalm 102:25-27

^{10} And, You, LORD, in the beginning hast laid the foundation of the earth; and the heavens are the works of Your hands: ^{11} They will perish; but You remain and they all will grow old like a garment; ^{12} And as a cloak You will fold them up, and they will be changed: but You are the same, and Your years will not fail. (Hebrews 1:10-12)

^{25} Of old You laid the foundation of the earth: and the heavens are the work of Your hands. ^{26} They will perish, but You will endure: yes, all of them will grow old like a garment; like a cloak You will change them, and they will be changed: ^{27} But You are the same, and Your years will have no end. (Psalm 102:25-27)

This passage emphasizes six things about the Son: (1) Yeshua is superior in His basic existence; (2) He is the Creator of the universe; (3) The Son is sovereign over the changes in the universe; (4) The Son is the unchangeable Lord in the midst of a changing universe; (5) The Son is eternal; and (6) While He is eternal, the universe will someday be discarded like an old piece of cloth (Revelation 6:14; II Peter 3:10); the universe is destined to be dissolved. While He is eternal, the universe in temporal.

Hebrews 1:13 Compared with Psalms 110:1 & 80:17

But to which of the angels has He said at any time, Sit on My right hand, until I make Your enemies Your footstool? (Hebrews 1:13)

The LORD said to my Lord, "Sit at My right hand, until I make Your enemies Your footstool." (Psalm 110:1)

Let Your hand be upon the man of Your right hand, upon the Son of Man whom You made strong for Yourself (Psalm 80:17).

These two verses from Psalms predict the Son's enthronement in glory and His seat at the right hand of the Father, alluded to in Hebrews 1:13. The Son is a partner with the Father in the Father's work. Because He is sitting, His work is completed. In the ancient world, the one who sits on the king's right hand is the king's equal.

Also, embedded in Hebrews 1:4, is a theme that will be picked up by the author in Hebrews 5, regarding the priesthood of Melchizedek:

Being made so much better than the angels, as He has by inheritance obtained a more excellent Name than they (Hebrews 1:4)

In summary, Hebrews 1:14 declares Messiah's status versus the status of angels: *Are they not all ministering spirits, sent forth to minister for those who shall be heirs of salvation?* While He is seated, showing His work is finished, angels, on the other hand, are still busy doing their work; for their work is never finished; for they are ministering spirits.[172]

As we move through the following passages, we will continue to see that Yeshua is God, He is superior to all things, He was the giver of the Law of Moses and **rendered it inoperative** when He **inaugurated** and mediated the **New Covenant**. Embedded in the **New Covenant** are the thirty-three positional truths[173] and the Law of Messiah.

The Superiority of Messiah to Angels (2:1-18)

In verses 1-4 you have the ***first warning passage***. The introductory word *therefore* reflects what has just been said in chapter 1. ***Not drifting away from the Faith*** that was established by the mediatorial work of angels in the giving of the Law is in focus. Those who drift away from the Faith will be judged physically. In the Torah there are two great examples in Leviticus 10 with Nahab and Abihu and in Leviticus 16 with the rebellion of Korah, Dathan, and Abiram concerning the supremacy of the Aaronic Priesthood. The idea behind this is: If that which was mediated by angels received the judgment of God, it is even more true when the Law is being given by the One who created the angels, who is sovereign and supreme over the angels. If His words are neglected, counted as unimportant, those who neglect them will also receive even greater judgment; for all this was confirmed through *signs and wonders* with many *miracles* and *the gift of the Ruach Ha-Kodesh.*

Then in verses 5-18, the author proceeds to show that the Creator of angels, Yeshua, was made *a little lower than the angels* (vv. 7, 9) and took upon Himself the *seed of Abraham* (v. 16) so that He could provide in His death salvation through His blood, the blood of the **New Covenant,** when He ***inaugurated*** it at the Cross. Remember, He tasted death (v. 9); He did not nibble at death as all four Gospel accounts clearly record. As God, He could not die; but as the God/Man He could and did die. At that time, He was glorified, returning to the Father where all things have been put in *subjection under His feet* (v. 8). He is sovereign over the angels who mediated the Law. Now the author of Hebrews recaps it by quoting Psalm 8:4-6:

> *⁴ What is man, that You are mindful of him: And the Son of Man, that You visited Him? ⁵ For You have made Him a little lower than the angels, and have crowned Him with glory and honor. ⁶ You made*

---

[172] Arnold Fruchtenbaum, *Ariel's Bible Commentary: The Messianic Jewish Epistles: Hebrews, James, 1 & II Peter, and Jude.* San Antonio, TX: Ariel Press, 2005, pp. 23-27.

[173] Arnold Fruchtenbaum, Manuscript #110 – "Thirty-Three Things: A Study of Positional Truth." San Antonio, TX: Ariel Press, n.d.

Him to have dominion over the works of Your hands; You have put all things under His feet.

Headship and authority were given to man, Adam, but that was lost to Satan through the Fall of man into sin (Genesis 3). This headship was won back by Messiah Yeshua at the Cross which was the death sentence for Satan as He provided salvation for man and to fulfill His Promises to Israel in the Messianic Kingdom. He is sovereign; He is supreme. The Law was a temporary standard that was removed and replaced by Yeshua in the **New Covenant** with the Law of Messiah. This passage is loaded with many points worthy of explanation but due to the context of this book, it will not be articulated.

The Superiority of Messiah to Moses (3:1-6)

Before reviewing Hebrews 3:1-6, let us analyze two huge background verses that help us understand Moses. We will first look at Numbers 12:5-10 and then Deuteronomy 18:15-19 so that we first understand Moses fully, his position and his person. Look together with me at Numbers. The background to these verses is the sibling rivalry between Miriam and Aaron against Moses. This was a direct challenge to Moses' authority and it was instigated primarily by Miriam with Aaron following her lead:

> [5] *And the LORD came down in the pillar of the cloud* [Shechinah glory], *and stood in the door of the tabernacle and called Aaron and Miriam: and they both came forth.* [6] *And He said, Hear now My words: If there is a prophet among you, I the LORD will make Myself known unto him **in a vision** and will speak unto him **in a dream**.* [7] *My servant Moses is not so who is **faithful in all My house**.* [8] *With him will I speak **Mouth to mouth**, even apparently, and not in dark speeches* [riddles]; *and the **similitude** [form] **of the LORD shall he behold:** why then were you not afraid to speak against My servant Moses?* [9] *And the anger of the LORD was kindled against them* [Miriam and Aaron]; *and He departed.* [10] *And the cloud departed from off the tabernacle; and behold, Miriam became leprous, white as snow: and Aaron looked upon Miriam, and behold she was leprous.* (Numbers 12:5-10)

The LORD makes three points here: *First,* Moses was faithful in all the LORD's house, which would be the whole house of Israel. Now the LORD makes two additional clarifications on Moses and how the LORD revealed Himself to him in comparison to future prophets. With other prophets like Isaiah, Jeremiah, Ezekiel, and Zechariah, the LORD spoke to them in visions and dreams, but not so with Moses. *Second*, the LORD spoke to Moses *Mouth to mouth* or Face to face, meaning personal one-on-one communication. *Third*, the LORD says that Moses beheld the very form of God in His essence through limited exposure. The two descriptions make Moses unique among all other prophets for no other prophet, and I mean no other prophet, could have put that on his personal resume. Rabbinic Judaism likes to make Deuteronomy 18 plural, prophet<u>s</u>; but God was clear. He was referring to a singular Prophet, like Moses. Moses was a unique and faithful servant; this plays into a very pertinent section of Scripture from Deuteronomy 18:15-19 (below) on *the Prophet like Moses* that would come. He has come.

> *[15] The LORD your God will raise up unto you a Prophet* [Moses, pointing to Yeshua] *from the midst of you, of your brethren,* **like unto Me**; *unto Him you shall hearken;* [16] *According to all that you desired of the LORD your God in Horeb in the day of the assembly,* [Israel] *saying let me not hear again the voice of the LORD my God, neither let me see this great fire any more, lest I die.* [17] *And the LORD said unto me* [Moses], *they have well spoken that which they have spoken.* [18] ***I will*** *raise them up a Prophet from among their brothers,* ***like unto you****, and will* ***put My words in His mouth****; and He shall speak unto them* ***all that I shall command Him***. [19] *And it shall come to pass, that whosoever will not* ***hearken unto My words*** *which* ***He shall speak in My Name****, I will require it of him*.

The LORD said to Moses I will raise up a *Prophet* from your brethren *like unto you* Moses. Because the people were scared to death with the appearance of the LORD as described in Exodus 19:9-11, 16-20, they requested that the LORD speak to Moses (v. 16) and then Moses to them for they were terrified. Now again comes the supremacy of Yeshua, for in verses 18-19 you have a First Coming Messianic prophecy of Messiah who will be *the Prophet like Moses*. That *Prophet* would be none other than Yeshua Ha-Mashiach; for the LORD says of Himself, I will require of Israel to listen, to hearken unto every word that He speaks, for He is God.

We understand from Matthew 5:17 that the promised Messiah is the *Prophet* Who would *fulfill* all that He gave to Moses at Mount Sinai and then ***rendered that Law inoperative*** at the Cross. Here the LORD is speaking of Himself, for this appearance to Moses was a theophany of God, of Messiah, as He, Himself, gave the Law to Moses. This same Prophet will later mediate a **New Covenant** because Israel violated and broke the *old covenant* (Jeremiah 31:32; Deuteronomy 31:16, 20; Ezekiel 16:59). I will deal later with the fact that Yeshua is the Author of the Law of Moses. Moses was unique, a great man who was the LORD's faithful servant. Because of how the LORD spoke to him, Moses would be used as the marker to point NOT to himself but to Yeshua, *the Prophet like Moses*. All the Scriptures focus on *the Prophet like Moses* so much so that at the end of Deuteronomy 34:10, the end of the Torah, we find the explanation that this *Prophet* had not come yet. So, in the Prophets (*Nevi'im*) section of the Scriptures it opens with the fact that since the *Prophet* has not yet come, therefore *meditate* on the Law of the LORD *day and night* (Joshua 1:8).

> *And there arose not a prophet since in Israel like unto Moses, whom the LORD knew Face to face* (Deuteronomy 34:10).

> *This book of the Law shall not depart from your mouth; but you shall meditate in it day and night, that you may observe to do according to*

> *all that is written in it: for then you will make your way prosperous, and then you will have good success.* (Joshua 1:8)

The Prophet section of the Scriptures (*Nevi'im*) ends with the fact in Malachi (4:5) that the Prophet has not come yet, for *Elijah the prophet* will come *before the Day of the LORD.*

Now Yeshua talks about fulfilling all three sections of the *Tanakh:* the Law, the Prophets, and the Writings (Kethuvim) (such as Psalms, history, and other wisdom material):

> *Then He said to them, "These* are *the words which I spoke to you while I was still with you, that all things must be fulfilled which were written in the Law of Moses and in* the *Prophets and in* the *Psalms concerning Me."* (Luke 24:44)

The Psalms, from the Writings, begin with mediating on *the Law of the LORD; and in His Law does he mediate day and night* (Psalm 1:2). The end of the *Kethuvim* (II Chronicles 36:21; Leviticus 26:32-35) references the Seventy Weeks of Daniel; and in Daniel 9:24-27 is given the timetable for the coming of the *Prophet like Moses*, the Messiah.[174] As said before, Yeshua is central to all Scripture and is the focus throughout the *Tanakh* leading up to the Gospels and His First Coming. The focus is on Him, not on Moses and not on the Law. Can you see that?

Now with this background behind us, let us move on to Hebrews 3:1-6 which confirms the fact that Moses is not the key, for Yeshua is superior to Moses in all ways.

> [1] *Wherefore, holy brethren,* **partakers** *of a heavenly calling, consider the* **Apostle** *and* **High Priest** *of our profession, even Yeshua Ha-Mashiach;* [2] *Who was faithful to Him who appointed Him, as also was Moses faithful in all His house* [3] *For this Man has been counted worthy of* **more glory than Moses**, *just as He Who has built the house has more honor than the house.* [4] *For every house is built by someone; but* **He that built all things is God.** [5] *And Moses indeed was faithful in all His house, as a servant, for a testimony of those things which were afterward to be spoken;* [6] *but Messiah as a son*

---

[174] Mediating on the Law of the LORD and the threefold division of the Tanakh is brought out by two authors:

John H. Sailhamer, *The Meaning of the Pentateuch*. Downers Grove, IL: Intervarsity Press, 2009, pp. 17-18, 31, 51, 201-203, 298.

Michael Rydelnik, *The Messianic Hope*. Nashville, TN: B&H Publishers, 2010, pp. 60-64.

over His own house; whose house are we [body of Messiah], *if we hold fast the confidence and the rejoicing of the hope firm unto the end.*

In verse 1, these brethren were partakers of His *heavenly calling*; they were true believers in Messiah Yeshua. *Partaker* is used of these believers in Messiah (3:14), *partakers* in the Holy Spirit (6:4), and *partakers* of divine judgment (12:8). Only here in this Epistle to the Hebrews 3:1 is Yeshua called an *Apostle*. Elsewhere, He is called a sent one of the Father (Isaiah 48:16), as well as He being *like Moses* and the *High Priest* who was *like Moses,* as the great intercessor who pleaded with the LORD his God on behalf of Israel (Exodus 32:11-14; Numbers 12:13; Deuteronomy 9:20). These partakers whom the author is addressing in his Epistle are to *consider*, which means "to make a careful study or investigation of" the superiority of Messiah over Moses. Verse 2 says that both Yeshua and Moses were appointed and found faithful in their service. Then in verse 3, a distinction is made showing that Messiah is superior to Moses. Moses was faithful in his service for God over the house of Israel. Messiah was faithful in His service to the Father and was worthy of more glory than Moses, for He that built the house has *more honor than the house*. As important as Moses was as the tool of God to Israel, the Messiah is the Creator and *builder of all things*.

In review up to this point, Yeshua the Son is the ultimate revelation of God. He is superior to the angels, and now we see that Yeshua is superior to Moses. Do you have any misplaced allegiance to the Law of Moses? Can you recognize that Yeshua as the Shechinah in the *Tanakh* was the Author of that Law, and is now the Author and Mediator of the **New Covenant?** He enacted this change by His offering of Himself as the ultimate sacrifice for sin that He used to replace the *old covenant* and has now given us the Law of Messiah.

Following the first warning, ***not to drift away from the faith*** (Hebrews 2:1-4) but to remember that Yeshua is superior to Moses, is the ***second warning.*** Hebrews 3:7-4:13 warns believers concerning disobedience and doubt. Hebrews 4:11-13 is quoted below, as a reminder.

> *[11] Let us therefore labor to enter that rest, lest anyone fall according to the same example of unbelief. [12] For the word of God is living and powerful, and sharper than any two-edged sword, piercing even to the division of soul and spirit, and of joints and marrow, and is a discerner of the thoughts and intents of the heart. [13] And there is no creature hidden from His sight, but all things* are *naked and opened to the eyes of Him to whom we* must give *account.*

Next, we will see that Yeshua is superior to Aaron the high priest.

The Superiority of Messiah to Aaron (4:14-5:10)

Yeshua has a better *position (4:14-16)*

> *¹⁴ Seeing then that we have a great high priest, that is passed into the heavens, Yeshua the **Son of God**, let us hold fast our profession. ¹⁵ For we have not a high priest who cannot be touched with the feeling of our infirmities; but was in all points **tempted like as we are, yet without sin**. ¹⁶ Let us therefore come boldly unto the throne of grace, that we may obtain mercy, and find grace to help in time of need.*

The Greek word *oun* means "therefore," thus tying Hebrews 4:14 to the preceding second warning passage. Yeshua is our *great high priest* with the word *great* in Greek being *megan* meaning "intensely awesome and most excellent." He is highly exalted; superior to Moses, to Aaron, and to the Levitical priests, for He is designated as the Son of God. He has passed through the heavens at His ascension (Acts 1:9-11) and we have continuous access to this ***better position***, with a ***better priest*** than the earthly priest who only had access to God once a year (Leviticus 16) on the Day of Atonement (Yom Kippur). He also was tested (Matthew 4:1-11; Mark 1:12-13; Luke 4:1-13) without sin, showing that He understands all the limitations of humanity, for He was tested in all areas (I John 2:15-17) as we are, *without sin*. He understands our weaknesses because He personally experienced the limitations of our frail humanity, He can and does sympathize with us, meaning His ***better position*** also makes Him a ***better*** priest than Aaron.

Yeshua Is a Better *Priest (5:1-7:28)*

To be a ***better priest*** there are four prerequisites for the priesthood in Hebrews 5:1-4. This passage speaks of the contrast between Aaron and *the Prophet Like Moses* – Yeshua – as He also deals with the ***third warning to avoid spiritual stagnation*** (5:11-6:12) before going to the comparison of Yeshua with Melchizedek.

> The *first* prerequisite for being a priest is that you must be human.
>
> The *second* is that a priest must function in a priestly order in which he *offers both gifts and sacrifices for sin*.
>
> *Third*, he must be compassionate and sympathetic, and Yeshua personally experienced infirmity.
>
> *Fourth*, He had to be appointed by God just as Aaron was (Exodus 16:33; 28:1; Numbers 17:8).

In Hebrews 5:5-10, the author covers the same prerequisites above, but in a different order to show that Yeshua is a Priest after the order of Melchizedek, who is mentioned twice in verses 5 and 10. In verse 9 you have the reality of the **New Covenant**, *and being made perfect, He became the Author of eternal salvation unto* *all them that obey Him. All they that obey Him* is not a reference to the Mosaic Law but to the Law of Messiah that He instituted through the **New Covenant**. Again, He provided what the Law of Moses could never accomplish.

After the interlude of the ***third warning,*** the author now returns to Abraham and not Moses to illustrate God's immutable Promises. He points to the birth of Yitzchak (Isaac) which was twenty-five years in coming. Here it is extremely important to understand the activity of the pre-incarnate Messiah. His appearances before His earthly birth are called theophanies.[175] He appeared in the *Tanakh* as He made the Abrahamic Covenant, quoting from Genesis 12:3, and swearing only by Himself (Genesis 15), for there was no one greater. Messiah also appears as a theophany in Genesis 22:16-17 referring to Hebrews 4:14, where he showed the *immutability of His counsel, confirmed it by an oath*, His oath (Judges 2:1; Isaiah 48:12, 16). He is the *anchor of our soul*, not angels, not Moses and the Law, and not Aaron. As prophesied of Him in one of the BRANCH passages of Zechariah (6:12-13), for the BRANCH will wear two crowns: a kingly crown and a priestly crown, which was completely unheard of and forbidden in the Law. He is a ***better priest*** after the order of Melchizedek (Genesis 14; Psalm 110:4).

Messiah Is after the Order of Melchizedek, Not of Aaron (7:1-28)

There are three major comparisons in this section between Messiah and Melchizedek. However, the material that forms the basis for Melchizedek is very limited material in the *Tanakh*. Melchizedek is mentioned twice in the Hebrews text, with the historical record (Genesis 14:18-20) and the poetical record (Psalm 110:4). From those two texts, the author of Hebrew builds his three comparisons which he develops in this chapter:

1. First Comparison: Melchizedek and Yeshua – 7:1-3
2. Second Comparison: The Orders of Melchizedek and Aaron – 7:4-10
3. Third Comparison: The Levitical Priesthood and the Priesthood of Yeshua – 7:11-25

First Comparison: Melchizedek and Yeshua – 7:1-3

The introduction of Melchizedek by the author declares that he was the *king of Salem*. The name of his kingdom, Salem, means "peace," and was later known as Jerusalem. Melchizedek's Canaanite, Jebusite dynastic name means *"king of righteousness."* Along with being a king of Salem, he was also a priest of *the most*

---

[175] There are several chapters by John B. Metzger in his book *Discovering the Mystery of the Unity of God* (San Antonio, TX: Ariel Press, 2010) showing the activity of Yeshua in the Tanakh. Yeshua was the Author of the Abrahamic Covenant and also the One who inaugurated the **New Covenant**.

high God, a faithful high priest who was independent of any other priestly order. According to Allen, below, there is a repetition of words used in verses 1-2 and then repeated in reversed order:

> These 10 verses are also given cohesion by the use of chiasm where "meeting," "blessing," and "tenth" (all in vv. 1-2) are mentioned in inverted order in vv. 4, 6, 10.[176]

In verse 1, Melchizedek *met* Abraham and *blessed* him; and Abraham gave him a *tenth* of his spoils from the slaughter of the Mesopotamian kings. We also learn from the author that Melchizedek was *without father, without mother, without descent, having neither beginning of days, nor end of life but was made **like** unto the Son of God*. Fruchtenbaum capsulizes this by saying:

> There is no record of his [Melchizedek's] death; there is no record of someone needing to succeed him. Melchizedek represents the living, not the dying. Insofar as the biblical record is concerned, he abides a priest continually; the Melchizedekian Priesthood is eternal.[177]

Some conclude from verse 3 that Melchizedek was the pre-incarnate Messiah, which simply cannot be the case as Steven Ger, a Jewish believer, emphasizes:

> The text states that Melchizedek is **like** the Son of God, not that he is the Son of God, describing Melchizedek's similarity to Jesus with the word *aphomoioo*, "to make like," not the words *charakter*, "image," or *hupostasis*, "essence" (1:3).[178]

> Josephus records that in the fifteen centuries that had ensued from the inauguration of the Levitical priesthood to the destruction of the second temple, Israel was served by 83 different high priests. Jesus, however, permanently holds his priesthood because He continues forever. His priesthood is *aparabaton*, "inviolable," "untransferable," and therefore, is completely permanent.[179] [Bolding is mine.]

---

[176] David L. Allen, *Hebrews: The New American Commentary: An Exegetical and Theological Expositional of Holy Scripture*, p. 407.

[177] Arnold Fruchtenbaum, *Ariel's Bible Commentary: The Messianic Jewish Epistles: Hebrews, James, 1 & II Peter, and Jude.* San Antonio, TX: Ariel Press, 2005, p. 100.

[178] Steven Ger, *The Book of Hebrews: Christ is Greater*. Chattanooga, TN: AMG Publishers, 2009, p. 113.

[179] Steven Ger, *The Book of Hebrews: Christ is Greater*. Chattanooga, TN: AMG Publishers, 2009, p. 120.

I went to great lengths in one of my books[180] to show why Melchizedek could not be the pre-incarnate Messiah giving eight points from James Borland:

(1) Theophanies are actual appearances and not imaginary;

(2) They are initiated by God;

(3) They are revelatory, meaning that God's primary purpose was to reveal, at least in a partial manner, something about Himself or His will, to the recipient;

(4) They were for individuals;

(5) They were intermittent in appearance;

(6) They were also temporary;

(7) They were audible and visible;

(8) And, last, they did vary in form.[181]

In emphasizing point six of Borland (above), Fruchtenbaum makes further clarification as to why Melchizedek could not be a theophany.

> Another reason why Melchizedek could not have been a theophany is that, in the Old Testament, theophanies appeared and disappeared; they held no long-term office. The Melchizedek of Genesis 14 was a king of the city-state of Jerusalem, which required a position and a permanent residency. Theophanies never held a position; they were always short and temporary manifestations.[182]

This introduction sets the basis for the rest of the Hebrews, chapter 7.

Second Comparison: The Orders of Melchizedek and Aaron – 7:4-10

Before going into the second comparison, we need to examine the biblical principle of *imputation* (see teaching block in Snapshots in Romans on Imputation, page 118). Paul lays out the principle of *imputation* in Romans 5:12-19. In using the terminology of *imputation,* you and I, and all of mankind, are in the loins of Adam; for it was from Adam that the sin nature was *imputed* to us. Now the author of

---

[180] John B. Metzger, *Discovering the Mystery of the Unity of God.* San Antonio, TX: Ariel Press, 2010, pp. 257-262.

[181] James Borland, *Christ in the Old Testament.* Ross-shire, Great Britain: Christian Focus Publications, 1999, pp. 21-30.

[182] Arnold Fruchtenbaum, *Ariel's Bible Commentary: The Messianic Jewish Epistles: Hebrews, James, 1 & II Peter, and Jude.* San Antonio, TX: Ariel Press, 2005, p. 98.

Hebrews picks up that principle as it related to Abraham and Levi (one of Abraham's descendants). Fruchtenbaum expresses it well:

> The entire human race originated in the loins of Adam. As a result of this seminal relationship, when Adam sinned, all humanity is viewed as having participated in the sin. Hence, Adam's sin is imputed to all humanity because it is also considered to be the sin of every individual since Adam. The author of Hebrews points out that when Abraham paid tithes, Levi, who was a descendant of Abraham, was also viewed as having paid tithes to Melchizedek by means of **imputation** through a seminal relationship. Nevertheless, because he was in the loins of his father, Abraham, Levi was viewed as having paid tithes to Melchizedek.[183]

Before moving on to Hebrews 7:4-10, there is a point to be understood by the reader. The author of Hebrews indicates that even with the introduction in verses 1-3, he expands on the significance of Melchizedek in the future plan of God. Genesis 14:17-20 is not the focal text of Hebrews 7 but rather Hebrews 7:1-3 explains the significance and dependence on Psalm 110:4 by its author David.[184] Genesis 14 merely introduces Melchizedek to the Genesis text; while David in Psalm 110 picks up the spiritual emphasis of Melchizedek with David's future Son and then the author of Hebrews amplifies David's words.

In Hebrews 7:4, Abraham is called a *patriarch*, emphasizing his inherent greatness. He had an esteemed position but was lesser because by his giving to Melchizedek a *tenth of the spoils of war*, he was recognizing that the high priest Melchizedek was greater than he was. What will be emphasized in this chapter (Hebrews 7) is that the Levitical order under Aaron was inferior to the Melchizedekian order because the Levitical priests died and would have to be replaced; whereas, the Melchizedekian Priesthood was eternal, needing no successor. In the latter part of verse 4 and in verse 5, he references a *tenth* of the spoils and in that he references that *Levi* was in the *loins of Abraham*, so that *Levi* paid tithes to Melchizedek who was superior to Abraham even though Abraham had the Promises of the Abrahamic Covenant. This will be developed later in the chapter.

As the author of Hebrews begins to put together his thrust in this passage (Hebrews 7:4-10) that addresses the relationship of Abraham and Melchizedek, several things become clear, as Fruchtenbaum states, concerning the *tenth* or tithe and being *blessed*, and the superiority of Melchizedek over Abraham:

---

[183] Arnold G. Fruchtenbaum, "Man and Sin: Understanding Biblical Anthropology and Hamartiology," *Come and See Series,* Vol. 6, 2022, p. 195.

[184] David L. Allen, Hebrews: *The New American Commentary: An Exegetical and Theological Exposition of Holy Scripture.* Nashville, TN: B&H Publishing Group, 2010, pp, 410-411.

> First, Abraham's tithe to Melchizedek was a one-time event; he did not give one regularly. Second, Abraham did not give these tithes from his income but from the spoils of war. [as to the blessing] In verse 6, Melchizedek blessed Abraham. Although it says that Melchizedek's genealogy was not from them – he had no racial connection to the Levites – he received tithes from Abraham and then blessed Abraham. The blessor is superior to the one being blessed; Melchizedek blessed Abraham who had the covenant Promises. In verse 7, the writer's point is that the blessor is superior. ... The lesser is blessed by the greater. Abraham did not bless Melchizedek. Melchizedek blessed Abraham and he is therefore superior.
>
> [With Melchizedek represented as being eternal] the fourth superiority in verses 9-10 is shown in respect to Levi, who is the founder of the Tribe of Levi. He paid tithes to Melchizedek through Abraham. In verse 9, the point the writer makes is that Levi, who received tithes, paid them. But Levi was not yet living when the tithes were paid. How did he pay tithes through Abraham? The answer ... is a theological deduction. Verse 10 contains a principle found in Scripture called the principle of imputation, which emphasizes a seminal relationship. It is true that Levi was not living at the time that Abraham paid tithes to Melchizedek, but he was in *the loins of Abraham*. Levi paid tithes to Melchizedek by means of imputation, for he was still in the loins of his father, Abraham, *when Melchizedek met him*. The writer's point is that, if the fathers like Abraham and Levi were obliged to recognize the superiority of the Melchizedekian Priesthood, the sons should also recognize this superiority.[185] [brackets mine]

So the whole point of the author in the first ten verses of Hebrews chapter 7 is to show that when Melchizedek *met* Abraham and *blessed* him, we have the greater blessing the lesser. By citing the *tenth* of the spoils, the author of Hebrews ties Levi to Abraham in paying his tithe to Melchizedek, meaning that Levi – through Abraham – was lesser than Melchizedek (the lesser to the greater). Now he will develop this thought further.

---

[185] Arnold Fruchtenbaum, *Ariel's Bible Commentary: The Messianic Jewish Epistles: Hebrews, James, 1 & II Peter, and Jude.* San Antonio, TX: Ariel Press, 2005, pp. 100-101.

Third Comparison: The Levitical Priesthood and the Priesthood of Yeshua – 7:11-25

The Inferiority of the Levitical Priesthood – 7:11-19

¹¹ Therefore, if perfection were through the Levitical priesthood (for under it the people received the Law), what further need was there that another priest should rise according to the order of Melchizedek, and not be called according to the order of Aaron? ¹² For the priesthood being changed, of necessity there is also a change of the Law. ¹³ For He [Messiah] of whom these things are spoken belongs to another tribe [Judah], from which no man has officiated at the altar.

¹⁴ For it is evident that our Lord arose from Judah, of which tribe Moses spoke nothing concerning priesthood. ¹⁵ And it is yet far more evident if, in the likeness of Melchizedek, there arises another priest ¹⁶ who has come, not according to the Law of a fleshly commandment, but according to the power of an endless life. ¹⁷ For He testifies: "You are a priest forever according to the order of Melchizedek."

¹⁸ For on the one hand there is an annulling of the former commandment because of its weakness and unprofitableness, ¹⁹ for the Law made nothing perfect; on the other hand, there is the bringing in of a better hope, through which we draw near to God. [Brackets are mine.]

In the Greek there are two words for *another* or *other* as we saw in Galatians 1. *Allos* [ἄλλος] means "another of the same kind," whereas *heteros* [ἕτερος] means "another of a different kind."[186] In verses 11, 13, and 15 the author uses *heteros*. In verses 11 and 15 the author is pointing to another priest of a different kind, contrasting the priesthood of Yeshua with the priesthood of Aaron. He uses the same term, *heteros*, again in verse 13 of *another* tribe, other than Levi, for by command in the Mosaic Law the priest had to be of the line of Aaron (Levi); whereas, Yeshua was of the tribe of Judah, a different tribe than Levi (Aaron).

There is another significant word in verse 12, for *change* and *changed* are both used; *metathesis* (μετατιθεμένης) means "transposition" or "a transference from one place to another."[187] All of this analysis is repeated by Allen.[188] Verse 12 simply states

---

[186] William D. Mounce, *Complete Expository Dictionary of Old and New Testament Words*. Grand Rapids, MI: Zondervan Publications, 2006, p. 490.

[187] W. E. Vine, *Vine's Expository Dictionary of Old and New Testament Words*. Old Tappen, NJ: Fleming H. Revell Co, 1981, vol. 1, p. 180.

that the priesthood has changed from the Levitical priesthood to the Melchizedekian priesthood. The author continues by saying that it also requires the Law to change to the Law of Messiah of the **New Covenant**. Many Messianics and all of Rabbinic Judaism claim that the Law of Moses is eternal, but God and His author in Hebrews along with Paul in Galatians (3:23-24) state that the Law and Levitical system are temporary, for Messiah is NOW the High Priest after a different order than Aaron.

In verse 11, the author starts out with the Greek word *oun,* meaning "therefore," building on the previous statements. Hebrews 7:11 states and Fruchtenbaum adds that God did not intend for perfection to come through the Levitical system. Furthermore, there is an **inseparable** connect-ion between the Levitical Priesthood and the Mosaic Law. For one to be done away with would also require the other to be done away with.[189] This is an extremely important point. Now go back and reread this paragraph and the previous paragraph. God never divided the Law into moral, civil, and priestly sections; it was given by God as a unit! James understood that when he said to violate or break one Law makes you guilty of breaking all 613 Laws [2:10]. You cannot dice the Law up or modify it and say this section is mandatory and the rest are not. Torah keepers do this by cherry-picking the laws they wish to keep while trying to make them mandatory for all believers to keep. Then they ignore other commandments of the Law. Torah keepers are also guilty of modifying the Law so that they can violate the Law by keeping it outside of the Land of Israel. That is exactly what Stern states in his commentary regarding Hebrews 7:12, that it allows for separating the Levitical and sacrificial portion of the Mosaic Law out of the Law, making it non-mandatory:

> The context makes it overwhelmingly clear that no change or transformation in Torah is envisioned other than in connection with the priesthood and the sacrificial system. The term "metathesis" implies retention of the basic structure of Torah, with some of its elements rearranged ("transformed"); it does not imply abrogation of either the Torah as a whole or of mitzvot not connected with the priesthood and the sacrificial system.[190]

Stern's statement is an example of a Torah-observant type of position that falsely attempts to separate out some of the Law that could then be ignored while keeping in place other parts of the Law, usually by modifying the Author's Law. Another paraphrase of a Torah-observant author implies that now God has modified part of

---

[188] David L. Allen, *Hebrews: The New American Commentary: An Exegetical and Theological Expositional of Holy Scripture,* 420.

[189] Arnold Fruchtenbaum, *Ariel's Bible Commentary: The Messianic Jewish Epistles: Hebrews, James, 1 & II Peter, and Jude.* San Antonio, TX: Ariel Press, 2005, p. 102.

[190] David H. Stern, *The Jewish New Testament Commentary.* Clarksville, MD: Jewish New Testament Publications, 1992, p. 681.

the Law *because of what Yeshua did on the Cross*, which is the same thing that Stern said concerning Hebrew 7:12, generally saying that the Law is only modified in regard to the priesthood and sacrificial system and *because of what Yeshua did on the Cross*.

Again, Stern and an unnamed author are separating or dicing up the Law to fit their Torah-observant biases, which completely opposes the position of the author of Hebrews as well as Paul and the Jerusalem Council. He also tries to say that if the Law is set aside or annulled, then what do you do with the prophecies of Ezekiel 40-48, as he says there is a re-establishment of the Levitical system in the Kingdom?

This again shows a complete bias against the ability of God, Who is the Master of all, to change His economies from Law to Grace, to Kingdom. He is not Dispensational in his thinking; whereas, God IS Dispensational in how He works with mankind in each of His economies. One further paraphrase of the Torah-observant author mentioned above is how he questions the use of Matthew 5:17 from his Torah keeping perspective:

> If you change the Law in discarding the importance of Sabbath observance, the observing of the Feasts and the eating of kosher foods and the Torah's commandments concerning human ethics and morality, you violate the Law and are in rebellion to God.

He continues to show his bias and lack of understanding what the Master of the Universe instigated, as the saying goes: God HOLDS ALL THE TRUMP CARDS, not Messianic Torah scholars. Steven Ger understands what the author of Hebrews is saying in his response to Stern and to this unnamed teacher who promotes Torah observance:

> Yet what Stern decries is exactly what the passage teaches. The author's use of the particular, loaded word *metathesis*, coupled with the context in which it is employed, makes it difficult to accept that the author intends a mere shuffling of the Torah's deck along with a few selected Levitical edits in order to create a modified, rearranged, abridgment of Torah. Practically speaking, it is a fallacy to suppose that the Torah can be neatly compartmentalized. It was given to Israel as a single legislative unit composed of consistently overlapping ceremonial, civic, and moral legislation. To break one law was to break them all (James 2:10). Indeed, the Torah itself forbids either augmenting of diminishing its content (Deuteronomy 4:2). ... The priestly system is inextricably entwined in the very fabric of the Mosaic Law, similar to a metastatic tumor so

extensively spread that it cannot be excised without killing the patient.[191]

David Allen adds a further important statement to this whole idea of separating the Law for the sake of one theological bias.

> Verses 13-14 further explain why there must be a change in the Law. The Law prescribed that all priests must be from the tribe of Levi. If there is another priesthood, which supersedes the Levitical, then there must be a change in the Law, otherwise the new priesthood would be in violation of the Law.[192]

In verse 18 there are three very important words used by the author to show that the Law was inferior and incapable, *for the law made nothing perfect*. The first word is *disannulling* (in verse 18) of the commandments. To annul, *atheteo* means "to abolish" "to reject, set aside, nullify."[193]

> *For on the one hand there is an **annulling** of the former commandment because of its weakness and unprofitableness* (Hebrews 7:18).

It is an interesting word, as Ger states that within the context of Hebrews that the same word *atheteo* is used in 9:26 referencing Yeshua having removed, set aside, or put away sin through His sacrificial death. Now why has sin been annulled? The reason is because the former commandments, the Law, and the Levitical priesthood were *weak* and *useless*.[194] Allen states the following:

> The adjectives *weak* and *useless* are used to indicate that the Law itself, concerning the Levitical priesthood, could not bring about final atonement and the spiritual reality of access to God. In context, both the Law itself and the Levitical priests were incapable of bringing this about. *Useless* conveys a similar notion to *weakness* and describes the ineffectiveness of the Law. This is brought out in

---

[191] Steven Ger, *The Book of Hebrews: Christ is Greater*. Chattanooga, TN: AMG Publishers, 2009, p. 116.

[192] David L. Allen, Hebrews: *The New American Commentary: An Exegetical and Theological Exposition of Holy Scripture*. Nashville, TN: B&H Publishing Group, 2010.p. 422.

[193] William D. Mounce, *Mounce's Complete Expository Dictionary of Old and New Testament Words*. Grand Rapids, MI: Zondervan Publishing, 2016, p. 23.

[194] Steven Ger, *The Book of Hebrews: Christ is Greater*. Chattanooga, TN: AMG Publishers, 2009, p. 118.

> Hebrews 9, where the Law only brought external cleansing and could not deal with matters of the heart."[195]

This is all being laid aside by Yeshua, our High Priest, for the old system simply could not accomplish what was necessary for redemption. It was annulled, it was weak, it was useless and Messiah Yeshua gives us a *better* hope. Again, as mentioned in Galatians 3:23-25, the Law was our (Jewish people's) tutor; to lead people to Messiah. The Law could only point out one's sin; in contrast, this work of our High Priest will bring us a *better* hope,[196] establishing constant and open communication with the Father through the eternal Son. Now that all this background has been laid down, we turn to the superiority of the Priesthood of Yeshua.

In summary, just as His death *put away sin*; in the same way, His death put away the Law of Moses. It was because the Law was *weak* and *unprofitable*, for it could not provide life, only *death* and *condemnation* (II Corinthians 3:7, 9). This gives a better understanding of Romans 8:1-2.

The Superiority of the Priesthood of Yeshua – 7:20-28

Now the author moves from Yeshua being *better* than the Levitical system to Yeshua being a *better hope* for He is eternal and the Law and Levitical priests were temporary. Again, the author quotes Psalm 110:4 as he refers to the LORD's oath (*Horkomosia*) being kept with Yeshua in verses 20 and 28 as an irrevocable divine oath! The significance of an oath by God has complete priority. Ger states that the Levitical priesthood was established by means of Law, and even the Law of God takes second place to the *horkomosia* (oath) of God.[197]

> *The LORD has sworn and will not repent, You are a Priest forever after the order of Melchizedek* (Hebrews 7:21b).

Then the author of Hebrews adds that because of this oath we have with certainty of a *better covenant* (*Kreittonos diatheke*), which is a direct reference to Jeremiah 31 (Isaiah 42:6; 59:1-2; Ezekiel 16:59-60; Matthew 26:28; Revelation 5:9). From 7:22, the author uses the word *diatheke,* meaning "covenant" a total of 17 times (7:22; 8:6, 8, 9 [2x], 10; 9:4 [2x], 15 [2x], 16, 17, 20; 10:16, 29; 12:24; 13:20).

---

[195] David L. Allen, *Hebrews: The New American Commentary: An Exegetical and Theological Exposition of Holy Scripture.* Nashville, TN: B&H Publishing Group, 2010, p. 425.

[196] Arnold Fruchtenbaum, *Ariel's Bible Commentary: The Messianic Jewish Epistles: Hebrews, James, 1 & II Peter, and Jude.* San Antonio, TX: Ariel Press, 2005, p. 104.

[197] Steven Ger, *The Book of Hebrews: Christ is Greater.* Chattanooga, TN: AMG Publishers, 2009, p. 119.

> *By so much more was Yeshua made a surety of a **better covenant**.*
> (Hebrews 7:22)

The *oath* to Yeshua from the Father makes certain that He had made a *better covenant*. **Better** than what covenant? Because He fulfilled the Law (Matthew 5:17) and was the perfect sacrifice, He provided salvation through His finished work on the Cross, establishing the ***better covenant*** or the **New Covenant** which takes the place of the *old covenant*, the Mosaic covenant. Throughout this book I have been italicizing the term *old covenant* to emphasize that term because we will now be entering the pinnacle of that discussion starting here, then followed up in chapters 8-9 of Hebrews, to completely cement the *old covenant* as disannulled, ***rendered inoperative***, abolished, terminated, and replaced by the **New Covenant**.

In Hebrews 7:23-24, the author emphasizes the humanity of Yeshua. For there have been many priests, eighty-three to be exact, who have not continued because of death, because of the weakness of the *old covenant*. But the God-Man continues because He is of an unchangeable priesthood, for it is eternal as the psalmist David stated. Now David lived 1000 years before Yeshua and the change of economies, yet in David's day it should have been realized that the *old covenant* was temporary because of what David wrote in Psalm 110:4.

In verse 25, we read that because of the *oath* of God, Yeshua made a *better covenant*, one that is irrevocable. He is therefore (*oun*) able to save (*sozein*) to the uttermost. Both Fruchtenbaum and Ger interact respectively with the words *saved* and *uttermost*.

> The Greek word for *uttermost* means "to arrive at a final destination with all these various aspects completed." It means "to be saved completely and to be saved forever." This is a good verse for eternal security. They have been saved to the uttermost; saved forever, saved totally, saved completely. Jesus guarantees that the believer will arrive at his final destination. Because there is a future facet of salvation which is the redemption of their bodies at the resurrection, and because the believer has already been saved to the uttermost, their resurrection is guaranteed.[198]
>
> In 7:25 the author reaches a logical conclusion based on the previous verses. Jesus is, therefore, "able to save forever." The present tense of *sozein*, the verb translated "to save," indicates that Jesus' work in salvation goes far beyond that of the single moment in time that the new believer initially received salvation. His salvation power extends throughout each moment of every believer's lifetime,

---

[198] Arnold Fruchtenbaum, *Ariel's Bible Commentary: The Messianic Jewish Epistles: Hebrews, James, 1 & II Peter, and Jude.* San Antonio, TX: Ariel Press, 2005, p. 106.

ensuring our salvation for today as well as our eventual arrival in His presence at our final tomorrow.[199]

In Hebrews 7:26, the author points to five things that are true of Yeshua our High Priest because of His nature.

> *First*, He is *holy*, He is pure and in His personal relationship with the Father.
>
> *Second*, He is *guileless,* for He did not practice evil but righteousness in all His dealings.
>
> *Third*, He was *undefiled;* unstained, and free from all kinds of defilement and as Fruchtenbaum[200] adds, this freedom was from all defilement; this is His relationship sinward (towards sin), and it refers to His sinlessness and moral purity in contrast to the Levitical priests who were concerned with ritual (physical) purity.
>
> *Fourth*, He is *separated from sinners* in His present ministry in the heavenly Tabernacles.
>
> *Last*, He was made higher than the heavens.

This verse (7:26) also starts out with the Greek word *gar* meaning "for." Allen says that the use of *gar* connected with the use to describe the high priest we have in Jesus likely refers both to what has been said in the immediately preceding verses and to what follows here in verses 27 and 28.[201]

In verse 27, the author makes a contrast between the Levitical priest and Yeshua's offering. The priest offered up daily and yearly sacrifices, first for himself before offering up for the people, as he is referencing the Day of Atonement. Yeshua did so once when He offered up Himself. Fruchtenbaum[202] makes an additional note saying:

> While His own death was a priestly act, He was not a priest at the time of His death, for it was God the Father who offered Him up

---

[199] Steven Ger, *The Book of Hebrews: Christ is Greater*. Chattanooga, TN: AMG Publishers, 2009, p. 120.

[200] Arnold Fruchtenbaum, *Ariel's Bible Commentary: The Messianic Jewish Epistles: Hebrews, James, 1 & II Peter, and Jude.* San Antonio, TX: Ariel Press, 2005, p. 107.

[201] David L. Allen, Hebrews: *The New American Commentary: An Exegetical and Theological Exposition of Holy Scripture.* Nashville, TN: B&H Publishing Group, 2010, p. 429.

[202] Arnold Fruchtenbaum, *Ariel's Bible Commentary: The Messianic Jewish Epistles: Hebrews, James, 1 & II Peter, and Jude.* San Antonio, TX: Ariel Press, 2005, p. 107.

(Psalm 22:15; Isaiah 53:10). Jesus did not become High Priest until the ascension, and that is why His priesthood is continuous.

In verse 28, we read that the Law made *men high priests* but they were full of weaknesses, and they died; but with *the word of the oath* of God *the Son is consecrated for evermore*. In the mind of the author, both the Levitical system and the Law itself were over, replaced by the Son who fulfilled all the expectations and requirements of God and mediated the **New Covenant**.

A summary of Hebrews 7 follows in eight points:

(1) Yeshua represents all, while Aaron represented Israel only.

(2) Aaron was only a priest, while Yeshua is both King and Priest.

(3) While Aaron was concerned with sin and judgment, the priestly ministry of Yeshua was characterized by righteousness and peace.

(4) Yeshua did not inherit or pass on His priesthood, while Aaron did pass on his priesthood, and his descendants inherited the priesthood from Aaron.

(5) Aaron's priesthood kept those he represented in a state of infancy, while the priesthood of Yeshua brings to maturity.

(6) The ministry of Yeshua resulted in blessing, while Aaron's only produced that which was weak and unprofitable.

(7) The Aaronic priesthood was based on the Law of Moses which functioned by an endless procession of dying men, while the priesthood of Yeshua is based on a covenant that made Him a priest forever, unchangeable and permanent.

(8) The priesthood of Yeshua is based on the sinlessness of the priest, while the Aaronic priesthood was carried on through sinful men.

The following chart (from Steven Ger's book on Hebrews, pages 122-123), compares the Levitical and Melchizedekian priesthoods.

Levitical Priesthood and Jesus' Melchizedekian Priesthood – page 223

Levitical	Melchizedekian	Hebrews
Serves as priest only	Serves as Priest and King	1:3, 8; 2:17; 3:1; 4:14-15; 5:5, 9-10; 7:1-2
Ministry is limited to Israel	Ministry is universal in scope	7:1-3
Subordinate to Abraham	Superior to Abraham	7:2, 4-7
Israel tithed to Levi	Levi tithed to Melchizedek	7:9-10
Dependent on Aaron[ic] genealogy	Independent of genealogy	7:3, 6, 11-16
Appointed by Law	Appointed by divine oath	7:28
Requires many appointed men	Requires one appointed Son	4:14; 5:1, 5; 7:23-28
Temporary and limited by death	Unlimited by time and duration through immortality	5:6, 9-10; 6:20; 7:3, 8, 15-19, 23-25
Priest needs atonement	Priest is source of atonement	2:9-10, 17; 5:3; 7:26-28
Priest has restricted access to Holy Of Holies	Priest has continual access to the Holy of Holies	9:7, 9-14, 24; 10:19-22
Priest serves in a copy of the divine Tabernacle	Priest serves in the divine Tabernacle	8:2-5; 9:1-8, 11-12, 24
Priest is chief officiate on the Day of Atonement	Priest is fulfillment of the Day of Atonement	9:7, 11-14
Priest sacrifices animals	Priest sacrifice Himself	2:9-10; 10:4, 10-14
Priest regularly offers a series of multiple sacrifices	Priest offers one ultimate sacrifice	7:27; 8:3; 9:26; 10:1-4, 10-14

Levitical Priesthood and Jesus' Melchizedekian Priesthood – page 224

Levitical	Melchizedekian	Hebrews
Priest continually standing	Priest now seated	10:11-12
No final remission of sin	Final remission of sin	2:9-10; 5:9-10; 7:27; 9:26; 10:1-4, 10-14, 18
Imperfect salvation results	Perfect salvation results	2:9-10, 17; 7:11-14, 18-19, 28; 10:1-4, 10-14
Provision of external cleansing	Provision of internal cleansing	9:13-14
Priest can never secure salvation	Priest secures eternal salvation	5:9-10; 7:25; 9:12; 10:1-4, 10-14
Appointment dependent on Mosaic Law	Appointment independent of Mosaic Law	5:6, 9-10; 7:1-3, 11-19; 8:4
Inherent deficiency of old legal basis	Inherent perfection of new legal basis	7:11-14, 18-19
Based on a good covenant	Based on a better covenant	7:22
Based on a good hope	Based on a better hope	7:19
One man possessed access to Divine Presence	All believers possess access to Divine Presence	9:7; 10:19-22

by Steven Ger, *The Book of Hebrews: Christ is Greater*. Chattanooga, TN: AMG Publishers, 2009, pp. 122-123.

The Superiority of the New Covenant over the *Old Covenant* (8:1-13).

Now the author has moved us along theologically and practically from the Son who is the final revelation, to the facts that He is superior to (*better* than) angels, superior to (*better* than) Moses, superior to (*better* than) Aaron and now superior to (*better* than) the whole Levitical system and the Law. It has all been laid aside, and our High Priest has *mediated* a ***better covenant***, the **New Covenant** with all its ramifications. As a reminder, the word for *new* in **New Covenant** means something brand new, and not something renewed, which we covered in Part One of this book. The New Priesthood is based on a ***better*** *covenant*.

The Basis of the New Covenant: Better Promises – 8:1-6

The Levitical priests and the Law of Moses that governs them are inferior, weak, unprofitable, and broken, but our High Priest is in a place of superiority at the right hand of the throne of God in the heavens, not on earth. He is not reigning from David's throne right now. His ministry now takes place in the true Tabernacle of which the earthly Tabernacle and later Temple are mere shadows, patterns (Exodus 25:9) or types of the real Tabernacle in heaven. In the author's day, the Temple was still standing in all of its beauty and glory; but because Messiah was of the tribe of Judah, He could not act as an earthly priest. Verse 6 is key; Messiah has a more excellent ministry, and the author makes three points:

First, Messiah is a *mesites*, a mediator, an arbitrator, or a go-between regarding the Father and mankind on earth, any who are lost in sin. In the Kingdom, He will be an arbitrator between individuals; but after His rejection at His First Coming, He refused to be an arbitrator or mediator between brothers (Luke 12:13-14).

Second, He mediated a *better covenant;* and the *better covenant* is the **New Covenant**. The ramifications of the **New Covenant** alone could fill a large book. The inferior Law cannot hold a candle to it.

Third, this *better covenant* was established upon *better promises*. I hope as you have gone through Hebrews you have taken notice of the author's use of the word *better*. Here is a summary of this section by Fruchtenbaum:

> Jesus serves in Heaven in a more excellent or ***better*** ministry. This ministry is based upon a ***better*** covenant, which is the theme for the rest of this chapter. Jesus has a superior [***better***] priesthood because of the superior basis on which it rests. The superior basis is ***better*** promises which are found in the ***better*** covenant, the **New Covenant.** Any covenant made between God and man demands a mediator. Moses was the mediator of the first covenant, and Aaron was the priest. However, Jesus is both the Mediator and the Priest of the **New Covenant**. The **New Covenant** is superior [***better***] to the *old*

covenant because it rests upon *better* promises. For example, the *old covenant*, the Mosaic Covenant, was based upon the Law. It brought blessing for obedience, but it brought cursing, and even death for disobedience. In contrast, the **New Covenant** is based upon grace, and it is able to impart righteousness and provide empowerment to keep its demands. It is this **New Covenant** that is the basis for His high priestly ministry in a *better* sanctuary.[203] [brackets and ***bolding*** mine]

Below is a chart by Steven Ger from his book on Hebrews.[204]

The Use of the Term *Better* in Hebrews	
Hebrews 1:4	Jesus has become *much **better** than angels*
Hebrews 6:9	***Better*** *things concerning you*
Hebrews 7:7	*Lesser is blessed by the greater*
Hebrews 7:19	*A **better** hope*
Hebrews 7:22; 8:6	*A **better** covenant*
Hebrews 8:6	***Better*** *promises*
Hebrews 9:23	***Better*** *sacrifices*
Hebrews 10:34	*A **better** possession*
Hebrews 11:16	*A **better** country*
Hebrews 11:35	*A **better** resurrection*
Hebrews 11:40	*God had provided something **better***
Hebrews 12:24	***Better*** *than the blood of Abel*
by Steven Ger	

The Proof of the Superiority of the New Covenant – 8:7-12

Fruchtenbaum[205] clearly points to the fact that the announcement of the **New Covenant** was a new and ***better covenant***, meaning that the Mosaic Covenant was

---

[203] Arnold Fruchtenbaum, *Ariel's Bible Commentary: The Messianic Jewish Epistles: Hebrews, James, 1 & II Peter, and Jude.* San Antonio, TX: Ariel Press, 2005, p. 110.

[204] Steven Ger, *The Book of Hebrews: Christ is Greater.* Chattanooga, TN: AMG Publishers, 2009, p.39.

old. Thus, the prophet Jeremiah declared that the *old covenant* was temporary and that it would end and be replaced by this **New Covenant.**

Verse 7 begins with the Greek *gar* meaning "for." The author of Hebrews was building his argument from verses 3 and 4 from the previous section which was an introduction to this section. If the Mosaic Law *was faultless*, there would be no need for a **New Covenant**; but the *old covenant* could not produce the power for justification. Repeating from before, the problem was not with the Law, for it was *holy, just and good* (Romans 7:12). The fault lay with Israel who had an incapacity to keep the Law, for the Law could not provide the power to keep it. Despite this deficit in Israel's ability to keep the Law, Torah-keeping Gentiles (and some Jewish believers) keep going back to a failed system to keep a Law that was never given to them in the first place. Notice in verse 8 the pronoun *them*. The *them* is Israel (not Gentiles for they are not even included in the context) as the author again uses *gar* or *for* as he moves into a powerful section of Scripture which is the largest intact passage quoted from the *Tanakh* (from Jeremiah 31:31-34) in all the New Testament:

> *⁸ For finding fault with them, He says, Behold, the days come, says the LORD, when I will make a **New Covenant** with the House of Israel and with the House of Judah: ⁹ Not according to the covenant that I made with their fathers in the day when I took them by the hand to lead them out of the land of Egypt; because they continued not in My covenant, and I regarded them not, says the LORD. ¹⁰ For this is the covenant that I will make with the House of Israel after those days, says the LORD; I will put My laws into their mind, and write them in their hearts: and I will be to them a God, and they shall be to Me a people: ¹¹ And they shall not teach every man his neighbor; and every man his brother, saying, Know the LORD: for all shall know Me from the least to the greatest. ¹² For I will be merciful to their unrighteousness, and their sins and their iniquities will I remember no more.*

The opening salvo is that, as Allen states, the Law was a failure and insufficient by design. Both the *old covenant* and the **New Covenant** originated in the will of God and served to express His single divine will, but was given in two consecutive and strategic parts to man.[206]

Let me explain it this way. For God was not ready to reveal His complete will to Israel, because in His progressive revelation of Himself and His Son, it was not yet time to fully reveal His plan and His Messiah. His plan was meant for the remedy of

---

[205] Arnold Fruchtenbaum, *Ariel's Bible Commentary: The Messianic Jewish Epistles: Hebrews, James, 1 & II Peter, and Jude.* San Antonio, TX: Ariel Press, 2005, p. 111.

[206] David L. Allen, Hebrews: *The New American Commentary: An Exegetical and Theological Exposition of Holy Scripture.* Nashville, TN: B&H Publishing Group, 2010, pp. 446-447.

sin and later to fulfill His Promises to Abraham, Israel, and David. Until then, Israel needed a tutor (Law) to guide and direct them in anticipation of His time to reveal His Son (Galatians 3:23-25), when His Son would take on flesh and dwell (John 1:14) among His people. They, of course, rejected *the Prophet Like Moses* (Deuteronomy 18:15-19), and had Him crucified, which set the stage to fully reveal God's redemptive program when He would regenerate (circumcise) the hearts of His people (Jeremiah 31:33; Ezekiel 36:26; Deuteronomy 30:6). Further, He would forgive all sin (Jeremiah 31:34) by the blood of the Lamb of God (John 1:29; Revelation 5:5-6, 9, 12-13), who is God's Son (Proverbs 30:4; Isaiah 9:6-7). By this plan, He would give all future Jews and Gentiles who believe in Him, the indwelling Ruach Ha-Kodesh (Ezekiel 36:26-27; John 14:17; I Corinthians 3:16; 6:19), with the Holy Spirit's sealing (Ephesians 1:13-14) and baptism (I Corinthians 12:13).

God **announced** His Plan through Jeremiah, but did not **inaugurate** it until the death of Messiah, Who was given to regenerate both Jews and Gentiles, to provide forgiveness, and to enable the indwelling of the Ruach Ha-Kodesh by His **inauguration** of the **New Covenant**. The fulfillment or the **ratification** of the **New Covenant** belongs to Israel alone at the end of the Tribulation period when they embrace Him and call for Him to come and deliver them from the Anti-christ, which He will do; and then He will set up the Kingdom and fulfill the Abrahamic, Land, Davidic, and **New** covenants.

What becomes even more interesting is that in the Masoretic Text for Jeremiah's prophecy, the Law is referenced in the singular, but the Septuagint text says Law**s** in the plural. Ger gives a plausible explanation:

> The standard Masoretic Hebrew text of Jeremiah's prophecy records that God will write on Israel's hearts His law (singular form), which is often taken to mean God's "Torah." However, we do not find in the corresponding section of the Septuagint's second-century BC Greek translation of Jeremiah a parallel reading of *nomos*, "law" (singular form), but instead, *nomous*, "laws" (plural form). ... The Jewish translators of the Septuagint intentionally translated Jeremiah 31:33 with a plural *nomous* to remove the possibility of misunderstanding it in reference to the Torah, intending that it instead be understood as a nonspecific set of God's laws that may or may not overlap with those of the Mosaic legislation. ... the plural *nomous* is not accident of translation, but rather the accurately safeguarded and transmitted Word of God.[207]

---

[207] Steven Ger, *The Book of Hebrews: Christ is Greater*. Chattanooga, TN: AMG Publishers, 2009, p. 130.

It clearly conveys that the translators of the Septuagint understood more than we give them credit for, that the system of Law would change to Law*s* which are given in the form of imperative commands in the New Testament Epistles, pointing to the Law of Messiah.

In Hebrews 8, verse 8 and verse 10, you have the phrases *the days come* and *after those days*. The question is after what days? In the Jeremiah text that phrase is in the prophetic future, meaning in the future He will establish the **New Covenant** with Israel but will do so in two parts, at two different times. What we know from God's progressive revelation is that Yeshua would *inaugurate* the **New Covenant** at His death, but will not *ratify* it at the same time, because that also has a qualifying phrase *after those days*. Torah keepers want to teach that the Law is eternal and that the **New Covenant** is a *renewed*[208] *old covenant*, that is modified. The second prophetic future stage of *after those days* refers to after Israel is purged of its rebels (Ezekiel 20:33-38), and those remaining believe in Him by Faith (Hosea 5:15-6:3) and call for His return. He will return and deliver them at the very end of the Tribulation period (Micah 2:12-13). *It will be only to a newly regenerated nation, saved in a day* (Zechariah 3:9; Romans 11:25-26) *that He will install His Law in their hearts and minds* (Joel 2:28-32), *not before!* Otherwise, the Scriptures contradict themselves, for Paul uses two imperative commands to believers, both Jews and Gentiles in Romans 12:2, that they are not to be *conformed to this world* but to be *transformed by the renewing of the mind*. **Why do believers have to renew their minds? It is because that New Covenant had not yet been ratified**, so they must be daily immersed in His Word and being obedient to the Law of Messiah. The same principle applies and is recorded in the *Tanakh*, to meditate on the Word of God day and night (Joshua 1:8; Psalm 1:1-2). Romans 12:2 would be useless if God had already implanted His Word in their hearts as Torah keepers claim. When Jeremiah and the author of Hebrews reference this passage, the author's intent should be easily understood, as Ger states:

> *Behold, days are coming.* Every Israelite should have anticipated that the Mosaic Covenant's days were numbered. It became antiquated in Jeremiah's day, and it was "ready to disappear" when [the Epistle of] Hebrews was written almost two millennia ago.[209] [brackets mine]

Now let me return to the two aspects of the **New Covenant** which involve two different time periods. First, when the **New Covenant** is *inaugurated,* it set the stage for both Jews and Gentiles to be regenerated, for forgiveness of sin and indwelling of the Ruach Ha-Kodesh. At that period in time, we only received this first phase of the

---

[208] See Part One of this book, "The Difference between New and Renew," p.51.

[209] Steven Ger, *The Book of Hebrews: Christ is Greater*. Chattanooga, TN: AMG Publishers, 2009, p. 135.

New Covenant. We will not receive the full application of the **New Covenant** that Jeremiah speaks of until after our death or the Rapture when we as believers all go to be in His presence. For us as Gentiles, the reality of the **New Covenant** will then be complete; the old nature ceases. Then at a different time period – still future and not from its *inauguration* 2000 years ago, the *ratification* of the **New Covenant** will be fulfilled when *all Israel* living at the end of the Tribulation period will believe and call for His deliverance. ***Then and only then will Israel have implanted in their hearts and minds His Law*** which is not the same as the *old covenant* Law system. There is so much more than can be said to confirm all that the Lord has written.

Conclusion – 8:13 – The Temporary Ceases; The New Covenant Is Permanent

> *In that He says, a New Covenant, He has made the first old. Now that which decays and waxes old is ready to vanish away.*

Our attention is drawn to the word *old* as Ger states:

> [The term *old*] in the Greek is *palaioo* which means obsolete, antiquated, useless through being worn out. The Mosaic covenant had automatically become the *old covenant*. Paul likewise employs the phrase *old covenant* (II Corinthians 3:14). ... The verb for *old*, *palaioo*, is employed twice in this verse, first conjugated as a perfect active indicative, *He has made old*, and again as a present passive participle *being made old*, both forms leading to the inevitable conclusion that God Himself was the responsible agent of the Mosaic Covenant's obsolescence. In short, God exercised His divine prerogative to pull the plug on His own covenant, but only after having established its superior replacement.[210]

Fruchtenbaum and Allen add to this context of understanding the words used and not used by the author:

> There are two different Greek words for *old*. The first is *archaios*, which is the origin of the English word "archaeology." This word means "old in point of time." If something is only old in the point of time, it may still be usable. ... The Second Greek word, the word used here is *palaios*, which is the origin of The English word "paleontology." It means "old in the point of use," it is "worn out," "useless," "obsolete." It is in the Greek perfect tense meaning it has been made *old* in the sense of uselessness and continues to be so.

---

[210] Steven Ger, *The Book of Hebrews: Christ is Greater*. Chattanooga, TN: AMG Publishers, 2009, p. 134.

> The **New Covenant** permanently antiquated the *old covenant*. It is obsolete, it is aged, and it has been rendered inoperative.[211]

> The use of the perfect tense of *palaioo*, "make obsolete," highlights the permanent antiquated status of the *old covenant*. Both participles in the final clause, literally, "what is growing old" and "what is aging," are governed by a single article, which indicates a single action is in view. The first participle is passive and the second is active: the Mosaic covenant has been declared old by God and is aging in the sense of being outdated.[212]

Ger[213] challenges his Messianic brothers in Messiah that regardless of the contextual and grammatical evidence, Torah keepers tenaciously hold to their position that there is only one Torah, even if they have to modify it to make it work, as if Torah was the premium hallmark of Jewish identity. He further adds that for Messianics, to be disloyal to Torah is to abandon their Jewish heritage and that abandonment of Torah is seen as rebellion against God. In reality, Torah observance has absolutely nothing to do with their Jewishness. One final point on this, they are also suffering from the residual effect from a well-known rabbi, Maimonides, who said in the ninth of his famous thirteen Principles of Faith, "I believe with a complete faith that this Torah will not be exchanged and there will be no other Torah from the creator." That is a blatant denial of Jeremiah as well as assuming the mind of the Creator by a finite rabbi. Further, according to Ger:

> The Melchizedekian priesthood of Yeshua was not designed to be inserted into the Mosaic covenant's preexisting mold; it broke the mold! ... Believers cannot swap out one priesthood for another, like upgrading the components of an obsolete computer. The **New Covenant** is not an upgrade but a comprehensive replacement. The reason that new wine cannot be poured into old wineskins.[214]

---

[211] Arnold Fruchtenbaum, *Ariel's Bible Commentary: The Messianic Jewish Epistles: Hebrews, James, 1 & II Peter, and Jude.* San Antonio, TX: Ariel Press, 2005, p. 112.

[212] David L. Allen, Hebrews: *The New American Commentary: An Exegetical and Theological Exposition of Holy Scripture.* Nashville, TN: B&H Publishing Group, 2010, p. 449.

[213] Steven Ger, *The Book of Hebrews: Christ is Greater.* Chattanooga, TN: AMG Publishers, 2009, p. 135.

[214] Steven Ger, *The Book of Hebrews: Christ is Greater.* Chattanooga, TN: AMG Publishers, 2009, p. 136.

Summary of Main Points in Hebrews

In reviewing Hebrews, look at the main points showing that the *old covenant* was completely *rendered inoperative* by God, not by Dispensationalists – we merely observe what God did and believe it.

> *First*, Messiah the Son is the final word, the final revelation from the Father (1:1-3).
>
> *Second*, he shows us from the *Tanakh* that Yeshua, the Son is superior to angels (1:4-14).
>
> *Third*, the Son is superior to Moses (3:1-6).
>
> *Fourth*, the Son is superior to Aaron (5:1-4).
>
> *Fifth*, the **New Covenant** is superior to the entirety of the Levitical priesthood and sacrifices (5:5-10; 6:13-20).
>
> *Sixth*, Yeshua is now a priest after a different order that replaces the Aaronic priestly order; He is of the Melchizedekian order (7:4-28).
>
> *Seventh*, Yeshua is the mediator of the **New Covenant** and all the spiritual blessings (Ephesians 1:3), and all the physical blessings Israel will enjoy as Messiah fulfills the Abrahamic, Land, Davidic and **New Covenants** in the Messianic Millennial Kingdom which will extend into the Eternal Order (8:1-13).

The Superiority of the Messiah's Priestly Service (9:1-10)

Components of the Levitical Sanctuary – 9:1-5

Here I offer only a brief summary of this section (see the chart on The **New Covenant** between God and Israel, page 237, for more detail.) Looking at Hebrews 9:1-5, first, the author makes a contrast between the earthly Tabernacle and the heavenly Tabernacle in 8:2.

> *¹ Then indeed, even the first* covenant *had ordinances of divine service and the earthly sanctuary. ² For a tabernacle was prepared: the first* part, *in which* was *the lampstand, the table, and the showbread, which is called the sanctuary; ³ and behind the second veil, the part of the tabernacle which is called the Holiest of All, ⁴ which had the golden censer and the ark of the covenant overlaid on all sides with gold, in which* were *the golden pot that had the manna, Aaron's rod that budded, and the tablets of the covenant; ⁵ and above it were the cherubim of glory overshadowing the mercy seat. Of these things we cannot now speak in detail.*

Remember that the author put forth in chapter 8 that the earthly Tabernacle was but a pattern or type of the heavenly Tabernacle. These verses deal with the approach to God. On the earth it was only once a year; whereas, with the **New Covenant** and the heavenly Tabernacle, we can continually approach Him because the *veil* at the death of Yeshua was *rent from top to bottom* (Matthew 27:51). In verses 1-5 you have a brief description of the Holy Place and the Holy of Holies and the fact that there were separations in dealing with all the components of the Levitical sanctuary. Fruchtenbaum[215] notes that under the old system there were barriers that separated the Jewish people in their worship of God. The Outer Court separated Gentiles from Jews. The Inner Court separated the Levites from the non-Levites. The first veil separated the priest from non-priest. The second veil separated the High Priest from common priests. However, we now understand that through the **New Covenant** that Yeshua mediated, there are no barriers or separations of peoples. Yeshua is superior to the *old covenant* system.

Components of Levitical or Priestly Service – 9:6-7

In verses 6-7, the first room and the second room of the Tabernacle / Temple deal with the Holy Place and the Holy of Holies:

> *⁶Now when these things had been thus prepared, the priests always went into the first part of the tabernacle, performing the services. ⁷But into the second part the high priest went alone once a year, not without blood, which he offered for himself and* for *the people's sins* committed *in ignorance;*

The emphasis in verse 6 on the first Tabernacle or the Holy Place was that the priests were continually doing their daily work, tending the Menorah, adding oil to it daily, trimming the wick, and changing the showbread. The emphasis is that the priests were never finished and there were no chairs for them to sit down. The contrast is clearly made as Fruchtenbaum states,[216] only one man, the high priest could enter. Only one man, out of one family, out of one clan, out of one tribe, out of one nation, out of one ethnicity of the Jewish people, out of all humanity ever had access to that room; and that was only on the Day of Atonement once a year and only with blood to be sprinkled on the mercy seat. The work of the priest went on and on because it was inadequate; whereas, the work of Yeshua is finished, and He is seated. The reason He is seated is because His work is done and completed; it is final. The contrast

---

[215] Arnold Fruchtenbaum, *Ariel's Bible Commentary: The Messianic Jewish Epistles: Hebrews, James, 1 & II Peter, and Jude.* San Antonio, TX: Ariel Press, 2005, pp. 114-115.

[216] Arnold Fruchtenbaum, *Ariel's Bible Commentary: The Messianic Jewish Epistles: Hebrews, James, 1 & II Peter, and Jude.* San Antonio, TX: Ariel Press, 2005, p. 115.

could not be clearer between the *old covenant* which was inferior to the superior and *better* **New Covenant** established by Yeshua, its mediator.

The Limitations of the Inferior Levitical Worship – 9:8-10

The author credits the illumination of the Ruach Ha-Kodesh that the way to holiness was not manifested, it was not revealed while the earthly Temple was still functioning.

> *⁸ ... the Holy Spirit indicating this, that the way into the Holiest of All was not yet made manifest while the first tabernacle was still standing. ⁹ It* was *symbolic for the present time in which both gifts and sacrifices are offered which cannot make him who performed the service perfect in regard to the conscience— ¹⁰ concerned only with foods and drinks, various washings, and fleshly ordinances imposed until the time of reformation.*

None of the offerings and sacrifices for sin had been accepted by God since the sacrifice of the Lamb of God at Calvary in AD 30; and the author of Hebrews is writing around AD 65. The Blood of the Lamb of God was the ONLY answer for sin. The Levitical system was inadequate. While the priest did fulfill the required sacrifices and responsibilities, it only covered their sin but did not remove their sin; so the consciousness of sin was still with them. The **New Covenant** changed all that. God was moving them from an inferior, inadequate system to a *better* system because of the finished work of Messiah as the *mediator* of the **New Covenant**. The Levitical system was inferior, and because of its structure, it had no power over sin and could not give eternal life and could not make Israel holy; in fact, the *Tanakh* revealed the opposite, it revealed their unholiness. The Law through the Levitical system with all its sacrifices, drink offerings, ritual cleansing, and carnal ordinances only involved the flesh. These were external only; they did not change the heart, only the **New Covenant** would change the heart (Jeremiah 31:33; Deuteronomy 30:6; Colossians 2:11). The last phrase of verse 10 says these rituals were imposed only *until the time of reformation.* Here is another word that only the author uses that is completely unique to the New Testament. The Greek word translated reformation is *diorthosis* means "to correct" or "to make right" or "to make straight."

To the author's point, Ger says that once this new age (age of Grace) of "making things right" between God and His people arrived, the Levitical system of worship became superfluous.[217]

---

[217] Steven Ger, *The Book of Hebrews: Christ is Greater*. Chattanooga, TN: AMG Publishers, 2009, p. 149.

Superiority of Messiah's Sacrifice (9:11-28).

> ¹¹ *But Messiah being come High Priest of good things to come, by a greater and more perfect Tabernacle, not made with hands, that is to say, not of this* [earthly] *building;* ¹² *Neither by the blood of goats and calves* [bulls]*, but by His own blood He entered in once into the Most Holy Place, having obtained eternal redemption for us.*

In these verses, notice the superiority of Messiah's sacrifice contrasted with the inferior sacrifices offered by earthly, human, flawed, sinful priests. The words *good things to come* reference the fulfillment of all the Messianic Promises through His blood, through the blood of the **New Covenant** (Isaiah 42:6; Matthew 26:28) and not from the *old covenant*. The author makes contrasts between the heavenly Tabernacle versus the earthly pattern. The heavenly was made *without hands* versus the earthly *made with hands*, meaning the earthly Tabernacle and the Temple that existed in the author's day – Herod's Temple, which was the fifth expression of the place of Levitical service.[218] He contrasts the offering of *the blood of goats* for the general Jewish populace and the offerings for the nation (*with* the blood of bulls) which was for the high priest, versus the one offering made *through* Messiah's blood. Notice the use of terms *by the blood* of goats and calves and *by His own blood* (Ephesians 1:7). The Day of Atonement (Leviticus 16) is referenced for the repeated continual offering of bulls and goats yearly in contrast to Messiah offering Himself *once*. *Once* is *ephapax*, the word for *once for all* in 7:27. Another contrast is that His blood *obtained eternal redemption* whereas the *old covenant* system did not. So, what is presented is the superiority of Messiah's offering and the superiority of Messiah's priestly work over and against the inferior offerings and inferior work of earthly priests.

The Results of the Messiah's Sacrifice – 9:13-14

> ¹³ *For if the blood of bulls and of goats, and the ashes of a* [red] *heifer sprinkling the unclean, sanctifies to the purifying of the flesh:* ¹⁴ *How much more shall the blood of Messiah, who through the eternal Spirit offered Himself without spot to God, purge your conscience from dead works to serve the living God?*

The author now uses the word *for* to reference what he said in verses 11-12 to show why our redemption is eternal. These sacrifices in the *Tanakh* were limited to only outward cleansing. It cleansed the flesh ceremonially but did not cleanse the heart;

---

[218] **Places of Worship:** [1] tabernacle in the wilderness and Shiloh, [2] Solomon's Temple – first temple era, [3] Zerubbabel's Temple – second temple era, [4] Maccabean enlargement with the [5] final restoration of Herod's Temple which was still standing in the author's day.

whereas, Yeshua's work is spiritual and results in our inward cleansing. Again, there is a contrast given by the author, the offerings of bulls and goats and the ashes of the red heifer only purified the flesh (the exterior); whereas, Messiah's offering would purge all defilement both external, and – more importantly – it would purify the internal, the *conscience* which the *old covenant* system did not purify. It did not purify the *conscience* of the load of sin that each individual bore (9:9). Fruchtenbaum summarizes this section with five points:

1. The means of cleansing was the blood of Jesus.

2. The basis of cleansing was the voluntary death of Jesus.

3. [The sacrifice] was without spot or blemish since there was no moral failure on His part (I Peter 1:19).

4. The object was to purge the conscience *from dead works*; these *dead works* were the works of the Levitical system; works which are now dead because they have come to an end as far as God is concerned.

5. The goal of Jesus' death was for the believers to serve *the living God;* they are not to return to the *dead works* of the Levitical system but *to serve the living God*.[219]

The *old covenant* filled its purpose until Messiah mediated the **New Covenant,** and all the ramifications far outstrip the *old covenant* and its lack of benefits. This next section is extremely important to understand what the author says. Torah keepers have little to say about this coming passage.

The following chart by Steven Ger in his book on Hebrews shows a summary of the aspects of how the **New Covenant** relates to Israel.[220]

---

[219] Arnold Fruchtenbaum, *Ariel's Bible Commentary: The Messianic Jewish Epistles: Hebrews, James, 1 & II Peter, and Jude.* San Antonio, TX: Ariel Press, 2005, p. 121.

[220] Steven Ger, *The Book of Hebrews: Christ is Greater.* Chattanooga, TN: AMG Publishers, 2009, pp. 132-133.

The New Covenant between God and Israel

Passages	[Provisions]
Jer 31:32	The New Covenant is separate and distinct from the Mosaic Covenant, which it was designed to replace.
Jer 31:33	God's new Laws will be internalized [in the future].
Jer 31:33-34; Ezek 36:25-27	There is a promise of Israel's spiritual regeneration.
Jer 31:33; Ezek 36:26-27	The Holy Spirit will indwell all [believers].
Jer 31:34; 33:8	There is a promise of Israel's sins being forgiven.
Jer 31:34	The covenant blessing extend[s] to every participating Jew.
Jer 31:33; 32:38; Ezek 37:28	The ideal covenantal relationship will be fully realized in the Kingdom.
Jer 31:38-40; 32:41-44; 33:7-13	Jerusalem will be gloriously rebuilt and Israel will be prosperous and secure in their Land.
Isa 55:3; 61:8; Jer 32:40; Ezek 16:60	Everlasting and irrevocable
Jer 33:14-15; Ezek 34:24-25	The Messianic King will rule over Israel and the whole earth.
Ezek 37:26-28	God will dwell in His sanctuary in the midst of Israel.

Passages	Importance
Gen 12:1-3, 7; 13:14-17; 15:1-21; 17:1-21; 22:16-18; Eph 2:11-16; 3:5-6	These references amplify and explain how both Jews and Gentiles participate in the application of the Abrahamic Covenant's blessing component.

Passages	Confirmation from the Gospels and New Testament
Mt 26:28; Mk 14:24; Lk 22:20; I Cor 11:25; Heb 10:29; 13:20	Jesus' shed blood is the means of [inaugurating and] ratifying the New Covenant.
Rom 11:26-27	The New Covenant is the guarantee of Israel's salvation.
2 Cor 3:6-7; Heb 8:6-13	There is need for the New Covenant and the new Law, [the Law of Messiah].
Heb 7:22; 8:6; 9:15; 12:24	Jesus is the guarantee and mediator of the superior covenant.
Heb 10:16-18	There is forgiveness through the New Covenant

Steven Ger, *The Book of Hebrews: Christ is Greater*. Chattanooga, TN: AMG Publishers, 2009, pp. 132-133.

The Ratification of a New Covenant – 9:15-22

Now, let us go to Hebrews 9:15-17 to see what God used to completely illumine my heart and put the final nail in the coffin of teachings of the Judaizers and Torah observance adherents for me. These three verses were the clincher for me in understanding this whole Torah-observant issue and Hebrew Roots for that matter. To me it is a slam dunk, I used to enjoy watching Michael Jordon when he played with the Chicago Bulls (1984-1998). He would appear to be flying through the air to make the score. What a joy it was to watch him, and what a joy it is for me to discover these verses in this completely unnecessary divisive issue in the Messianic Movement.

There are several concepts presented by the author that need special attention. Many long statements and dissertations could be given, so I will spare you that for now. For more information, check the three books that I referenced for your benefit at the beginning of this section on Hebrews (see page 196). This is not a full dissertation on the subject, but we will be camping out on several words to understand the author's intent. First let us look at this entire passage (Hebrews 9:15-22) but focusing especially on verses 15-17.

> *[15] And for this cause **He** is the **Mediator** of the **New Covenant**, that by means of death, for the redemption of the **transgressions** that were under the **first covenant**, they which are called might receive the promises of **eternal inheritance**. [16] For where a **testament** [will] is, there must also of necessity be the **death** of the **testator**, [17] For a testament [will] is of force after men are **dead**: otherwise, it is of no strength at all while the **testator lives**. [18] Therefore not even the first covenant was dedicated without blood. [19] For when Moses had spoken every precept to all the people according to the Law, he took the blood of calves and of goats, with water, and scarlet wool, and hyssop, and sprinkled both the book, and all the people. [20] Saying, This is the blood of the testament which God has commanded you. [21] Then likewise he sprinkled with blood both the tabernacle, and all the vessels of ministry. [22] And almost all things are by the Law purged with blood; and without shedding of blood is no remission.*

Identity of HE

He is the Messiah; *HE* is the Author; *HE* is the One Who made and confirmed the Abrahamic Covenant with Abraham (Genesis 12:1-3; Genesis 15); *HE* is the Angel of the LORD (Exodus 3:2-15); *HE* is the Shechinah Glory that gave the Law to Moses; and it is *HE* that the author of Hebrews identifies as the ***Mediator*** of the **New Covenant** that was ***announced*** by Jeremiah and ***inaugurated*** by Yeshua on the Cross with His blood. The **New Covenant** will be ***ratified*** at the end of the Tribulation period when *all Israel is saved* (Zechariah 3:9; Romans 11:26; Joel 2:28-32); then it will literally be fulfilled. The Church does NOT fulfill the *New Covenant*, NOR does the Church bring in the Kingdom, which is a very popular statement today made either purposely or in ignorance! The **New Covenant** is

ONLY fulfilled in Israel. We as Jewish and Gentile believers in the economy of Grace receive the spiritual benefits of the **New Covenant**; however, the promise was made **directly** and **primarily** to Israel and will be completed in Israel's future. When Yeshua **ratifies** the **New Covenant** in the hearts of Israel, He then will completely fulfill all the covenants when He sets up in the earthly, literal 1000-year Messianic Kingdom in the literal city of Jerusalem. When the **New Covenant** is ratified, then and only then will the Abrahamic, Land, and Davidic Covenants be fulfilled.

Now What is a Mediator?

A ***mediator*** is one who intervenes between two parties who are separated and need to be reconciled. Question: Why would ***He*** be the ***Mediator*** of the ***New Covenant*** if the *old covenant* was in still in force? ***He*** Who is God, the Shechinah (John 8:12), made ***His*** will known by the *first testament* given to Israel at Mount Sinai. However, now that *the fullness of time* (Galatians 4:4)[221] has come with ***His*** Coming in the flesh (John 1:14), *the Prophet like Moses*, the Messiah. He inaugurated the **New Covenant** as its mediator (Hebrews 8:6; 9:15; 12:24; Galatians 3:19-20; I Timothy 2:5).

Who Is the Transgressor and What Are the Transgressions?

The word *transgression* is Παράβασις / *parabasis* and is a compound word. Παρά or *para* means "contrary" and βασις or *baino* means to "go." To do a transgression or be a transgressor means to ***go contrary*** to God's commands.[222] The *Tanakh* and Gospels document clearly and unequivocally that Israel went "contrary" to His Law, His statutes, His ordinances, His commandments and His Voice. However, He – the Author of that Law – has freed Israel (Romans 7:4; Galatians 3:19-29), the Jewish people, from the curse of the Law and has given abundant life (John 10:10) through the **New Covenant** and the Law of Messiah, which is embedded in it.[223] In summary, it includes the idea of overstepping or deviating from God's holy standard – and in this case, it would be a transgressor of the Mosaic Law [or sin in general (Romans 5:12-19)]. The Mosaic Law was impotent, powerless, to help the transgressor, because the breaking of God's Law or the beaching of God's Law sealed the transgressor's doom (Galatians 3:19).

So for any transgressions today by Torah keepers, whether Jewish or Gentile believers in Messiah who still place themselves under the Mosaic Law, redemption is impossible and the gaining of the *promises* of our *eternal inheritance* is equally

---

[221] See John B. Metzger, *Discovering the Mystery of the Unity of God.* San Antonio, TX: Ariel Press, 2010. Chapters 6 and 7 on *Theophanies* and *The Shechinah of God.*

[222] *www.Biblehub.com/greek/3847.htm* (Last accessed 5/26/2025).

[223] It might seem that Torah-observant folks would rather continue to violate His Law and receive His condemnation (II Corinthians 3:7, 9) instead of being freed from condemnation (Romans 8:1).

impossible. So, along with the saints in the *Tanakh*, they would be stuck perpetually in Hell, the Paradise section (Luke 16:19-31),[224] and would NEVER be admitted to the very presence of God in heaven and never receive the covenants and promises of God without the work of Messiah. Today, Torah keepers would face the same fate, unless something happened to remove them from doom. Something needed to happen to pave the way from the condemnation of the Mosaic Law to receive *redemption* and *the promises of* our *eternal inheritance*. That promised inheritance could not happen if the Law were in effect. Do Torah keepers see and understand that they are practicing a system that perpetually condemns them with NO hope in sight? Except for God! How awesome is what comes next.

Who is the Testator, the Author of the Old Covenant?

This *first testament* is spoken of in Hebrews 9, when *He* (the pre-incarnate Messiah) made it; and it was in force until the day of *His* death as the *testator* of *His first covenant* or will. The Shechinah, the glorious presence of God, *He* made the covenant with Israel; but God cannot die!!! So God, the Shechinah Glory of Mount Sinai came in the flesh and *dwelt* among men (John 1:14; 8:12) so that *He* could die and bring the *first covenant* to an end (Romans 10:4), **rendering** His first testament **inoperative** and to establish *His* eternal unconditional **New Covenant** based on *His* blood, not on the blood of animals that had to be offered repeatedly (Hebrews 9:11-14). His sacrifice was made ONCE, NEVER having to be repeated! This means the *old covenant*, or the *first testament* as the author of Hebrews describes it, was fulfilled, **rendered inoperative** as clearly stated in several Epistles of Paul, and as stated by Yeshua, Himself, in Matthew 5:17, in order that the **New Covenant** could begin to function. So, with the annulling of all and not just part of the Mosaic Law at the Cross, Yeshua **inaugurated** another covenant, the **New Covenant,** **announced** in the prophecy of Jeremiah as the **New Covenant** (Jeremiah 31:31-34; Ezekiel 36:26-27).

To annul something means "to make void, to abolish; to cancel, invalidate, to bring to an end" as Paul stated in Romans 10:4. The reason why the *old covenant* had to end was because it had no teeth to provide salvation, or the *redemption* referenced in verse 15. Fruchtenbaum adds a further statement in connection to redemption for the past as well as now and in the future:

> The truth is the Old Testament sacrifices did not remove the sins of the Old Testament saints. The Hebrew word *kippur* for atonement simply means "to cover." Animal blood could not remove the sins of the Old Testament saints; it only covered them. That is why, when an Old Testament saint died, he would not go directly to Heaven. He instead went down to the Paradise or Abraham's Bosom section of

---

[224] Arnold G. Fruchtenbaum, *Yeshua: The Life of Messiah*. San Antonio, TX: Ariel Press, 2017. pp. 391-395.

> *Sheol* or *Hades* [Luke 16:19-31] and waited for the death of Jesus, which is the time when the saint's sins were removed. When Jesus died, He did not simply die for all the sins to be committed after His death. He also died for the sins that were committed before His death; for sins committed under the first covenant.[225] [bracketed reference mine]

This also briefly explained the need of the **New Covenant** because our *redemption* is directly tied to Yeshua's finished work on the Cross. The *old covenant* became obsolete, it was annulled or terminated, ***rendered inoperative*** because of His fulfillment of the Law (Matthew 5:17) and then becoming the sin sacrifice and *mediator* for all who have and would believe in Him by Faith. The answer or antidote to sin was finally accomplished, for there was now no further need for the Law as a system of Law or a standard, because He replaced it with a **New Covenant.** Through that **New Covenant,** we now have *redemption* and our *eternal inheritance*. This makes the Promises given a reality for all believers before and after Messiah. Again, quoting Fruchtenbaum as we approach verses 16-17:

> In verses 16-17, he [the author] switches in his thinking from the concept of a covenant to the concept of a will. The connection between the two is the concept of *inheritance*; a will provides for an inheritance. He points out that a will cannot be executed until the death of the testator, until the one who wrote the will dies. Until the testator dies, the contents of the will, with its benefits and provisions, are only promises. In human relations, a will or testament is only in force after the death of the one who made the will. In the same way, in God's bequeathing salvation to the lost sinner, the bequest is only operative after the sinner dies; he enters heaven only after he dies. They are saved now, but they enter heaven only upon death (the only exception is if the Rapture occurs in their lifetime). ... His [the author's] main point is that *a testament* or a will demands *death*. This helps to explain why, in verse 15, he speaks of the Messiah as the mediator of the **New Covenant** who made that covenant effective through His death and in the way lost sinners who accept salvation on the terms of the will or testament came into the inheritance.[226] [brackets mine]

Do Torah keepers understand that the Author of the Torah and the *old covenant* was none other than the Shechinah Glory of God, the very presence of God Who was the Second Person of the Godhead? This Second Person appeared to God's people at

---

[225] Arnold Fruchtenbaum, *Ariel's Bible Commentary: The Messianic Jewish Epistles: Hebrews, James, 1 & II Peter, and Jude.* San Antonio, TX: Ariel Press, 2005, p. 122.

[226] Arnold Fruchtenbaum, *Ariel's Bible Commentary: The Messianic Jewish Epistles: Hebrews, James, 1 & II Peter, and Jude.* San Antonio, TX: Ariel Press, 2005, p. 123.

Mount Sinai and to Moses, and we understand this Second Person to be the pre-incarnate Messiah, Yeshua, *the Prophet like Moses*. Since God cannot die, He became a man so He could die to give us our *redemption* and our *eternal inheritance*, making all the *promises* a reality in the **New Covenant**. So rather than Dispensationalists depreciating the Law of Moses by not obeying it, it is Torah-keeping adherents who are making the work of God, Messiah Yeshua, inferior by holding on to the *holy, just and good* Law that He, Himself, made obsolete, for it served its purpose being a *school master* (Galatians 3:24-25 – *Pedagogue*) to bring Israel to Messiah. Believers should not be reverting back to an obsolete Law system that was completely ineffective to give us *redemption* and our *eternal inheritance* which was *promised*.

The **New Covenant** replaces the *old covenant* or *first testament*. For this **New Covenant** is NOT a renewing of the *old* or *first testament* as many in the Messianic Movement try to push off on biblically uneducated believers who lack the viewpoint from the whole of God's plan. To refresh your mind, let us go back to Part One of this book in chapter six so you can completely understand what the Hebrew and Greek texts of Scripture say, and how the meaning is differentiated between the words *renew* and *new*. The **New Covenant** is a total replacement of the *old,* and the only spiritual and physical hope for Israel.[227] Their hope rests solely on their embracing Yeshua as their Messiah and King now before death or the Rapture; otherwise, salvation will occur to the whole of Israel living at the end of the Tribulation period (Matthew 23:39; Psalm 118:26).

The **New Covenant** will accomplish three things that the *old* covenant or *first testament* was completely incapable of doing. This was given in Part One of the book, but because of its importance, it will be given again because the Mosaic Law was incapable of achieving the results that the Messiah will produce in the **New Covenant,** so the *old* covenant or *first testament* was ***rendered inoperative*** by Him.

> ***First*** *of all,* the **New Covenant** promised a ***circumcised heart*** (Jeremiah 31:31-34a), a regenerated heart (Deuteronomy 30:6). The *old covenant* could not regenerate the Jewish heart, for the *old covenant* had proven throughout biblical history that it was impotent to change the heart of Israel.
>
> ***Second***, it promised the ***removal of sin*** (Jeremiah 31:34b), and not the covering of sin. The blood of animals only covered sin until the next sacrifice became necessary or until the next Day of Atonement. The blood of Messiah removed our sins, never to be brought up against us again – they are removed! No more sacrifice after

---

[227] See John Metzger's book, *Israel's Only Hope: The New Covenant* (Keller, TX: JHousePublishing. Purple Raiment, 2015), which can be purchased from Ariel Ministries or *www.jhousepublishing.com*.

sacrifice after sacrifice, which, in the *old* or *first testament* was an unending job of the Aaronic priests. Messiah's sacrifice of Himself would occur once, NEVER to be repeated.

Third, the **New Covenant** *promised the indwelling of the Ruach Ha-Kodesh* (Ezekiel 36:26-27; John 14:17b) upon every believer, not the coming upon a select few to fulfill a specific task (Exodus 31:2-6). The vast majority of Jewish people never experience the Ruach Ha-Kodesh coming upon them, but after the Cross, ALL believers have been sealed with the Ruach Ha-Kodesh (Holy Spirit) of promise *until the day of redemption* (Ephesians 1:13-14), at our new home with Him in glory.

Here the author of Hebrews speaks of the *first will* or testament. This document was in force until the Author of it died. What document did Yeshua put into place that was finished upon His death? The answer is the Mosaic Law. This was the *first testament* or will of the Shechinah of God who is the pre-incarnate Messiah Yeshua. He made the *first testament* with Israel at Sinai as Yahweh, the Shechinah glory who met repeatedly with Moses on the Mount (Exodus 20-31) and in the Tent of Meeting (Exodus 33:7-11). How do we arrive at that conclusion concerning Yeshua without writing a dissertation?

In John 1:18, Yochanan the Immerser (John the Baptist) clearly states that the Son, the Messiah, reveals the Father and that the Jewish people have never seen or heard the Father. Yeshua repeats approximately the same thing in John 5:37. So if it was not the Father Who spoke at Mount Sinai and gave the Law to Moses, then it was the pre-incarnate Son, Who appeared as the Shechinah Glory of God (Exodus 33:17-23). He was the very presence of the eternal God that made a conditional, temporal covenant with the people of Israel, which was confirmed or ratified in Exodus 24. Study through the Torah. Who spoke to Moses 154 times? *The Angel of the LORD, Yahweh* [LORD], the Shechinah Glory of God who was the pre-incarnate Messiah.[228]

Repetition is still the mother of learning, so I repeat it again, this time from Matthew 5:17. Yeshua was referencing the fact that the Pharisees accused Him of violating the Law. What they were accusing Him of was violating Rabbinic Law, manmade law, because they had elevated manmade law to the status of equal to, or greater than the Mosaic Law that the pre-incarnate Yeshua had given them. Yeshua, the *Prophet like Moses*, responds that He came to fulfill the Mosaic Law, which was God's standard. By His standard, He fulfilled every *jot and tittle* as His will of *first testament* required. Until He died, that *old testament* Law of the *testator* was in force

---

[228] See *Discovering the Mystery of the Tri-Unity of God* (San Antonio, TX: Ariel Press, 2010) available at *www.Ariel.org*. In said book, I unfold and unpack the activity of the Second Person of the Godhead in the *Tanakh* at great length. The second person is the one Whom we call *Yeshua* the Messiah in the Gospels and **New Covenant**.

and had to be fulfilled, and it could only come by the death of the *testator*, by His death. He was the *Testator* that the author of Hebrews referenced.

What Is a Testator?

A testator is one who makes a will or testament. That *first testament* of the Mosaic Law, by its very nature, would remain in force until Messiah's death. The will of *the testator* while living cannot be acted upon until the testator's death. However, when he dies, the will is discharged to the people named in the will (Romans 7:1-4). The people group named in the *first testament* was Israel, NOT the Gentiles, NOT believers living in the Dispensation of Grace, or the Church age. Paul reveals the purpose and plan of the mystery of God, His Church and the One New Man, which was hidden in the *Tanakh* (Ephesians 3:4-6; Colossians 1:24-27).

Developing a theological position is taking all of the revealed Word of God and putting it together, for God will not contradict Himself. To illustrate, how could Yeshua say to individuals who believe on Him (John 3:16; 5:24), they HAVE, as a possession everlasting life, with absolutely no qualification except to believe in Him by Faith? Then why do believers such as Calvinists and Armenians add works to the Scriptures as qualifications for salvation? Why do Torah keepers add to and subtract from His Word? In Salvation, works are important for believers; but works do not confirm your salvation. Salvation is by Faith Alone, plus nothing. Now, we recognize that in His progressive revelation, God did not reveal His plan all at once; He revealed pieces of it in increments of time, not all at once but over a period of sixteen centuries. There is a principle regarding how to teach your children found in Isaiah 28:13. Parents are to teach their children *precept upon precept, precept upon precept, line upon line, line upon line, here a little and there a little.*[229]

Yes, we would be wise to realize that humans are children in their understanding as it relates to God's knowledge and wisdom. Therefore, we would be even wiser to recognize our human limitations and adhere to the LORD as He speaks in His Word. If we instead elevate ourselves with theological biases over Scripture, such as Torah keeping, or Calvinism, or Armenianism (in naming a few), we will have incorrect doctrine that is not of God. The Church today is infested with these erroneous doctrines (Matthew 13:24-30, 36-43).

In Hebrews 9:18-22, the key phrase is the *sprinkling of blood*. It was used in the *first testament* to dedicate the Tabernacle and the furniture of the Tabernacle. Although the *first covenant,* which was a tool of God to lead Israel to their Messiah (Galatians 3:23-25), this *first testament* was inadequate to complete the process of God for *redemption* and *inheritance* because it was with inferior blood. However, the blood of *the Lamb of God* (John 1:29) was **better blood** (12:24; I Peter 1:17-21)

---

[229] This passage is prophecy concerning Israel and their coming Judgment. But tucked away in this passage is a principle that all parents used to teach their children.

that would bring in the reality of the *Promises* and the *inheritance* of *eternal life* that inferior blood could not accomplish. So why would anyone even consider returning to inferior blood when the Author of the *first covenant* ended the *old covenant* of inferior blood with His **better** blood to guarantee believers *redemption* and *eternal inheritance* that the *old covenant* could not provide?

The Ministry in the New Tabernacle (9:23-28)

Why do believers insist on clinging to Laws that come from inferior temporary blood compared to His **better** blood? His blood purified the heavenly Tabernacle made without hands, and He appeared before the Father as our **better** High Priest after the order of Melchizedek. By doing so, Messiah *put away our sin* which the *old covenant* was incapable of doing.

Hebrews 10:9

I am not trying to write a commentary on Hebrews here, for there is much more that can be said; but I will reframe the message, making one final point before closing. Let me quote Hebrews 10:9:

> *Then said He, Behold, I come to do Your will, O God. He takes away the first, that He may establish the second.*

In Hebrews 10:9, the author begins by quoting King David from Psalm 40:8: *I delight to do Your will, O my God: Yes, Your Law is within my heart*. The writer of Hebrews is saying for emphasis that He, the Messiah, is *come to do the will of the Father*. Chapters 10 through 13 of Hebrews have much valuable material, including the ***fourth warning*** passage to these believers (10:26-31) concerning following an inferior lifestyle of faithlessness by rejecting the sufficiency of Messiah's sacrifice. But look at verse 9 for the sake of emphasis on the preceding chapters concerning the significance the two covenants: the Mosaic Covenant, labeled as the *old covenant* involving the Law of Moses, contrasted by the **New Covenant** and the <u>Law of Messiah</u> that comes from it.

Biases are dangers whether it be Replacement (Fulfilled) Theology or Torah keeping, one guilty of spiritualizing the text so that they can place the Church in the *Tanakh* and replace Israel with themselves. The other guilty of wiggling around clear Scripture to push a bias that believers are to keep Torah which has been ***rendered inoperative*** by Messiah, Himself, the Author of the Law of Moses. Here in a clear crisp statement the author states that the *old covenant* has been *taken away* (Hebrews 10:9). Couple that simple statement with the words of Peter in Acts 10 and 15, the Jerusalem Council, and the numerous Epistles of Apostle Paul and all the material the author of Hebrews has given us. Then the second phrase, *that He may establish the second,* which is the **New Covenant**.

I have been a believer in Messiah for 65 years and I have discovered that the Word of God does not contradict itself. Only scholars who deny Scripture find fault with God and exalt their "opinion" over what an all-knowing God has clearly said. Others bring theological biases and twist Scripture to make it say what God never said by adding Torah keeping. This statement by the author of Hebrews capsulizes his point that the God has *taken away* the *old covenant* and replaced it by *establishing* the second, the **New Covenant**. Why do people make the Scriptures more difficult by exporting error and inhibiting God's desire to conform us to the image of His Son (Romans 8:29), not to the image of Moses and the *old covenant*.

Conclusion of Hebrews

One last reference to the author of the Book of Hebrews as he gives his apostolic benediction. I want to conclude with his words in 13:20-21.

> [20] *Now the God of peace, that brought again from the dead our Lord Yeshua, that Great Shepherd of the sheep, through the blood of the everlasting covenant* [**New Covenant**], [21] *Make you perfect in every good work to do His will, working in you that which is well pleasing in His sight, through Yeshua Ha-Mashiach; to whom be glory forever and ever. Amen.*

Notice the language that he uses: Yeshua is the *Great Shepherd of the sheep* (referencing John 10:16). Those sheep are both Jews and Gentiles united together in one body (Ephesians 2). Also, the sheep that He shepherds have been redeemed, purchased from the slave market of sin by His blood, and he specifies that it is directly a result of the **New Covenant**. Notice Who is supreme? Messiah is, not Moses and not the Law of Moses. This blood of the **New Covenant** makes us *perfect* [complete], and the works that we do will be *to do HIS WILL*.

After reading through all the evidence from Peter, James, the Jerusalem Council, Paul in numerous Epistles and now the author of Hebrews we can readily see that HIS WILL is the result of the **New Covenant** that brought life – abundant life – into our hearts and through the **New Covenant** we are now *well pleasing in His sight*. Yeshua is *better* and superior to all that the *Tanakh* referenced. He is the pinnacle, not Moses, not the Law of Moses that served its purpose but was found to be inadequate to go beyond the announcement of death to the violator. Yeshua was the Author of the Law of Moses with the purpose fulfilled in His coming and death. Now He is the Author and Mediator of a *better* covenant. May HE receive all the *glory forever and ever* (Hebrews 13:21). What an awesome conclusion to this Epistle on the supremacy of Messiah.

There is some much biblical evidence against the position of being Torah observant, especially regarding Torah-keeping Gentiles who were NOT part of the Mosaic Law to begin with. The evidence is in the words of Peter in Acts, the verdict from the Jerusalem Council, the Book of Romans, and the severe words given in the Book of Galatians and from other Epistles. Finally, the writer of the Letter to the Hebrews puts the finishing touches on one of the most detailed warnings against the position of Torah observance. The Letter to the Hebrews is the most Old Testament book in the New Testament, which is rooted in the book of Leviticus.

Yet stiffnecked Torah keepers, with hardened hearts, cling to their disobedience just like Israel did in worshipping the true God in "high places" instead of Jerusalem. Beware of them; their hearts are self-hardened like the heart of Pharaoh of the Exodus. I already know that they will not agree with this book, because their hardened heart has chosen to exalt Moses and the Law instead of its Author. Beware of them, for just as I am seeing in the political climate today, they will continue to pervert the Scriptures using slick, convincing words as they worship God in their "high places."

In general, the Messianic Movement often acts on a complete lack of understanding of God's purpose for God's Covenants and Dispensations. In the case of Torah observance and the Hebrew Roots movement, which is Torah observance on steroids, and all the various shades of it, we have immature Gentile believers who are children in their biblical understanding (Ephesians 4:14) holding onto something that has served God's purpose in the past but was never theirs to begin with. Messiah has now **rendered** His own Law, the Mosaic Law **inoperative**, finished by His death, the death of the *Testator* Who has *mediated* another covenant, the **New Covenant** by His blood to replace the *old*. As a result, immature spiritual children still want to be under a guardian, the *pedagogue* or *schoolmaster*, when physically they are fully grown.

The Dispensation of Law was added, as it states in Galatians, as a guardian to guide Israel until Messiah came to grow them up in the Faith. The whole purpose of the Law was to guide the Jewish people to the *Prophet Like Moses*, the Messiah who is the *Testator* of His will – the *old covenant* or the *first testament* – to bring the Jewish nation to Messiah. However, as history continues to repeat itself, believers and non-believers alike still rebel even when the Messiah has come and provided salvation to Jews and Gentiles through the **New Covenant**. Sadly, unbeknownst to first-century Judaism, His death secured the Promises of the *Tanakh* with His *redemption,* an *eternal inheritance* in Him through His death on the Cross. Fully understanding God's Word brings freedom and life!

APPENDIX ONE
General Categories of the Law of Messiah

This is an incomplete list of differences between the Law of Moses and the Law of Messiah. The Law of Messiah emphasizes living a godly character in conformity with the character of Messiah that believers are to emulate as we yield to the Ruach Ha-Kodesh. This appendix points to general categories of the Law of Messiah,[230] a code of discipleship which is frequently mentioned in the **New Covenant**, but infrequently acknowledged by His children.

The Law of Messiah gives LIFE.

The Law of Messiah gives the standards and qualifications for Elders and Deacons.

It also deals with how marriage should be regarded and how the family unit is to conduct itself.

It deals with how employers are to treat their employees.

It gives guidelines for the believer's response to government.

The Law of Messiah warns against false teachers and directs believers to be discerning.

It also deals with the issue of separation from sin.

Other instructions are given as to how to care for the widows and the poor and needy.

The Law of Messiah gives instructions concerning the Lord's Table.

It promises spiritual blessings in Messiah.

It deals with spiritual cleanliness rather than just physical cleanliness.

It gives the changes in the ministry of the Ruach Ha-Kodesh.

The Law of Messiah deals with the believer's integrity of heart in one's relationship to physical and spiritual issues.

Love is intensified.

---

[230] Headings come from John B. Metzger's book, *The Law, Then and Now: What About Grace?* Larkspur, CO: Grace Acres Press, 2019, pp. 263-288.

It gives instructions and warnings against Satanic adversaries and spiritual warfare.

The Law of Messiah gives instruction to put on Messiah and not to fulfill the desires of the flesh.

It instructs concerning spiritual discipline in light of sinning believers.

It instructs on living and walking under the control of the Ruach Ha-Kodesh.

It instructs on giving, not tithing.

The spiritual character of the believer is stressed.

The Law of Messiah is given to all the ethnicities of the earth, not just to one nation.

It deals with the issue of Christian Liberty.

Believers are to be conforming to spiritual lifestyles, not cultural lifestyles of one nation.

The system of Grace is emphasized.

Believers are to imitate Messiah.

Believers are given the gifts of the Ruach Ha-Kodesh.

Admonitions are specially given to believers in Messiah.

APPENDIX TWO
Law of Messiah – Greek
Imperative Commands

Listed below are all the imperative commands (bolded & underlined) that apply to the Dispensation of Grace. There are some commands that are personal in nature like between Paul and Timothy when he asks him to bring the parchments (Scriptures) and his cloak (his outer coat). Some of them are from the Hebrew Scriptures, especially from the book of Acts, in quotations from the Greek Septuagint like Acts 2:22, 24. There are other incidents, particularly in the book of Acts, that only applied to the individual addressed. I did not include the Gospels except where Yeshua made reference to the future Church. There are 614 verses referenced and 758 total imperative commands. For believers today, this Law of Messiah carries the same weight that the Law of the old economy carried.

Gospels

Matt 16:24   Then Yeshua said to His disciples, "If anyone desires to come after Me, let him *deny* himself, and *take* up his cross, and *follow* Me.

Matt 18:15   Moreover if your brother sins against you, *go* and *tell* him his fault between you and him alone. If he hears you, you have gained your brother.

Matt 18:16   But if he will not hear you, then *take* with you one or two more, that by the mouth of two or three witnesses every word may be established.

Matt 18:17   And if he refuses to hear them *tell* it to the church. But if he refuses even to hear the church, let him be to you like a heathen and a tax collector.

Matt 19:6   So then, they are no longer two but one flesh. Therefore, what God has joined together, let not man *separate*.

Matt 28:19   Go therefore and make *disciples* of all the nations, baptizing them in the Name of the Father and of the Son and of the Holy Spirit.

Matt 28:20   Teaching them to observe all things that I have commanded you; and *lo*, I am with you always, even to the end of the age. Amen.

Mark 16:15	And He said to them, "Go into all the world and **preach** the gospel to every creature."
John 14:1	Let not your heart be **troubled**; you **believe** in God, **believe** also in Me.
John 15:4	**Abide** in Me, and I in you. As the branch cannot bear fruit of itself, unless it abides in the vine, neither can you, unless you abide in Me.
John 15:7	If you abide in Me, and My words abide in you, you will **ask** what you desire, and it shall be done for you.
John 15:9	As the Father loved Me, I also have loved you; **abide** in My love.
John 15:18	If the world hates you, you **know** that it hated Me before it hated you.
John 15:20	**Remember** the word that I said to you, "A servant is not greater than his master." If they persecuted Me, they will also persecute you. If they kept My word, they will keep yours also.
John 17:11	Now I am no longer in the world, but these are in the world, and I come to You. Holy Father, **keep** through Your Name those whom You have given Me, that they may be one as We are.
John 17:17	**Sanctify** them by Your truth. Your Word is truth.
John 20:22	And when He had said this, He breathed on them, and said to them, "**Receive** the Holy Spirit."

Acts

Acts 1:10	And while they looked steadfastly toward heaven as He went up, **behold**, two men stood by them in white apparel,
Acts 1:20	"For it is written in the Book of Psalms: 'Let his dwelling place **be** desolate, and **let** no one live in it,' and, 'Let another take his office.'
Acts 1:24	And they prayed and said, "You, O Lord, who knows the hearts of all, **show** which of these two You have chosen."
Acts 2:7	Then they were all amazed and marveled, saying to one another, "**Look**, are not all these who speak Galileans?"
Acts 2:14	But Peter, standing up with the eleven, raised his voice and said to them, "Men of Judea and all who dwell in Jerusalem, let this **be** known to you, and **heed** my words."

Acts 2:22	"Men of Israel, *hear* these words: Yeshua of Nazareth, a Man attested by God to you by miracles, wonders, and signs which God did through Him in your midst, as you yourselves also know."
Acts 2:34	"For David did not ascend into the heavens, but he said himself: 'The LORD said to my Lord, "*Sit* at my right hand,"'
Acts 2:36	"Therefore let all the house of Israel *know* assuredly that God has made this Yeshua, whom you crucified, both Lord and Messiah.
Acts 2:38	Then Peter said to them, "*Repent*, and let every one of you be *baptized* in the name of Yeshua Messiah for the remission of sins; and you shall receive the gift of the Holy Spirit."
Acts 2:40	And with many other words he testified and exhorted them, saying, "Be *saved* from this perverse generation."
Acts 3:4	And fixing his eyes on him, with John, Peter said, "*Look* at us."
Acts 3:6	Then Peter said, "Silver and gold I do not have, but what I do have I give you: In the Name of Yeshua Messiah of Nazareth, *rise* up and *walk*."
Acts 3:19	*Repent* therefore and be *converted*, that your sins may be blotted out, so that times of refreshing may come from the presence of the Lord.
Acts 4:10	Let it *be* known to you all, and to all the people of Israel, that by the Name of Yeshua Messiah of Nazareth, whom you crucified, whom God raised from the dead, by Him this man stands here before you whole.
Acts 4:19	But Peter and John answered and said to them, "Whether it is right in the sight of God to listen to you more than to God, you *judge*."
Acts 4:29	Now, Lord, *look* on their threats, and *grant* to Your servants that with all boldness they may speak Your word.
Acts 5:8	And Peter answered her, "*Tell* me whether you sold the land for so much?" She said, "Yes, for so much."
Acts 5:9	Then Peter said to her, "How is it that you have agreed together to test the Spirit of the Lord? *Look*, the feet of those who have buried your husband are at the door, and they will carry you out."
Acts 5:20	"*Go*, stand in the temple and *speak* to the people all the words of this life."

Acts 5:25	So one came and told them, saying, "*Look*, the men whom you put in prison are standing in the temple and teaching the people."
Acts 5:28	Saying, "Did we not strictly command you not to teach in this Name? And *look*, you have filled Jerusalem with your doctrine, and intend to bring this Man's blood on us!"
Acts 5:35	And he said to them: "Men of Israel, take *heed* to yourselves what you intend to do regarding these men."
Acts 5:38	And now I say to you, keep *away* from these men and *let* them alone; for if this plan or this work is of men, it will come to nothing;
Acts 6:3	Therefore, brethren, *seek* out from among you seven men of good reputation, full of the Holy Spirit and wisdom, whom we may appoint over this business;
Acts 7:2	And he said, "Brethren and fathers, *listen*: The God of glory appeared to our father Abraham when he was in Mesopotamia, before he dwelt in Haran,"
Acts 7:3	And said to him, "Get *out* of your country and from your relatives, and come to a land that I will show you."
Acts 7:33	"Then the LORD said to him, 'Take your sandals *off* your feet, for the place where you stand is holy ground'"
Acts 7:40	Saying to Aaron, "*Make* us gods to go before us; as for this Moses who brought us out of the land of Egypt, we do not know what has become of him."
Acts 7:56	And said, "*Look*! I see the heavens opened and the Son of Man standing at the right hand of God!"
Acts 7:59	And they stoned Stephen as he was calling on God and saying, "Lord Yeshua, *receive* my spirit."
Acts 8:19	Saying, "*Give* me this power also, that anyone on whom I lay hands may receive the Holy Spirit."
Acts 8:22	*Repent* therefore of this your wickedness, and *pray* God if perhaps the thought of your heart may be forgiven you.
Acts 8:24	Then Simon answered and said, "*Pray* to the Lord for me, that none of the things which you have spoken may come upon me."

Acts 8:26	Now an angel of the Lord spoke to Phillip, saying, *"**Arise** and **go** toward the south along the road which goes down from Jerusalem to Gaza."* This is desert.
Acts 8:27	So he arose and went. And ***behold***, a man of Ethiopia, a eunuch of great authority under Candace the queen of the Ethiopians, who had charge of all her treasury, and had come to Jerusalem to worship,
Acts 8:29	Then the Spirit said to Philip, *"**Go** near and **overtake** this chariot."*
Acts 8:36	Now as they went down the road, they came to some water. And the eunuch said, *"**See**, here is water. What hinders me from being baptized?"*
Acts 9:6	So he, trembling and astonished, said, "Lord, what do You want me to do?" Then the Lord said to him, *"**Arise** and **go** into the city, and you will be told what you must do."*
Acts 9:10	Now there was a certain disciple at Damascus named Ananias; and to him the Lord said in a vision, "Ananias." And he said, *"**Here** I am, Lord."*
Acts 9:11	So the Lord said to him, "Arise and ***go*** to the street called Straight, and ***inquire*** at the house of Judas for one called Saul of Tarsus, for ***behold***, he is praying."
Acts 9:15	But the Lord said to him, *"**Go**, for he is a chosen vessel of Mine to bear My Name before Gentiles, kings, and the children of Israel."*
Acts 9:34	And Peter said to him, "Aeneas, Yeshua the Messiah heals you. ***Arise*** and ***make*** your bed." Then he arose immediately.
Acts 9:40	But Peter put them all out and knelt down and prayed. And turning to the body he said, "Tabitha, ***arise***." And she opened her eyes, and when she saw Peter, she sat up.
Acts 10:5	Now ***send*** men to Joppa and ***send*** for Simon whose surname is Peter.
Acts 10:13	And a voice came to him, "Rise, Peter, ***kill*** and ***eat***."
Acts 10:15	And a voice spoke to him again the second time, "What God has cleansed you must not ***call*** common."
Acts 10:17	Now while Peter wondered within himself what this vision which he had seen meant, ***behold***, the men who had been sent from Cornelius had made inquiry for Simon's house, and stood before the gate.

Acts 10:19	While Peter thought about the vision, the Spirit said to him, "***Behold***, three men are seeking you."
Acts 10:20	Arise therefore, ***go*** down and ***go*** with them, doubting nothing; for I have sent them."
Acts 10:21	Then Peter went down to the men who had been sent to him from Cornelius, and said, "***Yes***, I am he whom you seek. For what reason have you come?"
Acts 10:26	But Peter lifted him up, saying, "***Stand*** up; I myself am also a man."
Acts 10:30	So Cornelius said, "Four days ago I was fasting until this hour; and at the ninth hour I prayed in my house, and ***behold***, a man stood before me in bright clothing,"
Acts 10:32	"***Send*** therefore to Joppa and ***call*** Simon here, whose surname is Peter. He is lodging in the house of Simon, a tanner, by the sea. When he comes, he will speak to you."
Acts 11:7	And I heard a voice saying to me, 'Rise, Peter, ***kill*** and ***eat***.'
Acts 11:9	But the voice answered me again from heaven, 'What God has cleansed you must not ***call*** common.'
Acts 11:13	And he told us how he had seen an angel standing in his house, who said to him, '***Send*** men to Joppa, and ***call*** for Simon whose surname is Peter,'
Acts 12:7	Now ***behold***, an angel of the Lord stood by him, and a light shone in the prison; and he struck Peter on the side and raised him up, saying, "***Arise*** quickly!" And his chains fell off his hands.
Acts 12:8	Then the angel said to him, "***Gird*** yourself and ***tie*** on your sandals"; and so he did. And he said to him, "***Put*** on your garment and ***follow*** me."
Acts 12:17	But motioning to them with his hand to keep silent, he declared to them how the Lord had brought him out of the prison. And he said, "Go, ***tell*** these things to James and to the brethren." And he departed and went to another place.
Acts 13:2	As they ministered to the Lord and fasted, the Holy Spirit said, "Now ***separate*** to Me Barnabas and Saul for the work to which I have called them,"
Acts 13:11	And now, ***indeed***, the hand of the Lord is upon you, and you shall be blind, not seeing the sun for a time." And immediately a dark mist

	fell on him, and he went around seeking someone to lead him by the hand.
Acts 13:15	And after the reading of the Law and the Prophets, the rulers of the synagogue sent to them, saying, "Men and brethren, if you have any word of exhortation for the people, *say* on [*say* it]."
Acts 13:16	Then Paul stood up, and motioning with his hand said, "Men of Israel, and you who fear God, *listen:*"
Acts 13:25	And as John was finishing his course, he said, "Who do you think I am? I am not He. But *behold*, there comes One after me, the sandals of whose feet I am not worthy to loose."
Acts 13:38	Therefore let it *be* known to you, brethren, that through this Man is preached to you the forgiveness of sins;
Acts 13:40	*Beware* therefore, lest what has been spoken in the Prophets come upon you:
Acts 13:41	'*Behold*, you despisers, *Marvel* and *perish*! For I work a work in your days, A work which you will by no means believe, though one were to declare it to you.'
Acts 13:46	Then Paul and Barnabas grew bold and said, "It was necessary that the word of God should be spoken to you first; but since you reject it, and judge yourselves unworthy of everlasting life, *behold*, we turn to the Gentiles."
Acts 14:10	Said with a loud voice, "*Stand* up straight on your feet!" And he leaped and walked.
Acts 15:13	And after they had become silent, James answered, saying, "Men and brethren, *listen* to me:"
Acts 15:29	That you abstain from things offered to idols, from blood, from things strangled, and from sexual immorality. If you keep yourselves from these, you will do well. *Farewell*.
Acts 16:1	Then he came to Derbe and Lystra. And *behold*, a certain disciple was there, named Timothy, the son of a certain Jewish woman who believed, but his father was Greek.
Acts 16:9	And a vision appeared to Paul in the night. A man of Macedonia stood and pleaded with him, saying, "Come over to Macedonia and *help* us."

Acts 16:15	And when she and her household were baptized, she begged us, saying, "If you have judged me to be faithful to the Lord, come to my house and *stay*." So she persuaded us.
Acts 16:31	So they said, *"**Believe** on the Lord Yeshua Messiah, and you will be saved, you and your household."*
Acts 16:35	And when it was day, the magistrates sent the officers saying, "Let those men ***go**.*"
Acts 16:36	So the keeper of the prison reported these words to Paul, saying, "The magistrates have sent to let you go. Now therefore depart, and ***go*** in peace."
Acts 16:37	But Paul said to them, "They have beaten us openly, uncondemned being Romans, and have thrown us into prison. And now do they put us out secretly? No indeed! Let them come themselves and ***get*** us out."
Acts 18:9	Now the Lord spoke to Paul in the night by a vision, "Do not be ***afraid***, but ***speak***, and do not keep silent."
Acts 19:38	Therefore, if Demetrius and his fellow craftsmen have a case against anyone, the courts are open and there are proconsuls. Let them ***bring*** charges against one another.
Acts 20:10	But Paul went down, fell on him, and embracing him said, "Do not ***trouble*** yourselves, for his life is in him."
Acts 20:22	And ***see***, now I go bound in the spirit to Jerusalem, not knowing the things that will happen to me there,
Acts 20:25	"And ***indeed***, now I know that you all, among whom I have gone preaching the Kingdom of God, will see my face no more."
Acts 20:28	Therefore ***take*** heed to yourselves and to all the flock, among which the Holy Spirit has made you overseers, to shepherd the church of God which He purchased with His own blood.
Acts 20:31	Therefore ***watch,*** and remember that for three years I did not cease to warn everyone night and day with tears.
Acts 21:14	So when he would not be persuaded, we ceased, saying, "The will of the Lord be ***done**.*"
Acts 21:23	Therefore ***do*** what we tell you: We have four men who have taken a vow.

Acts 21:24	Take them and be *purified* with them, and *pay* their expenses so that they may shave their heads, and that all may know that those things of which they were informed concerning you are nothing, but that you yourself also walk orderly and keep the law.
Acts 21:28	Crying out, "Men of Israel, *help*! This is the man who teaches all men everywhere against the people, the law, and this place; and furthermore, he also brought Greeks into the temple and has defiled this holy place."
Acts 21:36	For the multitude of the people followed after, crying out, "*Away* with him!"
Acts 21:39	But Paul said, "I am a Jew from Tarsus, in Cilicia, a citizen of no mean city; and I implore you, *permit* me to speak to the people."
Acts 22:1	"Brethren and fathers, *hear* my defense before you now."
Acts 22:10	So I said, "What shall I do, Lord?" And the Lord said to me, "Arise and *go* into Damascus, and there you will be told all things which are appointed for you to do."
Acts 22:13	[Ananias] came to me; and he stood and said to me, 'Brother Saul, *receive* your sight.' And at that same hour I looked up at him.
Acts 22:16	And now why are you waiting? Arise and be *baptized*, and *wash* away your sins, calling on the Name of the Lord.
Acts 22:18	And [I, Saul] saw Him saying to me, 'Make *haste* and *get* out of Jerusalem quickly, for they will not receive your testimony concerning Me.'
Acts 22:21	Then He said to me, '*Depart*, for I will send you far from here to the Gentiles.'
Acts 22:22	And they listened to him until this word, and then they raised their voices and said, "*Away* with such a fellow from the earth, for he is not fit to live!"
Acts 22:26	When the centurion heard that, he went and told the commander, saying, "*Take* care what you do, for this man is a Roman."
Acts 22:27	Then the commander came and said to him, "*Tell* me, are you a Roman? He said, "Yes."
Acts 23:11	But the following night the Lord stood by him and said, "*Be* of good cheer, Paul; for as you have testified for Me in Jerusalem, so you must also bear witness at Rome."

Acts 23:15	Now you, therefore, together with the council, *suggest* to the commander that he be brought down to you tomorrow, as though you were going to make further inquiries concerning him; but we are ready to kill him before he comes near."
Acts 23:17	Then Paul called one of the centurions to him and said, "*Take* this young man to the commander, for he has something to tell him."
Acts 23:23	And he called for two centurions, saying "*Prepare* two hundred soldiers, seventy horsemen, and two hundred spearmen to go to Caesarea at the third hour of the night;"
Acts 23:30	And when it was told me that the Jews lay in wait for the man, I sent him immediately to you, and also commanded his accusers to state before you the charges against him. *Farewell*.
Acts 24:20	Or else let those who are here themselves *say* if they found any wrongdoing in me while I stood before the council,
Acts 24:25	Now as he reasoned about righteousness, self-control, and the judgment to come, Felix was afraid and answered, "Go *away* for now; when I have a convenient time, I will call for you."
Acts 25:5	"Therefore," he said, "let those who have authority among you go down with me and *accuse* this man, to see if there is any fault in him."
Acts 25:24	And Festus said: "King Agrippa and all the men who are here present with us, you *see* this man about whom the whole assembly of Jews petitioned me, both at Jerusalem and here, crying out that he was not fit to live any longer."
Acts 26:16	But *rise* and *stand* on your feet; for I have appeared to you for this purpose, to make you a minister and a witness both of the things which you have seen and of the things which I will yet reveal to you.
Acts 27:24	Saying, 'Do not be *afraid*, Paul; you must be brought before Caesar; and *indeed,* God has granted you all those who sail with you.'
Acts 27:25	Therefore take *heart*, men, for I believe God that it will be just as it was told me.
Acts 28:26	Saying, '*Go* to this people and *say*: "Hearing you will hear, and shall not understand; and seeing you will see, and not perceive;"
Acts 28:28	"Therefore let it *be* known to you that the salvation of God has been sent to the Gentiles, and they will hear it!"

Romans

Rom 2:17	*Indeed* you are called a Jew, and rest on the Law, and make your boast in God.
Rom 3:4	Certainly not! Indeed, *let* God be true but every man a liar. As it is written: "That you may be justified in Your words, and may overcome when You are judged."
Rom 6:11	Likewise you also, *reckon* yourselves to be dead indeed to sin, but alive to God in Christ Jesus our Lord.
Rom 6:12	Therefore do not let sin *reign* in your mortal body, that you should obey it in its lusts.
Rom 6:13	And do not *present* your members as instruments of unrighteousness to sin but *present* yourselves to God as being alive from the dead, and your members as instruments of righteousness to God.
Rom 6:19	I speak in human terms because of the weakness of your flesh. For just as you presented your members as slaves of uncleanness, and of lawlessness leading to more lawlessness, so now *present* your members as slaves of righteousness for holiness.
Rom 9:33	As it is written: "*Behold* I lay in Zion a stumbling stone and rock of offense, and whoever believes on Him will not be put to shame."
Rom 11:9	And David says: "Let their table *become* a snare and a trap, a stumbling block and a recompense to them."
Rom 11:10	"Let their eyes be *darkened*, so that they do not see, and bow down their back always."
Rom 11:18	Do not *boast* against the branches. But if you do boast, remember that you do not support the root, but the root supports you.
Rom 11:20	Well said. Because of unbelief they were broken off, and you stand by faith. Do not be *haughty*, but *fear*.
Rom 11:22	Therefore *consider* the goodness and severity [sternness] of God: on those who fell, severity [sternness]; but toward you, goodness, if you continue in His goodness. Otherwise, you also will be cut off.
Rom 12:2	And do not be *conformed* to this world, but be *transformed* by the renewing of your mind, that you may prove what is that good and acceptable and perfect will of God.
Rom 12:14	*Bless* those who persecute you; *bless* and do not curse.

Rom 12:16	Be of the same mind toward one another. Do not set your mind on high things, but associate with the humble. Do not *be* wise in your own opinion.
Rom 12:19	Beloved, do not avenge yourselves, but rather *give* place to wrath; for it is written, "Vengeance is Mine, I will repay," says the Lord.
Rom 12:20	Therefore "If your enemy is hungry, *feed* him; if he is thirsty, give him to *drink;* For in so doing you will heap coals of fire on his head."
Rom 12:21	Do not be *overcome* by evil, but *overcome* evil with good.
Rom 13:1	Let every soul be *subject* to the governing authorities. For there is no authority except from God, and the authorities that exist are appointed by God.
Rom 13:3	For rulers are not a terror to good works, but to evil. Do you want to be unafraid of the authority? *Do* what is good, and you will have praise from the same.
Rom 13:4	For he is God's minister to you for good. But if you do evil, be *afraid*; for he does not bear the sword in vain; for he is God's minister, an avenger to execute wrath on him who practices evil.
Rom 13:7	*Render* therefore to all their due: taxes to whom taxes are due, customs to whom customs, fear to whom fear, honor to whom honor.
Rom 13:8	*Owe* no one anything except to love one another, for he who loves another has fulfilled the Law [of Messiah].
Rom 13:14	But put *on* the Lord Yeshua Messiah, and *make* no provision for the flesh, to fulfill its lusts.
Rom 14:1	*Receive* one who is weak in the faith, but not to dispute over doubtful things.
Rom 14:3	Let not him who eats *despise* him who does not eat, and let not him who does not eat *judge* him who eats; for God has received him.
Rom 14:5	One person esteems one day above another; another esteems every day alike. Let each be *fully* convinced in his own mind.
Rom 14:13	Therefore let us not judge one another anymore, but rather *resolve* this, not to put a stumbling block or a cause to fall in our brother's way.

Rom 14:15	Yet if your brother is grieved because of your food, you are no longer walking in love. Do not ***destroy*** with your food the one for whom Messiah died.
Rom 14:16	Therefore do not let your good *be* spoken of as evil.
Rom 14:20	Do not ***destroy*** the work of God for the sake of food. All things indeed are pure, but it is evil for the man who eats with offense.
Rom 14:22	Do you have faith? ***Have*** it to yourself before God. Happy is he who does not condemn himself in what he approves.
Rom 15:2	Let each of us ***please*** his neighbor for his good, leading to edification.
Rom 15:7	Therefore ***receive*** one another, just as Messiah also received us, to the glory of God.
Rom 15:10	And again he says: "***Rejoice***, O Gentiles, with His people!"
Rom 15:11	And again: "***Praise*** the LORD, all you Gentiles! ***Laud*** Him, all you peoples!"
Rom 16:3	***Greet*** Priscilla and Aquila, my fellow workers in Messiah Yeshua.
Rom 16:5	Likewise greet the church that is in their house. ***Greet*** my beloved Epaenetus, who is the firstfruits of Achaia to Messiah.
Rom 16:6	***Greet*** Mary, who labored much for us.
Rom 16:7	***Greet*** Andronicus and Junia, my countrymen and my fellow prisoners, who are of note among the apostles, who also were in Messiah before me.
Rom 16:8	***Greet*** Amplias, my beloved in the Lord.
Rom 16:9	***Greet*** Urbanus, our fellow worker in Messiah, and Stachys, my beloved.
Rom 16:10	***Greet*** Apelles, approved in Messiah. Greet those who are of the household of Aristobulus.
Rom 16:11	***Greet*** Herodion, my countryman. Greet those who are of the household of Narcissus who are in the Lord.
Rom 16:12	***Greet*** Tryphena and Tryphosa, who have labored in the Lord. Greet the beloved Persis, who labored much in the Lord.

Rom 16:13	***Greet*** Rufus, chosen in the Lord, and his mother and mine.
Rom 16:14	***Greet*** Asyncritus, Phlegon, Hermas, Patrobas, Hermes, and the brethren who are with them.
Rom 16:15	***Greet*** Philologus and Julia, Nereus and his sister, and Olympas, and all the saints who are with them.
Rom 16:16	***Greet*** one another with a holy kiss. The churches of Messiah greet you.
Rom 16:17	Now I urge you, brethren, note those who cause divisions and offenses, contrary to the doctrine which you learned, and ***avoid*** them.

I Corinthians

I Cor 1:31	… that, as it is written, "He who glories, let him ***glory*** in the LORD."
I Cor 3:10	According to the grace of God which was given to me, as a wise master builder I have laid the foundation, and another builds on it. But let each one ***take*** heed how he builds on it.
I Cor 3:18	Let no one ***deceive*** himself. If anyone among you seems to be wise in this age, let him become a fool that he may become wise.
I Cor 3:21	Therefore let no one ***boast*** in men. For all things are yours:
I Cor 4:1	Let a man so ***consider*** us, as servants of Messiah and stewards of the mysteries of God.
I Cor 4:5	Therefore ***judge*** nothing before the time, until the Lord comes, who will both bring to light the hidden things of darkness and reveal the counsels of the hearts. Then each one's praise will come from God.
I Cor 4:16	Therefore I urge you, ***imitate*** me [Paul].
I Cor 5:7	Therefore ***purge*** out the old leaven, that you may be a new lump, since you truly are unleavened. For indeed Messiah, our Passover, was sacrificed for us.
Cor 6:9-10	Do you not know that the unrighteous will not inherit the kingdom of God? Do not be ***deceived***. Neither fornicators, nor idolaters, nor adulterers, nor homosexuals, nor sodomites, nor thieves, nor covetous, nor drunkards, nor revilers, nor extortioners will inherit the kingdom of God.

I Cor 6:18	***Flee*** sexual immorality. Every sin that a man does is outside the body, but he who commits sexual immorality sins against his own body.
I Cor 6:20	For you were bought at a price; therefore, ***glorify*** God in your body and in your spirit, which are God's.
I Cor 7:2	Nevertheless, because of sexual immorality, let each man ***have*** his own wife, and let each woman ***have*** her own husband.
I Cor 7:3	Let the husband render to his wife the affection ***due*** her, and likewise also the wife to her husband.
I Cor 7:5	Do not ***deprive*** one another except with consent for a time, that you may give yourselves to fasting and prayer; and come together again so that Satan does not tempt you because of your lack of self-control.
I Cor 7:9	But if they cannot exercise self-control, let them ***marry***. For it is better to marry than to burn with passion.
I Cor 7:11	But even if she does depart, let her ***remain*** unmarried or be ***reconciled*** to her husband. And a husband is not to divorce his wife.
I Cor 7:12	But to the rest I, not the Lord, say: If any brother has a wife who does not believe, and she is willing to live with him, let him not ***divorce*** her.
I Cor 7:13	And a woman who has a husband who does not believe, if he is willing to live with her, let her not ***divorce*** him.
I Cor 7:15	But if the unbeliever departs, let him ***depart***; a brother or a sister is not under bondage in such cases. But God has called us to peace.
I Cor 7:17	But as God has distributed to each one, as the Lord has called each one, so let him ***walk***. And so I ordain in all the churches.
I Cor 7:18	Was anyone called while circumcised? Let him not ***become*** uncircumcised. Was anyone called while uncircumcised? Let him not be ***circumcised***.
I Cor 7:20	Let each one ***remain*** in the same calling in which he was called.
I Cor 7:21	Were you called while a slave? Do not be ***concerned*** about it; but if you can be made free, rather ***use*** it.
I Cor 7:23	You were bought at a price; do not ***become*** slaves of men.

I Cor 7:24	Brethren, let each one *remain* with God in the state in which he was called.
I Cor 7:27	Are you bound to a wife? Do not *seek* to be loosed. Are you loosed from a wife? Do not *seek* a wife.
I Cor 7:36	But if any man thinks he is behaving improperly toward his virgin, if she is past the flower of youth, and thus it must be, let him *do* what he wishes. He does not sin; let them *marry*.
I Cor 8:9	But *beware* lest somehow this liberty of yours become a stumbling block to those who are weak.
I Cor 9:24	Do you not know that those who run in a race all run, but one receives the prize? *Run* in such a way that you may obtain it.
I Cor 10:7	And do not *become* idolaters as were some of them. As it is written: "The people sat down to eat and drink and rose up to play."
I Cor 10:10	… nor *complain*, as some of them also complained, and were destroyed by the destroyer.
I Cor 10:12	Therefore let him who thinks he stands take *heed* lest he fall.
I Cor 10:14	Therefore, my beloved, *flee* from idolatry.
I Cor 10:15	I speak as to wise men; *judge* for yourselves what I say.
I Cor 10:18	*Observe* Israel after the flesh: Are not those who eat of the sacrifices partakers of the altar?
I Cor 10:24	Let no one *seek* his own, but each one the other's well-being.
I Cor 10:25	*Eat* whatever is sold in the meat markets, asking no questions for conscience' sake.
I Cor 10:27	If any of those who do not believe invites you to dinner, and you desire to go, *eat* whatever is set before you, asking no question for conscience sake.
I Cor 10:28	But if anyone says to you, "This was offered to idols," do not *eat* it for the sake of the one who told you, and for conscience sake; for "the earth is the LORD's, and all its fullness."
I Cor 10:31	Therefore, whether you eat or drink, or whatever you do, *do* all to the glory of God.

I Cor 10:32	*Give* no offense, either to the Jews or to the Greeks or to the church of God.
I Cor 11:1	*Imitate* me, just as I also imitate Messiah.
I Cor 11:6	For if a woman is not covered, let her also be *shorn*. But if it is shameful for a woman to be shorn or shaved, let her be covered.
I Cor 11:13	*Judge* among yourselves. Is it proper for a woman to pray to God with her head uncovered?
I Cor 11:24	And when He had given thanks, He broke it and said, *"Take, eat*; this is My body which is broken for you; *do* this in remembrance of Me."
I Cor 11:25	In the same manner He also took the cup after supper, saying, "This cup is the **New Covenant** in My blood. This *do*, as often as you drink it, in remembrance of Me."
I Cor 11:28	But let a man *examine* himself, and so let him *eat* of the bread and *drink* of the cup.
I Cor 11:33	Therefore, my brethren, when you come together to eat, *wait* for one another.
I Cor 11:34	But if anyone is hungry, let him *eat* at home, lest you come together for judgment. And the rest I will set in order when I come.
I Cor 12:31	But earnestly *desire* the best gifts. And yet I show you a more excellent way.
I Cor 14:1	*Pursue* love, and *desire* spiritual gifts, but especially that you may prophesy.
I Cor 14:12	Even so you, since you are zealous for spiritual gifts, let it be for the edification of the church that you *seek* to excel.
I Cor 14:13	Therefore let him who speaks in a tongue *pray* that he may interpret.
I Cor 14:20	Brethren, do not *be* children in understanding; however, in malice be babes, but in understanding *be* mature.
I Cor 14:26	How is it then, brethren? Whenever you come together, each of you has a psalm, has a teaching, has a tongue, has a revelation, has an interpretation. Let all things be *done* for edification.
I Cor 14:27	If anyone speaks in a tongue, let there be two or at the most three, each in turn, and let one *interpret*.

I Cor 14:28	But if there is no interpreter, let him *keep* silent in church, and let him *speak* to himself and to God.
I Cor 14:29	Let two or three prophets *speak*, and let the others *judge*.
I Cor 14:30	But if anything is revealed to another who sits by, let the first *keep* silent.
I Cor 14:34	Let your women *keep* silent in the churches, for they are not permitted to speak; but they are to be submissive, as the Law also says.
I Cor 14:35	And if they want to learn something, let them *ask* their own husbands at home; for it is shameful for women to speak in church.
I Cor 14:37	If anyone thinks himself to be a prophet or spiritual, let him *acknowledge* that the things which I write to you are the commandments of the Lord.
I Cor 14:38	But if anyone is ignorant, let him be *ignorant*.
I Cor 14:39	Therefore, brethren, *desire* earnestly to prophesy, and do not *forbid* to speak with tongues.
I Cor 14:40	Let all things be *done* decently and in order.
I Cor 15:33	Do not be *deceived*: "Evil company corrupts good habits."
I Cor 15:34	*Awake* to righteousness, and do not *sin*; for some do not have the knowledge of God, I speak this to your shame.
I Cor 15:51	*Behold*, I tell you a mystery: We shall not all sleep, but we shall all be changed.
I Cor 15:58	Therefore, my beloved brethren, *be* steadfast, immovable, always abounding in the work of the Lord, knowing that your labor is not in vain in the Lord.
I Cor 16:1	Now concerning the collection for the saints, as I have given orders to the churches of Galatia, so you must *do* also:
I Cor 16:2	On the first day of the week let each one of you *lay* something aside, storing up as he may prosper, that there be no collections when I come.
I Cor 16:10	And if Timothy comes, *see* that he may be with you without fear; for he does the work of the Lord, as I also do.

I Cor 16:11	Therefore let no one despise him. But **send** him on his journey in peace, that he may come to me; for I am waiting for him with the brethren.
I Cor 16:13	***Watch***, ***stand*** fast in the faith, be brave, be strong.
I Cor 16:14	Let all that you do be ***done*** with love.
I Cor 16:18	For they refreshed my spirit and yours. Therefore ***acknowledge*** such men.
I Cor 16:20	All the brethren greet you. ***Greet*** one another with a holy kiss.
I Cor 16:22	If anyone does not love the Lord Yeshua Messiah, let him ***be*** accursed. ***O Lord, come****!*

II Corinthians

II Cor 5:17	Therefore, if anyone is in Christ, he is a new creation; old things have passed away; ***behold***, all things have become new.
II Cor 5:20	Now then, we are ambassadors for Christ, as though God were pleading through us: we implore you on Christ's behalf, be ***reconciled*** to God.
II Cor 6:2	For He says: "In an acceptable time I have heard you, and in the day of salvation I have helped you." ***Behold***, now is the accepted time; ***behold***, now is the day of salvation.
II Cor 6:9	… as unknown, and yet well known; as dying, and ***behold*** we live; as chastened, and yet not killed;
II Cor 6:13	Now in return for the same (I speak as to my children), you also be ***open***.
II Cor 6:14	Do not ***be*** unequally yoked together with unbelievers. For what fellowship has righteousness with lawlessness? And what communion has light with darkness?
II Cor 6:17	Therefore "Come out from among them and be ***separate***, says the Lord. Do not ***touch*** what is unclean, and I will receive you."
II Cor 7:2	***Open*** your hearts to us. We have wronged no one, we have corrupted no one, we have cheated no one.
II Cor 7:11	For ***observe*** this very thing, that you sorrowed in a godly manner: What diligence it produced in you, what clearing of yourselves, what indignation, what fear, what vehement desire, what zeal, what

	vindication! In all things you proved yourselves to be clear in this matter.
II Cor 8:11	But now you also must *complete* the doing of it; that as there was a readiness to desire it, so there also may be a completion out of what you have.
II Cor 8:24	Therefore *show* to them, and before the churches, the proof of your love and of our boasting on your behalf.
II Cor.10:7	Do you look at things according to the outward appearance? If anyone is convinced in himself that he is Messiah's, let him again *consider* this in himself, that just as he is Messiah's, even so we are Messiah's.
II Cor 10:11	Let such a person *consider* this, that what we are in word by letters when we are absent, such we will also be in deed when we are present.
II Cor 10:17	But "he who glories, let him *glory* in the LORD."
II Cor 11:16	I say again, let no one think me a fool. If otherwise, at least *receive* me as a fool, that I also may boast a little.
II Cor 12:13	For what is it in which you were inferior to other churches, except that I myself was not burdensome to you? *Forgive* me this wrong!
II Cor 12:14	*Now* for the third time I am ready to come to you. And I will not be burdensome to you; for I do not seek yours, but you. For the children ought not to lay up for the parents, but the parents for the children.
II Cor 12:16	But *be* that as it may, I did not burden you. Nevertheless, being crafty, I caught you by cunning!
II Cor 13:5	*Examine* yourselves as to whether you are in the faith. *Test* yourselves. Do you not know yourselves, that Yeshua Messiah is in you? – unless indeed you are disqualified.
II Cor 13:11	Finally, brethren, *farewell*. Become *complete*. Be of *good* comfort, be *of* one *mind*, *live* in peace; and the God of love and peace will be with you.
II Cor 13:12	*Greet* one another with a holy kiss.

Galatians

Gal 1:8	But even if we, or an angel from heaven, preach any other gospel to you than what we have preached to you, let him *be* accursed.
Gal 1:9	As we have said before, so now I say again, if anyone preaches any other gospel to you than what you have received, let him *be* accursed.
Gal 1:20	(Now concerning the things which I write to you, *indeed*, before God, I do not lie.)
Gal 3:7	Therefore *know* that only those who are of faith are sons of Abraham.
Gal 4:12	Brethren, I urge you to *become* like me, for I become like you. You have not injured me at all.
Gal 4:21	*Tell* me, you who desire to be under the Law, do you not hear the Law?
Gal 4:27	For it is written: "*Rejoice*, O barren, you who do not bear! Break *forth* and *shout*, you who are not in labor! For the desolate has many more children than she who has a husband."
Gal 4:30	Nevertheless what does the Scripture say? "*Cast* out the bondwoman and her son, for the son of the bondwoman shall not be heir with the son of the freewoman."
Gal 5:1	*Stand* fast therefore in the liberty by which Messiah has made us free, and do not be *entangled* again with a yoke of bondage.
Gal 5:2	*Indeed* I, Paul, say to you that if you become circumcised, Messiah will profit you nothing.
Gal 5:13	For you, brethren, have been called to liberty; only do not use liberty as an opportunity for the flesh, but through love *serve* one another.
Gal 5:15	But if you bite and devour one another, *beware* lest you be consumed by one another!
Gal 5:16	I say then: *Walk* in the Spirit, and you shall not fulfill the lust of the flesh.
Gal 6:1	Brethren, if a man is overtaken in any trespass, you who are spiritual *restore* such a one in a spirit of gentleness, considering yourself lest you also be tempted.

Gal 6:2	**Bear** one another's burdens, and so ***fulfill*** the <u>Law of Messiah</u>.
Gal 6:4	But let each one ***examine*** his own work, and then he will have rejoicing in himself alone, and not in another.
Gal 6:6	Let him who is taught the word ***share*** in all good things with him who teaches.
Gal 6:7	Do not be ***deceived***, God is not mocked; for whatever a man sows, that he will also reap.
Gal 6:11	***See*** with what large letters I have written to you with my own hand!
Gal 6:17	From now on let no one ***trouble*** me, for I bear in my body the marks of the Lord Yeshua.

Ephesians

Eph 2:11	Therefore ***remember*** that you, once Gentiles in the flesh – who are called Uncircumcision by what is called Circumcision made in the flesh by hands.
Eph 4:25	Therefore, putting away lying, "Let each one of you ***speak*** truth with his neighbor," for we are members of one another.
Eph 4:26	"Be ***angry***, and do not ***sin***": do not let the sun ***go*** down on your wrath,
Eph 4:27	Nor ***give*** place to the devil.
Eph 4:28	Let him who stole ***steal*** no longer, but rather let him ***labor***, working with his hands what is good, that he may have something to give him who has need.
Eph 4:29	Let no corrupt word ***proceed*** out of your mouth, but what is good for necessary edification, that it may impart grace to the hearers.
Eph 4:30	And do not ***grieve*** the Holy Spirit of God, by whom you were sealed for the day of redemption.
Eph 4:31	Let all bitterness, wrath, anger, clamor, and evil speaking be put ***away*** from you, with all malice.
Eph 4:32	And ***be*** kind to one another, tenderhearted, forgiving one another, even as God in Messiah forgave you.
Eph 5:1	Therefore ***be*** imitators of God as dear children.

Eph 5:2	And *walk* in love, as Messiah also has loved us and given Himself for us, an offering and a sacrifice to God for a sweet-smelling aroma.
Eph 5:3	But fornication and all uncleanness or covetousness, let it not even be *named* among you, as is fitting for saints.
Eph 5:6	Let no one *deceive* you with empty words, for because of these things the wrath of God comes upon the sons of disobedience.
Eph 5:7	Therefore do not *be* partakers with them.
Eph 5:8	For you were once darkness, but now you are light in the Lord. *Walk* as children of light.
Eph 5:11	And have no *fellowship* with the unfruitful works of darkness, but rather expose them.
Eph 5:14	Therefore He says: "*Awake*, you who sleep, *Arise* from the dead, and Messiah will give you light."
Eph 5:15	*See* then that you walk circumspectly, not as fools but as wise.
Eph 5:17	Therefore do not *be* unwise but understand what the will of the Lord is.
Eph 5:18	And do not be *drunk* with wine, in which is dissipation; but be *filled* with the Spirit,
Eph 5:22	Wives, *submit* to your own husbands, as to the Lord.
Eph 5:25	Husbands, *love* your wives, just as Messiah also loved the church and gave Himself for her.
Eph 5:33	Nevertheless let each one of you in particular so *love* his own wife as himself, and let the wife see that she respects her husband.
Eph 6:1	Children, *obey* your parents in the Lord, for this is right.
Eph 6:2	"*Honor* your father and mother," which is the first commandment with promise.
Eph 6:4	And you, fathers, do not *provoke* your children to wrath, but *bring* them up in the training and admonition of the Lord.
Eph 6:5	Bondservants, be *obedient* to those who are your masters according to the flesh, with fear and trembling, in sincerity of heart, as to Messiah.

Eph 6:9	And you, masters, *do* the same things to them, giving up threatening, knowing that your own Master also is in heaven, and there is no partiality with Him.
Eph 6:10	Finally my brethren, be *strong* in the Lord and in the power of His might.
Eph 6:11	*Put* on the whole armor of God, that you may be able to stand against the wiles of the devil.
Eph 6:13	Therefore take *up* the whole armor of God, that you may be able to withstand in the evil day, and having done all, to stand.
Eph 6:14	*Stand* therefore, having girded your waist with truth, having put on the breastplate of righteousness.
Eph 6:17	And *take* the helmet of salvation, and the sword of the Spirit, which is the word of God.

Philippians

Phil 2:2	*Fulfill* my joy by being like-minded, having the same love, being of one accord, or one mind.
Phil 2:4	Let each of you *look* out not only for his own interests, but also for the interests of others.
Phil 2:5	Let this *mind* be in you which was also in Messiah Yeshua.
Phil 2:12	Therefore, my beloved, as you have always obeyed, not as in my presence only, but now much more in my absence, *work* out your own salvation with fear and trembling;
Phil 2:14	*Do* all things without complaining and disputing.
Phil 2:18	For the same reason you also be *glad* and *rejoice* with me.
Phil 2:29	*Receive* him therefore in the Lord with all gladness, and hold such men in esteem;
Phil 3:1	Finally, my brethren, *rejoice* in the Lord. For me to write the same things to you is not tedious, but for you it is safe.
Phil 3:2	*Beware* of dogs, *beware* of evil workers, *beware* of the mutilation!
Phil 3:17	Brethren, join in following my example, and *note* those who walk, as you have us for a pattern.

Phil 4:1	Therefore, my beloved and longed-for brethren. my joy and crown, so **stand fast** in the Lord, beloved.
Phil 4:3	And I urge you also, true companion, **help** those women who labored with me in the gospel, with Clement also, and the rest of my fellow workers, whose names are in the Book of Life.
Phil 4:4	***Rejoice*** in the Lord always. Again I will say ***rejoice!***
Phil 4:5	Let your gentleness be ***known*** to all men. The Lord is at hand.
Phil 4:6	Be ***anxious*** for nothing, but in everything by prayer and supplication, with thanksgiving, let your requests be ***made*** known to God;
Phil 4:8	Finally, brethren whatever things are true, whatever things are noble, whatever things are just, whatever things are pure, whatever things are lovely, whatever things are of good report, if there is any virtue and if there is anything praiseworthy – ***meditate*** on these things.
Phil 4:9	The things which you learned and received and heard and saw in me, these ***do***, and the God of peace will be with you.
Phil 4:21	***Greet*** every saint in Messiah Yeshua. The brethren who are with me greet you.

Colossians

Col 2:6	As you therefore have received Messiah Yeshua the Lord, so ***walk*** in Him,
Col 2:8	Beware lest anyone ***cheat*** you through philosophy and empty deceit, according to the tradition of men, according to the basic principles of the world, and not according to Messiah.
Col 2:16	So let no one ***judge*** you in food or in drink, or regarding a festival or a new moon or sabbaths,
Col 2:18	Let no one ***cheat*** you of your reward, taking delight in false humility and worship of angels, intruding into those things which he has not seen, vainly puffed up by his fleshly mind,
Col 3:1	If then you were raised with Messiah, ***seek*** those things which are above, where Messiah is, sitting at the right hand of God.
Col 3:2	Set your ***mind*** on things above, not on things on the earth.

Col 3:5	Therefore put to ***death*** your members which are on the earth: fornication, uncleanness, passion, evil desire, and covetousness, which is idolatry.
Col 3:8	But now you yourselves are to ***put*** off all these: anger, wrath, malice, blasphemy, filthy language out of your mouth.
Col 3:9	Do not ***lie*** to one another, since you have put off the old man with his deeds,
Col 3:12	Therefore, as the elect of God, holy and beloved, ***put*** on tender mercies, kindness, humility, meekness, longsuffering;
Col 3:15	And let the peace of God ***rule*** in your hearts, to which also you were called in one body; and ***be*** thankful.
Col 3:16	Let the word of Messiah ***dwell*** in you richly in all wisdom, teaching and admonishing one another in psalms and hymns and spiritual songs, singing with grace in your hearts to the Lord.
Col 3:18	Wives, ***submit*** to your own husbands, as is fitting in the Lord.
Col 3:19	Husbands, ***love*** your wives and do not be ***bitter*** toward them.
Col 3:20	Children, ***obey*** your parents in all things, for this is well pleasing to the Lord.
Col 3:21	Fathers, do not ***provoke*** your children, lest they become discouraged.
Col 3:22	Bondservants, ***obey*** in all things your masters according to the flesh, not with eyeservice, as men-pleasers, but in sincerity of heart, fearing God.
Col 3:23	And whatever you do, ***do*** it heartily, as to the Lord and not to men.
Col 3:24	Knowing that from the Lord you will receive the reward of the inheritance; for you ***serve*** the Lord Messiah.
Col 4:1	Masters, ***give*** your bondservants what is just and fair, knowing that you also have a Master in heaven.
Col 4:2	***Continue*** earnestly in prayer, being vigilant in it with thanksgiving;
Col 4:5	***Walk*** in wisdom toward those who are outside, redeeming the time.
Col 4:10	Aristarchus my fellow prisoner greets you, with Mark the cousin of Barnabas (about whom you received instructions: if he comes to you, ***welcome*** him),

Col 4:15	**Greet** the brethren who are in Laodicea, and Nymphas and the church that is in his house.
Col 4:16	Now when this epistle is read among you, **see** that it is read also in the church of the Laodiceans, and that you likewise read the epistle from Laodicea.
Col 4:17	And **say** to Archippus, "Take **heed** to the ministry which you have received in the Lord, that you may fulfill it."
Col 4:18	This salutation by my own hand – Paul. **Remember** my chains. Grace be with you. Amen.

I Thessalonians

I Thess 4:18	Therefore **comfort** one another with these words.
I Thess 5:11	Therefore **comfort** each other and edify one another, just as you also are doing.
I Thess 5:13	And to esteem them very highly in love for their work's sake. Be at **peace** among yourselves.
I Thess 5:14	Now we exhort you, brethren, **warn** those who are unruly, **comfort** the faint-hearted, **uphold** the weak, be **patient** with all.
I Thess 5:15	**See** that no one renders evil for evil to anyone, but always **pursue** what is good both for yourselves and for all.
I Thess 5:16	**Rejoice** always.
I Thess 5:17	**Pray** without ceasing.
I Thess 5:18	In everything **give** thanks; for this is the will of God in Messiah Yeshua for you.
I Thess 5:19	Do not **quench** the Spirit.
I Thess 5:20	Do not **despise** prophecies.
I Thess 5:21	**Test** all things; **hold** fast what is good.
I Thess 5:22	**Abstain** from every form of evil.
I Thess 5:25	Brethren, **pray** for us.
I Thess 5:26	**Greet** all the brethren with a holy kiss.

II Thessalonians

II Thess 2:15   Therefore, brethren, **stand** fast and **hold** the traditions which you were taught, whether by word or our epistle.

II Thess 3:1   Finally, brethren, **pray** for us, that the word of the Lord may run swiftly and be glorified, just as it is with you,

II Thess 3:10   For even when we were with you, we commanded you this: If anyone will not work, neither shall he *eat*.

II Thess 3:14   And if anyone does not obey our word in this epistle, **note** that person and do not **keep** company with him, that he may be ashamed.

II Thess 3:15   Yet do not **count** him as an enemy, but **admonish** him as a brother.

I Timothy

I Tim 2:11   Let a woman **learn** in silence with all submission.

I Tim 3:10   But let these also first be **tested**; then let them **serve** as deacons, being found blameless.

I Tim 3:12   Let deacons **be** the husbands of one wife, ruling their children and their own houses well.

I Tim 4:7   But **reject** profane and old wives' fables, and **exercise** yourself toward godliness.

I Tim 4:11   These things **command** and **teach**.

I Tim 4:12   Let no one **despise** your youth, but **be** an example to the believers in word, in conduct, in love, in spirit, in faith, in purity.

I Tim 4:13   Till I come, **give** attention to reading, to exhortation, to doctrine.

I Tim 4:14   Do not **neglect** the gift that is in you, which was given to you by prophecy with the laying on of the hands of the eldership.

I Tim 4:15   **Meditate** on these things; **give** yourself entirely to them, that your progress may be evident to all.

I Tim 4:16   **Take** heed to yourself and to the doctrine. **Continue** in them, for in doing this you will save both yourself and those who hear you.

I Tim 5:1   Do not rebuke an older man, but **exhort** him as a father, younger men as brothers,

I Tim 5:3	***Honor*** widows who are really widows.
I Tim 5:4	But if any widow has children or grandchildren, let them first ***learn*** to show piety at home and to repay their parents; for this is good and acceptable before God.
I Tim 5:7	And these things ***command*** that they may be blameless.
I Tim 5:9	Do not let a widow under sixty years old be ***taken*** into the number, and not unless she has been the wife of one man.
I Tim 5:11	But ***refuse*** the younger widows; for when they have begun to grow wanton against Messiah, they desire to marry.
I Tim 5:16	If any believing man or woman has widows, let them ***relieve*** them, and do not let the church be ***burdened***, that it may relieve those who are really widows.
I Tim 5:17	Let the elders who rule well be ***counted*** worthy of double honor, especially those who labor in the word and doctrine.
I Tim 5:19	Do not ***receive*** an accusation against an elder except from two or three witnesses.
I Tim 5:20	Those who are sinning ***rebuke*** in the presence of all, that the rest also may fear.
I Tim 5:22	Do not lay hands ***on*** anyone hastily, nor ***share*** in other people's sins; ***keep*** yourself pure.
I Tim 5:23	No longer ***drink*** only water, but ***use*** a little wine for your stomach's sake and your frequent infirmities.
I Tim 6:1	Let as many bondservants as are under the yoke ***count*** their own masters worthy of all honor, so that the name of God and His doctrine may not be blasphemed.
I Tim 6:2	And those who have believing masters, let them not ***despise*** them because they are brethren, but rather ***serve*** them because those who are benefited are believers and beloved. ***Teach*** and ***exhort*** these things.
I Tim 6:5	Useless wranglings of men of corrupt minds and destitute of the truth, who suppose that godliness is a means of gain. From such ***withdraw*** yourself.
I Tim 6:11	But you, O man of God, ***flee*** these things and ***pursue*** righteousness, godliness, faith, love, patience, gentleness.

I Tim 6:12	*Fight* the good fight of faith, lay *hold* on eternal life, to which you were also called and have confessed the good confession in the presence of many witnesses.
I Tim 6:17	*Command* those who are rich in this present age not to be haughty, nor to trust in uncertain riches but in the living God, who gives us richly all things to enjoy.
I Tim 6:20	O Timothy! *Guard* what was committed to your trust, avoiding the profane and idle babblings and contradictions of what is falsely called knowledge.

II Timothy

II Tim 1:8	Therefore do not be ashamed of the testimony of our Lord, nor of me His prisoner, but *share* with me in the sufferings for the gospel according to the power of God.
II Tim 1:13	*Hold* fast the pattern of sound words which you have heard from me, in faith and love which are in Messiah Yeshua.
II Tim 1:14	That good thing which was committed to you, *keep* by the Holy Spirit who dwells in us.
II Tim 2:1	You therefore, my son, be *strong* in the grace that is in Messiah Yeshua.
II Tim 2:2	And the things that you have heard from me among many witnesses, *commit* these to faithful men who will be able to teach others also.
I Tim 2:3	You therefore must *endure* hardship as a good soldier of Yeshua Messiah.
II Tim 2:7	*Consider* what I say, and may the Lord give you understanding in all things.
II Tim 2:8	*Remember* that Yeshua Messiah, of the seed of David, was raised from the dead according to the gospel.
II Tim 2:14	*Remind* them of these things, charging them before the Lord not to strive about words to no profit, to the ruin of the hearers.
II Tim 2:15	Be *diligent* to present yourself approved to God, a worker who does not need to be ashamed, rightly dividing the word of truth.
II Tim 2:16	But *shun* profane and idle babblings, for they will increase to more ungodliness.

II Tim 2:19	Nevertheless the solid foundation of God stands, having this seal: "The Lord knows those who are His," and, "Let everyone who names the name of Messiah *depart* from iniquity."
II Tim 2:22	*Flee* also youthful lusts; but *pursue* righteousness, faith, love, peace with those who call on the Lord out of a pure heart.
II Tim 2:23	But *avoid* foolish and ignorant disputes, knowing that they generate strife.
II Tim 3:1	But *know* this, that in the last days perilous times will come.
II Tim 3:5	Having a form of godliness but denying its power. And from such people *turn* away!
II Tim 3:14	But you must *continue* in the things which you have learned and been assured of, knowing from whom you have learned them.
II Tim 4:2	*Preach* the word! Be *ready* in season and out of season. *Convince*, *rebuke*, *exhort*, with all longsuffering and teaching.
I Tim 4:5	But you be *watchful* in all things, *endure* afflictions, *do* the work of an evangelist, *fulfill* your ministry.
II Tim 4:9	Be *diligent* to come to me quickly.
II Tim 4:11	Only Luke is with me. Get Mark and *bring* him with you, for he is useful to me for ministry.
II Tim 4:13	*Bring* the cloak that I left with Carpus at Troas when you come – and the books, especially the parchments.
II Tim 4:15	You also must *beware* of him, for he has greatly resisted our words.
II Tim 4:19	*Greet* Prisca [Pricilla] and Aquila, and the household of Onesiphorus.
II Tim 4:21	*Do* your utmost to come before winter. Eubulus greets you, as well as Pudens, Linus, Claudia, and all the brethren.

Titus

Titus 1:13	This testimony is true. Therefore *rebuke* them sharply, that they may be sound in the faith.
Titus 2:1	But as for you, *speak* the things which are proper for sound doctrine.
Titus 2:6	Likewise, *exhort* the young men to be sober-minded.

Titus 2:15	*Speak* these things, *exhort*, and *rebuke* with all authority. Let no one *despise* you.
Titus 3:1	*Remind* them to be subject to rulers and authorities, to obey, to be ready for every good work.
Titus 3:9	But *avoid* foolish disputes, genealogies, contentions, and striving about the Law; for they are unprofitable and useless.
Titus 3:10	*Reject* a divisive man after the first and second admonition.
Titus 3:12	When I send Artemas to you, or Tychicus, be *diligent* to come to me at Nicopolis, for I have decided to spend the winter there.
Titus 3:13	*Send* Zenas the lawyer and Apollos on their journey with haste, that they may lack nothing.
Titus 3:14	And let our people also *learn* to maintain good works, to meet urgent needs, that they may not be unfruitful.
Titus 3:15	All who are with me greet you. *Greet* those who love us in the faith. Grace be with you all. Amen.

Philemon

Phil 1:12	I am sending him back. You therefore *receive* him, that is, my own heart.
Phil 1:17	If then you count me as a partner, *receive* him as you would me.
Phil 1:18	But if he has wronged you or owes anything, put that on my *account*.
Phil 1:20	Yes, brother, let me have joy from you in the Lord; *refresh* my heart in the Lord.
Phil 1:22	But, meanwhile, also *prepare* a guest room for me, for I trust that through your prayers I shall be granted to you.

Hebrews

Heb 1:6	But when He again brings the firstborn into the world, He says: "Let all the angels of God *worship* Him."
Heb 1:13	But to which of the angels has He ever said: "*Sit* at My right hand, till I make Your enemies Your footstool."
Heb 2:13	And again: "I will put My trust in Him." And again: "*Here* am I and the children whom God has given Me."

Heb 3:1	Therefore, holy brethren, partakers of the heavenly calling, ***consider*** the Apostle and High Priest of our confession, Yeshua Messiah.
Heb 3:12	***Beware***, brethren, lest there be in any of you an evil heart of unbelief in departing from the living God.
Heb 3:13	But ***exhort*** one another daily, while it is called "Today," lest any of you be hardened through the deceitfulness of sin.
Heb 6:10	For God is not unjust to forget your work and labor of love which you have ***shown*** toward His Name, in that you have ministered to the saints, and do minister.
Heb 7:4	Now ***consider*** how great this man was, to whom even the patriarch Abraham gave a tenth of the spoils.
Heb 8:5	Who serve the copy and shadow of the heavenly things, as Moses was divinely instructed when he was about to make the tabernacle. For He said, *"**See** that you make all things according to the pattern shown you on the mountain."*
Heb 8:8	Because finding fault with them, He says: *"**Behold**, the days are coming, says the LORD, when I will make a **New Covenant** with the house of Israel and with the house of Judah."*
Heb 8:11	None of them shall teach his neighbor, and none his brother, saying, *"**Know** the LORD,"* for all shall know Me, from the least of them to the greatest of them.
Heb 10:7	"Then I said, *'**Behold**, I have come – In the volume of the book it is written of Me – to do Your will, O God.'"
Heb 10:9	Then He said, *"**Behold**, I have come to do Your will, O God."* He takes away the first that He may establish the second.
Heb 10:32	But ***recall*** the former days in which, after you were illuminated, you endured a great struggle with sufferings:
Heb 12:3	For ***consider*** Him who endured such hostility from sinners against Himself, lest you become weary and discouraged in your souls.
Heb 12:5	And you have forgotten the exhortation which speaks to you as to sons: *"My son, do not **despise** the chastening of the LORD, nor be discouraged when you are rebuked by Him."*
Heb 12:12	Therefore ***strengthen*** the hands which hang down, and the feeble knees,

Heb 12:13	And *make* straight paths for your feet, so that what is lame may not be dislocated, but rather be healed.
Heb 12:14	*Pursue* peace with all people, and holiness, without which no one will see the Lord.
Heb 12:17	For you *know* that afterward, when he wanted to inherit the blessing, he was rejected, for he found no place for repentance, though he sought it diligently with tears.
Heb 12:25	*See* that you do not refuse Him who speaks. For if they did not escape who refused Him who spoke on earth, much more shall we not escape if we turn away from Him who speaks from heaven.
Heb 13:1	Let brotherly love *continue*.
Heb 13:2	*Do* not forget to entertain strangers, for by so doing some have unwittingly entertained angels.
Heb 13:3	*Remember* the prisoners as if chained with them – those who are mistreated – since you yourselves are in the body also.
Heb 13:7	*Remember* those who rule over you, who have spoken the word of God to you, whose faith *follow*, considering the outcome of their conduct.
Heb 13:9	Do not be *carried* about with various and strange doctrines. For it is good that the heart be established by grace, not with foods which have not profited those who have been occupied with them.
Heb 13:16	But do not *forget* to do good and to share, for with such sacrifices God is well pleased.
Heb 13:17	*Obey* those who rule over you, and be *submissive*, for they watch out for your souls, as those who must give account. Let them do so with joy and not with grief, for that would be unprofitable for you.
Heb 13:18	*Pray* for us; for we are confident that we have a good conscience, in all things desiring to live honorably.
Heb 13:22	And I appeal to you, brethren, *bear* with the word of exhortation, for I have written to you in few words.
Heb 13:23	*Know* that our brother Timothy has been set free, with whom I shall see you if he comes shortly.
Heb 13:24	*Greet* all those who rule over you, and all the saints. Those from Italy greet you.

James

James 1:2	My brethren, *count* it all joy when you fall into various trials.
James 1:4	But let patience *have* its perfect work, that you may be perfect and complete, lacking nothing.
James 1:5	If any of you lacks wisdom, let him *ask* of God, who gives to all liberally and without reproach, and it will be given to him.
James 1:6	But let him *ask* in faith, with no doubting, for he who doubts is like a wave of the sea driven and tossed by the wind.
James 1:7	For let not that man *suppose* that he will receive anything from the Lord.
James 1:9	Let the lowly brother *glory* in his exaltation.
James 1:13	Let no one *say* when he is tempted, "I am tempted by God"; for God cannot be tempted by evil, nor does He Himself tempt anyone.
James 1:16	Do not be *deceived*, my beloved brethren.
James 1:19	So then, my beloved brethren, let every man *be* swift to hear, slow to speak, slow to wrath.
James 1:21	Therefore lay aside all filthiness and overflow of wickedness, and *receive* with meekness the implanted word, which is able to save your souls.
James 1:22	But *be* doers of the word, and not hearers only, deceiving yourselves.
James 2:1	My brethren, do not *hold* the faith of our Lord Yeshua Messiah, the Lord of Glory, with partiality.
James 2:3	And you pay attention to the one wearing the fine clothes and say to him, "You *sit* here in a good place," and say to the poor man, "You *stand* there," or, "*Sit* here at my footstool."
James 2:5	*Listen*, my beloved brethren: Has God not chosen the poor of this world to be rich in faith and heirs of the kingdom which He promised to those who love Him?
James 2:12	So *speak* and so *do* as those who will be judged by the law of liberty.
James 2:16	And one of you says to them, "*Depart* in peace, be *warmed* and *filled*," but you do not give them the things which are needed for the body, what does it profit?

James 2:18	But someone will say, "You have faith, and I have works." **Show** me your faith without your works, and I will show you my faith by my works.
James 3:1	My brethren, let not many of you *become* teachers, knowing that we shall receive a stricter judgment.
James 3:3	*Indeed*, we put bits in horses' mouths that they may obey us, and we turn their whole body.
James 3:4	*Look* also at ships: although they are so large and are driven by fierce winds, they are turned by a very small rudder wherever the pilot desires.
James 3:5	Even so the tongue is a little member and boasts great things. *See* how great a forest a little fire kindles!
James 3:13	Who is wise and understanding among you? Let him *show* by good conduct that his works are done in the meekness of wisdom.
James 3:14	But if you have bitter envying and self-seeking in your hearts, do not *boast* and *lie* against the truth.
James 4:7	Therefore *submit* to God. *Resist* the devil and he will flee from you.
James 4:8	*Draw* near to God and He will draw near to you. *Cleanse* your hands, you sinners; and *purify* your hearts, you double-minded.
James 4:9	*Lament* and *mourn* and *weep*! Let your laughter be *turned* to mourning and your joy to gloom.
James 4:10	*Humble* yourselves in the sight of the Lord, and He will lift you up.
James 4:11	Do not *speak* evil of one another, brethren. He who speaks evil of a brother and judges his brother, speaks evil of the Law and judges the Law. But if you judge the Law, you are not a doer of the Law but a judge.
James 4:13	*Come* now, you who say, "Today or tomorrow we will go to such and such a city, spend a year there, buy and sell, and make a profit."
James 5:1	*Come* now, you rich, weep and howl for your miseries that are coming upon you!
James 5:4	*Indeed* the wages of the laborers who mowed your fields, which you kept back by fraud, cry out; and the cries of the reapers have reached the ears of the Lord of Sabaoth.

James 5:7	Therefore be *patient*, brethren, until the coming of the Lord. *See* how the farmer waits for the precious fruit of the earth, waiting patiently for it until it receives the early and latter rain.
James 5:8	You also be *patient*. *Establish* your hearts, for the coming of the Lord is at hand.
James 5:9	Do not grumble against one another, brethren, lest you be condemned. *Behold*, the Judge is standing at the door!
James 5:10	My brethren, *take* the prophets, who spoke in the Name of the Lord, as an example of suffering and patience.
James 5:11	*Indeed* we count them blessed who endure. You have heard of the perseverance of Job and seen the end intended by the Lord – that the Lord is very compassionate and merciful.
James 5:12	But above all, my brethren, do not *swear*, either by heaven or by earth or with any other oath. But let your "Yes" *be* "Yes," and your "No," "No," lest you fall into judgment.
James 5:13	Is anyone among you suffering? Let him *pray*. Is anyone cheerful? Let him *sing* psalms.
James 5:14	Is anyone among you sick? Let him *call* for the elders of the church, and let them *pray* over him, anointing him with oil in the Name of the Lord.
James 5:16	*Confess* your trespasses to one another, and *pray* for one another, that you may be healed. The effective, fervent prayer of a righteous man avails much.
James 5:20	Let him *know* that he who turns a sinner from the error of his way will save a soul from death and cover a multitude of sins.

I Peter

I Peter 1:13	Therefore gird up the loins of your mind, be sober, and rest your *hope* fully upon the grace that is to be brought to you at the revelation of Yeshua Messiah.
I Peter 1:15	But as He who called you is holy, you also *be* holy in all your conduct.
I Peter 1:16	Because it is written, "*Be* holy, for I am holy."

I Peter 1:17	And if you call on the Father, who without partiality judges according to each one's work, *conduct* yourselves throughout the time of your stay here in fear.
I Peter 1:22	Since you have purified your souls in obeying the truth through the Spirit in sincere love of the brethren, *love* one another fervently with a pure heart.
I Peter 2:2	As newborn babes, *desire* the pure milk of the word, that you may grow thereby.
I Peter 2:6	Therefore it is also contained in the Scripture, "*Behold*, I lay in Zion a chief cornerstone, elect, precious, and he who believes on Him will by no means be put to shame."
I Peter 2:13	Therefore *submit* yourselves to every ordinance of man for the Lord's sake, whether to the king as supreme,
I Peter 2:17	*Honor* all people. *Love* the brotherhood. *Fear* God. *Honor* the king.
I Peter 3:3	Do not let your adornment *be* merely outward – arranging the hair, wearing gold, or putting on fine apparel.
I Peter 3:10	For "He who would love life and see good days, let him *refrain* his tongue from evil, and his lips from speaking deceit."
I Peter 3:11	"Let him *turn* away from evil and *do* good; Let him *seek* peace and *pursue* it."
I Peter 3:14	But even if you should suffer for righteousness' sake, you are blessed. "And do not be *afraid* of their threats, nor be troubled."
I Peter 3:15	But *sanctify* the Lord God in your hearts, and always be ready to give a defense to everyone asks you a reason for the hope that is in you, with meekness and fear."
I Peter 4:1	Therefore, since Messiah suffered for us in the flesh, *arm* yourselves also with the same mind, for he who has suffered in the flesh has ceased from sin,
I Peter 4:7	But the end of all things is at hand; therefore be *serious* and *watchful* in your prayers.
I Peter 4:12	Beloved, do not *think* it strange concerning the fiery trial which is to try you, as though some strange thing happened to you.

I Peter 4:13	But *rejoice* to the extent that you partake of Messiah's sufferings, that when His glory is revealed, you may also be glad with exceeding joy.
I Peter 4:15	But let none of you *suffer* as a murderer, a thief, an evildoer, or as a busybody in other people's matters.
I Peter 4:16	Yet if anyone suffers as a Christian, let him not be *ashamed*, but let him *glorify* God in this matter.
I Peter 4:19	Therefore let those who suffer according to the will of God *commit* their souls to Him in doing good, as to a faithful Creator.
I Peter 5:2	*Shepherd* the flock of God which is among you, serving as overseers, not by compulsion but willingly, not for dishonest gain but eagerly.
I Peter 5:5	Likewise you younger people, *submit* yourselves to your elders. Yes, all of you be submissive to one another, and be *clothed* with humility, for "God resists the proud, but give grace to the humble."
I Peter 5:6	Therefore *humble* yourselves under the mighty hand of God, that He may exalt you in due time.
I Peter 5:8	Be *sober*, be *vigilant*; because your adversary the devil walks about like a roaring loin, seeking whom he may devour.
I Peter 5:9	*Resist* him, steadfast in the faith, knowing that the same sufferings are experienced by your brotherhood in the world.
I Peter 5:14	*Greet* one another with a kiss of love. Peace to you all who are in Messiah Yeshua. Amen.

II Peter

II Peter 1:5	But also for this very reason, giving all diligence, *add* to your faith virtue, to virtue knowledge,
II Peter 1:10	Therefore, brethren, be even more *diligent* to make your call and election sure, for if you do these things, you will never stumble.
II Peter 3:8	But, beloved, do not *forget* this one thing, that with the Lord one day is as a thousand years, and a thousand years as one day.
II Peter 3:14	Therefore, beloved, looking forward to these things, be *diligent* to be found by Him in peace, without spot and blameless;

II Peter 3:15	And *consider* that the longsuffering of our Lord is salvation – as also our beloved brother Paul, according to the wisdom given to him, has written to you.
II Peter 3:17	You therefore, beloved, since you know this beforehand, *beware* lest you also fall from your own steadfastness, being led away with the error of the wicked.
II Peter 3:18	*But* grow in the grace and knowledge of our Lord and Saviour Yeshua Messiah. To Him be the glory both now and forever. Amen.

I John

I John 2:15	Do not *love* the world or the things in the world. If anyone loves the world, the love of the Father is not in him.
I John 2:24	Therefore let that *abide* in you which you heard from the beginning. If what you heard from the beginning abides in you, you also will abide in the Son, and in the Father.
I John 2:27	But the anointing which you have received from Him abides in you, and you do not need that anyone teach you: but as the same anointing teaches you concerning all things, and is true, and is not a lie, and just as it has taught you, you will *abide* in Him.
I John 2:28	And now, little children, *abide* in Him, that when He appears, we may have confidence and not be ashamed before Him at His coming.
I John 3:1	*Behold* what manner of love the Father has bestowed on us, that we should be called children of God! Therefore, the world does not know us, because it did not know Him.
I John 3:7	Little children, let no one *deceive* you. He who practices righteousness is righteous, just as He is righteous.
I John 3:13	Do not *marvel*, my brethren, if the world hates you.
I John 4:1	Beloved, do not *believe* every spirit, but *test* the spirits, whether they are of God; because many false prophets have gone out into the world.
I John 4:2	By this you *know* the Spirit of God: Every spirit that confesses that Yeshua Messiah has come in the flesh is of God,
I John 5:21	Little Children, *keep* yourselves from idols. Amen.

II John

II John 1:8   ***Look*** to yourselves, that we do not lose those things we worked for, but that we may receive a full reward.

II John 1:10   If anyone comes to you and does not bring this doctrine, do not ***receive*** him into your house nor ***greet*** him.

III John

III John 1:11   Beloved, do not ***imitate*** what is evil, but what is good. He who does good is of God, but he who does evil has not seen God.

III John 1:14   But I hope to see you shortly, and we shall speak face to face. Peace to you. Our friends greet you. ***Greet*** the friends by name.

Jude

Jude 14   Now Enoch, the seventh from Adam, prophesied about these men also, saying, "***Behold***, the Lord comes with ten thousands of His saints."

Jude 17   But you, beloved, ***remember*** the words were spoken before by the apostles of our Lord Yeshua Messiah.

Jude 21   ***Keep*** yourselves in the love of God, looking for the mercy of our Lord Yeshua Messiah unto eternal life.

Jude 22   And on some have ***compassion***, making a distinction.

Jude 23   But others ***save*** with fear, pulling them out of the fire, hating even the garment defiled by the flesh.

Revelation

Rev 1:7   ***Behold***, He is coming with clouds, and every eye will see Him, even they who pierced Him. And all the tribes of the earth will mourn because of Him. Even so. Amen.

Rev 1:11   Saying, "I am the Alpha and the Omega, the First and the Last," and, "What you see, ***write*** in a look and ***send*** it to the seven churches which are in Asia: to Ephesus, to Smyrna, to Pergamos, to Thyatira, to Sardis, to Philadelphia, and to Laodicea."

Rev 1:17   And when I saw Him, I fell at His feet as dead. But He laid His right hand on me, saying to me, "Do not ***be*** afraid; I am the First and the Last."

Rev 1:18	"I am He who lives, and was dead, and **behold**, I am alive forevermore. Amen. And I have the keys of Hades and of Death."
Rev 1:19	"***Write*** the things which you have seen, and the things which are, and the things which will take place after this."
Rev 2:1	"To the angel of the church of Ephesians ***write***, 'These things says He who holds the seven stars in His right hand, who walks in the midst of the seven golden lampstands."
Rev 2:5	"***Remember*** therefore from where you have fallen; ***repent*** and ***do*** the first works, or else I will come to you quickly and remove your lampstand from its place – unless you repent."
Rev 2:7	"He who has an ear, let him ***hear*** what the Spirit says to the churches. To him who overcomes I will give to eat from the tree of life, which is in the midst of the Paradise of God."
Rev 2:8	"And to the angel of the church of Smyrna ***write***, 'These things says the First and the Last, who was dead, and came to life.'"
Rev 2:10	Do not ***fear*** any of those things which you are about to suffer. ***Indeed***, the devil is about to throw some of you into prison, that you may be tested, and you will have tribulation ten days. Be faithful until death, and I will give you the crown of life.
Rev 2:11	"He who has an ear, let him ***hear*** what the Spirit says to the churches. He who overcomes shall not be hurt by the second death."
Rev 2:12	"And to the angel of the church in Pergamos ***write***, 'These things says He who has the sharp two-edged sword."
Rev 2:16	"***Repent***, or else I will come to you quickly and will fight against them with the sword of My mouth."
Rev 2:17	"He who has an ear, let him ***hear*** what the Spirit says to the churches. To him who overcomes I will give some of the hidden manna to eat. And I will give him a white stone, and on the stone a new name written which no one knows except him who receives it."
Rev 2:18	"And to the angel of the church in Thyatira ***write***, 'These things says the Son of God, who has eyes like a flame of fire, and His feet like fine brass."
Rev 2:22	"***Indeed*** I will cast her into a sickbed, and those who commit adultery with her into great tribulation, unless they repent of their deeds."

Rev 2:25	"But hold *fast* what you have till I come."
Rev 2:29	"He who has an ear, let him **hear** what the Spirit says to the churches."
Rev 3:1	"And to the angel of the church in Sardis **write**, 'These things says He who has the seven Spirits of God and the seven stars: "I know your works, that you have a name that you are alive, but you are dead."'"
Rev 3:2	"***Be*** watchful, and ***strengthen*** the things which remain, that are ready to die, for I have not found your works perfect before God."
Rev 3:3	"**Remember** therefore how you have received and heard; **hold** fast and **repent**. Therefore if you will not watch, I will come upon you as a thief, and you will not know what hour I will come upon you."
Rev 3:6	"He who has an ear, let him **hear** what the Spirit says to the churches."
Rev 3:7	"And to the angel of the church in Philadelphia **write**, 'These things says He who is holy, He who is true, "He who has the key of David, He who opens and no one shuts, and shuts and no one opens."
Rev 3:8	"I know your works. **See**, I have set before you an open door, and no one can shut it; for you have a little strength, have kept My word, and have not denied My Name."
Rev 3:9	"**Indeed** I will make those of the synagogue of Satan, who say they are Jews and are not, but lie – **indeed** I will make them come and worship before your feet, and to know that I have loved you."
Rev 3:11	"**Behold**, I am coming quickly! Hold *fast* what you have, that no one may take your crown."
Rev 3:13	"He who has an ear, let him **hear** what the Spirit says to the churches."
Rev 3:14	"And to the angel of the church of the Laodiceans **write**, 'These things says the Amen, the Faithful and True Witness, the Beginning of the creation of God.'"
Rev 3:18	"I counsel you to buy from Me gold refined in the fire, that you may be rich; and white garments, that you may be clothed, that the shame of your nakedness may not be revealed; and **anoint** your eyes with eye salve, that you may see."

Rev 3:19	"As many as I love, I rebuke and chasten. Therefore, be *zealous* and *repent*."
Rev 3:20	"*Behold*, I stand at the door and knock. If anyone hears My voice and opens the door, I will come into him and dine with him and he with Me."
Rev 3:22	"He who has an ear, let him *hear* what the Spirit says to the churches."

Total Verses – 614   Total Imperative Commands – 758

APPENDIX THREE
The *Tanakh* Is Not Neglected or Depreciated by the New Covenant

In my study of this topic I have read over and over again from Torah observance proclaimers that we who are Dispensationalist disregard the whole of the Torah and the *Tanakh* when we say that the *old covenant* has been annulled, terminated, replaced and **rendered inoperative** as a working standard for believers to live by today. We interpret the Scriptures literally; it is not what we say – it is what God said.

There is a total mishandling of Matthew 5:17 and Romans 10:4 in that these verses are completely and purposely mishandled in teaching that since Yeshua kept the Law of Moses so are we to do the same. Because they look at Dispensational teaching as false, they purposely do not understand that God used different economies as He worked with mankind as He progressively revealed Himself and His redemptive plan and program. They will not because of their bias prohibits them from seeing that God Himself set the law system aside, **not** Dispensationalist. They do not see or realize that yes, Yeshua did keep the Law of Moses because that was the economy of Law that He lived under and was required to live by it. He fulfilled it, which is exactly what He did and in so doing He mediated a **New Covenant**, completely different from the *old covenant*. The following comes from the dictionary[231] on how the word *fulfill* is generally used and understood (also go back and reread the chapter entitled "Snapshot of Matthew" p. 106); it means:

> ***To bring to completion***: Yeshua fulfilled the Law and completed its purpose.
>
> ***To bring to an end***: Yeshua brought the Law to an end; its purpose is fulfilled. ***To put into effect – to execute***: Since no one kept the Law of Moses, it was in effect, but unrealized until Yeshua obeyed it completely. He executed the law and fulfilled it.
>
> The word *fulfillment* is "the act or process of fulfilling." When all saints from the days of the *Tanakh* failed to keep the law, Yeshua was the only one to fulfill it as He lived out His life flawlessly.

---

[231] *Merriam-Webster's Collegiate Dictionary: Eleventh Edition*, Springfield, MA: Merriam-Webster, Incorporated, 2008, p. 505.

Thus, He brought the law to completion, to an end; He executed what no other human could do.

Torah keepers repeatedly make statements that the Law is eternal or that the Torah is eternal, that the **New Covenant** is nothing more than an extension of the *old covenant*. I made one mistake in the reading of their books and that was not recording how many times they say that the Law is still the authority for believers to obey, both for Jews and Gentiles, they are legion.

Rather than being accused of diminishing the Law, as was pointed out in Part One, chapter 3, subheading "The Continued Value of the Law," p. 32, we believe that the *Tanakh* should be used lawfully as Paul tells Timothy (I Tim 1:8) *but we know that the law is good, if a man use it lawfully,* and that would mean in its context. The author of Hebrews upholds the *Tanakh* with around 137 quotations and references from the *Tanakh* and the Torah, as referenced in the long list[232] compiled by Steven Ger that follows. The author affirms the Superiority of Messiah and His establishment of the **New Covenant** and the annulling of the *old covenant*.

Since this is such a huge issue with Torah keepers I will follow this whole issue with a list I have compiled of quotations and allusions to the *Tanakh* from Romans, Galatians, James, Peter, and John as he records the Revelation of Yeshua Ha-Mashiach.

List of Used Passages in Hebrews from the Torah and *Tanakh*

Hebrews Chapter One

Heb	*Tanakh*	Subject
1:2	Psalm 2:8	The Son as Heir of creation
1:3	Psalm 110:1	The divine authority of the Son
1:5	Psalm 2:7	The sonship of the Messiah
1:5	2 Sam 7:14; I Chron 17:13	The sonship of the Messiah
1:6	Psalm 97:7	Worship of the Son by angels
1:7	Psalm 104:4	The position of angels
1:8-9	Psalm 45:6-7	Deity of the Son

---

[232] Taken from teaching blocks from each chapter in Steven Ger's Commentary on Hebrews, *The Book of Hebrews: Christ Is Greater,* (Volume 13) (21st Century Biblical Commentary Series). Ed Hindson (Series Editor). Mel Couch (Series Editor), Chattanooga, TN: AMG Publishers, 2009, pp. 48, 52, 68, 83, 94, 104, 113, 127, 140, 162, 188-189, 205, 220.

1:10-12	Psa 102:25-27	Deity of the Son
1:13	Psalms 110:1	The divine authority of the Son

Hebrews Chapter Two

2:6-8	Psalm 8:5-7	The divine authority of the Son
2:12	Psalm 22:22	The Purpose of the Son
2:13	Isaiah 8:17-18	The Purpose of the Son
2:13	Isaiah 12:2	The Purpose of the Son
2:16	Isaiah 41:8-9	Messiah as Son of Abraham

Hebrews Chapter Three

3:2-5	Number 12:7	The Position of Moses
3:7-11	Psalm 95:7-11	Israel's wilderness rebellion
3:8	Exodus 17:7	Israel's wilderness rebellion
3:15	Psalm 95:7-8	Admonition to faithfulness
3:16-18	Number 14:1-35	Israel's wilderness rebellion

Hebrews Chapter Four

4:3	Psalm 95:11	God's rest denied to the faithless
4:4	Genesis 2:2	God's rest following creation
4:5	Psalm 95:11	God's rest denied to the faithless
4:8	Joshua 22:4	Israel's conquest of the Land
4:10	Genesis 2:2	God's rest following creation

Hebrews Chapter Five

5:3	Lev 9:7 & 16:6	The Levitical high priest's need for atonement
5:4	Exodus 28:1	The commissioning of Aaron as high priest
5:5	Psalm 2:7	The sonship of the Messiah
5:6 & 10	Psalm 110:4	The Son's Melchizedekian priesthood
5:9	Isaiah 45:17	Eternal salvation

Hebrews Chapter Six

6:8	Genesis 3:17-18	The divine curse of the earth

6:13	Genesis 22:16	The binding of Isaac
6:14	Genesis 22:17	The Abrahamic Covenant
6:16	Exodus 22:11	The Mosaic Law concerning oaths
6:18	Number 23:19	The unchangeable purpose of God
6:18	I Samuel 15:29	The unchangeable purpose of God
6:19	Leviticus 16:2	The high priest's role on the Day of Atonement
6:20	Psalm 110:4	The Son's Melchizedekian priesthood

Hebrews Chapter Seven

7:1-2	Genesis 14:17-20	Melchizedek and Abraham
7:3	Psalm 110:4	Melchizedekian Priesthood
7:5	Numbers 18:21	The Mosaic Law concerning Israel's Levitical Tithe
7:14	Genesis 49:10	Prophecy regarding Messiah's descent from Judah
7:14	Isaiah 11:1	Prophecy regarding Messiah's descent from Jesse
7:17 & 21	Psalm 110:4	The Son's Melchizedekian Priesthood
7:27	Leviticus 9:7; 16:6	The Levitical high priest's need for atonement

Hebrews Chapter Eight

8:1	Psalm 110:1	The Divine Authority of the Son
8:5	Exodus 25:40	The Tabernacle
8:8-12	Jeremiah 31:31-34	The **New Covenant**

Hebrews Chapter Nine

9:2	Exod 25:23-26:30	The Tabernacle and its components
9:3	Leviticus 16:3	The Holy of Holies
9:4	Exodus 16:33	The jar of manna
9:4	Exodus 30:1-6	The altar of incense
9:4	Numbers 17:8-10	The rod of Aaron
9:4	Deut 10:3-5	The two stone tablets
9:4-5	Exodus 25:10-22	The Ark of the Covenant

9:6	Numbers 18:2-6	The service of the Levitical priesthood
9:7	Leviticus 16:2	The High Priest's role on the Day of Atonement
9:10	Leviticus 10:2	The Mosaic Law concerning food
9:10	Lev 11:25; 15:18; Num 19:13	The Mosaic Law concerning uncleanness
9:13	Leviticus 16:6-7	The Day of Atonement
9:13	Numbers 19:9	The ashes of the red heifer
9:19-20	Exodus 24:3-8	The ratification of the Mosaic covenant
9:21	Leviticus 8:15	The consecration of the Levitical priesthood
9:22	Leviticus 17:11	The necessity of blood for atonement
9:28	Isaiah 53:12	Isaiah's suffering servant

Hebrews Chapter Ten

10:4	Leviticus 16:6-7	The Day of Atonement
10:5-9	Psalm 40:6-8	The Levitical sacrificial system
10:11	Exodus 29:38	The Levitical priestly service
10:12	Isaiah 53:10-12	Isaiah's suffering servant
10:12-13	Psalm 110:1	The divine authority of the Son
10:16-17	Jeremiah 31:33-34	The **New Covenant**
10:22	Ezekiel 36:25	The **New Covenant**
10:25	Lev 23:27; 25:9	The Day of Atonement
10:26	Numbers 15:30-31	The sin of defiance
10:27	Isaiah 26:11; 20-21	Divine judgment against God's enemies
10:28	Deut 17:6; 19:15	The Mosaic Law concerning testimony
10:29	Exodus 24:8	The ratification of the Mosaic Covenant
10:30	Deut 32:35-36	Divine judgment against God's enemies
10:30	Psalm 135:14	Divine justice for God's people
10:37-38	Habakkuk 2:3-4	Admonition to faithfulness

Hebrews Chapter Eleven

11:3	Psalm 33:6-9	Divine creation
11:4	Genesis 4:3-10	Cain and Abel
11:5	Genesis 5:24	Enoch
11:7	Genesis 6:13-7:1	Noah
11:8	Genesis 12:1-5	Abraham
11:9	Genesis 23:4; 26:3; 35:12-27	The patriarchs
11:11	Genesis 18:11-14	Sarah
11:12	Genesis 22:17	The Abrahamic Covenant
11:13	Genesis 23:4	The Patriarchs
11:17	Genesis 22:1-10	The binding of Isaac
11:18	Genesis 21:12	The Abrahamic Covenant
11:20	Genesis 27:27-29; 39-40	Isaac's blessing of Jacob and Esau
11:21	Gen 47:31; 48:15-16	Jacob's blessing of Joseph's sons
11:22	Genesis 50:24-25	The death of Joseph
11:23	Exodus 1:22-2:2	The birth of Moses
11:24	Exodus 2:10-15	The maturity of Moses
11:28	Exodus 12:21-30	The Passover
11:29	Exodus 14:21-31	The Exodus
11:30	Joshua 6:12-21	The conquest of Jericho
11:31	Joshua 2:11-12; 6:21-25	Rahab
11:32	Judges 6-8	Gideon
11:32	Judges 4-5	Barak
11:32	Judges 13-16	Samson
11:32	Judges 11-12	Jephthah
11:32	1-2 Sam; I Chron.	David
11:32	I Samuel 1-16	Samuel
11:33	Daniel 6:1-27	Daniel
11:34	Daniel 3:23-25	Shadrach, Meshach, and Abednego
11:35	II Kings 4:32-37	Elisha and the Shunammite's son

11:36	Jer 20:2; 37:15	Jeremiah
11:37	II Chronicles 24:21	Zechariah the son of Jehoiada

Hebrews Chapter Twelve

12:2	Psalm 110:1	The divine authority of the Son
12:5-6	Proverbs 3:11-12	Divine discipline
12:7-9	Deuteronomy 8:5	Divine discipline
12:12	Isaiah 35:3	Encouragement to live a sanctified life
12:13	Proverbs 4:26	Encouragement to live a sanctified life
12:16-17	Genesis 25:33-34; 27:30-40	Jacob and Esau
12:18-19	Deut 4:11-12; 5:22-27	Israel's Sinai experience
12:18-20	Exodus 19:12-23; 20:18-21	Israel Sinai experience
12:21	Deuteronomy 9:19	Israel's Sinai experience
12:23	Genesis 18:25	God as Judge
12:24	Genesis 4:10	Cain and Abel
12:24	Jeremiah 31:31	The **New Covenant**
12:26	Exodus 19:18	Israel's Sinai experience
12:26	Haggai 2:6	Divine judgment against God's enemies
12:29	Deuteronomy 4:24	Divine judgment against God's enemies

Hebrews Chapter Thirteen

13:2	Gen 18:1-8; 19:1-3	Abraham, Lot, and the angels
13:5	Deuteronomy 31:6-8	The promise of God's abiding presence
13:6	Psalm 118:6	The promise of God's abiding presence
13:11	Leviticus 16:27	The Day of Atonement
13:15	Hosea 14:2	Worship
13:17	Ezekiel 3:17	Community responsibilities
13:20	Isaiah 53:3	The **New Covenant** and Davidic Covenant
13:20	Jeremiah 32:40	The **New Covenant**
13:20	Zechariah 9:11	The **New Covenant**

| 13:20 | Zechariah 13:7 | Prophecy regarding the Messiah's death |

List of Used Passages in Romans from the Torah and *Tanakh*

Romans	*Tanakh*	Subject
1:2	Moses, David, Isaiah, Jeremiah; etc.	His Prophets in the *Tanakh*
1:2	Gen. through Malachi	Holy Scriptures
1:3	Genesis 3:15; 22:18; II Samuel 7:12-16	The Seed of David
1:4	Psalm 16:10-11	Resurrection
1:17	Habakkuk 2:4	Just shall live by Faith
1:18	Genesis 3; 6-8; 19; Exodus 7-12	Wrath of God revealed
1:20	Genesis 1	Creation
1:21-23, 25	Exodus 3:2; Jeremiah 2:11	Hearts and minds darkened
	Psalm 106:19-20; I Kings 12:28-31	Worship of golden calf
1:26-27	Genesis 19	Sodomy
2:5	Zephaniah 1:14-18	Seventieth Week of Daniel
2:11	Deuteronomy 10:17	No respecter of persons
2:17-18	Exod 24; Ezra 8:1-13	Jew and Law
2:21	Exodus 20:15	Do not steal
2:22	Exodus 20:14	Do not commit adultery
2:24	Exodus 20:7; Ezek 36:17-27	His Name blasphemed
2:25-28	Genesis 17:1-14	Circumcision
2:27, 29	I Samuel 17:43; 18:25-27	Uncircumcision
2:29	Deut 10:16	Circumcision of the heart
3:4	Psalm 51:4	Difference between God and man
3:10	Psalm 14:1, 3	All men are sinners
3:11	Psalm 14:2	Man does what is right in his own eyes
3:12	Psalm 14:3	All men are sinners

3:13	Psalm 5:9; 10:7; 140:3	The tongue is the revealer of the heart
3:14	Psalm 10:7	The tongue is the revealer of the heart
3:15	Isaiah 59:7	Cain killed Abel
3:16	Psalm 36:1	Illustrated by kings Ahab, Ahaz and Manasseh
3:17	Isaiah 59:7-8	May refer to King Manasseh and his evil ways
3:19-20	Psalm 143:2	The Law reveals the sinful heart
3:21		Law and prophets
3:25	Leviticus 16:14	Propitiation
3:25	Leviticus 17:10	Remission
3:31		Law of Moses
4:1-3	Genesis 15:6	Abraham's righteousness by Faith
4:2	Genesis 15:6	Abraham justified
4:6	Psalm 32:1-2	David
4:9-10	Genesis 15	Circumcision & Abraham
4:9-12	Genesis 15	Circumcision
4:13, 16, 20-21	Genesis 12, 13, 15, 17, and 22	Promise to Abraham and his seed
4:13-15	Genesis 12, 13, 15, 17 and 22	Promise to Abraham did not come through Law
4:17-22	Genesis 17:5; 15:5	Abraham and seed
5:5	Ezekiel 36:28	Holy Spirit promised
5:12	Genesis 2-3	Sin of Adam imputed to all men
5:12	Genesis 3	Adam's sin
5:13	Exodus 20	Deuteronomy Law
5:14	Genesis 3-4	Death
5:14-15	Gen 3 – Exod 20	Adam to Moses
5:15-20	Genesis 3, 4, 6, 11	Adam and Messiah, both through one
5:20	Exodus 20-24	Sin abounded
6:3		Baptized / ritual immersion
6:4	Jeremiah 31:31-34	Newness of life
6:14-15		Law system to Grace

7:1-8, 14		Law
7:12, 24-25		Law
8:11	Ezekiel 36:26-27	Spirit indwells
8:20-21	Genesis 3	Creation / our bodies groan for redemption
8:36	Psalm 44:22	We suffer persecution and trouble daily
9:4	Genesis 17:19	Promise of Yitzchak [Isaac]
9:4	Exodus 20	Deuteronomy Law
9:5	Exodus 2:24	Fathers
9:5	Genesis 49:10; Ruth 4:17-22	Abraham & David
9:7	Genesis 17:19	Seed of Abraham
9:7	Genesis 26:4	Isaac
9:8		Promise / believing remnant
9:9	Genesis 18:10	Sarah
9:10	Genesis 25:19-23	Rebecca & Isaac
9:12	Genesis 25:23	Elder / younger
9:13	Malachi 1:2-3	Jacob I loved
9:15	Exodus 33:19	Moses
9:17	Exodus 9:16	Pharaoh
9:21	Jer 18; Isa 64:8; Isa 29:16; 45:9	Potter
9:24	Genesis 12:1-3; Isaiah 48:12	Us – Called
9:24	Genesis 12:3; 26:4; 28:12-13	Gentiles
9:25-26	Hosea 2:23	Salvation of Israel at the end of the Tribulation
9:27	Isaiah 10:20-22	A remnant
9:29	Isaiah 1:9	Isaiah
9:33	Psa 118:22; Isa 8:14; Zech 3:9-10	Zion, Stumbling stone
10:4	Exodus 20-23, 25-31, 33-40	Law
10:5	Leviticus 18:5	Moses and Law

10:6-7	Deut 30:12-13; Proverbs 30:4	Righteous man cannot say
10:8	Deuteronomy 30:14	Word is nigh
10:11	Isaiah 29:16; 49:23	The righteous shall not be ashamed
10:15	Isaiah 52:7	Proclaimers
10:16	Isaiah 53:1	Israel disobeyed the Gospel
10:19	Deuteronomy 32:21	Moses
10:20	Isaiah 65:1	Isaiah a faithful prophet
10:21	Isaiah 65:2	To Israel, a rebellious people
11:2-4	I Kgs 19:10, 14, 18	Elijah
11:8	Isa 29:10; Jer 6:10	Written – eyes & ears
11:9	Psalms 69:22	David
11:11	Deuteronomy 32:21	Provoke
11:26	Deuteronomy 30:3	Messiah
11:27	Jeremiah 31:31-34	My Covenant
11:34	Isaiah 40:13	NO one is His Counselor
12:19	Deut 32:35	Written
13:8	Leviticus 19:18; Proverbs 22:7	Fulfiller of the Law
13:9	Exodus	Adultery
13:9	Exodus	Kill
13:9	Exodus	Steal
13:9	Exodus	False testimony
13:9	Exodus	Covet
13:9	Leviticus	Love neighbor
15:3	Psalm 69:9	Written
15:8	Genesis 17:9-14	Pre-incarnate Messiah ministered to His people
15:9	Psalm 18:49	Gentiles
15:10	Deuteronomy 32:43	Gentiles
15:11	Psalms 17:1	Gentiles
15:12	Isaiah 11:1, 10	Gentiles
15:21	Isaiah 52:15	The nations and the Jews shall hear of Him

List of Used Passages in Galatians from the Torah and *Tanakh*

Galatians	*Tanakh*	Subject
2:3, 7	Genesis 17	Titus not circumcised
2:16	Habakkuk 2:4	Not justified by the works of the Law
3:6, 8	Genesis 15:6	Abraham
3:10	Exodus - Deut	Law a unit
3:13	Deuteronomy 21:23	Messiah became a curse for us
3:14	Genesis 12:3	Blessing
3:14, 17-22	Genesis 12:3	Promise
3:16	Genesis 22:18	Abraham & Seed
3:19	Genesis 3:18	Seed
3:29	Genesis 12:2-3c	Abraham seed & Promise
4:10	Leviticus 23	Major and minor feasts of the Law
4:22-25	Genesis 21	Abraham and two sons
4:27	Isaiah 54:1	Blessed are the barren that conceived not
4:28	Genesis 12:2; 17:19	Isaac
4:30	Genesis 21:10	Cast out the bond woman and her son not part of the Promise
5:2-3	Genesis 12:3	Circumcision and the curse of the Law
5:14	Leviticus 19:18	Law is fulfilled

List of Used Passages in James from the Torah and *Tanakh*

James	*Tanakh*	Subject
1:10	Psalm 103:15-16	Flower
1:27	Ex 22:22; Deut 14:28-29; Isa 58:7; Psa 68:5; 82:3; 146:9	Fatherless and widows
2:1-9	Deut 10:17	Respecter of persons
2:11	Exodus 20:14	Adultery

2:11	Exodus 20:13	Kill
2:21-23	Genesis 15:6	Abraham
3:5	Proverbs	Tongue
3:8	Proverbs	Tongue

List of Used Passages from I & II Peter from the Torah and *Tanakh*

I & II Peter	*Tanakh*	Subject
I Peter 1:2	Lev 16:14-19	Sprinkling of blood
1:2	Isaiah 42:6; 49:6	New Covenant
1:10	Daniel 12:4, 9	Prophets of old who desired to understand
1:11	Isaiah 53; Psa 22	Sufferings
1:15	Isaiah 48:12	Called you
1:15-16	Leviticus 11:44	Written – Holy
1:17	Deuteronomy 10:17	Respect of persons
1:19	Exodus 12:5	Without blemish
1:23	Jeremiah 31:31-34	Born again – Circumcised heart
1:24	Isaiah 40:6-8	Flower and grass
1:25	Psalm 119:39	Word is forever
2:4	Psalm 118:22	Living stone
2:6	Isaiah 28:16	Cornerstone
2:8	Psa 118:22; Isa 8:14	Stone of stumbling
2:8	Deuteronomy 32; I Samuel 2:2 others	Messiah is the Rock
2:9	Exod 19:6; Isa 61:6	Royal Priesthood
2:21-25	Isaiah 53:6	Suffering Servant
3:6	Genesis 18:12	Sarah
3:20	Genesis 6	Noah
3:22	Psalm 80:17	Right hand of God
4:1	Isaiah 53	Messiah suffered
II Peter 2:1	Deut 18:20; I Kgs 18:19-29;	False prophets – false teachers

	22:6-7; Ezek 13; Jer 28; Zech 13:2-5	
2:4	Genesis 6	Angels not spared judgment
2:5	Genesis 6	Old world
2:5	Genesis 6-8	Global flood
2:6	Genesis 19	Sodom and Gomorrah
2:7-8	Genesis 19	Righteous Lot
2:15	Numbers 22-24	Balaam
2:16	Numbers 22:22-34	Balaam's donkey
2:22	Proverbs 26:11	Dog returns to vomit
2:22	Proverbs 26:11	Pig returns to the mud after being washed
3:2	Isaiah – through minor prophets	Holy prophets
3:5	Genesis 1:2	World standing in water
3:10	Isaiah 2:12-22	The Day of the LORD

List of Used Passages from the Torah and *Tanakh* in Revelation

In the book of Revelation there are no direct quotations from the *Tanakh*. In the book there are many borrowed phrases and motifs taken from the *Tanakh*, and are the Book of Revelation develops them. There are over 500 such references from the *Tanakh*. Arnold Fruchtenbaum has them listed in his book *The Footsteps of Messiah*.[233] I am not going to list them all but simply give you a sampling.

Revelation	***Tanakh***	**Subject**
1:4	Isaiah 11:2	Seven spirits
1:7	Daniel 7:13; Zech. 12:10-14	2nd Coming of Messiah
1:8	Isaiah 41:4	First and the last
1:17	Isaiah 48:12	First and the last
2:7	Genesis 2:9	Tree of Life

---

[233] Arnold Fruchtenbaum. The Footsteps of Messiah: A Study of the Sequence of Prophetic Events. San Antonio, TX: Ariel Press, 2021, pp. 765-771.

2:14	Numbers 25:1-3	Doctrine of Balaam
2:18	Daniel 10:6	Feet like brass
2:27	Psalm 2:7-9	Rule with rod of iron
3:5	Exod. 32:32-33	Blot out his name
3:7	Isaiah 22:22	Key of David
4:3	Ezekiel 1:26, 28	Throne of God
4:5	Isaiah 11:2	Seven spirits
4:6	Ezekiel 1:5	Four living creatures - cherubim
4:7	Ezek. 1:5-28; 10:1	Cherubim
4:11	Genesis 1:1	Creator
5:5	Genesis 49:9-10	Tribe of Judah
5:6	Zechariah 3:8-9	Seven spirits of God
5:9	Psalm 40:3	New Song
5:11	Daniel 7:10	1,000's & 10,000's
6:14	Isaiah 34:4	Judgment of God on the earth
6:16	Hosea 10:8	Hills fall on us
7:4	Genesis 49	Tribes of Israel
8:3	Psalm 141:2	Incense before the throne
8:7	Exodus 9:23-24	Hail and fire
9:2-3	Joel 2	Locust / demons
10:4	Danicl 8:26	Seal up
10:7	Amos 3:7	His servants, the prophets
10:9	Jeremiah 15:16	Eating the book
11:1	Zech 2:1-2	Measuring rod
11:4	Zech 4:1-3, 11-14	Two witnesses
11:6	I Kings 17:1	Drought
11:7	Daniel 7:3, 7-8, 21	Beast
12:1	Genesis 37:9	Woman, moon and 12 stars
12:3	Daniel 7:7, 20, 24	Great red dragon
12:7	Daniel 10:13, 21	War in heaven
12:9	Genesis 3:1; Job 1:6	Serpent
12:14	Exod 19:4; Deut 32:11	Eagles wings

12:17	Genesis 3:15	Her seed
13:1	Daniel 7:3, 7-8	Seven heads – 10 horns
13:2	Daniel 7:12	Leopard, bear, lion
13:3	Daniel 7:8	Wounded unto death
13:7	Daniel 7:21	War against the saints
13:13	I Kings 1:9-12	Fire from heaven
14:1	Ezekiel 9:4	Mark on foreheads
14:3	Psalm 144:9	Sang new song
14:8	Jeremiah 51:7-8	Babylon is fallen
14:18	Joel 3:13	Sickle, harvest
15:3	Exodus 15:1-18	Song of Moses
15:8	Exodus 40:34; I Kgs 8:10-11	Glory filled the temple
16:2	Exodus 9:8-11	Grievous sores
16:3	Exodus 7:17-25	Sea as blood
16:6	Isaiah 49:26	drink blood
16:14	Joel 3:9-16	Armageddon
16:21	Exodus 9:18-25	Great hail
17:1	Nahum 3:4	Mother of harlots
17:4	Jeremiah 51:7	Cup of abominations
17:12	Daniel 7:24-25	Ten horns
18:2	Isa 21:9; Jer 51:37	Babylon is fallen
18:3	Jeremiah 51:7	Nations are drunk
18:9-19	Ezekiel 26:16-18; 27:26-31	Mourning over Babylon
19:3	Isaiah 34:9-10	Smoke of Babylon
19:11	Psalm 18:10;	White horse
19:13	Isaiah 63:3	Garments with blood
19:15	Psalm 2:8-9	Rod of iron
19:17	Ezekiel 39:17	Fowls drink blood
20:12	Psalm 69:28	Written in the book
20:15	Daniel 12:1	Written in the book
21:3	Hosea 2:23	He will be their God

21:4	Isaiah 25:8	Wipe away tears
22:2	Gen 2:9; 3:22-24; Ezek 47:12	Tree of Life
22:18-19	Deut 4:2; 12:32	Written in the book

When reading through all the references from the *Tanakh* found in the Epistles on through Revelation, it is utterly fruitless to say we diminish the Torah and the *Tanakh* after seeing all the quotations recorded by Paul, James, Peter, John, and the author of Hebrews. Again, we do not diminish what God has recorded through the guidance of the Holy Spirit (II Peter 1:20-21).

APPENDIX FOUR
Thirty-Three Positional Truths

The purpose of listing all the Positional Truths is because most of these truths come as a direct result of the outworking of the **New Covenant** that Messiah mediated and are not possible under the Mosaic Law that Torah keepers want to observe. The ramifications of the benefits of the **New Covenant** are the outworking of God's Grace, Regeneration, Imputation, Redemption, Reconciliation, Propitiation, Justification, Sanctification[234] and all the other Positional Truths simply are not possible under the Law of Moses. Yet with all the enormous benefits coming from the **New Covenant,** some wish to marginalize, minimize, and depreciate the work of the Creator in the **New Covenant** by placing all His work listed in this section subservient to the Law of Moses. They are simply following the lead of unbelieving rabbinic rabbis of Judaism at the Council at Yavneh who modified and attempted to extend the Law which God Himself dismantled as a system to be lived by. Their modified Law does not give life, only condemnation for sin; however, they insist on selectively picking the laws they want to obey while violating the laws they could obey, which is the greatest disrespect to Messiah imaginable. By way of application, drawn from Hebrews 10:29, they have *trodden underfoot the Son of God, and have counted the BLOOD of the* [**New**] *Covenant wherewith they were sanctified, an unholy thing.* Yes, they present the BLOOD of Messiah, the BLOOD of the **New Covenant**, the BLOOD of *the Lamb of God* as an unworthy thing. They lift up Moses and demote Yeshua Ha-Mashiach to the level of Moses! Now let us look at the thirty-three Positional Truths, summarized from the work of Arnold Fruchtenbaum.[235] At the end of each of the thirty-three Positional Truths, I will add my personal bullet point to contrast it against what the Law of Moses does not provide.

1. Redemption

The Scriptures, which make redemption a part of positional truth, are Romans 3:24; I Corinthians 1:30; Ephesians 1:7; and Colossians 1:14. The price of redemption was the blood of the Messiah. The very concept of redemption means, "to purchase out of." In the Spiritual realm, it means, "to purchase out of the slave market of sin." To purchase something always requires a purchase price. The purchase price

---

[234] All these concepts are illustrated in Teaching blocks in this book.

[235] Fruchtenbaum. *Thirty-Three Things: A Study of Positional Truth: Manuscript 110.* San Antonio, TX: Ariel Press. This quotation has been re-phrased and abridged.

was the blood of the Messiah. There are three different Greek words all meaning "to redeem." Each has a slightly different shade of meaning.

> The first one is *agorazo*, which means "to purchase," "to pay the price sin demanded so that one can be redeemed" (II Peter 2:1; Revelation 5:9).
>
> The second word is *exagorazio*, which means, "to purchase out of the marketplace." In the spiritual realm, it means, "to purchase out of the slave market of sin" (Galatians 3:13; 4:5).
>
> The third Greek word is *lutroo*, and it means "to release and set free" (Matthew 20:28; I Timothy 2:6; Titus 2:14).

By combining these three Greek words, *redemption* means that the redeemed person is purchased by the payment of a price, the blood of the Messiah; he is removed out of the marketplace, the slave market of sin; then he is set free so that he can serve the Lord.

- The Law of Moses has NO redeeming or salvific qualities; it only points to the fact that mankind is comprised of sinners.

2. Reconciliation

Means that the position of the world, which was in a state of alienation from a holy God, was changed by the Messiah's death so that all men are now able to be saved by Grace through Faith (Romans 5:10-11; II Corinthians 5:18-19; Colossians 1:20-22). Biblically speaking, offending mankind is being reconciled back to the offended God.

- The Mosaic Law showed man that he is in active rebellion and alienation from a holy God, the Law had no answers or provision to unite sinful man with a holy God, only *condemnation* and *death*.

3. Propitiation

The term *propitiation* means that the wrath of a holy God was satisfied by Messiah's voluntary blood sacrifice which enabled God to act on man's behalf (Romans 3:25; I John 2:2; 4:10).

- The offering at Yom Kippur was only a temporary measure, with inferior blood which had to be done year after year for 1,500 years with NO permanent results.

4. Forgiveness

The term *forgiveness* means that all of believers' sins, past, present, and future, have been totally forgiven (Ephesians 1:7; Colossians 1:14; 2:13) by God because of the finished work of Messiah on the Cross. It also means that there is no sin that a believer can commit which will cause him to lose his salvation.

- It is only in the **New Covenant** that forgiveness is ultimately given, for their God no longer remembers our sin but completely removes it. Forgiveness in the Mosaic Law code was temporary; it was by animal blood (a shadow of that which was to come) which covered the sin but did not remove it.

5. Justification

The definition of *justification* is "to be declared righteous" (Romans 3:24; 5:19; 8:30) by a holy, righteous God. That righteousness is imparted to man by Grace through Faith in Messiah and His finished work on the Cross.

- Under the Mosaic Law there was no permanent justification; which was because of inferior blood. Abraham was justified by God but that was 500 years before the Mosaic Law system. No one else in the *Tanakh* was declared to be righteous by God.

6. Glorification

It means being glorified in the sight of God, which is His assurance of the ultimate imparting of Messiah's glory (Romans 8:18, 30; 9:23; Colossians 3:4; I John 3:2). Positionally, being glorified means that the believer is certainly going to be practically and experientially glorified in that future day.

- The Mosaic Law provided no glorification to the saints in the *Tanakh*, for upon death they went to Hades, a holding tank for believers, also called "Paradise," until Messiah's death, burial, and resurrection on the Cross.

7. Deliverance

Deliverance specifically refers to being delivered from the *power of darkness* (Acts 26:18; Ephesians 2:1-2; Colossians 1:13; Hebrews 2:14-15). The fact that the believer has been delivered from the power of darkness means that he is no longer under any obligation whatsoever to serve Satan. The believer has been transferred from the kingdom of darkness to the Son's kingdom of light.

- *Deliverance* in the *Tanakh* dealt only with physical deliverance from an enemy. The Law of Moses had no ability to deliver man from the power of darkness.

8. Circumcision

This does not refer to physical circumcision, the circumcision of the flesh, but it refers to the circumcision of the heart, spoken of in Colossians 2:11 (Deut. 10:6). This circumcision of the heart involves the putting off of the deeds of the flesh.

- In the *Tanakh* circumcision was a sign of Jewishness under the Abrahamic Covenant and of being a "son of the commandments," placing him under the Law of Moses. Only God will circumcise man's heart. Circumcision was only a physical sign in two covenants, it had NO salvific qualities.

9. Being Acceptable to God

The believer has been made righteous by (five things): the imputation of Messiah's righteousness (Romans 5:11-21; I Corinthians 1:30; II Corinthians 5:21), by his new sanctified position (I Corinthians 1:2, 30; 6:11), he has been *perfected forever* (Hebrews 10:14) because he is not now condemned any longer by his sin (John 3:18; 5:24; Romans 8:1) which makes him qualified to be accepted by God (Colossians 1:12).

- There is no counterpart for being accepted by God, for everything in the Law was temporary.

10. The Firstfruits of the Holy Spirit

The believers have the firstfruits of the Holy Spirit: They have been **regenerated** (John 3:5-6; Titus 3:5), **baptized** or placed into the body of Messiah (Romans 6:1-10; I Cor 12:13), **indwelt** by the Ruach Ha-Kodesh (Holy Spirit) meaning he is now the temple of God (Romans 5:5; 8:9; I Corinthians 3:16; 6:19; Galatians 4:6; II Timothy 1:14; I John 2:27; 3:24), and **sealed** by the Ruach Ha-Kodesh (II Corinthians 1:22; Ephesians 1:3-14; 4:30) and has eternal security, and each believer is filled with the Ruach Ha-Kodesh (5:18).

- The Mosaic Law offers nothing that is comparable to or even comes close to what the Ruach Ha-Kodesh does in this present economy or Dispensation.

11. In the Eternal Plan of God

Believers are in the eternal plan of God which is shown by the five facets of His will: We are **foreknown** (Romans 8:29; Ephesians 1:5, 11-12; I Peter 1:1-2), **predestined** (John 6:65; Romans 8:29-30), **elect** (Romans 8:33; Colossians 3:12; I Thessalonians 1:4; Titus 1:1; I Peter 1:1-2), **chosen** (Ephesians 1:4; II Thessalonians 2:13) and **called** (Romans 8:30; 9:24; I Thessalonians 5:24; II Thessalonians 2:14; II Timothy 1:9; Hebrews 3:1).

- Once again, the Law does not provide this at all for Gentiles!

12. Based on the Rock: The Messiah

Based upon this position, the believer has a sure foundation upon which he can stand; he can build his life upon a foundation of the Rock, not upon a foundation of sand (Matthew 7:24-27; I Corinthians 3:9-15; Ephesians 2:20-22; I Peter 2:4-6).

- Moses referred to God (Messiah) as their Rock, but they refused to stand on the solid Rock (Deuteronomy 32:18) and chose the shifting sands of man's religion, culture, and philosophy. The Law of Moses did not help them.

13. Made Nigh

This relates specifically to Gentile believers. Being *made nigh* means we are now brought into a position where we can enjoy Jewish spiritual blessings. By Faith in the Messiah, the Gentile believer has been drawn near to enjoy not the physical, material benefits of the Jewish covenants, but the spiritual benefits of the Jewish covenants according to Ephesians 2:13.

- Under the Law of Moses, you as Gentiles were on the outside looking in but could not participate in the covenants to Israel. The Law did absolutely nothing for you. The Law of Moses did not bring you *nigh*; the **New Covenant** and the Blood of Messiah brought you *nigh*.

14. Members of the Holy and Royal Priesthood

Believers have become members of a holy and royal priesthood; this results in the priesthood of all believers. This is true particularly of Jewish believers in I Peter 2:5, 9, but it is also true of Gentile believers according to Revelation 1:5-6 and 5:9-10.

- As a Gentile, you had no standing as a priesthood unto God; the Law made absolutely no provisions for you.

15. Transferred into God's Kingdom

Believers are no longer a part of the kingdom of darkness but are part of the Kingdom of God according to II Peter 1:11. Two ramifications are that believers have been delivered out of the power of darkness; the powers of darkness have no legal authority over the believer any longer. This is also the basis for the believer to walk consistently in an orderly manner, in the kind of lifestyle that the Bible Commands (I Thessalonians 2:12).

- Observing Torah does not transfer believers into God's kingdom; it is only the result of the **New Covenant**.

16. A Chosen Generation: A Holy Nation: A Peculiar People

This position is more true of Jewish believers than of Gentile believers according to I Peter 2:9. It should be kept in mind that Peter did not write to the Church as a whole, but specifically to Jewish believers.

> The Church is not a chosen generation; it is comprised of *people of all generations*.

> The Church is not a holy nation; it is comprised of *people from all nations*.

> The Church is not a peculiar, singular people; it is comprised of members from *all peoples, tribes, and tongues*.

Keeping in mind that Peter wrote specifically to Jewish believers, this particular position means that Jewish believers are the chosen generation; they are the holy nation; they are the peculiar people. The point that Peter makes in the context is that the nation of Israel as a whole has failed to fulfill its calling of Exodus 19. However, the Remnant of Israel, the Jewish believers within the nation, known as *the Israel of God*, have fulfilled their calling. So they are the chosen generation, the holy nation, and the peculiar people.

- Gentiles, the Law left you out. It is only through the **New Covenant** that you share these titles with believing Jewish people.

17. Citizen of Heaven

A practical application of having citizenship in heaven (Luke 10:20; II Corinthians 5:1-2; Ephesians 2:19; Philippians 3:20; Hebrews 12:22-24; I Peter 2:11-12) is that it should result in keeping one's mind on heavenly things, not on earthly things. The believer on this earth is merely a pilgrim, an alien, a foreign resident, simply passing through. While the believer has every encouragement to participate in those things in the world in which believers should and need to participate, one should always remember that more important than being a citizen from any nation on earth, we are believers together – "co-citizens" – in Heaven.

- For a Torah-observant believer, does Torah keeping of the Law of Moses make anyone a citizen of heaven; or did you become a citizen of Heaven through the **New Covenant**, His finished work of the Cross?

18. In the Family of God

As a result of the **New Covenant** and believing on Messiah Yeshua, you are now part of God's household, part of God's building (I Corinthians 3:9; 6:10; Ephesians 2:19-20; I Peter 2:5).

- Being Torah observant does not make you part of the household of God; this only came through the inauguration of the **New Covenant** by the mediator of that **New Covenant**.

19. Adoption

The believer has been adopted as a child of God (Romans 8:15; Galatians 4:5; Ephesians 1:4-5). The advantage of being adopted is that, while natural children are in the family because they were born into it, adopted children are chosen to be loved. Being the adopted children of God means that God has chosen to love each believer.

- The Law did not make Israel or Torah keepers the adopted children of God, but by Faith in Him we were all adopted into God's family as a direct result of the **New Covenant**.

20. The Children of God

Since we are adopted, we are now the children of God. Our adoption is seen in four facets (John 1:12; Romans 8:16; I John 3:1-2). *First*, it means that the believer has been begotten (I John 5:1; I Peter 1:23). *Second*, is that believers who were once dead in their trespasses and sins have been quickened or made alive by God. They are no longer spiritually dead, but they have been quickened, made spiritually alive, to become the children of God (II Corinthians 5:14-15; Ephesians 2:5; Colossians 2:13). *Third*, believers are now the sons (children) of God, followers of God (Romans 8:14; II Corinthians 6:18; Galatians 3:26; 4:6-7; I John 3:2). *Fourth*, believers are now a new creation or a new creature; the believer has been created anew to become a child of God (II Corinthians 5:17; Galatians 6:15; Ephesians 2:10; 4:24; Colossians 3:10).

- Did the Law of Moses make you spiritually alive? Did it make you a new creation? Only the **New Covenant** could do that.

21. Part of the Fellowship of the Saints

Believers are part of the fellowship of the saints (John 17:11, 21-23; I John 1:3, 7). The practical application is that this fellowship becomes the basis for unity among believers. Believers can be unified because they are all part of the fellowship of the saints.

- You will never be accepted in the fellowship of Israel as long as you proclaim the Name of Yeshua. However, you are through Messiah enjoying the fellowship of the saints, both Jew and Gentile together as one, but again that only comes through the **New Covenant** not the Mosaic code of Law.

22. Light in the LORD

Believers are not only the light of the world, they are also light in the Lord according to Ephesians 5:8. Believers are the children of light, and being the children of light, they are to walk in light. The believer's practice must be conformed in his position. Positionally, believers are the children of light; therefore, in practice, they should be walking in the light (I Thessalonians 5:4-9).

- Did being Torah keepers make you light or did Messiah?

23. Heavenly Associations

This gives the believer seven heavenly positions: *First* you are a partner with the Messiah in life (Galatians 2:20; Colossians 3:3-4; I John 5:11-12). *Second,* the believer is a partner with the Messiah in the believer's position (Ephesians 2:6; Colossians 3:1-3). *Third,* believers are partners with Messiah in service (John 7:18; 20:21). *Fourth,* it means believers are partakers with the Messiah in His suffering (Romans 8:17; II Corinthians 1:5; Philippians 1:29; 3:10; II Timothy 2:12). *Fifth,* you are partners with Him in prayer. *Sixth,* believers are partners in betrothal as the Bride of the Groom, the Messiah (II Corinthians 11:2; Ephesians 5:25-27). *Last of all,* believers are partners with the Messiah in the expectation of His return (Titus 2:13; Hebrews 9:28).

- Does the Law of Moses give you these associations with Messiah? The Law does not.

24. Completion

The believer is complete in the Messiah according to Colossians 2:10. This means that the believer has been made full. The believer is complete in Him, though in practice there may be many things lacking in his life. But because of the believer's position, he is complete.

- Did the Law of Moses make you full or complete in anything? Only the **New Covenant** did.

25. In Possession of Every Spiritual Blessing

The believer does not have to agonize for spiritual blessings. He does not have to "tarry" or wait for spiritual blessing; He does not have to "pray through" to get his spiritual blessings. He is already in possession of every spiritual blessing (I Corinthians 3:23; Ephesians 1:3).

- In the **New Covenant,** you are blessed in heavenly places; but the Law only gave a blessing if obeyed. Now Yeshua has made it impossible to keep the

Law; instead, we are to keep the Law of Messiah because of the **New Covenant**.

26. A Gift from God the Father to God the Son

The believer is a gift from God the Father to God the Son (John 6:37-40; 17:2, 6, 9, 24). The main application of this position is the assurance of eternal security. Because he is a gift from God the Father to God the Son, he cannot be snatched out of the hand of either the Father or the Son.

- The Law does not view you as a gift but as a transgressor.

27. Messiah's Inheritance

The believer has been willed to the Messiah, and therefore the believer is His inheritance according to Ephesians 1:18. Yeshua has inherited the believer; because of this, the believer is the peculiar, private, individual possession of the Messiah.

- Through the Law there is no spiritual inheritance, only condemnation and death! Under the Law you could only inherit the physical Land, but that inheritance could be and was lost because of violating the Law of Moses.

28. Heirs

The believers are not only an inheritance, but they are also heirs; believers are "co-heirs" with the Messiah. This means that believers will someday receive their inheritance (Romans 8:17; Galatians 4:7; Ephesians 1:11, 14; Colossians 1:12; 3:24; Titus 3:7; Hebrews 9:15; I Peter 1:4). This inheritance includes the resurrection body and a position in the Messianic Kingdom.

- The Law of Moses made no provision for inheritance; that inheritance ONLY comes through the **New Covenant**, which is the ONLY thing that can regenerate or circumcise the human heart.

29. Freed from the Law

Believers are freed from the Law. While in one sense this relates to all believers, it is particularly true of Jewish believers, simply because Gentile believers were never under the Law of Moses. ... So especially the Jewish believers in the Body of the Messiah have been freed from the Law (Romans 6:14; 10:4; II Corinthians 3:2-11; Galatians 3:19; Ephesians 2:11-15; Hebrews 7:11-12). Positionally, the Jewish believer has been freed from the Law.

- The **New Covenant** has freed Jewish believers from the old standard, the Mosaic Law, and has accepted Gentiles because of the **New Covenant**, a new standard of living, the Law of Messiah.

30. The Judgment of the Old Man unto a New Walk

The believer's *old man*, his sin-nature, has now been judged; therefore, he is now able to walk a new walk [Law of Messiah], and he is called upon to do so. The practical application of this position is that it provides the power to *walk in newness of life* according to Romans 6:1-11 and Galatians 2:20. By saying that the *old man* was judged, it also teaches that the believer's *old man* has been "co-crucified" with the Messiah. Therefore, the old nature, the sin nature or the *old man*, no longer has any binding, legal authority over the believer. The believer no longer has any obligation to obey the old sin nature. For this reason, he has the power *to walk in newness of life.* [Brackets mine.]

- The Law of Moses could not deal with the sin nature of man; only the **New Covenant** could deal with it and give victory over it.

31. United to the Father and to the Son and the Holy Spirit

Believers are united to the Father, to the Son and to the Ruach Ha-Kodesh according to Acts 17:28 and II Corinthians 6:16 in six ways. *First,* the believer is in God the Father (John 17:21; I Thessalonians 1:1; II Thessalonians 1:1). *Second*, the Father is also in the believer. On the one hand, the believer is in the Father; on the other hand, the Father is in the believer (John 14:23; Ephesians 4:6). *Third*, the believer is in the Son (John 14:20; 17:21; Romans 8:1; II Corinthians 5:17). *Fourth,* not only is the believer in the Son, but the Son also indwells the believer (John 14:20, 23; Colossians 1:27). *Fifth,* the believer is in the Ruach Ha-Kodesh (Romans 8:9; Ephesians 2:22); and, last of all, the Ruach Ha-Kodesh is in the believer (John 14:16-17; Romans 8:9, 11; I Corinthians 2:12; 3:16; 6:19; II Timothy 1:14).

- This aspect was completely unheard of in the Law of Moses.

32. Access to God

First, the believer has immediate access to the grace of God according to Romans 5:2. Second, the believer has access to God the Father (Ephesians 2:18). Third, one of the purposes of granting the believer access to Him is so that the believer can have assurance of one's salvation (Ephesians 3:12; Hebrews 4:16; 10:19, 22). Fourth, this access to God provides fellowship with God (I Corinthians 1:9; I John 1:3).

- Under the Law, you only had the access of prayer to the Father; only the high priest had direct access to God and that was only once a year at Yom Kippur. Now in Messiah you have direct access with the Son and the Father all the time.

33. Within the Much More Care of God

First, the believer is the object of God's divine love (John 17:23; Romans 5:8; 8:35-39; Ephesians 2:4; 5:2; II Thessalonians 2:16; I John 3:1, 16; 4:10). *Second*, the believer is the object of His grace. *Third*, the believer is the object of His power in that the power of God is often manifested through the saints (Ephesians 1:19). *Fourth*, the believer is the object of His faithfulness; and, *fifth*, the believer is the object of His peace. *Sixth*, the believer is the object of God's consolation and comfort; and, *last of all*, the believer is the object of God's intercession. It is because of this position that the Messiah is continually interceding on behalf of the believer (Romans 8:27, 34; I Timothy 2:5; Hebrews 7:25; I John 2:1).

- Where in the *Tanakh* – the Law of Moses – can you find such provisions?

APPENDIX FIVE
The Eternal Nature of the Mosaic Law

by Robert Morris of HaDavar Ministries
An Unpublished Manuscript

Now, what about the "eternal nature of the Mosaic Law?" First we need to define what the word *Torah* means; and then, to be precise and clear, use that meaning when we are discussing issues.

Define Torah:

The word Torah contains a broad range of meaning in the Bible, as seen from the BDB[236] entry below.

> תּוֹרָה **n.f. direction, instruction, law** — **1.** *instruction*: **a.** human: of a mother; of a father; of sages; of a poet; תּוֹרַת חֶסֶד *kind instruction* (of a wise wife). **b.** divine; through his servants. **c.** *a body of prophetic* (or sometimes perh. priestly) *teaching*; in the heart; myriads of precepts. **d.** *instruction in Messianic age*. **e.** *a body of priestly direction* or *instruction* relating to sacred things. **2.** *law* (prop. *direction*): viz. **a.** of *special laws*, sg. of Feast of Maṣṣoth, sabbath; of direction given by priests in partic. case; of statutes of priest's code; pl. תּוֹרוֹת *laws*; (of decisions in civil cases given by Moses); the laws of the new temple; those laws in which men should walk. **b.** of *codes of law*, (1) הַתּוֹרָה as *written in the code of the covenant*; (2) *the law of the Deuteronomic code*. (3) *the law of the Priest's code*. **3.** *custom, manner*: תּוֹרַת הָאָדָם *the manner of man*, not of God, i.e. deal with me as man with man.

We have to determine the biblical meaning of the word *Torah* from the context. Does it mean direction, instruction, or law? In addition to these biblical meanings, we have to determine if Asher Norman is using a cultural meaning as well. In Rabbinic

---

[236] **BDB**: Stands for Briggs, Driver, and Brown who compiled a Hebrew English Lexicon of the Old Testament.

Judaism, a reference to *The Torah* is a reference to the written biblical material and the oral, traditional material (the Mishnah and the Gemara [Talmud]). In addition, in the Jewish community we often refer to *The Torah,* and we mean the entire Bible (an alternative reference to the entire Bible is *Tanakh*). So, you can see, a writer or speaker can use the term *Torah* and be referring to five different possibilities. To avoid confusion I will use the term *Law of Moses* rather than *Torah*. Unfortunately, Asher appears to use the term *Torah* without distinguishing what meaning of Torah he is referring to, which can be quite confusing.

With all the above stated, I would say that we have good reason to reject the statement that the Law of Moses is eternal in nature. It had a beginning in 1446 BC at Mount Sinai, and it had an end in 30 AD with the ministry of Yeshua. What's the Biblical evidence?

Evidence from Language

Let us start with by examining two key Hebrew words: *olam* and *ad*. *Olam* and *ad* are words that you have to be very, very careful with and not assume simplistic definitions. Their meaning has to be determined from the context in which they are used (like most Hebrew words, for example – Torah). Let me begin by presenting some material from a well-respected lexicon, *The Theological Wordbook of the Old Testament,* and from Dr. Arnold G. Fruchtenbaum, the Director of Ariel Ministries. I realize this is a bit technical but it is necessary.

Olam

Jenni holds that its basic meaning "most distant times" can refer to either the remote past or to the future or to both as due to the fact that it does not occur independently (as a subject or as an object) but only in connection with prepositions indicating direction (*min* "since," *ad* "until," *lĕ* "up to") or as an adverbial accusative of direction or finally as the modifying genitive in the construct relationship. In the latter instance *ōlām* can express by itself the whole range of meanings denoted by all the prepositions "since, until, to the most distant time"; i.e. it assumes the meaning "(unlimited, incalculable) continuance, eternity." (THAT II, p. 230).

The LXX generally translates *ōlām* by *aiōn* which has essentially the same range of meaning. That **neither the Hebrew nor the Greek word in itself contains the idea of endlessness** is shown both by the fact that they sometimes refer to events or conditions that occurred at a definite point in the past, and also by the fact that sometimes it is thought desirable to repeat the word, not merely saying "forever," but "forever and ever."

Both words came to be used to refer to a long age or period – an idea that is sometimes expressed in English by *world*. Post-biblical Jewish writings refer to the present world of toil as *hā ōlām hazzeh* and to the world to come as *hā ōlām habbā*.

‘ad

‘ad (q.v.) has substantially the same range of meaning as ‘ōlām (usually, long continuance into the future, but cf. Job 20:4).

Dr. Fruchtenbaum covers the territory in his manuscript on the Sabbath as well (Ariel Ministries Manuscript 176).[237] His material on the Sabbath is 100 percent applicable to our examination of the Law of Moses. In his manuscript, he examines the perpetuity of the Sabbath. In *26 Reasons* the issue is the perpetuity of the Mosaic Law. The point I am stressing is point "c. The Concept of Eternity." Just substitute *Mosaic Law* for *Sabbath* in most cases.

The Concept of Eternity.

The third key phrase is *for ever*. The simple, basic truth is that Classical Hebrew, the Hebrew of the Old Testament Scriptures, has no term that carries the concept of *eternity*. There are phrases that carry this concept, such as *without end,* but there is not a single word that carries the concept of eternity as there is in English.

To focus on the meaning of the term *for ever*, six things should be kept in mind. First, the Hebrew word is *olam*. The word itself simply means "long duration," "antiquity," "futurity," "until the end of a period of time." That period of time is determined by the context. Sometimes it is the length of a man's life, sometimes it is an age, and sometimes it is a Dispensation.

The second thing to keep in mind is that there are two Hebrew forms of *olam*. The first form is *le-olam*, which means "unto an age." And the second form is *ad-olam*, which means "until an age." However, neither of these forms carries the English meaning of "forever." Although it has been translated that way in English, the Hebrew does not carry the concept of *eternity* as the English word *forever* does.

The third thing to keep in mind is that the word *olam, le-olam,* or *ad-olam,* sometimes means only up "to the end of a man's life." For example, it is used of someone's lifetime (Exodus 14:13), of a slave's life (Exodus 21:6; Leviticus 25:46; Deuteronomy 15:17), of Samuel's life (I Samuel 1:22; 2:35), of the lifetimes of David and Jonathan (I Samuel 20:23), and of David's lifetime (I Samuel 27:12; 28:2; I Chronicles 28:4). While the English reads *for ever,* obviously from the context it does not mean "forever" in the sense of "eternity," but only up to the end of the person's life.

---

[237] Arnold G. Fruchtenbaum, The Sabbath, Manuscript #176, San Antonio, TX: 2014, pp. 31-33.

The fourth thing to keep in mind about the meaning of *olam* is that it sometimes means only "an age" or "Dispensation." For example, Deuteronomy 23:3 uses the term *for ever* but limits the term to only ten generations. Here it obviously carries the concept of an age. In II Chronicles 7:16, it is used only for the period of the First Temple. So, again, the word *for ever* in Hebrew does not mean "eternal" as it does in English; it means "up to the end of a period of time, either a man's life, or an age, or a Dispensation."

The point of presenting this technical material is the fact that the Biblical Hebrew words used to describe the Law of Moses allow for the Law of Moses to be temporary rather than eternal. We are not contradicting the vocabulary or grammar when we say that the Law of Moses is temporary. When dealing with the Law of Moses, a more correct translation would be that it is an "age-long" covenant rather than an "eternal" covenant (and similar statements).

Evidence from Jeremiah 31:31-34

Our position that the Mosaic Law is a covenant that will last for an age or Dispensation (the Dispensation of Law) is confirmed by the fact that Jeremiah states that the **New Covenant** replaces the Law of Moses. There are a number key ideas to notice that support the temporary nature of the Law of Moses. Let's take them sentence by sentence.

Jeremiah 31:31 "Behold, days are coming," declares the Lord, "when I will make a new covenant with the house of Israel and with the house of Judah,

In verse 31 the term "New" means "brand new" as the Theological Wordbook of the Old Testament explains.

חָדָשׁ (*ḥādāš*). *New, new thing, fresh*. This **adjective**, usually attributive, describes, as in English, a variety of physical objects (e.g., house, wife, cords, sword, garment, cruse, meal offering, king, gate, etc.). It is also used for non-material things as name (Isa 62:2), song (Ps 149:1), covenant (Jer 31:31), God's mercies (Lam 3:23), heart, and spirit (Ezek 36:26). While suffering, Job longed for the time when his glory was "fresh" in him (Job 29:20).

Some like to claim that the word means to renew or repair and is therefore describing a renewed Mosaic Law in Jeremiah 31:31. Their mistake is to miss the fact that the form of the word in Jeremiah is an **adjective**. It is true that the noun form of the word means renew or repair but the noun is not in the text, the adjective is.

Evidence From Rabbinic Literature

This would be a good place to share some Rabbinic Quotes that recognize that the **New Covenant** is brand new and not something renewed or repaired.

The Jewish Messiahs, **Harris Lenowitz, page 270ff** (Harris Lenowitz, to the best of my knowledge is not a Jewish Christian)

The notion that the days of the messiah, the messiah's apocalyptic reign, will be served by a new law is a Jewish one. Paul is quite Jewish in seeking to extend his new, more accessible, religion to Gentiles in the interest of time as did some of his contemporaries among the rabbis. In his essay, "The Crisis of Tradition in Jewish Messianism," G. Scholem reviews the most important rabbinic statements that look forward to a utopian messianic age governed by a new, relaxed law:

Lev. Rabbah 9:7—All sacrifices will be abolished except for the offer of thanksgiving

Yalkut and Midrash Mishle on Prov. 9:2—All festivals will be abolished except for Purim which will never be abolished (and the Day of Atonement will be like Purim)

Midrash Tehillim in regard to Psalm 146:7—The Lord allows the forbidden ... and will one day allow the eating of all animals now forbidden to be eaten ... In the time to come he will allow every thing that he has forbidden.

Lev. Rabbah 13:3—A new Torah shall go forth from me.

Yalkut in regard to Isaiah 26:2—the messiah himself will teach it (the new Torah)

The Messiah Texts, **Raphael Patai, pages 247-257** (Again, to the best of my knowledge Raphael Patai is not a Jewish Christian)

Eccl. Rabbah 11:1—R Hizqiya in the name of R. Simon bar Zibdi said: "The whole Tora which you learn in This World is vanity as against the Tora of the World to Come. For in This World a man learns Tora and forgets, but in the Future to Come (he will not forget) as it is written, *I will put My Tora in their inward parts and in their heart will I write it* (Jer. 31:33). (One of seventeen similar entries)

Return to Jeremiah 31:31-34

To say that the **New Covenant** is indeed something brand new is totally consistent with the Biblical text and the comments of the rabbis. Let's go on to the next verse.

Jeremiah 31:32

> *"... not like the covenant which I made with their fathers in the day I took them by the hand to bring them out of the land of Egypt, My covenant which they broke, although I was a husband to them,"* declares the Lord.

The **New Covenant** is distinct from the Mosaic Covenant. Verse 32 is a reference to the Law of Moses given at Mount Sinai 430 years after the Abrahamic Covenant

(Galatians 3:17). Please notice that God states that the Law of Moses was broken by the Jewish people. The problem did not lie with God – He was a husband to us. The responsibility for breaking the Mosaic Covenant is ours – we became an adulterous wife (Jer 5:7, 8. 7:9. 9:2. Ezek 22:9-11. 23:9-12. Hos 4:2, 3; etc.). Let's move on to verse 33.

Jeremiah 31:33

> *"But this is the covenant which I will make with the house of Israel after those days," declares the Lord, "I will put My law within them and on their heart I will write it; and I will be their God, and they shall be My people."*

God will put into place a brand new arrangement **after** Jeremiah's time (circa 600-580 BC). It cannot be the Law of Moses. That law was broken **before** Jeremiah's time. What is the law he is referring to here if it is not the broken Law of Moses? A formal name is not given here, just a description regarding the nature of this brand new arrangement – it will be internal.

This is in contrast with the broken Law of Moses which was external in nature. Under the Mosaic Covenant it was incumbent upon man to place God's Word in his heart. A righteous man, like the psalmist, would do his best to accomplish that task through study, meditation, memorization, etc. (Psalm 119:11 *Your word I have treasured in my heart, That I may not sin against You.*) But it was up to the man and that means that his efforts, while admirable, would always fall short because of mankind's limitations. However, in Jeremiah 31:33, placing the **New Covenant** in the heart of man would not face human limitations because God states that He will personally do it. This statement emphasizes why the **New Covenant** is so new and different from what came before. Under the **New Covenant** God Himself takes on the responsibility and task of placing His law within the core of a person's being. Due to the perfect all-powerful nature of God, we can be sure that his workmanship is complete and perfect. It will not fall short due to human limitations as the Mosaic Law did. The Mosaic Law is holy and righteous and good, but God never endued it with the power to enter a man's heart.

From our New Testament perspective we know what this law is. We can give it two names. It is the Law of the Messiah (Galatians 6:2) or The Law of the Spirit of Life (Romans 8:2). The internal nature of the **New Covenant** is enabled because the **New Covenant** believer is indwelt by the Holy Spirit (Jn 14:17; Rom 8:9–11; 1 Cor 3:16, 17; 6:19; 2 Cor 6:16; 1 Jo 2:27). When the **New Covenant** Believer is indwelt by the Ruach HaQodesh then God's law is truly in his heart. Finally, let's look at the last verse.

Jeremiah 31:34

> *"They will not teach again, each man his neighbor and each man his brother, saying, 'Know the Lord,' for they will all know Me, from the*

least of them to the greatest of them," declares the Lord, "for I will forgive their iniquity, and their sin I will remember no more."

Two key features of the **New Covenant** [are] knowledge of God and forgiveness of sins which [are] the basis for the Spirit's indwelling. Again, this is very different from the Mosaic Covenant. Under the Mosaic Covenant the tribe of Levi was assigned the job of teaching his neighbor and brother (2 Chron 17:8, 9; 30:22; 35:3; Neh 8:7.) When the **New Covenant** is finally fulfilled, when all Israel enters into the **New Covenant** (Romans 11:25-27), this teaching ministry will not be necessary.

Asher Norman is confusing you when he states on page 16 that "the Torah will be in effect in the Messianic age." That statement is vague and imprecise. That statement makes it appear that the Mosaic Law or the Mosaic Law plus the Talmud, that we know today, since it is "eternal," will be in effect during the Messianic Kingdom. If that is what he means, he is incorrect. The Mosaic Law will not be in effect during the Messianic age.

Evidence From Zechariah 14:16-19

If the Mosaic Law is not in effect during the Messianic Kingdom, then what law will be in effect? The answer is that the **New Covenant** or Millennial Law will be in effect at that time, just as Jeremiah stated. Just one example (of many) of the difference between Mosaic Law and **New Covenant** or Millennial Law is found at the end of the book of Zechariah. Under the Mosaic Law the Feast of Tabernacles was mandatory for the Jewish people only. However, under Millennial Law/**New Covenant** the observance of Tabernacles will be mandatory for the entire world. Any nation that does not obey will be punished.

Zechariah 14:16-19

> *^{16} Then it will come about that any who are left of all the nations that went against Jerusalem will go up from year to year to worship the King, the Lord of hosts, and to celebrate the Feast of Booths.*
>
> *^{17} And it will be that whichever of the families of the earth does not go up to Jerusalem to worship the King, the Lord of hosts, there will be no rain on them.*
>
> *^{18} If the family of Egypt does not go up or enter, then no rain will fall on them; it will be the plague with which the Lord smites the nations who do not go up to celebrate the Feast of Booths.*
>
> *^{19} This will be the punishment of Egypt, and the punishment of all the nations who do not go up to celebrate the Feast of Booths.*

This is one example of the fact that the Mosaic Law is not operating in the Kingdom. A new system is – Kingdom Law.

Evidence from The Soncino Books of the Bible

This factor is especially apparent in the concluding chapters of the book of Ezekiel. The rabbis tore their hair out trying to reconcile the statements in Ezekiel with the Mosaic Law. The classic Jewish commentary, the Soncino Books of the Bible, explains this phenomenon with these comments:

Page xi: The text of the concluding chapters, dealing with the Temple of the future, presents almost insurmountable difficulties. The types and number of sacrifices prescribed there differ from those mentioned in the Pentateuch; and there are many innovations which, according to the accepted law, are normally beyond the authority of a prophet to institute (Shab 104a). With reference to these difficulties the Rabbis said that only Elijah, the prophet who is to herald the final redemption, will be able to explain them satisfactorily (Men. 45a).

Page xiii: The Talmud reveals the fact that the Book of Ezekiel was at one time in danger of being suppressed and excluded from the Scriptural canon. In Shab. 13b the following passage occurs: 'Rab Judah said in the name of Rab: In truth, that man is to be remembered for blessing; his name is Chananiah son of Hezekiah. Had it not been for him, the Book of Ezekiel would have been withdrawn, because its words seem to contradict the teachings of the Torah. What did he do? Three hundred barrels of oil were provided for him (for lighting and food) and he sat in an upper chamber where he reconciled all discrepancies.'

Page xiv: (In regard to Chananiah, above) Yet, despite this Rabbi's efforts at harmonization, many divergences were detected between the Book and the Mosaic code which baffled all attempts at reconciliation ...

Page 265: These closing chapters present almost insuperable difficulties. They contain discrepancies, contradictions with Pentateuchal laws, and terms which do not occur elsewhere.

All the "discrepancies" which "baffle" the rabbis unsuccessful attempts at harmonization would evaporate if they would concede that there is a new law, a new covenant in operation during the Messianic Kingdom. Instead they stubbornly stick to the doctrine that the Mosaic Law is eternal. In truth, the Mosaic Law or Mosaic Covenant was never designed to be eternal in the first place. It was designed to be temporary in nature.

The Position of the New Testament

The New Testament is totally consistent with the data from the Hebrew Bible. This consistency is summed up in Galatians 3:19:

> [19] *Why the Law then? It was added because of transgressions, having been ordained through angels by the agency of a mediator, until the seed would come to whom the promise had been made.*

Paul is talking about the Mosaic Law in verse 19. He notes that it had a beginning. It was "added." Added to what? Added to the Abrahamic Covenant that preceded it by 430 years. When did the Mosaic Law begin? It began in 1446 BC at Mount Sinai. It was added to the Abrahamic Covenant for a purpose; to deal with the sin issue (because of transgressions). It was added "until." The little word "until" tells us that the Law of Moses had an end. The end of the Mosaic Law is tied into the coming of the seed. The seed is a reference to the Messiah. Yeshua came as a Jew, living under the Law of Moses, in order to fulfill it (Galatians 4:4; Matthew 5:17). When Yeshua completed His mission the purpose for the Mosaic Law was fulfilled and it was rendered inoperative. It was replaced by the **New Covenant** and all the imperatives found in the New Testament that apply to Believers today. There are over 600 commands in the New Testament that we are supposed to obey today.

So what is the status of the Mosaic Law today? The Mosaic Law is still holy and righteous and good (Romans 7:12) and relevant (2 Tim 3:16-17) but it is not required. It is not the mandatory rule of life for the Believer living under the **New Covenant**. The Mosaic Law should be referred to for principles that will instruct us and give us wisdom. However, if a Believer today does not obey a precept of the Mosaic Law he will not find himself under the curse of the Law (Deut 28, Lev 26). In a similar manner, if a Believer obeys a precept in the Mosaic Law God is not obligated to bless him either (Deut 28; Lev 26). Remember the Mosaic Law requires God to bless or curse according to obedience or disobedience. We are not under that arrangement today. The Word of God abides forever (Psalm 119:89-91) but the Mosaic Law portion of God's eternal revelation is not operating as the rule of life for the Believer any more. It was never intended to be eternal. Our rule of life today is the **New Covenant** (the New Testament).

Incidentally, if the Mosaic Law is operating today, then Yeshua cannot be our High Priest. Under the Mosaic Law the priest functioned under the order of Aaron. Under that order the priest had to be from the tribe of Levi and the King had to be from the tribe of Judah. If Yeshua is our Messiah/King and our High Priest He cannot function under the stipulations of the Mosaic Covenant. He has to function under a different system. That is the point of the book of Hebrews. Yeshua functions under the order of Melchizedek (Psalm 110). Under that order the High Priest can also be the King. A quick perusal of some of the key points of the book of Hebrews will verify that.

> Hebrews 5:10: *being designated by God as a high priest according to the order of Melchizedek.*
>
> Hebrews 6:20: *where Jesus has entered as a forerunner for us, having become a high priest forever according to the order of Melchizedek.*
>
> Hebrews 7:12: *For when the priesthood is changed, of necessity there takes place* a change of law also.
>
> Hebrews 7:18-19: [18] *For, on the one hand, there is a setting aside of a former commandment because of its weakness and uselessness* [19]

(for the Law made nothing perfect), and on the other hand there is a bringing in of a better hope, through which we draw near to God.

Asher Norman stated that we cannot add to or subtract from God's Word and we agree totally with that concept. However, The **New Covenant** is not a man-made addition to God's Word. It was predicted by the prophet Jeremiah and came into operation as stated. Ironically, Yeshua's evaluation of the situation is that the rabbis are the ones who have added to the Mosaic Law. Yeshua did not view the Oral Law (the Mishnah) as a valid part of the Mosaic Law. In fact He discerned that in many cases the Mishnah actually invalidated the Mosaic Law.

> [13] *"thus invalidating the word of God by your tradition which you have handed down; and you do many things such as that."* [Mark 7:13]

Conclusion

Based on this perspective and this evidence, which Asher Norman does not refer to in his book, I feel I can state that the rabbinic concept of an eternal Law of Moses is incorrect. It is apparent that many ancient rabbis held to the position of the New Testament. The Law of Moses, the Mosaic Covenant was designed from the beginning to be temporary in nature. It will reach its goal and a brand new covenant will replace it.

BIBLIOGRAPHY

Allen, David L. *Hebrews: The New American Commentary: An Exegetical and Theological Exposition of Holy Scripture*. Nashville, TN: B&H Publishing Group, 2010.

Baleston, Mottel. DVD's – *The Eight Covenants of the Bible* and *The Plan of the Ages*. San Antonio, TX: Ariel Ministries, 2008.

Bauer, William. William F. Arndt and F. William Gingrich, eds. *A Greek-English Lexicon of the New Testament and Other Early Christian Literature*. Chicago, IL: University of Chicago Press, 1957.

Borland, James. *Christ in the Old Testament*. Ross-shire, Great Britain: Christian Focus Publications, 1999.

Brenton, Sir Lancelot C. L. *The Septuagint with Apocrypha Greek and English*. Grand Rapids, MI: Zondervan Publishing House, 1980.

Brown, Colin. *New International Dictionary of New Testament Theology*, Grand Rapids, MI: Zondervan Publishing, 1986, vol 1, pp. 733-734.

Brown, Michael L. *Our Hands are Stained with Blood: The Tragic Story of the "Church" and the Jewish People*. Shippensburg, PA: Destiny Image Publishers, 1990.

Cairns, Earle. *Christianity Through the Centuries*. Grand Rapids, MI: Zondervan Press, 1967.

Cooper, David L. *The God of Israel: Messianic Series Number One*. Los Angeles, CA: Biblical Research Society, 1945. Available through *PromisesToIsrael.org*.

———. Volume two: *Messiah: His Nature and Person*. Los Angeles, CA: Biblical Research Society, 1933.

———. Volume three: *Messiah: His Redemptive Career*. Los Angeles, CA: Biblical Research Society, 1932.

———. Volume four: *Messiah: His First Coming Scheduled*. Los Angeles, CA: Biblical Research Society, 1939.

———. Volume five: *Messiah: His Historical Appearance*. Los Angeles, CA: Biblical Research Society, 1958.

———. Volume six: *Messiah: His Glorious Appearance Imminent*. Los Angeles, CA: Biblical Research Society, 1961.

———. Volume seven: *Messiah: His Final Call to Israel*. Los Angeles, CA: Biblical Research Society, 1962.

———. *Future Events Revealed according to Matthew 24-25*. Los Angeles, CA: Biblical Research Society, 1935.

———. *The 70 Weeks of Daniel*. Los Angeles, CA: Biblical Research Society, 1941.

———. *When Will Wars Cease?* Los Angeles, CA: Biblical Research Society, 1941.

———. *Why God's Interest Is in the Jew*. Los Angeles, CA: Biblical Research Society, 1941.

———. *Man: His Creation, Fall, Redemption and Glorification*. Los Angeles, CA: Biblical Research Society, 1950.

———. *What Men Must Believe or God's Gracious Provision for Man*. Los Angeles, CA: Biblical Research Society, 1953.

———. *The Shepherd of Israel*. Los Angeles, CA: Biblical Research Society, 1962.

———. *When Gog's Armies Meet the Almighty in the Land of Israel: Exposition of Ezekiel 38-39*. Los Angeles, CA: Biblical Research Society, 1970.

———. *An Exposition of the Book of Revelation*. Los Angeles, CA: Biblical Research Society, 1972.

C. S. Lewis Institute: "The Bible and the American Founders," *https://www.cslewisinstitute.org/resources/the-bible-and-the-american-founders/,* last accessed on 5/26/25.

Fruchtenbaum, Arnold G. *Come & See Series, Vol 1, The Word of God*. San Antonio, TX: Ariel Ministries Press, 2019.

———. *Come & See Series, Vol 6, Man and Sin: Understanding Biblical Anthropology and Hamartiology*. San Antonio, TX: Ariel Ministries Press, 2022.

———. *Come & See Series, Vol 7, The Soteriology of the Bible*. San Antonio, TX: Ariel Ministries Press, 2023, pp. 68-74.

———. *Faith Alone: The Condition of Our Salvation - An Exposition of the Book of Galatians*. San Antonio, TX: Ariel Ministries, 2014.

———. *Ha-Mashiach*: The Messiah of the Hebrew Scriptures. San Antonio, TX: Ariel Press, 2019.

———. *Israelology: The Missing Link in Systematic Theology*. San Antonio, TX: Ariel Ministries, 2018.

———. Lecture given in the fall of 2022 at Tacoma Bible Church on "The Law of Moses and the Law of Messiah," *https://www.youtube.com/watch?v=Htd6lhiglIY*. (Last accessed 5/26/2025.)

———. *Manuscript #110 – Thirty-Three Things: A Study of Positional Truth*. San Antonio, TX: Ariel Press, n.d.

———. *The Book of Romans: Exposition from a Messianic Jewish Perspective*. San Antonio, TX: Ariel Press, 2022.

———. *The Footsteps of Messiah: A Study of the Sequence of Prophetic Events*. San Antonio, TX: Ariel Press, 2021.

———. *The Messianic Jewish Epistles: Hebrews, James, I & II Peter, and Jude*. San Antonio, TX: Ariel Press, 2005.

———. *The Sabbath*. San Antonio, TX: Ariel Press, 2012.

———. *Yeshua: The Life of Messiah from a Messianic Jewish Perspective – Abridged Version*. San Antonio, TX: Ariel Ministries, 2017.

Ger, Steven. *The Book of Hebrews: Christ is Greater*. Chattanooga, TN: AMG Publishers, 2009.

Gibbs, David C. *Understanding the Constitution*. Flower Mound, TX: National Center of Life and Liberty, 2014.

Goldberg, Louis. *God, Torah, Messiah*. San Francisco, CA: Purple Pomegranate Productions, 2009.

Ham, Ken. *The Lie of Evolution*. Green Forest, AR: Masters Books, 2006.

———. *Six Days: The Age of the Church and the Decline of the Church*. Green Forest, AR: Masters Books, 2014.

Heinrich, William. *In the Shame of Jesus: The Hidden Story of Church Sponsored Anti-Semitism*. Witmer, PA: Evidence of Truth Ministries, 2016. Available through *www.PromisesToIsrael.org*.

Hill, Richard. *Freedom in Messiah: A Messianic Jewish Roots Commentary on the Book of Galatians*. Las Vegas, NV: S-E-L-F Publishing, 2015.

Hogg, C.F. & W.E. Vine. *The Epistle to the Galatians*. Grand Rapids, MI: Kregel Publications, 1921.

Institute for Creation Research (ICR) website in Dallas, TX. *https://discoverycenter.icr.org/* (Last accessed 05/26/2025.)

Kittel, Gerhard. *Theological Dictionary of the New Testament*. Grand Rapids, MI: Eerdmans Publishing Co., Vol. 1, p. 453, 1964.

Kohlenberger III, John R., Edward W. Goodrick and James A. Swanson. *The Greek English Concordance to the New Testament*. Grand Rapids, MI: Zondervan Publishing House, 1997.

Levy, David. *Guarding the Gospel of Grace*. Bellmawr, NJ: Friends of Israel Gospel Ministry, 1997.

Levytam, Gideon. *I Am Not Ashamed of the Gospel of Messiah: Romans 1:16*. Hawkesbury, Ontario, Canada: The Holy Scriptures and the Israel Bible Society of Canada, 2013.

MacArthur, John. *The MacArthur New Testament Commentary on Galatians*. Chicago, IL: Moody Press, 1987.

Merriam-Webster's Collegiate Dictionary: Eleventh Edition. Springfield, MA: Merriam-Webster, Inc, 2008.

Metzger, John B. *Discovering the Mystery of the Unity of God*. San Antonio, TX: Ariel Press, 2010.

——. *Israel's Only Hope: The New Covenant*. Keller, TX: JHousePublishing, Purple Raiment, 2015.

——. *Poking God's Eye: A Theological and Historical View of Anti-Semitism Based on the Blessings and Cursings of Genesis 12:3*. Keller, TX: JHousePublishing / Purple Raiment, 2018.

——. *The Law, Then and Now: What About Grace*. Larkspur, CO: Grace Acres Press, 2019.

Mills, Sanford C. *A Hebrew Christian Looks at Romans*. Grand Rapids, MI: Durham Publishing, 1968.

Morris, Robert. *Messiah and the Tabernacle: Exodus 25-30, A 16-Part Bible Study*. Huntington Beach, CA: JHousePublishing (Purple Raiment label), 2010.

———. "The Eternal Nature of the Mosaic Law. HaDavar Ministries, n.d.

———. *The Law of Messiah*. HaDavar Messianic Ministries, Irvine, CA, n.d.

Mounce, William. *Mounce's Complete Expository Dictionary of Old and New Testament Words*. Grand Rapids, MI: Zondervan Publishing, 2016.

Nadler, Sam. *The Messianic Ten Commandments: A Study in the Relationship between Grace and Law*. Charlotte, NC: The Word of Messiah Ministries, 2023.

Oxford University Press blog entitled "How the Bible Influenced the Founding Fathers," *https://blog.oup.com/2016/11/bible-influenced-founding-fathers*, last accessed 5/26/202.

Pentecost, Dwight. *Things which Become Sound Doctrine*. Westwood, NJ: Fleming Revell Publishing, 1965.

Postell, Seth; Eian Bar; and Erez Soref. *Reading Moses, Seeing Jesus*. Wooster, OH: Weaver Book Company, 2017.

Poyner-Levison, Alan. *The Law of Moses and the Law of Messiah*. (Messianic Jewish Author and Director and Messianic Teacher of Beit Shalom Ministries in the UK.), n.d.

Robinson, Andrew W. *Israel Betrayed, Vol 1: The History of Replacement Theology*. San Antonio, TX: Ariel Ministries, 2018.

Rydelnik, Michael. *The Messianic Hope: Is the Hebrew Bible Really Messianic?* Nashville, TN: B&H Publishing Group, 2010.

Rydelnik, Michael & Michael Vanlaningham. The Moody Bible Commentary. Chicago, IL: Moody Press, 2014.

Ryle, J. C. *Are You Ready For The End of Time?* Fearn, Scotland: Christian Focus, 2023.

Ryrie, Charles. *Dispensationalism*. Chicago, IL: Moody Press, 1995,

———. *Dispensationalism Today*. Chicago, IL: Moody Press, 1965.

———. *Dispensationalism, Revised and Expanded*. Chicago, IL: Moody Press, 2007.

Sailhamer, John H. *The Meaning of the Pentateuch*. Downers Grove, IL: Intervarsity Press, 2009.

Showers, E. *There Really is a Difference!: A Comparison of Covenant and Dispensational Theology*. Bellmawr, NJ: Friends of Israel Gospel Ministry, 1990.

Stern David H. *The Jewish New Testament Commentary*. Clarksville, MD: Jewish New Testament Publications, 1992.

Strauss, Lehman. The Epistles of John. Neptune, NJ: Loizeaux Brothers, 1972.

———. *Galatians & Ephesians*. Port Colborne, Ontario, Canada: Gospel Folio Press, 2010.

Strong, James. *A Concise Dictionary of the Words in the Greek New Testament with their Renderings in the Authorized English Version*. Peabody, MA: Hendrickson Publishers, 1988.

Symes, Kenneth. *Understanding God's Program for the Ages: A Study of Biblical Covenants & Dispensations*. London, Ontario, Canada: Bethel Baptist Printing Ministry, 2012.

Thayer's Greek-English Lexicon of the New Testament. Grand Rapids, MI: Zondervan Publishing House, 1963.

The Federalist: "How the Bible Inspired the American Founding from the Beginning," See *https://thefederalist.com/2020/11/23/how-the-bible-inspired-the-american-founding-from-the-beginning/* (last accessed 05/26/25).

Vine, W. E. *Vine's Expository Dictionary of the Old and New Testaments Words*. Old Tappan, NJ: Fleming H. Revell Co, 1981.

Whitcomb, John C. & Henry M. Morris. *The Genesis Flood: The Biblical Record and Its Scientific Implications*. Phillipsburg, NJ: P&R Publishing, 2011.

Wiersbe, Warren. *Be Free: A New Testament Study on Galatians*. Colorado Springs, CO: Chariot Victor Publishing, 1975.

Wilkin, Robert. *The Grace New Testament Commentary, Vol 2*. Denton, TX: Grace Evangelical Society, 2010.

Woods, Andy. *Ever Reforming: Dispensational Theology and the Completion of the Protestant Reformation*. Taos, NM: Dispensational Publishing House, Inc, 2018.

Wuest, Kenneth. *New Testament: An Expanded Translation*. Grand Rapids, MI: Eerdmans Publishing Co, 1962.

———. *Wuest's Word Studies: Vol 1, Galatians*. Grand Rapids, MI: Eerdmans Publishing Co, 1969.

Vlach, Michael J. *Dispensational Hermeneutics: Interpretation Principles that Guide Dispensationalism's Understanding of the Bible's Storyline*. Oxford University Press, 2023.

Yarbrough, Mark, "*Israel and the Story of the Bible*," Grand Rapids, MI: Kregel Publishing, 2018.

Youngblood, Ronald F. *Nelson's New Illustrated Bible Dictionary*. Nashville, TN: Nelson Publishers, 1986.

Magazines

Friedman, Doug. "The Mosaic Law: A New Perspective on an Old Problem," *Ariel Magazine,* Winter 2016, issue #21.

Sibley, Jim. "Serving Messiah, Serving Yeshua," *Ariel Magazine,* Winter 2023, issue #49.

www.ingramcontent.com/pod-product-compliance
Lightning Source LLC
Chambersburg PA
CBHW080330170426
43194CB00014B/2513